ROCKHURST COLLEGE LIBRARY

D0987221

A Gift of
ROCKHURST COLLEGE
Library
Guild

PSYCHOLOGY IN ORGANIZATIONS:
Integrating Science and Practice

SERIES IN APPLIED PSYCHOLOGY

Edwin A. Fleishman,George Mason University
Series Editor

Psychology in Organizations: Integrating Science and Practice
Kevin R. Murphy and Frank E. Saal

Teamwork and the Bottom Line: Groups Make a Difference
Ned Rosen

Patterns of Life History: The Ecology of Human Individuality
Michael D. Mumford, Garnett Stokes, and William A. Owens

Work Motivation
Uwe E. Kleinbeck, H.-Henning Quast, Henk Thierry,
and Hartmut Häcker

PSYCHOLOGY IN ORGANIZATIONS:
Integrating Science and Practice

Edited by

KEVIN R. MURPHY
Colorado State University

FRANK E. SAAL
Kansas State University

LEA LAWRENCE ERLBAUM ASSOCIATES, PUBLISHERS
1990   Hillsdale, New Jersey   Hove and London

Copyright © 1990 by Lawrence Erlbaum Associates, Inc.
All rights reserved. No part of this book may be reproduced in
any form, by photostat, microform, retrieval system, or any other
means, without the prior written permission of the publisher.

Lawrence Erlbaum Associates, Inc., Publishers
365 Broadway
Hillsdale, New Jersey 07642

Library of Congress Cataloging-in-Publication Data

Psychology in organizations : integrating science and practice /
   edited by Kevin R. Murphy, Frank E. Saal.
      p.   cm. — (Series in applied psychology)
   Includes bibliographical references.
   ISBN 0-8058-0477-3
   1. Psychology, Industrial.   I. Murphy, Kevin R., 1952–
II. Saal, Frank E., 1947- .   III.   Series.
HF5548.8.P777   1990
158.7—dc20

                                                    90-3053
                                                    CIP

Printed in the United States of America
10 9 8 7 6 5 4 3 2

HF
5548.8
P777
1990

Contents

40.09

Foreword

There is a compelling need for innovative approaches to the solution of many pressing problems involving human relationships in today's society. Such approaches are more likely to be successful when they are based on sound research and applications. This *Series in Applied Psychology* offers publications which emphasize state-of-the-art research and its application to important issues of human behavior in a variety of societal settings. The objective is to bridge both academic and applied interests.

Applied psychologists must often balance the role of a scientist, concerned with developing and evaluating general theories of behavior, with the role of a practitioner, attempting to solve real-world problems. This is especially true in the field of industrial and organizational psychology. We agree with the editors that science informs the practice of psychology in organizations by identifying general psychological principles that can be used to explain behavior in organizations, and that practice informs science by identifying problems that need to be solved by scientific theories and research. This volume, *Psychology in Organizations: Integrating Science and Practice,* illustrates that a true interaction between science and practice is absolutely necessary to have a viable field of I/O psychology.

The book shows that many I/O psychologists do function as true scientist-practitioners, and that the field is richer because of this interaction. It is clearly easier to link science and practice in some areas of I/O psychology (e.g., personnel selection) than in others (e.g., organizational development). However, after reading this book, one comes away more optimistic about the state of the scientist-practitioner model. The various authors are able to point to a number of success stories in various subdisciplines of I/O psychology, and they identify areas in which it would be realistic to expect progress in a reasonably short time.

The field of I/O psychology has grown significantly over the last ten years. Evidence of this is shown in the number of Ph.D. programs, the number of applicants, and the number of graduates of these programs. The Society of Industrial and Organizational Psychology has established the scientist-practitioner model as the accepted basis for Ph.D. training in this field. However, the emphasis in many programs is still decidedly academic. This emphasis is important, but we need to find ways to sustain a genuine interest in applications and to develop the skills needed to apply psychology in organizations. As our programs become bigger and more competitive, this becomes increasingly challenging. This book may help provide students in I/O psychology with some good examples of the scientist-practitioner model in action.

Most of the chapter authors, and both of the editors, are academics who do applied work, but who devote more time and energy to research that does not necessarily have immediate application. I know that the authors tried to achieve more symmetry in the contributions to the book from both practitioners and academics. Does this mean that scientists seem to be more willing to go halfway in forging links between science and practice? It seems worth pointing out that practitioners may need to do more to facilitate these links.

It is appropriate that the authors have dedicated this book to Professor Joseph M. Madden, who was the major professor of both editors and many of the authors of chapters in the book. Matt Madden trained a large number of I/O psychologists and had a significant impact on the development of their scientific skills and values and on their appreciation of good application.

The book does show that I/O psychologists do practice what they preach about the scientist-practitioner model. It should be a valuable text for professionals and students in organizational psychology and related fields. The book should also be of interest to managers in personnel, human resources, and management development areas.

Edwin A. Fleishman, Editor
Series in Applied Psychology

Preface

This book grew out of a conference held in honor of Joseph M. (Matt) Madden, on the occasion of his retirement from the Department of Psychology of Rensselaer Polytechnic Institute. Most of the conference participants (and authors in the present volume) were former students or colleagues of Matt's. Although this book was conceived of as a tribute to Matt, and a partial recognition of his personal and professional impact on the field of industrial/organizational psychology, the project grew into something of broader significance—an exploration of the interaction of science and practice in I/O psychology.

The authors of this volume point out many of the problems and opportunities in integrating science and practice in I/O psychology. Perhaps the most fitting tribute to Matt is the fact that his students, colleagues, and associates share his vision that I/O psychology is fertile ground for the effective interplay of science and practice. As many chapters will point out, we still have a long way to go in establishing and maintaining a truly effective integration. However, the book contains many examples of successful integration, and specific suggestions for improvement.

On a more personal note, both of us would like to express our gratitude and affection for Matt. He served as a graduate advisor to both of us during our tenure at RPI, and helped to shape our visions of the field of I/O psychology. This book is a very small token of our esteem and respect for Matt Madden.

One of our contributors, Larry Reid, deserves special recognition. Larry initiated and organized the conference that led to this volume; without his forethought and effort, we would not have been able to pull together this group of authors and contributions. We also appreciate the contributions of the Rensselaer Polytechnic Institute, in particular, those of Dean Phelan and the Department of Psychology. RPI founded and hosted the conference, and several members of the Psychology faculty participated as program moderators.

Kevin R. Murphy
Frank E. Saal

Introduction

Applied psychology has a definite public relations problem, especially when the area of application is in organizations. Managers often believe that half of what psychologists know is nothing more than common sense, and that the other half is wrong. This evaluation probably *does* describe some of the activities of psychologists in organizations, but we believe it does not describe the state of the art in Industrial/Organizational (I/O) psychology. At its best, I/O psychology represents the successful application of basic scientific findings to practical problems. At their worst, I/O and other areas of applied psychology represent nonscientific guesswork on the part of people who should know better. The integration of science and practice is a critical issue in evaluating applications of psychology, and is especially relevant to the field of I/O psychology.

This book deals with two key questions. First, is there a firm scientific basis for the major applications of psychology in organizations? A related issue is whether or not it is possible to develop organizational applications for research in the behavioral sciences. Second, does the practice of psychology in organizations contribute in any meaningful way to psychological research? This book attempts to answer these questions by describing some of the ways in which I/O psychologists integrate science and practice in applying psychology in organizations.

There are at least two models for combining science and practice. First, there is the largely one-way interaction between pure scientists and engineers. Here the scientists supply the principles and the engineers supply the technology. This model works well for a wide variety of purposes, but it is not optimal when applying psychology in organizations. Although the reasons are complex, they include the facts that our "technology" is often relatively primitive, that organizations are living systems that do not simply and passively accept our interventions, and that our scientific knowledge is not sufficiently advanced to supply precise principles that can guide the development of useful technologies (Banks & Murphy, 1985).

The second model for combining science and practice features a two-way interaction between science and practice. In this model, individuals are trained to both generate and apply knowledge. Science informs practice by developing general principles that may apply to a particular situation. Practice informs science by identifying problems that need to be solved, as well as shortcomings in the current "solutions" that science has been able to provide in a particular situation. The scientist-practitioner functions somewhat like the Wright brothers did in inventing the airplane—by experimenting, by applying the results to a real problem, and by using the outcomes to generate new experimentation. As this example implies, the scientist-practioner model may be more appropriate for a *young* science like psychology than for the more established sciences. Although most of us would like to see the field move toward the status of a mature science, the division between relatively pure knowledge and technology is still not distinct in many areas of psychology, and the separation of scientific and practical roles in many areas of psychology is premature.

Applied psychologists attempt to balance two very different roles, that of a scientist who is concerned with developing and testing general theories of behavior, and that of a practitioner who is concerned with solving real-world problems. Although all of the applied branches of psychology pay homage to some version of the scientist-practitioner model, it is clear that much of this is lip-service. This is most obvious among clinical psychologists, where the true scientist-practitioner is a rare bird indeed, but some critics suggest that it applies to all branches of psychology. Their argument is that the scientist-practitioner model is so full of contradictions that it simply cannot work. Thus, some critics of the scientist-practitioner model (e.g., Frank, 1984) have suggested that there has always been and will always be a separation between science and practice in psychology, and that efforts to combine the two are futile.

We believe that the scientist-practitioner model is alive and well, and that it lies at the heart of the field of Industrial/Organizational psychology. That is, we believe that science informs the practice of psychology in organizations by identifying general psychological principles that can be used to explain behavior in organizations, and that practice informs science by identifying problems that need to be solved and complexities that need to be taken into account in scientific research and theories. Furthermore, we believe that I/O psychologists often function in both the scientist and the practitioner roles. That is, many I/O psychologists *do* function as true scientist-practitioners. In fact, we suggest that the scientist-practioner model is a *necessary* part of the field of I/O psychology, and that without the model, it would be difficult to answer the question "Why is there a field of I/O psychology at all?".

Although we believe that the scientist-practitioner model works well for I/O psychology, there are many ambiguities. First, is applied science really science, or is it really a process of technology development? The answer to this question may have implications for how we train scientist-practitioners. Second, do psychologists' roles in organizations allow them to apply the scientific method, or to draw from psychological research in solving organizational problems? The answer to this question may have implications for our evaluation of the scientist-practitioner model, because some of the failures of the model might more closely reflect specific organizational constraints than the weakness of the approach. Third, does the scientist-practitioner model describe multiple roles that *different* members of the field take on (i.e., some I/O psychologists may be pure scientists and others may be pure practitioners), or multiple roles that *each* I/O psychologist (or the majority of I/O psychologists) takes on. These questions are addressed by several authors representing different areas of expertise and different segments of the I/O community.

There are clearly problems in putting the scientist-practitioner model into operation, and several chapters in this book discuss those problems as they relate to psychology in organizations. The model also holds some promise. There is increasing concern in I/O psychology over the gap between research and practice (e.g., Banks & Murphy, 1985). This gap can only grow larger if science and practice are segregated into two separate communities. Doing both science and practice helps I/O psychologists to keep in touch with two very different bodies of knowledge: (a) knowledge about how organizations actually work and function; and (b) knowledge about human psychology. Indeed, we believe that the combination of science and practice in a single field is the only practical way to stay in touch with both of these aspects. This does not mean that every *individual* I/O psychologist must do equal amounts of science and practice, but it does suggest to us that the *field* must accommodate both ends of the spectrum, and that graduate programs in I/O psychology must train individuals who can speak to both the scientific and the practitioner communities. This book is designed to illustrate some of the problems and advantages of the scientist-practitioner model as it applies to I/O psychology.

Plan of the Book

This book is divided into four sections. The first section includes chapters by a practitioner and an academic scientist that describe problems with the scientist-practitioner model in I/O psychology. The third chapter of this section attempts to put the problems noted in the first two chapters into perspective, and argues that some of our problems with the scientist-practitioner model are due to unrealistic or poorly articulated expectations.

The second and third sections represent the body of the book. Our second section discusses the interaction between science and practice in personnel psychology, and uses the applications of psychology in assessment and evaluation in organizations to illustrate this process. Chapters in this section discuss applications of psychology in predicting managerial potential, assessment centers, job performance measurement, and productivity measurement and enhancement.

The third section discusses the interaction between science and practice in organizational psychology, and uses applications of psychology that relate to the psychological climates of organizations to illustrate this process. This section includes chapters dealing with corporate culture, conflict in organizations, sexual harassment in the workplace, and employee drug testing.

The final section of the book consists of some introductory remarks, and a chapter by Joseph M. Madden summing up the current and future status of the scientist-practitioner model in I/O psychology. This chapter is written from the perspective of an individual who has been involved with the application of psychology in the military and in other organizations for over 45 years, and helps to put our current debates about the scientist-practitioner model in I/O psychology into perspective.

Kevin R. Murphy
Frank E. Saal

REFERENCES

Banks, C. G., & Murphy, K. R. (1985). Toward narrowing the research-practice gap in performance appraisal. *Personel Psychology, 38,* 335–345.

Frank, G. (1984). The Boulder model: History, rationale, and critique. *Professional Psychology: Research and Practice, 15,* 417–435.

THE SCIENTIST-PRACTITIONER MODEL: PROBLEMS AND PROSPECTS

In this section, we describe some of the challenges of integrating science and practice when applying psychology in organizations. Jean Lapointe's chapter examines this problem from the perspective of a psychologist in an organization, while Robert McIntyre examines it from the perspective of an academician. These two chapters highlight a wide variety of problems in integrating science and practice, from the lack of relevant skills to the operation of reward systems that discourage integration. The chapter by Kevin Murphy and Frank Saal is somewhat less pessimistic in tone, and suggests that some of our frustration over the difficulties of integrating science and practice in I/O psychology result from unrealistic expectations. This third chapter suggests that the scientist-practitioner model is alive and well in I/O psychology. The chapters in Sections Two, Three, and Four of this book examine this possibility in some detail.

1 Industrial/Organizational Psychology: A View From the Field

Jean B. Lapointe
United Brands Company

This chapter is a product of my belief that Industrial/Organizational (I/O) psychology can be and should be directly applicable to improving organizational performance. This belief shaped my decision to study I/O psychology in graduate school and pursue its application as an internal and external consultant. After 17 years of experience in large, complex organizations (i.e., military, graduate school, and three Fortune 500 corporations), I believe more firmly than ever in the potential for I/O psychology to contribute to practical organizational improvement. I am, however, more skeptical than ever that its contribution will be realized without some fundamental changes in I/O psychology.

This skepticism is born of personal experience. The more I have tried to be an I/O psychologist, the less I have been able to be of practical value to the organizations with and for whom I have worked. As a "practitioner," I have focused on day-to-day organizational problems and opportunities: starting-up new plants, reorganizations, increasing teamwork, selecting and developing managers, improving morale, etc. The more I have focused on solving these practical organizational problems, the more I have found myself drawn away from the I/O psychology community.

My identification with I/O psychology has waned during my tenure as a practical problem solver. My interests have shifted from knowledge for its own sake to knowledge for action, from correct methodology to activity that is results-oriented, from what isn't being done perfectly to what can be done better. I am much more likely to read *Harvard Business Review* than *Journal of Applied Psychology*. My ongoing professional development has included improving my influence skills and learning the basics of finance rather than attending the

American Psychological Association (APA) or the Society for Industrial and Organizational Psychology (SIOP) conventions.

I have observed an analogous contrast in entire internal consulting departments. One department I observed was led by an I/O psychologist and staffed with three other I/O psychologists and an industrial sociologist. These individuals were well trained and genuinely concerned that their work be rigorous and up to I/O psychology's standards. Three of the staff were oriented primarily to the more traditional I/O areas: measurement, selection, and performance appraisal. Although never articulated, the department saw its primary mission as developing and installing human resource systems to be used by others. The department's reputation rested on the development and wide-spread use of a single, very successful assessment center.

A second department was staffed with a mix of I/O psychologists, business school graduates, sociologists, and experienced managers. I/O psychologists were always in the minority and the department was led by an MBA. This staff also viewed themselves as professionals and had a strong concern for the quality of their work. However, quality was measured primarily by results: Did they succeed in helping the organization perform better? The staff members prided themselves not on adhering to the standards of I/O psychology, but on being "close to the business" and contributing to its success. The department's mission was explicitly stated as contributing to the profitability of the business. Its reputation rested on having done that time and time again.

The second department was decidedly more successful. It averaged six to eight projects per staff member compared with two to four in the first department. The second department's projects were usually conducted for senior-level executives and routinely had major impact on employee relations and profitability. The first department worked most often at middle levels and, except for the assessment center, rarely affected the firm's operations. The second department grew while the first did not. The second department was very successful in attracting highly qualified staff, including experienced I/O psychologists. Openings in the first department were difficult to fill, except with entry level professionals. Staff from the second department were often promoted to other departments, a rare event in the first department.

This contrast, like my own experience, is limited yet clear. I/O psychology did not provide me or either of these departments with the skills and knowledge necessary to effectively and consistently contribute to improved organizational functioning. The first department limited itself to I/O psychology, did without these tools, and minimized its impact. The second department went beyond I/O psychology to find the tools it needed to have an impact.

Others have made similar observations. Boehm (1982) contrasted two models for I/O research. One is a model of "what should be" according to the norms and standards for rigorous scientific research. The other is a model of "what is"—

research as it actually takes place in "real world" organizations. In comparing these models, Boehm observed:

> In short, the 'what is' model is scientifically, distinctly messy in terms of methodology, complexity, statistical analysis, and the conclusions that can be drawn. Yet, at the same time, it seems to present a more accurate picture of organizational reality than a model based on 'what should be.' (p. 30)

She concluded that:

> By and large, the reaction of behavioral scientists, when faced by the realities of the organizational research environment, has been either to attempt modification of the environment to fit the traditional model of inquiry or else to opt out of the scientific establishment. (pp. 30–31)

The incompatibility between our methods and our subject matter frequently limits I/O research to areas where it is at least possible to more-or-less conform to the model of "what should be." These areas exclude many, if not most, opportunities to achieve maximal impact on the bottom-line performance of organizations. This is exactly what happened to the first department described earlier.

But why should we, as a field of inquiry, concern ourselves with contributing to improved effectiveness? Isn't this whole issue simply a matter of values? If I/O psychology chooses to value scientific rigor over practical applicability, then so be it. We know from the physical sciences that scientific rigor will eventually produce results that can be productively applied in the "real world." So, if some individuals want to sacrifice rigor in return for short-term solutions, maybe they *should* opt out of the scientific establishment.

The difference between practical and scientific orientations *is* a value difference. But it is more than that. We depend on organizations for access to the phenomena we seek to study. Organizations have their own interests, their own goals, their own problems. Unless we contribute to their interests, we will not have access. Especially in today's competitive environment, organizations do not have the luxury of devoting resources—time, money, people, attention—to academic research that does not benefit them in some demonstrable manner.

The importance to I/O psychology of access to organizations cannot be overstated. Kuhn (1977) described "normal science" as puzzle solving. The key to a thriving, vital science is interesting puzzles. These puzzles are to be found in real organizations. Gaining access requires that we provide a product of value.

Insisting on rigor and the pursuit of our own interests frequently deprives our field of its most important asset—interesting, meaningful work. Argyris (1980) and others (e.g., Kelman, 1969) have criticized rigorous research as being inconsistent with the objective of obtaining accurate data and developing valid theory. Boehm (1982) reminded us that "organizations do not exist primarily as research laboratories for behavioral scientists (p. 36)." Failure to recognize and act on this basic fact will, in her words, lead to "stagnation of the field . . . and widening of the communication gap between academic and organizational I/O psychologists (pp. 36–37)."

In his editorial review of this chapter, Murphy (Personal communication, September 29, 1988) suggested that I/O psychology is turning away from organizations as a source of puzzles. As an example, he noted that most of the recent performance appraisal research has drawn its inspiration from cognitive psychology, not from observations of appraisal in organizations. Murphy's observation highlights the extremes to which I/O psychologists will go to study phenomena that lend themselves to "scientific" methods, rather than using or developing methods which suit the phenomena. "Performance appraisal" is not a natural phenomenon. It is an artifact of organizational life, which occurs only after considerable structuring of time, attention, and effort. Balzer and Zulsky's chapter later in this volume shows how divorcing performance appraisal research from its organizational context has led to a sterile, disorganized body of research which ill serves I/O scientists and organizational practitioners alike. These authors call for reconnecting the research to its organizational context by incorporating the interests of the scientist *and* the organization in every stage of the research process.

Whether we wish to understand organizations or improve them, we must deal with the realities of organizational life rather than treating them as inconvenient obstacles to the techniques, programs, or research we wish to conduct. Doing so requires three elements. From a practical perspective, we simply must do better at working with real organizations on *their* business problems. Second, we need a science that directs and guides consultants, managers, and others involved in the creation and improvement of organizations. Finally, the dichotomy between science and practice, between academic and organizational I/O psychologists, cannot continue to exist. Thought and action, theory and practice, must be more closely integrated. The balance of this chapter briefly addresses each of these requirements.

REQUIREMENTS FOR EFFECTIVE PRACTICE

I/O psychologists who strive to improve organizational functioning do so primarily in the role of consultant. As consultants, we have the opportunity to get directly involved with significant organizational issues, to improve organizational functioning, and to observe and experience organizational life first hand. The consultant role provides a bridge between a body of knowledge and particular situations, problems, or opportunities. Effectively applying that body of knowledge within a particular setting requires an additional set of skills, attitudes, and knowledge. If we are serious about contributing to and learning from "real world" organizations, then our ability to consult effectively must be given the same attention as our ability to do research.

A practical attitude is perhaps the most important characteristic of effective consultants. This practical attitude is characterized by a genuine interest in a particular situation and a concern for and appreciation of the client organization's interest in that situation. I find I am effective when I focus on the client's legitimate interests and try to understand the situation in terms that are meaningful to the client. Theories, techniques, programs, and methods are all potentially useful, but only to the extent that they help in understanding and advancing the client's interests. A practical attitude is nothing more and nothing less than putting the client's interests first. Let me illustrate.

I often use employee surveys to diagnose an organization and to help prepare it to change. I have analyzed and reported survey results in many forms—means, percentages, two-by-two tables, with norms, without norms, gap scores, and so on. A few years ago I came across a survey that used a type of score that was new to me. The score is computed by asking employees to respond to each item three times: first, rating the item as it *is now* in the organization; second, rating it as it *should be;* and, finally, rating *how important* the item is to the employee. Each item is scored by taking the difference between the "is now" and "should be" scores. The difference is then multiplied by the "importance" score to produce a "need-for-change" score. Means on the need-for-change score are then computed and reported for different employee groups.

Statistically, this procedure is, at best, less than ideal. Many measurement experts would probably say it is less than acceptable. The need-for-change score not only relies on the ever-troublesome difference measure, it also multiplies that measure and averages the result. However, the need-for-change score has exceptional face validity with client groups—both management and employees. The survey, and more important, the results are readily understood and accepted by the organization. At a practical level, the quality of measurement is very good. The survey works superbly to identify strengths and weaknesses and provides a way for managers and employees to discuss, understand, and solve problems. Thus, when viewed from the ideal scientific perspective, this survey is far from the most technically sophisticated. But when viewed from the practical perspective of what helps improve an organization, it is very effective.

Because this practical attitude is so important to effective consulting, one human resource development group tried to capture it as part of their Mission Statement:

> The Organization Development Department exists to improve the profitability and long-term success of (our Company), and its subsidiaries. We consult with managers to help them better understand the "people side" of their business and to design

and implement changes which will make their organizations stronger, more flexible, and better able to meet their business objectives. Managers who work with us can expect:

- An objective perspective on their organization;
- A genuine respect for their concerns and for the realities of their business environment;
- A broad focus on their business as a whole system;
- Support and encouragement to make their organization better than it is;
- Expertise in management, general business, human resources, leadership, psychology, organizational behavior and development; and,
- Consulting and management expertise in (this Company) and other industrial and service organizations.

Beer (1987), in his keynote address at the Organization Development Network Conference in Seattle, referred to this practical attitude as "a concern for the critical path." The critical path consists of the one or two things an organizational unit must do well in order to achieve its business objectives. The path might include manufacturing efficiency, quality, customer service, or similar items.

Based on his research, Beer concluded that programmatic efforts to transform organizations are doomed to failure. By definition, staff (or consultant) programs such as performance appraisal, selection systems, quality circles, mission definition, training and development, and so on are not on most organizational units' critical paths. Such programs place additional requirements on managers and distract their attention from the critical path. These programs and techniques provide stability and structure for those who initiate them. They do not improve managers' ability to get the job done, unless they are in response to business objectives as defined by the organizational unit.

A practical attitude and its emphasis on client needs and interests makes salient two issues: (1) the legitimacy of client interests, and (2) the definition or criteria of improved performance. A key assumption underlying the value I place on client interests is that the client's interest is, in fact, to improve organizational performance. This broad assumption encompasses at least three more specific assumptions:

1. That improved organizational performance is desirable—that the unit and ultimately the total organization to which this unit contributes is engaged in activity that is legal, sanctioned by society, and is morally acceptable to the consultant.

2. That the client manager is pursuing legitimate goals—goals that can reasonably be expected to improve the performance of the unit and the larger organization, that the manager has some authority or charter to pursue, and that the consultant does not object to on moral or other grounds.

3. That the methods being used or contemplated are also legitimate and have some reasonable chance of achieving the intended outcome.

One advantage of a practical attitude is that it highlights the consultant's responsibility for the organizations and assignments with which he or she chooses to work. By emphasizing client interests, a practical attitude reduces the possibility that a well-intentioned consultant will deceive her or himself that "scientific ends" justify the "practical means" of a particular assignment. The consultant must also be concerned with the "practical ends" of the assignment.

The assumed link between client interests and improved organizational performance raises the question of criteria—what is improved performance? The practical attitude I have espoused means that the client's answer to this question is, in the end, the answer that must prevail. This does not mean that the consultant cannot or should not influence the answer. In fact, influencing the client's objectives may in some cases be the most important service a consultant performs.

If the client and consultant cannot agree on their "practical ends," the consultant is not free to say in effect "I know better than the client what is best for this organization." The consultant, in fact, may know better, but is not free to unilaterally impose that knowledge. Working in the client's interests means working in a way that client and consultant *agree* are in the client's interests. Similarly, when organizational objectives conflict with the consultant's personal or professional objectives (e.g., research objectives), the consultant is not free to unilaterally resolve those conflicts in favor of the personal or professional objectives.

Thus, a practical attitude not only raises the question of what the client's interests are and how improved performance is defined. It also points to the source of the answer: the client and consultant working together. In case of disagreement, the client must prevail; the consultant then either adjusts his or her objectives accordingly or, if necessary, withdraws.

A "practical attitude" is essential to successful consulting, but it is far from sufficient. Cullen, Klemp, and Rossini (1981) developed a systematic, research-based model of the requirements for superior performance as an organizational effectiveness (OE) consultant. Their research and the resulting model is based on the competency approach described by Boyatzis (1982).

A competency is "an underlying characteristic of a person which results in effective and/or superior performance in a job" (Boyatzis, 1982, p. 21). Competencies can include motives, traits, skills, self-image, definitions of role, and knowledge. Competencies are not simply behaviors; nor are they effective performance. Competencies do not artificially separate the person from the job. Rather, competencies are the personal characteristics that lead to superior performance in a particular job in a particular context.

Table 1. summarizes Cullen et al.'s (1981) OE consultant competency model. The model consists of 34 consulting competencies grouped into nine clusters:

TABLE 1.1
Organizational Effectiveness Consulting Competencies

FUNCTIONAL KNOWLEDGE	DIAGNOSTIC SKILLS
1. Knowledge of organization effectiveness theory 2. Knowledge of client system as an organization	21. Obtains multiple perspectives on situations/problems 22. Diagnostic use of concepts
STRONG SELF-CONCEPT	23. Uses metaphors and analogies
3. Self-confidence 4. Low fear of rejection 5. Exercises restraint 6. Perceptual objectivity 7. Accepts responsibility for failure	24. Rapid pattern recognition
	TACTICAL PLANNING
	25. Cause and effect thinking
PROFESSIONAL SELF-IMAGE	26. Identifies key themes in data
8. Sees self as substantive expert 9. Understands and works to overcome limits of own expertise 10. Develops others	27. Identifies and uses influence patterns 28. Accurately gauges the reactions of others
	TACTICAL FLEXIBILITY
DEVELOPS COMMON UNDERSTANDING	29. Assumes and differentiates multiple roles
11. Concern for clarity 12. Values client input 13. Establishes professional rapport 14. Surfaces and discusses key concerns	30. Responds consciously to client norms and expectations 31. Takes advantage of opportunities
PERSONAL INFLUENCE	32. Problem focused adaptation of techniques and procedures
15. Concern for impact 16. Use of unilateral power 17. Creates positive image 18. Uses interpersonal influence strategies 19. Understands own impact on others 20. Oral and written presentation skills	RESULTS AND ORIENTATION
	33. Concern for measurable outcomes 34. Time consciousness

From Cullen, Klemp, and Rossini (1981).

Functional Knowledge, Strong Self-Concept, Professional Self-Image, Develops Common Understanding, Personal Influence, Diagnostic Skills, Tactical Planning, Tactical Flexibility, and Results Orientation.

These 34 competencies distinguish superior from average OE consultants. The more of these competencies the consultant possesses, the more likely she is to perform in a superior manner. The sheer number of characteristics suggests that the job of OE consultant is particularly complex and demanding. In comparison, Boyatzis' (1982) management competency model includes 20 competencies in four clusters. Specific competency models developed for two positions (one in sales, one in management) with which I am familiar include four clusters and 10 to 13 competencies each. The relative complexity of the OE consultant model parallels Boehm's conclusion that the model describing "real world" research is much more complex than the model describing research the way "it should be."

Nine competencies (the professional self-image and diagnostic skills clusters plus knowledge of OE theory and identifies key themes in data) seem likely to be developed through education in I/O psychology programs. Other competencies, particularly those in the strong self-concept and results orientation clusters, may be more appropriately identified through selection rather than developed through training. But how many I/O psychology programs consider selecting even a portion of their students with these types of characteristics in mind?

The remaining competencies provide direction for I/O psychology to improve the effectiveness of consultants in our field. Three of the clusters stand out as particularly relevant to my own experience: knowledge of the client system, the develops mutual understanding cluster, and the personal influence cluster.

Knowledge of the client system speaks to the need to understand and work within a particular organization with particular business objectives and particular problems. In his OD Network address, Beer put "know the business" at the top of his list of prescriptions for those of us who would help organizations improve.

Much of this knowledge is obtained while working within specific organizations. However, understanding of different industries and of general business functions such as finance, marketing, and human resources can be obtained through reading, study, and traditional classroom education.

The ability to "speak the language" of business helps a consultant both to establish credibility and to understand how specific programs and techniques might or might not contribute to a given critical path. One company I worked with was in the midst of a diversification effort. I understood the rationale behind this effort in general terms. However, after attending a short course in finance, I was able to talk about the business reasons for diversification in the same language my clients used. This helped me to understand why the ability to innovate and diversify was central to long-term financial success. I have no doubt we would be more effective as a field if the major business functions were not a "foreign language" to us.

Two other competency clusters—develops common understanding and personal influence, both have to do with exercising influence. It is no accident that 10 of the 34 competencies relate directly to influence. Pettigrew (1982) emphasized the political nature of organizations and of working within them. The competency model provides concrete definitions of the influence skills needed to succeed in this environment.

Developing common understanding is a strategy of mutual influence. The client and the consultant develop a shared definition of the situation, the goals they will pursue together, and their expectations for each other's activities. The very process of developing this common understanding creates a situation where the client and consultant can work together to achieve common goals.

The competency of valuing client input is directly related to having a practical attitude. Behaviors such as actively involving the client in the design of activities, and consulting him or her before taking action, demonstrate a genuine concern for his or her interests in the situation. Such behaviors also increase the probability of discovering any conditions that could interfere with the success of the planned activities.

Establishing professional rapport and identifying key concerns are two sides of the same coin. By attending to the client's concerns, the consultant models candor and trust. Establishing rapport involves the ability to have the client talk about issues important to her.

Concern for clarity is, in my experience, the most important of the four competencies in this cluster. Until client and consultant can clearly state their goals, expectations, and understandings, it is impossible to know whether a common understanding exists. The best way I know to achieve clarity is to commit the understanding to a written "contract" which specifies project goals, responsibilities, timelines, and parameters in plain English.

The written contract should emerge from discussions with the client. These discussions might take 1 hour or several months. During the discussions, the consultant learns about the client, her view of the situation, her concerns, what she hopes to achieve, and how those achievements will contribute to her business objectives. The client learns about the consultant, how he will approach their work together, what the "deliverables" will be, and what the work will require from the client and her organization.

In addition to providing clarity for the client and consultant, the contract is very useful for providing clarity to others involved in the work. If a project involves the formation of an employee team, I typically review the contract with them to help all of them understand their roles.

Although the contract should be clear, it must not be inflexible. Changing conditions often require its modification during the project. The times I have gotten into trouble, however, were usually the times when I assumed the necessary modification was so simple or so obvious that I made it unilaterally. When there is a change in the project, it is important to make sure the change is clear and is acceptable to everyone involved.

The written contract speaks to the need for clarity and common understanding at a "macro" or project level. Ambiguous situations often exist before the contract is developed, or within the framework of the overall project. For example, a project might call for several meetings to negotiate roles. The first step of clarifying existing roles, and the ultimate goal of clear, mutually accepted roles, would be clear. However, the number and agenda of meetings or other actions required to achieve that goal may not be known until the work is underway. In such situations, one of the most useful rules of thumb I know is to always have "a clear next step"—a clear understanding of what will be done next, by whom, and when. A particular role negotiation meeting, for example, would end by developing the agenda for the next meeting. A clear next step allows progress to continue, even though all the steps necessary to reach the goal are not yet known.

The six competencies in the personal influence cluster speak to the paramount importance of influence skills for effective consulting. Organizations that do not influence their members cease to be organizations. Consultants who do not influence their clients cease to be consultants. Because the consultant usually lacks formal authority or power, his or her personal ability to exercise influence becomes even more important.

The six personal influence competencies can be divided into two groups. Concern for impact, creates positive image, and understands own impact on others all focus on the consultant's image as an influential person. The superior consultant thinks about how she can personally influence others. She knows that for her work to have an impact, *she* must have an impact. She actively creates a positive, successful image of herself. She recognizes that her enthusiasm and confidence are a source of energy and confidence for others. Effective consultants recognize that their mere presence acts as a signal or stimulus to others for certain types of behavior.

The other three personal influence competencies—use of unilateral power, use of interpersonal influence strategies, and oral and written skills—all focus on the exercise of influence. Use of unilateral power, for example, involves telling others what to do, taking control of meetings, and insisting on following the agreed upon plan or objectives.

Using interpersonal influence strategies requires going beyond the rational argument and analysis we value so highly as scientists. Co-opting others, bargaining, building alliances, and even withdrawing are influence strategies that can be used effectively. Being a source of energy, enthusiasm, and positive reinforcement for clients is frequently a very effective influence strategy. This strategy, while easy to execute, is often forgotten. It runs counter to both the academic emphasis on critical evaluation and to the diagnostic role of identifying client problems.

Oral and written presentation skills merit special attention. In a consulting situation, influencing others is the *primary* purpose of much of one's formal communication. The neutrality, the wealth of detail, the numerous qualifying statements, the technical jargon, and the inevitable "further research is needed" characteristic of our scientific communications are an anathema to getting business people to do what you want. Brevity, persuasiveness, and simplicity are valued. Knowing exactly what you want to say and saying it with confidence are essential. If you do not believe in what you are saying, neither will your audience. In watching myself and others, I have seen that "unlearning" the academic style and learning a concise, direct, unambiguous style is a necessary first step for success in "real world" settings.

There is one additional competency which, while not included in the model, distinguishes between successful and unsuccessful consultants, at least in my experience: thorough preparation. The better prepared I am for meetings, discussions, working sessions, or any other personal contact with the client organization, the more successful I am.

Preparing for client meetings focuses on three elements: (1) clarity about what I want to accomplish in the meeting; (2) a plan for how I expect to accomplish it, and (3) contingencies. The goals and plan must be simple—simple enough to share with the client or to remember and monitor while I am working with him. The contingencies include what I know about the situation, the participants, and how they might react. The contingencies also include priorities; if there is not enough time to accomplish all my objectives, I know in advance which ones I will let go until the next opportunity.

Thorough preparation helps in two ways. Of course, it provides a road map that increases the chances of my getting wherever it is I want to go. Just as important, however, thorough preparation allows me to focus on the client and her situation. By preparing, I have already taken care of what is important to me. In the meeting,then, I am able to forget myself and concentrate on understanding and responding to what is going on around me. For those of you who play golf or tennis, it is much like mentally rehearsing a stroke in advance, and then being able to focus entirely on the ball during the game.

The OE consultant competency model provides direction for improving I/O psychologists' ability to work in organizations and contribute to their success. Those working with organizations on their problems have the opportunity to observe and experience organizational life first hand. They are the ones who can test concepts and theories through application. We must, in my view, alter and expand our definition of I/O psychology so that competence in contributing directly to improved organizational performance is as much a part of our field as is research and teaching.

A SCIENCE FOR PRACTICE

The discussion to this point can be summarized in a single statement: Competence as an Industrial/Organizational psychologist does not necessarily include competence as an organizational practitioner, i.e., consultant, manager, or employee. This statement is not simply a conclusion about the training of I/O psychologists. It is a conclusion about the body of theory, methods, and data that define our science.

In contrast to I/O psychology, the experimental physical sciences require competence at manipulating the appropriate tools, equipment, and materials to produce the phenomena of interest. Chemists must be able to go into the lab and do chemistry. Nuclear physicists must know how to operate and often construct the esoteric equipment their discipline requires. As experts in organization, should not we be competent in the practice of organization? Is it reasonable that as experts in organization, we cannot be relied upon to know how to create organization?

Our current tension between science and practice exists, I believe, because I/O psychologists approach organizations with the same taken-for-granted assumptions as organizational practitioners: Organizations exist as objective realities that can be studied and understood apart from one's own interaction with them. This assumption results in the construction of theories of explanation (Argyris and Schon, 1978), which may explain and predict organizational phenomena but which cannot be used to create or control those phenomena. As a result, being an I/O expert requires expertise only in studying and explaining organization, not in creating organization.

Action theory (Silverman, 1971) starts with a different assumption about the nature of organizations: that they are continually created and recreated by organizational actors. These actors are continually engaged in making sense of, or enacting (Weick, 1969), their organizations. They perceive and interpret events so that they become sensible and they act and react to events in a way that is sensible. What is sensible, of course, depends on what one knows, believes, assumes, and expects about the situation. In short, the creation or enactment of organizational reality is a product of organizational actors' knowledge.

Many different terms have been used to refer to different types of knowledge or cognitive structures: scripts (Schank & Abelson, 1977), schemata (Neisser, 1976), and theories (Argyris & Schon, 1974, 1978; Nisbett & Ross, 1980) to name a few. Here, I use the general term "knowledge," or "cognitive structures," and the specific term "theory of action" to refer to a particular type of organizational knowledge.

> A theory of action is a theory of deliberate human behavior which is for the agent a theory of control but which, when attributed to the agent, also serves to explain or predict his behavior. (Argyris & Schon, 1974, p.6).

Action theory, therefore, goes beyond seeking to merely explain and predict organizations "objectively." Action theory seeks to understand the theories and processes that guide the deliberate behavior of human actors and, therefore, the creation of the organization.

This is not to say that all behavior in organizations is deliberate. Schank and Abelson (1977), for example, used the term "script" to refer to the cognitive structures underlying routine, well programmed behavior sequences, such as going to a restaurant. Much of what goes on in organizations may be determined by scripts, and may or may not be deliberate. Similarly, other types of structures may be involved in the perception and processing of organizational events. The perceiving and processing of events, people, etc. might not be described as "deliberate" in the usual sense of the word. Theories of action are thus a special type of organizational knowledge which, because they control deliberate behavior, assume special importance in the context of improving organizational performance.

Theories of action not only control the actor's behavior, they are also used to explain and predict behavior. Nisbett and Ross (1980) have shown that social actors attribute causes of behavior not only to others but also to themselves. Furthermore, these self-attributions are subject to many of the same errors as attributions to others. Consequently, an actor may attribute or espouse a theory of action for himself which is different from the theory that actually controls his behavior.

Argyris and Schon (1974, 1978) recognized these erroneous self-attributions by distinguishing between one's espoused theories of action and one's "theory-in-use." These terms recognize the potential incompatibility between the way we say we would behave and the way we do behave. Furthermore, Argyris and Schon (1974) pointed out that the actor may or may not be aware of the incompatibility between theory-in-use and espoused theory. Nisbett and Ross (1980) reported a similar finding from studies of social cognition. Consequently, we cannot simply ask actors for their theories of action. Rather, we must infer their theories from observable behaviors, and then test those theories against further behaviors.

Adopting an action theory perspective would benefit I/O psychology in a number of ways. It would draw our science and our practice closer together and, in so doing, improve both. Expertise in action theory I/O psychology would require expertise in the knowledge it takes to create, maintain and change organizations. And, as with the physical sciences, a certain amount of this knowledge would *have* to be practical, or capable of being put into practice by the I/O psychologist. Thus, the practice of I/O psychology would be grounded in our science, rather than in conflict with it.

Systematically articulating the knowledge used by managers, consultants, and other organizational actors would have tremendous impact on management education and organizational effectiveness. What would business schools and executive education programs look like if we knew what knowledge managers actually use in their work?

Consider the impact of McGregor's "Theory X" and "Theory Y." In my experience, this is one I/O topic with which nearly every manager is familiar, and which they use to describe other managers, themselves, and behavior. "Theory X" and "Theory Y" are nothing more than theories of action. The discovery or invention of only a few such general theories could have a tremendous impact on how organizations actually function.

An action theory perspective would also improve I/O science. The unspoken everyday assumptions and common sense knowledge I/O psychologists share with organizational actors would become an explicit part of our science which would be tested, rather than an implicit belief hidden from inquiry. For example, Balzer and Sulsky's chapter later in this book calls for incorporating client interests into performance appraisal research. These interests comprise one component of a theory of action. As another example, Murphy's chapter calls for recognition that productivity is, by definition, a ratio measure. If I/O psychology had taken the time to understand managerial knowledge, we would have known that managers define productivity, as well as many of their other key financial measures, as ratios. Simon's (1987) call for the development of expert systems of managerial knowledge is another example of the benefit of an action theory approach.

An action theory perspective would require a dramatic increase in the use of qualitative methods. Even an elementary understanding of managerial thought strongly suggests it is primarily qualitative, despite the emphasis on "numbers" in today's environment. For example, managers are typically more concerned with the direction of change (increase or decrease) than with the specific magnitude of the change. It seems likely that qualitative methods will most often be appropriate to study qualitative phenomena. Furthermore, the requirement that our results be understandable and credible to managers also argues for qualitative methods that are generally simpler and more straightforward than quantitative ones. The competency methodology mentioned earlier seems well suited to the task of identifying important knowledge used by actors. Newer quantitative methods such as confirmatory factor analysis and nonmetric scaling are also useful to study managerial knowledge structures (e.g., Lapointe, 1981; Walsh, 1989).

Finally, an action theory perspective will help integrate action and thought, practitioner and scientist in our field. Consultants' and managers' "soft," qualitative knowledge of organizations will become legitimate grist for the scientific mill instead of a mere description of the research site. It is almost as if we have always known this descriptive information about organizations really is important, but our theories and methods had no place for it. An action theory perspective not only has room for this type of information, but requires it.

The hours consultants spend learning about their client will have practical *and* scientific value for research into that client's theories of action. The consultant's access to intense client contact will become a requirement for identifying and testing theories of action. The practical demands to solve problems will become opportunities for the scientist-practitioner to invent new, more effective theories of action as well as to document existing ones.

INTEGRATION OF THEORY AND RESEARCH
WITHIN I/O PSYCHOLOGY

Within I/O psychology, there are encouraging signs that thought and action *are* coming closer together. This book is certainly one such sign. Others signs include the publication by The Society for Industrial and Organizational Psychology (SIOP) of books like *Making It Happen—Designing Research with Implementation in Mind* (Hakel, Sorcher, Beer, & Moses, 1982) and articles in *The Industrial Psychologist* about consultants and consulting practices.

We need to continue and expand efforts that bring together the academic and applied members of I/O psychology. I suggest that we also need to go further and bring these two orientations together in individual members of our field. Rather than having some people who are practitioners or "doers," and some who are academics or "thinkers," we need people who are both. The chances of truly integrating thought and action in I/O psychology will be much greater if we have the same people functioning as both consultants and scientists. The tools we have to achieve this are the standard ones: selection, training, rewards, and career paths.

The predominant path of entry into I/O psychology is through graduate programs. The dominant criteria for admission to these programs are academic aptitude and performance. We must expand these criteria to include consulting and/or managerial competencies. For selection purposes, we might focus especially on competencies that are difficult to develop through training, such as strong self-concept and a results orientation. Significant experience in business or other organizations could be a prerequisite for entry into I/O psychology graduate programs.

Training in I/O psychology, both in graduate school and afterwards, must include training in both consulting and research competencies. Just as a basic competence in statistics is required now, so should a basic competence in consulting be required in the future. Internships and other types of field experience are essential, and deserve at least as much focus and attention as any other aspect of graduate training. Business writing needs to be taught along with scientific writing. To provide this training, we need to forge closer links between industry and academia. One way is to encourage or require I/O psychology faculty to have an active consulting practice, rather than simply permitting or even discouraging such practice.

We need to alter the reward systems in our field to make it clear that we value excellence in consulting and in the science for practice described above. Nontraditional, qualitative research needs to be accepted and recognized as readily as quantitative work. Practitioners need to be able to contribute what they know about organizations to I/O psychology in a way that is respected, valued, and rewarded by the rest of the field. We need awards and rewards for excellence in research, teaching, *and* consulting. SIOP's Professional Practice Award is a step in this direction.

Most important, careers in I/O psychology need to transcend the traditional boundaries between industry and academia. Practitioners need time and resources to think and reflect on what they have learned, and opportunities to teach it to others. Academics need to ground their prescriptions and theories in real organizations.

At present, moving back and forth between the two communities is difficult. Graduates of our programs who wish to consult in industry must now spend several years battling the stereotype of the detached, impractical academic. Once accepted as contributing members of the business community, they are unlikely to have the necessary credentials to reenter the academic community. We need to develop career patterns where movement between academia and business is not only acceptable but desirable. Such movement would incorporate more of the consultant and managerial perspectives in our academic programs. It would also allow for our scientific knowledge to be incorporated into operating businesses more quickly.

In closing, if there is one message I hope to leave, it is this: If I/O psychology is serious about helping organizations improve, we must have the inclination and the ability to "get our hands dirty" by helping managers solve day-to-day business problems and learn new ways of managing. By putting this hands-on involvement at the core of what we do, we cannot help but develop a science that is interesting, valid, and useful to ourselves and to our clients.

REFERENCES

Argyris, C. (1980). *Inner contradictions of rigorous research*. New York: Academic Press.

Argyris, C., & Schon, D. (1974). *Theory in practice: Increasing professional effectiveness*. San Francisco: Jossey-Bass.

Argyris, C., & Schon, D. (1978). *Organizational learning: A theory of action perspective*. Reading, MA: Addison-Wesley.

Beer, M. (1987). *Keynote Address at the Organizational Development Network 1987 Conference*. Seattle, WA.

Boehm, V. R. (1982). Research in the "real world"—A conceptual model. In M. D. Hakel, M. Sorcher, M. Beer, & J. L. Moses, (Eds.), *Making it happen*. Beverly Hills, CA: Sage Publications.

Boyatzis, R. E. (1982). *The competent manager*. New York: Wiley.

Cullen, B. J., Klemp, G. O., Jr., & Rossini, L. A. (1981). *Competencies of organizational effectiveness consultants in the U.S. Army*. Alexandria, VA: U.S. Army Research Institute for the Behavioral and Social Sciences, Research Note 83-13.

Hakel, M. D., Sorcher, M., Beer, M., & Moses, J. L. (1982). *Making it happen*. Beverly Hills, CA: Sage Publications.

Kelman, H. C. (1968). *A time to speak*. San Francisco: Jossey-Bass.

Kuhn, T. (Ed.). (1977). Second thoughts on paradigms. In T. Kuhn, *The essential tension*. Chicago: University of Chicago Press.

Lapointe, J. (1981). *Organizational schemata: Cognitive structures underlying organizational climate perceptions*. Unpublished doctoral dissertation, University of Michigan.

Neisser, U. (1976). *Cognition and reality*. San Francisco W. H. Freeman.

Nisbett, R. E., & Ross, L. (1980). *Human inference: Strategies and shortcomings of social judgment*. Englewood Cliffs, NJ: Prentice-Hall.

Pettigrew, A. M. (1982). Towards a political theory of organizational intervention. In M. D. Hakel, M. Sorcher, M. Beer, & J. L. Moses (Eds.), *Making it happen*. Beverly Hills, CA: Sage Publications.

Schank, R., & Abelson, R. (1977). *Scripts, plans, goals and understanding.* Hillsdale, NJ: Lawrence Erlbaum Associates.

Silverman, D. (1971). *The theory of organizations.* New York: Basic Books.

Simon, H. A. (1987). Making management decisions: The role of intuition and emotion. *The Academy of Management Executive, 1,* 57–64.

Walsh, J. P. (1988). Selectivity and selective perception: An investigation of managers' belief structures and information processing. *Academy of Management Journal, 31,* 873–896.

Weick, K. (1969). *The social psychology of organizing.* Reading, MA: Addison Wesley.

2 Our Science-Practice: The Ghost of Industrial-Organizational Psychology Yet to Come

Robert M. McIntyre
Old Dominion University

Work is a central focus in many peoples' lives. It serves as their reason for education, their self-identity, their symbol of contribution in life, and the source of sustenance and even wealth. Industrial-Organizational (I/O) psychology is the study of human behavior at *work*. Therefore, given the centrality of work to humankind, one might expect that I/O psychology has high visibility in the world. Surprisingly, its impact on the world—both perceived and real—is rather minor. In this chapter I attempt to explain why this is the case. In the course of doing so, I present predictions for the future of our field.

I/O psychology is a "science-practice." This label is never used, although it seems quite useful in understanding who we are. A science-practice is a hybrid of two aligning professions. Before scrutinizing the hybrid further, it is important to examine each of its constituents.

Science is an intellectual endeavor to know, learn, and propagate knowledge by a particular method we refer to as the scientific method. The scientific method involves knowing the universe by observing it and by reasoning about what has been observed. Specifically, questions are asked, hypotheses are formulated, data are collected, and conclusions pertinent to the hypotheses are drawn. Notice that there is no mention of the *content* of the questions in this description of science. Yet most people, if asked to give an example of a science, would undoubtedly name chemistry, physics, or biology. Rarely, if ever, would economics, psychology, or sociology be identified. The social sciences, every bit as scientific in their methods, do not share the aura of scientific respect enjoyed by the hard sciences.

Practice is a professional endeavor to render services pertaining to important human problems or needs that require special expertise and "artisanship." As such, pure practice is problem- or service-oriented. Practice exists for the purpose of alleviating problems. Accountancy is an example of a practice because it requires special expertise to alleviate special problems or provide special services.

Science-practice refers to a field that combines both the art of practice and the scientific method's implicit goal of knowing. The term science-practice suggests the following: (1) The art involved in practice is anchored in the scientific method. (2) The questions addressed through the scientific method emanate from the problems within the scope of the practice.

A common example of science-practice is medicine, although not all practicing physicians behave as scientist-practitioners. Medicine exists as a *practice* to cure humankind's illnesses. It exists as a *science* under the guise of "medical research" to gather knowledge that pertains to humankind's health-related problems. It exists as a *science-practice* in dealing with health problems through scientific means and stimulating understanding of scientific questions about health through the provision of services. To the extent possible, therefore, science-practice uses the scientific method to solve real problems and uses these problems and results of the practice as a source of learning and knowing.

Strictly speaking, therefore, the science-practice of I/O psychology exists for the purpose of studying and solving work-related problems. Anything less is not I/O psychology.

Forces that Affect the Face of I/O Psychology

Modern geology describes the earth's crust as consisting of continental plates floating on a sea of molten magma—hot oceans of energy. At certain junctures or faults the plates grind against each other in fits and starts creating friction, tremors, and quakes. The result of these tensions is an ever-changing and ever-shifting earth crust: Mountains and valleys are born, earthquakes and volcanoes are stirred, and continental masses slowly shift across the earth's surface.

Three institutions—science, the workplace, and the university—similarly influence I/O psychology. As the substrata of our field, these traditions, like powerful ideological plates, grind at each other and create the tensions and conflict that many of us experience in our professional lives. If we can grasp the extent of influence of these subsurface forces, we might come to a more complete understanding of where I/O psychology has come from and where it is going.

As was already stated, science is an endeavor to know, learn, and propagate knowledge through the scientific method. As a way of ascertaining truth about the world, science presents us with certain opportunities and certain constraints. There are opportunities for us to ask and pursue questions about anything in the universe, including the world of work. The opportunities, however, are not the major issue here. The constraints are.

\ There are constraints in the *way* that we acquire knowledge. The scientific method requires time and patience. From the point when the scientist asks the first question about the universe to the point when he or she finds the answer through the scientific method, there usually is an enormous lapse of time. In addition, questions must be articulated precisely, hypotheses must be formulated based on careful reasoning, data must be gathered (usually with great fastidiousness), and conclusions and new hypotheses must be generated. It is important to recognize that strict adherence to the scientific way of acquiring knowledge conflicts with other, less patient methods of knowing and learning, methods that nonscientists regularly use. Scientists, therefore, find themselves in an intellectual tangle when they attempt to solve problems in circumstances where there are not sufficient data or time to collect data to answer questions in a scientific way.

The *workplace* also presents opportunities and constraints to the I/O psychologist. It encompasses the domain of behaviors that we seek to understand and problems that we seek to solve. As practitioners we are presented with the opportunity to solve important problems within this domain. As scientists we are offered the opportunity to comprehend human behavior in one of its most important activities—work.

The workplace imposes constraints as well. Its *raison d'etre* is to survive profitably. To most organizations comprising the world of work, the search for knowledge is only of interest to the extent that it contributes to creating goods or services, and creating wealth—the primary ingredients to profit and surviveability. Therefore, lack of understanding and lack of knowledge take on great prominence to most organizations only when they become obstacles to profit. This means that the workplace is much less patient about the scientists' goals and ways of operating. Organizations view research, data collection, and hypothesis testing, at best, as bothersome means to an end and, at worst, wastes of resources and precious time.

The third ideological foundation on which I/O psychology rests is the university. By "university" I mean the composite of traditions and management practices that comprise the major institutions of learning. If the reader is surprised to find the university occupying a place of prominence within I/O psychology, consider its various roles. First, it is the only legitimate *source* of full members of this field. There is no entry into the profession except through the Ph.D. bestowed by the university. Second, it serves as a major *employer* of many of its members. Finally, the university is the primary *regulator* of the writings that codify "legitimate" I/O psychology.

As the source of new I/O psychologists and as a primary employer of I/O psychologists, the university passes on to the field current university-based values and attitudes concerning the place of scientific method, technology, and practice. As a regulator, the university is society's gatekeeper for most fields—not just I/O psychology. The university sets the rules for what constitutes scholarship. For the most part, the university dictates the type of product that all academic fields will produce, how this product will be evaluated, and how often such products should be rolled off the academic assembly line.

Concretely, of course, the university carries out this regulation through its monitoring of faculty performance. The university says that good science is that which is published in good professional journals. Scientific product that does not readily fit into such journals is either nonscience or poor science. The university states that good scientists produce on *some regular schedule* in the professional journals. Scientists who fail to yield products according to this "tempo" are either nonscientists or poor scientists.

The typical university is not wholly concerned with scholarship in the "regulation" that it does. As an organization that itself is interested in its own "profitable" survival, the university does not (and, perhaps, *should* not) abide by the credos of good science. When the workplace provides fewer job openings for a particular scientific field, universities often intervene to reduce the extent of support for that discipline. Alternatively, when problem *solution* acquires a higher status in the world than problem *understanding,* universities are inclined to provide more support to, and place higher value on, the problem-solving disciplines like engineering and management than the scientific disciplines like physics or psychology. In other words, the university views the *questions* of science as less critical than the *solutions* provided by the more practical disciplines because *solutions* attract extramural support and recognition.

Perspectives on the fault.   Three cultures percolate beneath the "crust" of I/O psychology. At times, the fundamental concerns of each are at odds with the others. What science views as the critical element to its existence—adherence to the scientific method—is a frivolous and esoteric concern to the workplace. The workplace demands answers to questions about how to profit and survive. To science, these are viewed as either the wrong or less important questions. Organizations constituting the workplace pose questions with an impatient spirit. Hence, science's strategy for answering these questions—based on data collection, data analysis, and cautious conclusions—are perceived in the workplace as "irrelevant." Because their basic goals differ, science and the workplace are fundamentally incompatible.

Finally, the university must be considered. In pursuing its agenda as an organization, the university may downplay the important pursuits of science. Faculty positions may be cut due to exigencies. Although pure science views all intellectual pursuits as equally worthy, the university may selectively support disciplines that have acquired greater extramural visibility. Laboratory or research space may be handed over to the more conspicuous "problem solving" disciplines. Paradoxically, the university might very well find itself grating against one of its prestigious members—science.

Further, what the university defines as "scientific product" constrains I/O psychology to a "hard" or laboratory science model—a model that fails to take into account the practice side of the field. In other words, the university has a controlling function that grates against and antagonizes the field. The university naturally expects I/O psychology faculty, because they view themselves as scientists, to generate journal articles, to acquire external grant or contract funds, and to teach. Yet, the workplace, the focal point of our field, expects from I/O psychology nothing more than simple, quick answers to profit-relevant questions without all of the niceties so characteristic of university-spawned products. Because their goals differ, the workplace and the university are fundamentally incompatible.

One might say that the field of I/O psychology rests on a sort of "ideological fault" where these three cultural "plates" grind constantly against each other. I believe that many of the characteristics of our field—the debates we engage in, our struggle for professional identity, the nature of the products we offer the world—largely derive from this ideological fault, this struggle that exists among these three powerful forces.

Facets of the Ideological Fault

This ideological fault, as I have called it, is responsible for a number of frustrations and problems that we, as practicing I/O psychologists, must confront. I discuss three of the particularly troublesome ones.

Nature of research questions.   What constitute real scientific questions? It is useful to consider the cultural biases of our three constituent forces on this issue. The sciences accept any issue as legitimate for scientific inquiry, provided that it is amenable to scrutiny by the scientific method. Organizations in the workplace, for the most part, regard scientific questions, in and of themselves, as unimportant except as these questions directly affect their primary purposes. Universities send mixed messages on this issue. They protect the academic freedom of all scholars to pursue any avenue of knowledge. Yet they selectively reinforce research endeavors involving hard-science and engineering-related questions. It is not so much that universities are awed by the technical sophistication of the questions. Sadly, it is that such questions attract the financial support of outside agencies.

One consequence of universities' attraction to technology (or to the financial support that accompanies it) is a message that I/O psychologists' scientific contributions and capabilities are much less significant than are those of the other technologically oriented scientists. The result is a certain self-consciousness on our part. We must prove to the university that we do "real science," despite the questions we ask!

The dual roles of science-practice.   As a science-practice, I/O psychology has dual concerns and dual roles, and this creates conflict. First, this duality creates some problem for the traditions of science. Although the sciences accommodate all sorts of questions, they deplore constraints in the inquiry. In contrast, our science-practice, as a matter of course, faces constraints in its inquiries posed by the exigencies of the workplace. Organizations need answers *now,* not sometime in the future after data are collected. "Best-guess" solutions to problems are perfectly appropriate and applauded. Esoteric excuses and inconclusiveness are inappropriate.

Traditional science has difficulty complying with these requirements and constraints. Its way of answering questions requires data. The scientific method will not be pushed by exigencies. It is a fundamental thwarting of scientists' primary beliefs to gather fewer data than are needed or to provide answers to questions on less than the amount of evidence that "should be gathered." Essentially, then, the scientist role conflicts with the practitioner role.

Publish or perish.   Universities have established amazingly universal criteria for assessing the success of their faculty members. Although the number varies from one institution to the next, the fact is that a successful university faculty member is one who generates some particular *number* of professional publications. Consider the effect of this criterion on the development of good science. It encourages university faculty to concern themselves with *quantity* of publications that, in turn, has little directly to do with the development of good science. Concern for quality of ideas is often replaced by a concern for number of entries on a curriculum vitae.

This may appear to be a university issue and, therefore, of little concern to organizations in the workplace. On the contrary, the negative effects for the workplace are substantial. The publish-or-perish management philosophy invites I/O psychology faculty members to strive for visibility in the scientific press rather than to provide solutions to workplace problems. Under this philosophy, work-related problems are much less important than *multiple discussions* of these problems, no matter how impotent or cogent these discussions may be. To those in industry, university-based I/O psychology retains an image of "stuck in the ivory tower." The consequence of this image is serious: *All* (or most) ideas coming from university scientists are considered irrelevant by the workplace because a *subset* of these ideas are the sterile result of the publish-or-perish system. The creative thinking carried out within the walls of the university loses its credibility and, therefore, its potential to make a difference.

For those of us who work in industry, the publish-or-perish criterion may seem little more than a minor annoyance. It may appear not to affect our professional lives very much. We should reconsider. In light of the fact that most I/O psychology publications come from the university setting, I believe that the publish-or-perish system is a serious issue for nonacademics as well. It curtails the quality and diversity of published ideas and thereby leaves practicing I/O psychologists to fend for themselves. It dilutes the impact of good I/O psychology research because it induces the common belief among practitioners that publications are the product of academics' efforts to appease the demands of a performance management system.

MANIFESTATIONS OF I/O PSYCHOLOGY

We I/O psychologists have three "masters"—science, the workplace, and the university. Because of this, the field's demands on its professionals are challenging. I believe that few of us balance the roles of scientist and practitioner. Most of us play the scientist role at some point or another in our careers and the practitioner role at other points. This is our way of coping with the ever-present challenge to balance the practice and science. It may be informative to consider some of the roles we adopt.

The basic researcher.   At times or in certain circumstances, we play the "pure or basic researcher" role. In some ways, this role comprises a most comfortable set of work activities, particularly if they take place in the laboratory. The basic I/O psychology researcher is allowed to think abstractly about issues in the workplace, without having to deal with the practical limitations that the workplace imposes. Much laboratory-based research that the basic researcher carries out is critically important, particularly in new *programs* of research. In these endeavors, ideas need to be tested. Measures need to be developed and scrutinized.

On the other hand, there are times when we become *too* comfortable in the laboratory and forget the fact that, as I/O psychologists, our bailiwick is the workplace. I refer to this role as the "disconnected basic researcher." During this phase of our professional existence, the *comfort* of the university-based laboratory prevents us from the real business of I/O psychology. It is so easy to sample from the available "colony" of virgin minds (undergraduate psychology students) for whom the research topics—performance appraisal, leadership, work motivation, to name a few—have only abstract significance. In discussing this basic research of convenience, Dunnette (1966) pointed out that our choice to engage in pure research

> . . . seems to arise out of the early recognition that gathering data from real people emitting real behaviors in the day-to-day world proves often to be difficult, unwieldy, and just plain unrewarding.

The danger, of course, in buckling under to this recognition is that

> we retreat to relative security of experimental or psychometric laboratories where new laboratory or test behaviors may be concocted to be observed, measured, and subjected to an endless array of internal analyses. (Dunnette, 1966, p. 346.)

It is simplistic and cynical to blame our tendency to be the disconnected basic researcher solely on the "difficulties of real-world research." A consideration of our "substrata" provides additional insights. Recall that science as a tradition requires that scientists control extraneous variables and isolate the problem to be solved in an unconfounded research design. As social scientists, this "requirement" is a part of our intellectual heritage, and we believe in it strongly. On the other hand, organizations are much too fluid for us to control all sources of "extraneous" variation while we seek to isolate a single work-related phenomenon. This frustrating realization pushes us to the laboratory setting. Furthermore, the university community reinforces expeditious work that leads to professional publications. The laboratory-based researcher can abide by an expeditious schedule much more readily than can the field researcher.

In commenting on the disconnected basic researcher role, Dunnette (1966) stated that we often

> . . . lose sight of the essence of the problems that need to be solved and the questions that need answers. The questions that get asked are dictated—all too often—by investigators' pet theories or methods, or by the need to gain "visibility" among one's colleagues. (p. 348)

He cites the following personal communication from John Campbell:

> Psychologists seem to be afraid to ask really important questions. The whole Zeitgeist seems to encourage research efforts that earn big grants, crank out publications frequently and regularly, self-perpetuate themselves, don't entail much difficulty in getting subjects, don't require the researchers to move from behind their desks or out of their laboratories except to accept speaking engagements, and serve to protect the scientist from all the forces that can knock him out of the secure "visible circle." (p. 348)

Campbell blamed our inclination to carry out basic research on the Zeitgeist. His statements were made nearly a generation ago. Apparently, the Zeitgeist has remained stable.

The Provider of Services—the Pure Practitioner.   We also provide I/O psychology services. Some of us do this at different stages of our professional lives. Others of us provide services as the primary part of our careers. I am speaking of practicing the *art* of I/O psychology, whereby we offer solutions to problems in the workplace with the technologies of our field. Too often, we leave our scientific heritage behind in these sojourns, along with our interest in developing knowledge and, importantly, our interest in providing services based on the scientific method. For this reason, I refer to this as the "disconnected practitioner role," implying that this type of practice is disconnected from the science of our field. There are several reasons for assuming the disconnected practitioner role. We feel frustrated that our field is doing less than an adequate job in solving workplace problems. We are driven by a strong desire to serve the organizations that employ us on their terms, and to provide service to people. Finally, we may be bent on increasing our monetary wealth.

There are positive and negative repercussions of the so-called disconnected practitioner role. First, we are intent on paying attention to the real problems, the ones that affect the bottom line. This is praiseworthy, provided that we guard against translating "real problems" into "problems that our technologies can readily handle." Second, we are intent on serving our clients, in giving them what they ask for. This is legitimate, provided that we clarify for the clients that what they want may not be what they need. Third, we avow an allegiance to clear communication, and use language that clients can understand. This is laudable, provided that our clear language openly discloses what our science-practice can *legitimately* provide and what it cannot. Fourth, we market our technologies (like assessment centers, behaviorally anchored rating scales, management-by-objectives systems). Marketing these techniques is fine to the extent that they address clients' problems. To the extent that they are replacements for sound data-based interventions, such marketing is off base.

The scientist-practitioner.   There are times when we play the fully connected, integrated, scientist-practitioner role. Showing a tolerance for ambiguity and a willingness to put up with frustration, we balance the urgency of workplace demands and the tenets of scientific investigation. There is no simple formula for doing this. Nor are there many rewards. The work itself—not publications, fame, or wealth—is the scientist-practitioner's reward.[1]

THE PRODUCTS OF I/O PSYCHOLOGY

Published Basic Research

On the one hand, the term "basic I/O psychology research" refers to the investigation of an issue that is *temporarily* scrutinized in the laboratory and, therefore,

---

[1]Even though there are many famous, well-to-do, and well published scientist-practitioners, the scientist-practitioner role, in my opinion, is an inefficient means of acquiring fame, wealth, or publications.

temporarily disconnected from the real world. The problems investigated in this "pure research" begin as real world issues, however. The scientist-practitioner decides to engage in "basic research" because, in the course of a program of research, he or she discovers that certain facets of a problem require attention independent and separate from the practical problem. For example, questions about what makes an individual a successful jet pilot might generate basic research issues related to visual acuity or structures of the intellect.

On the other hand, too often what is thought of as "basic I/O psychology research" evolves from several generations of other "pure research." Laboratory studies of this sort abound in the I/O psychology literature. Essentially, they ignore and are disconnected from real problems in the workplace. Such basic research too often involves *the* standard research paradigm in psychology: a 2-hour experiment with college students participating in make-believe settings. Little or no attention is paid to the differences between this type of "research" setting and the workplace. Ultimately, this type of research becomes and remains forever severed from the practical issues to which it was supposed to relate. Guion (1988a) blamed the proliferation of such studies on "publication fever," a condition he claims exists in epidemic proportions within university settings.

The problem with disconnected basic I/O psychology research is not the fact that it takes place in the laboratory. The key problems are, first, that basic researchers pay insufficient attention to the fidelity of the research conditions in the design of the study; second, they fail to take infidelity into account when interpreting the results. This leads to overgeneralizations regarding the applicability of results. I/O psychologists in industry who seek answers to work-related questions read this type of basic research and have difficulty ascertaining the implications and limitations of the findings for working organizations. Referring to this problem, Guion (1988a) pointed out that we pay insufficient attention to the boundary conditions of the research.

Disconnected basic research lacks the relevance to the workplace necessary to make a difference. Consequently, it merely contributes to the frictions of our field. I know I/O psychologists working in industry who are increasingly disenchanted. They look for guidance from published research and find more questions than answers. They speak of the lack of realism of the research. They show beginning signs of doubt in the science-practice's capability in negotiating real world problems. (See Lapointe's chapter in this volume for a discussion of this point.)

Gizmology

Science and technology use methods, techniques, and tools designed to accomplish their ends. When these methods, techniques, and tools become the "cart before the horse," or "the tail that wags the dog," gizmology is born.

Gizmology has long been a specialty product of I/O psychologists. We are known for our penchant for gizmos. In most psychology departments across the country, the resident experts in statistical methods, computer techniques, personal computer software and, probably in this day and age, desktop publishing are the I/O psychologists. There are two general types of gizmos with which we have become enamored: *tools of the trade* and *techniques.*

Tools of the trade.   The tools of our science-practice are quantitative and statistical methods. A review of the major journals in our field reveals one striking message: We are up to our intellectual ears in esoteric statistical methods. The faint of heart had better bring a thesaurus of statistical methods (and a thermos of strong coffee) before attempting serious perusal of any issue of the "top-tier journals."

Echoing the points of other writers, I have several concerns on the proliferation of quantitative methods. My first is that we have adopted an implicit "philosophy" that places quantitative methods and statistics in a niche above the problems that they are intended to help us solve. Instead of tools, they have become legitimate problems in and of themselves. Our science-practice is steadily becoming "methodology."[2] This often begins in graduate school where statistical expertise among the students assumes symbolic significance of power and more general expertise.

An anecdote brings this point home. One of the first things I learned in graduate school was the importance of "regression" for us "I/O types." As a new graduate student, I found myself conversing with one of the psychology department's elders, an experimental psychologist of Tichnerian vintage. In the course of this conversation, I mentioned my budding enthusiasm for "regression," perhaps in an attempt to impress him with my heartiness and maturity. Harkening back to memories of (or perhaps *conversations with*) Sigmund Freud, the wizened professor responded with a perplexed look. I had difficulty deciphering his nonverbal message of confusion. Was he disapproving of my interest and enthusiasm for statistics? His follow-up quip about my interest in reverting to childhood led me to believe that he was out of touch with what was happening in the real world of psychological research. Today, I draw a different conclusion about this incident. Not only are we as a field enthralled with our quantitative methods for their own sake, but our fascination with these methods begins at the earliest stage of our development, often in place of a fascination with the content of the field.

William L. Hays, a respected statistician and methodologist, has admonished readers of his classic text, *Statistics,* that it is all too easy for researchers, particularly young ones, to misunderstand the place of statistical methods in their careers. In warning against allowing the statistical method to take precedence over the scientific problem, Hays (1988) states that although statistical inference

---

[2]I am using the word "methodology" here in the strict sense of the word: a study of methods.

is a valuable tool in research, "it is never the arbiter of good research" (p. 282). Dunnette (1966) described our preoccupation with statistics more incisively as "statistical pet keeping." Among the "favorite pets" that Dunnette enumerated nearly 23 years ago were "factor analysis, complex analysis of variance designs, the concept of statistical significance, [and] multiple regression analysis." The list of pets today would include *far* more exotic creatures.

My second concern about quantitative methods pertains to the correctness and appropriateness of their use. Because quantitative methods have assumed a status equal to the problems that our science-practice purports to address, and because of the increasing user-friendliness of computers, we occasionally use these methods ignorantly and inappropriately. One of the most common violations entails the use of large-sample statistical methods—for example, LISREL, factor analytic techniques, multiple regression, and discriminant analysis—on small samples of convenience with no attempt or mention of "replication of results."

Thankfully, I am not alone in my tirade concerning the inappropriate use of quantitative methods. In discussing the very same issue, Guion (1988a) blamed the problem in part on the explosive arrival of so many *new* statistical techniques. He also blamed the problem on a deficiency in our graduate students' education. He believes that every graduate student in psychology should enter graduate school with the equivalent of an undergraduate major in mathematics. Although this may address the ignorance component of the problem, I wonder how much of it is actually attributable to pure mathematical ignorance. For example, the researcher might choose an inappropriate statistical method not out of ignorance but because, as a technique in vogue, it will impress reviewers and readers of the research.

My third concern with quantitative paraphernalia is that they distract us from one of the primary purposes of I/O psychology—understanding people at work. Stagner (1982) suggested that sophisticated quantitative methods dehumanize our science-practice by covering up the very human element of the problems. Leadership, motivation, training, equity of reward systems—all of these are human problems with human consequences. We often begin with full awareness of these kinds of problems, but then lose sight of the human aspect by hiding behind the pseudoscientific sophistication of numerical procedures.

Techniques.   Another, perhaps more subtle, form of gizmology concerns the techniques that we lavish on our clients, customers, and students. I say "subtle" because I am convinced that there is a not-so-silent majority of us who define our science-practice as a set of techniques for solving work-related problems. There is an illusion that we are dealing with content when we emphasize such techniques. In fact, we are reducing the profession from science-practice to technology. In emphasizing method over problem, the tail wags the dog.

Consider some of the common techniques: assessment centers, behaviorally anchored rating scales, brainstorming, the delphi method, management by objectives, policy capturing, and survey feedback (to name just a few). Does emphasis on these areas result in negative outcomes for the science-practice? The answer is "yes" and "no." Although the techniques serve an important purpose in our profession, there is danger in being so driven to use a technique that we neglect the very problem we are asked to solve. Another anecdote provides a case in point.

As a graduate student, I accompanied two consultants, neither of whom were members of the psychology department, to a meeting with a nearby business. In discussing the proposal that they would present to the prospective client, one of these individuals said the following: "I propose that we give them MBO . . . they'll *like* it and, besides, it can't *hurt* anyone." This proposal was formulated well before the meeting began with the prospective clients, and well before the clients' needs were completely understood.

This incident points to an important point about our methods. We become believers in ourselves as providers and proponents of techniques. We pigeonhole the workplace's problems in terms of the "standard" techniques for solving them. We neatly package the solutions to the problems that the workplace presents to us with ready "answers." Herein lies the real danger of gizmology: Replacing our scientific capabilities with ready answers without regard for the real questions. Quantitative methods and measurement techniques are valuable tools that facilitate our science-practice. They must not *replace* the science-practice.

Why gizmology? Why have many of us strayed into gizmology? Although many possible reasons can be listed, I believe there is one *overriding* reason: We are *self-conscious* about our role in the world. We doubt our scientific credibility because we recognize the dominance of the workplace's influence in our science-practice. (We think, "No respectable science would let itself be pushed around by the exigencies of the workplace.") The university community cannot quite figure us out. We call our work scientific, yet produce fewer publications than our laboratory-based colleagues. We bring in far fewer dollars than they. What's more, our subject matter seems more like "common-sense stuff" than the "stuff" of science. The workplace is suspicious of our pursuits, too. Other professions that serve the workplace wield esoteric mathematical wands to solve abstract financial, econometric, operations research, and accountancy-related problems. In contrast, we make up paper forms and administer them to "random samples," interview samples of incumbent workers, generate job descriptions on the basis of such interviews, and design training programs for the company's staff . . . all pretty mundane activities.

If this is even a partly accurate portrayal of our self-image, then it makes sense that dabbling in the esoterica of quantitative methods and in elaborate techniques may serve as a way to "make ourselves feel respectable." Consciously or unconsciously, we develop expertise in quantitative and measurement techniques partly to impress upon our "scientific selves" that we really have some legitimacy as a science, to convince the university that we really have the same sophistication as biology or chemistry or any of the other "hard" sciences, and to convince the workplace that we are every bit as effective (and abstruse) as the wielders of management science. In other words, gizmology serves as a defense against a poor, underdeveloped self-image.

Beneficial Products of the Field

In spite of its many diversions, the field of I/O psychology has benefited human-kind. The benefits are often subtle and overlooked, and sometimes hidden away in a place that the world will not notice. Take, for example, the truly valuable ideas in our technical reports or the articles in trade journals that translate technically detailed theories into practical solutions to the workplace's problems. Consider the experiences built into graduate programs that instill in students a curiosity and respect for organizations. Include undergraduate courses that provide students with new perspectives on the world of work, on management, on quality of work life, on meaning of pay, and so on. Nor should we neglect the professional journal articles reporting systematic and replicated research that has evolved from the laboratory to the field setting.

Other important products of our field are less tangible. Through our scientific yet practical approach to workplace problems, we instruct people to gain an appreciation for solving problems by means of the scientific (data-oriented) approach. We have created greater insight into the concept of cultural bias of tests, fairness to ethnic groups, gender bias, and sexual harassment. We have contributed to insights on the meaning of work, and the importance of money and other rewards in the workplace. We have worked to keep the human element on equal status with the advanced technology. We have raised questions concerning the effects of this burgeoning technology on the morale of workers. We have *not* rendered definitive answers in these problem areas. There are few definitive answers. Rather, our contribution has involved getting the workplace to *recognize* that these problems exist, that they need to be dealt with in the course of managing the workplace, and that they *can* be managed, to some extent anyway, through I/O psychology.

As scientist-practitioners, we have important things to offer organizations over and above our gizmos. We have an arsenal of ideas that, after translation into the terms and contexts of the workplace, will make them all the better. Many of the things we deem our major accomplishments are esoterica. But much of what we have in our arsenal of ideas really can make a difference.

THE FUTURE OF I/O PSYCHOLOGY

In invited addresses at three different meetings of the American Psychological Association, Lawshe (1959), Dunnette (1966), and Guion (1988a)—all past presidents of Division 14, Society for the Industrial and Organizational Psychology, spoke of the influence of our field on the world. Over the 29-year timespan that these addresses cover, one message remains amazingly (and disconcertingly) consistent: We, as a profession, are not effecting what we could effect. The question is, "why?" My answer is that ours is a "tough act." As a science-practice, we expend energy coping with the sometimes opposing forces of our scientific heritage and our practical goals, and have little energy left for bringing about the kind of changes that we could bring about.

It is tempting to respond to our plight by carrying out an historical analysis—a sort of postmortem on years gone by—to identify our many failings over the years. But this is just what the addresses by Lawshe, Dunnette, and Guion, referenced earlier, accomplished. They provided a critical accounting of where the field has been and where it was at the times of the addresses. I believe two, more important questions remain unexplored: (1) Where *will* the science-practice of I/O psychology go in the future? (2) Where *could* the field go (with some tweaking)?

THE "GHOST OF SCIENCE-PRACTICE YET TO COME"

Let us assume that we continue to be influenced by science, the workplace, and the university. Let us further assume that the goals, values and, importantly, our understanding of these three cultural influences remain constant. What will the future of I/O psychology be in, say, 25 years? Will the world know the accomplishments of our field, or will the field remain just another obscure academic discipline? Will universities recognize our contributions to knowledge and understanding of the world of work, or will we still be struggling to define for friends (and even family) what I/O psychology is all about? Will organizations hold the field of I/O psychology in high regard for a contribution to their welfare and that of their workers, or will they regard us as those people who fret about the impracticalities of test validation, rating forms, and attitude surveys?

My prediction is that we will continue to do a less-than-adequate job highlighting our *important* past contributions and garnering credit for the ideas that we have cultivated over the years. In other words, I predict that in 25 years the critiques of the field by Guion, Dunnette, and Lawshe will remain every bit as pertinent as they were in the past and are today.

I base my prediction on the conservative theory that the three most important forces on our field—our scientific heritage, the workplace, and the university community—will retain their discordant influence. The values of science will continue to create self-doubt when we engage in practice—that less-than-scientific side of our field that stands as a primary reason for our existence. The university will dictate by its tradition what constitutes acceptable evidence of success in our field. And the workplace will remain, for the most part, ignorant and unimpressed with all of our seeming folderol and esoterica.

At this point I am reminded of Ebenezer Scrooge, having communed with the third of three spirits:

> Before I draw nearer to the stone to which you point . . . answer me one question. Are these the shadows of the things that Will be, or are they shadows of the things that May be only? . . . Men's [sic] courses will foreshadow certain ends, to which, if persevered in, they must lead . . . But if the courses be departed from, the ends will change. Say it is thus with what you show me! (Dickens, 1843)

Following Ebenezer's memorable soliloquy, Dickens' third ghost remained "immovable as ever." I, however, will budge a little and make some recommendations for altering the future. These recommendations are directed at the university and the workplace.[3]

Directions for the Future in the University Community

Educate the educators. Because our field intends to provide practical answers to practical problems while retaining a strong allegiance to the traditions of science, it faces certain challenges that other scientific fields do not face. For the most part, other scientific fields do not have to convince their constituencies of the importance of collecting data. Yet I/O psychologists often find themselves creating crafty subterfuges within organizations so that they can collect real field data. They combine research with consulting if possible; they ask additional questions besides the ones they are paid to ask; they beg and borrow in order to gain the kinds of data required of field research. As a result, these data come with sweat and blood. What is most frustrating is that even after the data arrive, they often fail to provide the level of assurance that "cleaner" laboratory-spawned research data provide. The difficulties of the I/O scientist-practitioner directly result from a simple fact: The ways of the workplace—the primary target of our science—are not necessarily consonant with the ways of science. This point, and all of its corollaries, needs to be communicated to the university community.

Therefore, we must engage in a campaign to educate the university community about what we are as a science-practice, the questions that we ask, why they are scientifically tractable questions, what makes us *different* from other scientific fields of science, and what makes us *similar* to these fields. This educational campaign should remain just that—educational—with no agenda but to educate. It should not be presented as a "sales pitch" for increasing our office space, the number of faculty positions, the number of computers, the number of secretaries,

---

[3]I do not make recommendations for science because I believe that the *essential* scientific philosophy cannot and will not change. This is not to say that certain current beliefs regarding the implementation of the scientific method are unchangeable. Paradigm shifts in the field exemplify changes within a field that could lead to innovative ways by which science is implemented.

or the number of graduate assistantship slots. This campaign needs to be systemic and systematic. We need to reach the university president, the academic vice-president, and the entire community. It might even be wise to bring this "dog-and-pony show" to each university department. Finally, the student body should be educated about our field. We should take advantage of opportunities to talk about our field to groups of students, to discuss the important problems that our field tackles, and to impress them with our ideas!

Develop liaisons between the university and industrial communities.   One obstacle to academics' participation in research that is relevant to the world of work has been access and accessibility to the workplace. It is difficult for some faculty, either because of geographic location or lack of a "track record" in industry, to develop relationships with organizations to carry out field research.

To address this need, consider the movement among some of us to develop research consortia (Bracken & Stutzman, 1988). These consortia are designed to allow scientist-practitioners working in industry to share data, resources, and products. I recommend that university faculty become integrated into these industrially based research groups not so much for consulting purposes, as for the purpose of carrying out field research. Further, I recommend that our field formally support such consortia as a way of unifying the science-practice and cultivating greater understanding of the important problems that exist in the workplace.

Disseminate.   There is an almost universal tendency on the part of non-academics to resist writing about their work. Guion (1988a) refers to this as "publication paralysis." Folklore explains this state of affairs with the claim that the "real world" provides neither the time nor incentives for professional writing. Consider another explanation that supersedes time constraints and lack of incentives: There is no outlet for applied publications. A journal is needed that provides a forum for discussing the broadest range of I/O psychology topics.[4] Guardians of this journal should consist of a panel of nonacademics and academics. The journal should target scientist-practitioners within industry and academia as the primary audience. Topics covered should include "problems in the world of work" as our science-practice views them. How-to articles, case studies, think pieces, as well as applied field research should be fair game for this journal. The think pieces might include articles in which professionals clearly articulate the questions—and perhaps the answers—concerning practice or research in the field. For this journal, two rules should be enforced: (1) Write clearly; and (2) Respect, but don't fear, the science-practice. Finally—and this is why this recommendation appears within university-related future directions—

---

[4]Perhaps Landy's *Test Validity Yearbook* is a step in the right direction.

the journal should be sponsored by a university or a consortium of universities. Among other benefits, this would give the material discussed within the journal official legitimacy among the academic community. I believe that the journal would serve the science-practice immensely.

Making this journal work will not be easy. The first problem concerns the "home base" of this journal. Why would nonacademics accept a university-based publication? Two things will make this happen. (1) The editorial board, balancing the roles of science and practice, must be a *mix* of university- and industry-employed. (2) Nonacademics will have to be actively solicited to participate in the writing as well as the reviewing of articles.

"Publication paralysis," as Guion (1988a) has called it, is the second problem. It is an affliction that has had a long time to entrench itself. To make the journal work, we must deal with this problem by the following means:

1. We need to change our conception of what constitutes publishable work. If we encourage the variety of types of writing that I recommended earlier, this necessarily implies such a change.

2. We will have to begin by inviting authors from industry to write for the journal. While it is still new, I would anticipate that editors will spend a substantial portion of their time soliciting contributions.

3. We should encourage *teams* of academics and nonacademics to author submissions to the journal.[5]

Educate our new professionals.   In highlighting the word "educate," I exhume an old question. Are we educating or just "training" our new Ph.D.s? It is worth stepping back and taking stock of what is happening in education in general. The entire system of higher education in the 1980s seems to be *vocational* in nature. Students have transformed their intellectual curiosities about subject matter into questions like "Why do I have to know this?" and "How is this going to help me get a job?"

Although understanding the connection between formal courses and professional work is a legitimate concern for students, "why-do-I-have-to-know-this" types of questions speak to an ever-spreading attitude toward education. The belief is that knowledge and courses provide official credentials to gain access to some type of job. This attitude toward learning is becoming more and more

---

[5]Some have argued that no such journal will work because practitioners are not interested in publication. As evidence in support of this argument, Robert Guion has described the difficulty of getting manuscripts from applied psychologists for the last issue of the *Journal of Applied Psychology* under his editorship (Guion, 1988b). My response to this will probably sound like wishful thinking: I believe that this journal breaks tradition with the academically oriented journals (like *Journal of Applied Psychology*)and provides a new forum for professionals. Therefore, I believe it will work given sufficient time, patience, and commitment to this different journal philosophy that I describe.

common, even among those who pursue graduate-level education. The interest in knowledge for its own sake, in understanding aspects of the world just because they exist, is an endangered species of intellectual existence at all levels.

If we are to instill a deeper inquisitiveness and interest in the science of I/O psychology within our new professionals, we must deal with several basic issues concerning our programs. Do our doctoral programs provide clear treatment of what it means to be a scientist-practitioner? My impression is that, more often than not, our programs speak of and legitimize the existence of different "camps" within the field of I/O psychology: the "practitioner camp" and the "academic camp." In fact, many I/O psychology programs are informally known to produce primarily practitioners or primarily academics. Such an orientation is bound to give new I/O psychologists the destructive impression that one can separate the science from the practice, and the practice from the science.

These concerns imply certain recommendations for educating our new professionals: (1) We should educate our graduate students on the science-practice, in all courses and contacts with them. These interactions should instill a sense of professional identity within the neophyte. (2) We should educate students broadly and avoid spreading "publication fever." Guion (1988a) warned us about some of the worst of our practices as "educators": encouraging students, by example, to do "little, quick, and not-too-dirty studies that can be published somewhere" (pp. 3–4). Guion went on to say that when this practice manifests itself as early as the graduate level, it may prove incurable. (3) To the extent possible, reduce the number of required courses if the existence of these requirements leads students to believe that courses in the program are equivalent to hurdles that must be jumped rather than experiences in intellectual growth.[6] (4) Select students based on scientific inquisitiveness about the nature of things. Look for evidence of this in applicants' letters of recommendation, independent projects, and course papers. (5) Emphasize the importance of understanding the world of work in students' professional preparation. In this regard, encourage them to learn the language, issues, and concerns of the workplace. Encourage students to take courses in business schools or, even better, to become exposed to these topics in some practical way.

Evaluate the important products of our field.   In a scorching criticism of the publish-or-perish philosophy underlying current tenure systems that exist in most universities, Guion (1988a) forcefully reminded all of us that, in contrast to what the typical tenure review system entails, we as a field know something about a worker's "measuring up." Guion's point is that we need to bring the misguided practices of faculty evaluation and scientific product evaluation back on track with the ideas and tools we have so capably developed for nonuniversity organi-

---

[6]Thanks to Dr. Albert Glickman, Eminent Professor at Old Dominion University, for this insight.

zations. Guion took the opportunity to suggest several dimensions of faculty performance including the following:

1. pursuit and attainment of knowledge,
2. development of new knowledge "about *some* things,"
3. organization of existing knowledge,
4. dissemination of knowledge,
5. promotion of the use of knowledge, and
6. service to the university and general community.

Guion also suggested specific ways that these six performance dimensions can be assessed. His paper is worth reviewing.

I strongly believe that the faculty evaluation that goes on in the university setting is an issue for our field *as a whole,* for those who think of themselves as "applied" as well as the "academics." What happens in the university setting, because of the major influence that the university wields on our field, affects the research that is carried out and the new knowledge that is propagated. In other words, all scientist-practitioners are affected by what happens in the university setting. If this premise is accepted, then the next recommendation is quite logical: The Society for Industrial and Organizational Psychology (SIOP) needs to take a proactive, definitive, and organizationally based position on the evaluation of faculty in the field. This position would best be summarized in a "white paper" by SIOP and distributed to all universities that have programs in I/O psychology.

The following points should be among those covered in this paper:

1. Our field's expectations that its scientist-practitioners understand and learn from the problems that exist in the workplace;

2. The importance of a *variety* of written products generated by our scientist-practitioners, including technical reports written for organizations;

3. The importance of service to the community and organizations;

4. The significance of longitudinal programs of research in spite of the fact that the present system discourages such programs;

5. The importance of *descriptive* studies in real work settings (like those carried out by modern anthropologists involved in investigations of primitive societies) as well as field and laboratory experiments;

6. The importance of communicating with and educating organizations in presentations, seminars, technical reports, and the like; and

7. The importance of publications in the "lay press."

For other reforms, particularly those relevant to faculty evaluation, we must rely on the more experienced members of our field who have acquired necessary influence to motivate such changes. For example, consider the role of external reviewer of candidates for promotion and tenure. I believe that we as a society should take a proactive stance to articulate what should be considered in these external reviews. Guidelines are needed to assess the general impact that each candidate has had *within the context in which he or she is working.* Implicit in this statement is a particular philosophy of performance appraisal: The faculty member ought to be evaluated with respect to the goals and expectations of the university within which he or she has served. I would anticipate that these guidelines would help the reviewer evaluate the relative worth of

1. written technical reports,
2. written research proposals to organizations,
3. oral presentations to organizations,
4. publications in "trade journals,"
5. published writings in refereed professional journals,
6. advising and working with graduate students,
7. advising and working with undergraduate students,
8. providing professional service to community organizations, and
9. teaching graduates and undergraduates.[7]

Directions for the Future Relevant to the Workplace

Educate the workplace. Most organizations are not sufficiently aware of I/O psychology. They do not understand its purpose and do not comprehend its mission. Our primary response to this state of affairs is to sell ourselves and our science-practice. This word "sell" has an awful ring to it. It calls up images of fast talk and charlatanism. I use it here in the best sense of the word. Note that educating others about something is equivalent to selling that something in its entirety. In this sense, we must continue at a greater pace to sell ourselves, to explain what we as scientist-practitioners are about and what our professional mission is, and to describe what we uniquely offer to the workplace. To have an impact in this educational process, we must take on a sense of pride in our profession, and openly display this pride to organizations on every possible occasion. We need to educate organizations about the *unique* frustrations of scientist-practitioners, while at the same time espousing the value of the scientific method to solve their problems.

What vehicles are available to serve this educational end? First, formal presentations. As a society, we should decide to make formal presentations to our employers that describe our science-practice as it fits into their environments,

---

[7]By promulgating such proper methods for evaluating faculty contribution, I predict spinoff benefits to *all* university disciplines.

their universes. Those of us who are employed by large organizations should regularly "work in" presentations to organization members at all levels of the organizational hierarchy. These presentations should explain the kinds of problems we can address, the kinds of methods we use, the philosophy behind these methods, the successes we have enjoyed, the failures we have suffered, the utility of our interventions, the kinds of education we use in preparing future generations of I/O psychologists, and in this latter regard, the importance of the internship experiences that many organizations presently support. The point of these presentations is to communicate clearly and convincingly what we are about, and to explain the critical role of the workplace in our field.

There are other vehicles. We should make an effort to publish articles in company newsletters and magazines where they exist. We should view every interaction with organization representatives as a chance to educate, and we should take care to educate well. All of us, academics and nonacademics alike, should identify, promote, and publish in "trade journals" that treat issues within our field. Finally, we should include in our formal job descriptions activities that support our science-practice, including reading the professional literature and writing for this literature base.

This suggestion may seem naive. Yet, I recall that the job description of my first position with Bell Canada indicated that 10% of my time should be devoted to keeping up with developments in the field by reading professional journals. Lest readers think that this is a recounting of ancient history, my 2-year stint in Bell Canada ended in 1980.

Keeping up with the field and contributing to it by our writings involve a professional responsibility. This makes another comment about "scientific responsibility" appropriate at this point (Guion, 1988a). Many of us treat the practice side of our professional selves as our own personal business. Guion (1988a) caustically described this phenomenon as an "almost sociopathic freedom from any sense of responsibility to science." He stated that some of us (or all of us at times?) view ourselves as "tradesmen for whom the march of science is important only insofar as [we] can use advances made by others." Further, he hit on a most important point: We too often excuse ourselves from sharing our findings "by saying that [our] behavior is due to an environmental obstacle ('The boss won't let me share this information')." Guion explained that he has become increasingly skeptical of the excuse that employers treat the products of their professionals as proprietary. I agree. There is no question that there are *occasions* where organizations will not budge from such a policy. I question whether we have taken the necessary steps to educate these organizations about the value of scientific dissemination. I wonder if we do not cave in a little too soon on the issue. If our science-practice is to build on the momentum that it has already accumulated, and make a significant impact, we must adopt an ethic to work for the betterment of our science as well as for organizations and our personal fortunes.

Collaborate with fellow professionals.   We will remain isolated within organizations to the extent that fellow professionals remain uninvolved in the things that we do within organizations. Bridges connecting the management scientists, industrial engineers, economists, lawyers, and accountants would serve to increase the impact of our science-practice. Shaped by the knowledge and techniques of these fields, we might adopt new perspectives on solving old problems. Influenced by our clarity of purpose in understanding the human worker, these professionals may change their approaches to dealing with their own issues and problems. Of course, the difficulty in all of this involves educating ourselves to be able to "connect" with these professionals. This is where the education of our new graduating professionals might help.

THE BOTTOM-LINE

When this chapter was first conceived, I must admit that my mood was sullen. Setting out on a course to criticize the scientist-practitioner model, I was skeptical about its value and its usefulness. Perhaps you have shared some of these ambivalent feelings. The task of writing has brought about a sort of metamorphosis within me. Faced with the possibility that the scientist-practitioner model may be less than adequate, I was forced to identify another, more useful process to guide our (my?) professional existence. I discovered that we have no alternative. From the very beginning of modern I/O psychology, we were a science-practice. We are so by definition, by virtue of what we study and the methods we use.

We continue to feel the repercussions of opposing forces—science, the workplace, and the university—that grate against each other like three ideological "plates." These forces explain who we are, where we have come from, and possibly where we are heading. These forces explain why the field has failed to make the difference that a science-practice like ours *could* and *should* make. Will we continue only blandly affecting the world of work? Yes . . . if we continue on the present course. "Are these the shadows that Will be, or are they shadows that May be only?" That is up to us.

REFERENCES

Bracken, D. W., & Stutzman, T. M. (1988). The research consortium: Sharing data, resources, and headaches. *The Industrial-Organizational Psychologist, 26,* 49–54.

Dickens, C. (1843). *A Christmas Carol.* New York: Weathervane books.

Dunnette, M. D. (1966). Fads, fashions, and folderol in psychology. *American Psychologist, 21,* 343–352.

Guion, R. M. (1988a, August). *Pratfalls in the march of science.* Invited address (upon the award for the distinguished scientific contributions) to the Society for Industrial and Organizational Psychology, Meetings of the American Psychological Association, Atlanta, Georgia.

Guion, R. M. (1988b, August). Comments made during the invited address entitled *"Pratfalls in the march of science."* Invited address (upon the award for the distinguished scientific contributions) to the Society for Industrial and Organizational Psychology, Meetings of the American Psychological Association, Atlanta, Georgia.

Hays, W. L. (1988). *Statistics (4th Ed.)*. New York: Holt, Rinehart, and Winston.

Lawshe, C. H. (1959). Of management and measurement. *American Psychologist, 14*, 290–294.

Stagner, R. (1986). Past and future of industrial/organizational psychology. In F. J. Landy (Ed.), *Readings in industrial and organizational psychology*. Chicago: Dorsey Press.

3 What Should we Expect From Scientist-Practitioners?

Kevin R. Murphy
Colorado State University

Frank E. Saal
Kansas State University

The preceding chapters highlighted many of the problems encountered when we try to integrate science and practice in Industrial/Organizational (I/O) psychology. These problems notwithstanding, there are several reasons to believe that the effective integration of science and practice is indeed possible, and that the scientist-practitioner model is appropriate and viable for I/O psychology. In this chapter, we hope to put the problems noted in Chapters 1 and 2 into a useful perspective, and we suggest that some of our current frustration over roadblocks to integrating science and practice may be the result of unrealistic expectations. First, we review the essential features of the scientist-practitioner model, and discuss criticisms of this model in both clinical and non-clinical areas of psychology. Next, we discuss the conditions that are necessary for the effective integration of science and practice. Third, we examine the extent to which these conditions are present in both the academic and organizational contexts where the science and practice of I/O psychology are carried out, and suggest changes in research and practice that are needed to facilitate the integration of science and practice in I/O psychology. Finally, we outline what we believe are reasonable and achievable expectations for a field of psychology that attempts to follow the scientist-practitioner model.

THE SCIENTIST-PRACTITIONER MODEL

The scientist-practitioner model is, in theory, the dominant model for training and practice in American applied psychology. This model has been reaffirmed at virtually every major conference on graduate education (Bickman, 1987; Hoch,

Ross, & Winder, 1959; Raimy, 1950; Roe, Gustad, Moore, Ross, & Skodak, 1959; Strother, 1956). For example, the recent National Conference on Graduate Education in Psychology adopted several resolutions that are relevant to this model, including:

1.3 "It is essential in the graduate education of applied and professional psychologists to include education and training in the conduct of scientific research as well as the application of products of psychological research"

8.8 "Faculty members should demonstrate and/or support the integration of science-practice-teaching roles . . ."

9.1 ". . . Synergy between science and its application in psychological practice can help bridge the diversity which characterizes psychology."[1]

Although these conferences have concentrated more on clinical psychology and related fields than on nonclinical areas, the sheer number of clinicians, counselors, and other health care providers suggests that even if they were the sole proponents of this model, the scientist-practitioner model would still dominate.

The scientist-practitioner model prescribes that: (a) psychologists be trained and skilled in both the conduct and the application of psychological research, (b) science provides the basis for practice, in that the knowledge and techniques that are applied to solve practical problems should have a firm scientific basis, and (c) practice contributes to science, by identifying problems that need to be solved, and by providing a testing ground for the products of scientific research. The model discourages both practice that has no scientific basis and research that has no clear implications for practice.

One difficult issue in defining the role of a scientist-practitioner is whether the integration of science and practice should occur *within* persons or *between* persons. Different ways of integrating science and practice could be arranged on a continuum, where one extreme is the case in which all members of a discipline undertake both scientist and practitioner roles, and the other extreme is the case in which members of the same subfield are divided into two camps, pure scientists and pure practitioners. Neither extreme is likely to be encountered in reality. First, it is unrealistic to expect that all members (or even a large majority) of a particular subfield will actively pursue both science and practice roles. It is equally unrealistic to expect that two separate but equal groups (the scientific group and the practitioner group) will develop in a given field, or to imagine that two such disparate groups could work together well. It seems, therefore, that a field that truly follows the scientist-practitioner model will include some members who are primarily researchers, some who are primarily practitioners, and

---

[1]These resolutions are reprinted in *American Psychologist, 42,* 1070–1084.

some who combine both roles in a more balanced proportion. That is, scientist-practitioner fields are likely to be characterized by *both* within- and between-person integration of science and practice.

Although the scientist-practitioner model is formally endorsed by most applied psychologists, individuals who regularly combine research and practice roles are quite rare. This is most evident in the health-service areas of psychology (e.g., clinical, counseling, psychotherapy), but is also true in some nonclinical areas of psychology. The question that arises, then, is whether the scientist-practitioner model really is (or ever was) a viable one. We think there is evidence that this model is becoming less relevant for many applied psychologists.

Trends for Science and Practice

One concrete indication of the decline of the scientist-practitioner model is the dramatic increase in the number of psychologists who adopt exclusively practice-oriented roles, as opposed to research-oriented roles, or roles that emphasize both science and practice. American psychology is quickly moving in the direction of becoming a practice-oriented health-care field, a trend that is illustrated in Fig. 3.1. Although some health service psychologists are both producers and consumers of research, the majority appear to focus almost exclusively on developing and applying their skills as practitioners (Frank, 1984). Recent changes in the nature and mission of the American Psychological Association (APA) also mirror the trend shown in Fig. 3.1. Many research-orientated psychologists feel that this trend has gone so far that a new national society is necessary to represent scientific psychology, and have formed the American Psychological Society (APS) for this purpose.

A second piece of evidence comes from studies of the research activities of psychologists. It is clear that research and publication are rare activities for the great majority of Ph.Ds in psychology (Frank, 1984; Hoch et al., 1966). Most Ph.Ds never publish any empirical research, and for many of those who *do* publish, the dissertation is the first and last contribution to the published research literature. Even among clinical psychology faculty, research typically has a low priority (Goldfried, 1984). Among students, the priority given to research is even lower; it is widely believed that most Ph.D students in subfields of psychology oriented toward health care would simply not do research if it was not formally required of them (Frank, 1984). Finally, the research that is done appears to have little impact on clinical practice; practitioners frequently complain that clinical research is irrelevant to clinical practice (Kupfersmid, 1987).

The foregoing problems are not confined to the clinical community. One could argue that most I/O psychologists do not function as scientist-practitioners. The field is characterized by longstanding tension between those in the I/O community who are primarily oriented toward research, and those who are primarily oriented toward practice. A quote that is attributed to Bruce V. Moore

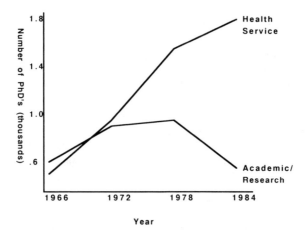

FIG. 3.1.   Ph.D's awarded to health service versus academic research psychologists. *Note.* Data are reported in Howard, Pion, Gottfredson, Flattau, Oskamp, Bray, and Burstein (1986). The changing face of American psychology: A report of the committee on employment and human resources. American Psychologist, 41, 1131–1327.

(thought to be the first person to receive a Ph.D in I/O psychology) nicely illustrates the extent and nature of this tension. Although World War I represented the first successful large-scale application of psychology in this country, Moore showed little interest in solving applied problems, and at the end of the war was reputed to say, "Now we can get back to the real business of psychology."

Like clinicians, I/O psychologists formally accept the scientist-practitioner model (Moses, 1986). However, I/O psychology also seems to be divided into two communities, one that is research-oriented, and another that is practice-oriented. Furthermore, most nonacademic I/O psychologists are not actively engaged in research or research publication. In the 1950s and 1960s, approximately 30–40% of the published research in the I/O psychology literature was contributed by nonacademics. Currently, only 15% is carried out by non-academic I/O psychologists (Sackett, Callahan, DeMeuse, Ford, & Kozlowski, 1986). Again like clinicians, practice-oriented I/O psychologists have complained that current I/O research is not relevant to practice, and does not help them solve problems in organizations (see, however, Banks & Murphy, 1985; Feldman, 1986. Also see chapters by Lapointe and McIntyre in this volume).

When one considers the problems raised in Chapters 1 and 2, along with these trends, one might wonder whether the scientist-practitioner model is viable at all. We believe that the answer is a qualified "yes." The model can work well if the necessary conditions for the integration of science and practice are present. Many of the failures of this model in clinical and I/O psychology may be attributable to a lack of the prerequisites for integrating science and practice rather than to a fundamental weakness of the model. It becomes essential, then, to examine these prerequisites and to assess the degree to which they are likely to be present in the various settings where psychologists (especially I/O psychologists) are likely to be employed.

PREREQUISITES FOR INTEGRATING SCIENCE AND PRACTICE

The successful implementation of the scientist-practitioner model depends on a careful (or fortuitous) match between the characteristics of psychologists and the characteristics of the settings in which they do and apply research. Three essential prerequisites can be identified. First, psychologists (and students of psychology) must have values that are compatible with the dual roles of scientist and practitioner. Second, they must have the skills to do and apply scientific research. Third, and perhaps most important, the settings in which they work must allow them opportunities to do relevant research and/or to apply the results of the research.

Values

The scientist-practitioner model requires the integration of two distinct value systems, one that emphasizes precision and scientific caution, and another that emphasizes action and the solution of practical problems (Spence, 1987). This integration is especially difficult for clinical and other health-service psychologists, because the humanistic value system that often characterizes practice is fundamentally different from the scientific value system that usually characterizes research (Kimble, 1984). However, this integration is probably difficult in *any* applied area of psychology (for discussion of this integration in social psychology, see Chein, 1966; McGuire, 1967; Ring, 1967; Streufert, 1987), and the problem of value incompatibility may help to explain the relative rarity of individuals who are seriously engaged in both research and practice, as well as the obstacles to communication between scientists and practitioners. As Spence (1987) noted, very few psychologists have the inclination or the flexibility to be comfortable in both scientist and practitioner roles.

Several studies suggest that scientists and practitioners differ not only in their values, but also in terms of their interests, personalities, and temperaments (Frank, 1984; Hoch et al., 1966). Put simply, different people seem to be drawn to science-oriented than to practice-oriented roles. If the choice of science-oriented vs. practice-oriented roles is determined in part by highly stable individual differences (e.g., basic values, personality, temperament), there may be strict limits on the extent to which the integration of science and practice roles *by a single psychologist* is possible, and it may even be difficult to encourage meaningful interactions between scientists and practitioners in the same area. We do not believe that research on personality differences among and between scientists and practitioners is sufficiently advanced to draw firm conclusions about the inherent plausibility of integrating scientist and practitioner roles. This literature does suggest, however, that there is likely to be a "ceiling effect" when counting the number of psychologists who take on both science and practice roles as compared to those who concentrate entirely on one role rather than the other. If personality places some limit on a person's ability to effectively integrate these roles, it may be unrealistic to expect that the majority of psychologists in *any* area will be *both* scientists and practitioners.

It is easier to describe value systems that would prevent one from effectively integrating the roles of scientist and practitioner than to describe the value system that would facilitate this integration. First, there is the belief, sometimes expressed by psychologists in nonapplied fields, that applied psychology is not "real" psychology. There is some merit to this point of view; virtually all applications of psychology involve activities and interventions that are not solely psychological in nature. For example, a psychologist who designs a performance appraisal system strictly on the basis of the most recent research on cognition and judgment will not be successful. A successful application of psychology in this instance will require the psychologist to be aware of and to take into account organizational realities, such as the political pressures faced by raters who wish to give either unusually high or unusually low ratings (Murphy & Cleveland, 1990), and it is unlikely that the system that is optimal in the specific organization will be the same as the system that is best from the perspective of scientific research. Nevertheless, the recognition that applied areas of psychology differ from nonapplied areas does not imply that one is good and the other is bad. A value system that gives a markedly less favorable evaluation to applied activities than to research that is not conducted with application in mind is fundamentally incompatible with the scientist-practitioner model.

Value systems that are sometimes associated with practice can prevent the successful integration of science and practice. In particular, the belief that the *process* of doing research is irrelevant to one's activities as a practitioner appears to be widespread (Frank, 1984; Kimble, 1984); this belief will clearly hinder the integration of science and practice.[2] One's beliefs about the fundamental causes of behavior might also have direct implications for the value that is attached to research. The belief that the causes of behavior are completely idiosyncratic, and that they can be understood only from the subjective perspective of the actor (and perhaps only in hindsight) will make it impossible for one to do psychological research, or to use the results of other psychologists' research. Being a scientist-

---

[2]Discontent with the utility of the results of current research is another matter. A psychologist who fully accepts the validity of the scientific approach may nevertheless conclude that research in a particular area does not help in solving a broad class of practical problems.

practitioner requires that one believe that research is possible and that research can help solve practical problems.

A related value system is sometimes encountered among managers, and to a lesser extent, among practitioners. Personal experience is often viewed as a necessary and sufficient prerequisite for solving practical problems. This value system has two components: (a) that knowledge and results from other settings do not apply in one's own setting, and (b) that people learn to solve problems simply by being repeatedly exposed to them. Both components will lead to distrust of research as a process for addressing real-world problems, and will greatly hinder the integration of science and practice.

Skills

The second requirement for the effective integration of science and practice is that psychologists have the skills necessary to successfully perform in both roles. Research skills include: (a) problem definition, (b) design of experiments and studies, (c) operationalization of variables, (d) data collection, and (e) data analysis and interpretation.[3] Most graduate students in psychology receive some training in all five areas, although the amount of coursework involved and the centrality of these skills to the student's training vary considerably across different areas of psychology. Even in graduate programs that offer a professional degree (such as the Psy.D–Doctor of Psychology) rather than a Ph.D, students are likely to receive some exposure to these topics. Thus, it is safe to assume that most psychologists will have *some* skills as researchers, although many seldom-used skills may dissipate over time.

The set of skills that are needed to practice psychology will depend greatly on the nature of the practice, and also on the context in which the psychologist works. Health-service psychologists will need a different set of skills than will I/O or Human Factors psychologists. The skills needed to work effectively in a large organization may be different than those needed to function in a small one. An I/O psychologist working as an external consultant to a large organization may need different skills than one who is working as an internal consultant in the same organization. Because of the diversity of skills required in different settings, we focus here on one type of psychologist and on one setting, and discuss skills required of I/O psychologists employed as members of an organization's human resources department.

Howard (1984) described the role of the I/O psychologist in industry, and noted that several skills that are not taught in graduate school are highly relevant to success in organizations. First, psychologists must "sell their services," or convince other organizational members or units that their services will be useful

---

[3]Specific areas of psychology may require additional skills. For example, surgical skills may be needed by a researcher who is studying the physiological regulation of hunger.

in solving practical problems. As psychologists in organizations quickly learn, there is usually little spontaneous demand for their services, nor is there clear recognition of the types of problems psychologists might be able to solve. Second, psychologists in organizations usually function as managers rather than as autonomous professionals. They must therefore be skilled in supervising others, delegating authority and tasks, planning, and other typical managerial functions. Third, they must be able to communicate the results and implications of their work to a nonprofessional audience, and must be able to translate jargon into understandable prose. Fourth, and perhaps most important, they must understand the context. That is, they must learn or know how the organization functions and why, and must understand the goals, the culture, and the climate of the organization. Understanding the context is essential to recognizing and avoiding constraints on one's ability to effectively address problems in the organization.

For both organizational staff and external consultants, one additional critical skill is to know the limits of one's knowledge and expertise, as well as how to bring others' expertise to bear in solving problems encountered in organizations. The ethical principles accepted by most psychologists, and many state licensing regulations, require that they do not practice outside of areas in which they are competent. Psychologists working in organizations are very likely to encounter problems that are outside of their areas of expertise, especially because the role of "psychologist" is likely to be poorly defined and poorly understood in most organizations. We believe that graduate programs in I/O psychology do not provide enough training in recognizing and dealing with the ethical dilemmas that are likely to be encountered in organizations. More training in translating the ethical principles for psychologists into concrete guidelines for ethical behavior as a manager is needed.

Skills in problem definition and diagnosis are especially critical for external consultants. It is common for consultants to find that the *real* problem is substantially different than the problem that is presented to them when they are contacted by the organization. For example, what managers describe as a problem with their performance appraisal scales may in fact reflect problems with rater motivation, or with communication between different levels of the organization. External consultants are less likely to know, in any detail, the context of the organization (although they may know the contexts of organizations in general), and thus cannot draw upon their knowledge of the particular situation to diagnose organizational problems.

There is clearly an imbalance in graduate training in research vs. practice skills for I/O psychologists. Virtually every I/O psychologist will take courses dealing with statistics and research design, and will have many opportunities to develop and demonstrate research skills, but few will have more than an occasional seminar on the practice of I/O psychology. Other training devices, such as internships, may provide additional training in practice-related skills, but these experiences are clearly not seen by many faculty as equally important as research training activities. Whether this is good or bad is hard to say; we believe that training *should* be imbalanced, and that the tilt should be strongly toward developing first-class research skills. However, the training of I/O psychologists cannot safely ignore the development of practice-oriented skills. I/O psychologists who lack skills in applying their research to organizational problems will not be effective as scientist-practitioners, or as credible sources of information for their practice-oriented colleagues.

Opportunities

No matter what one's values or skills, science and practice cannot be effectively integrated if the setting in which one works does not allow this. For example, many psychologists working in organizations have few, if any opportunities to do research, and must devote all of their time to solving practical problems. Similarly, a clinician in private practice may not have access to the data needed to test his or her hypotheses. Many academics have limited opportunities to apply their knowledge of psychology, or are discouraged from devoting time and energy to application. If it is true that many of the contexts in which psychologists work do not allow science *and* practice, it may be a good thing that relatively few psychologists share values that emphasize both roles. Indeed, we are not at all sure that the proportion of psychologists engaged in both science and practice is any larger than the proportion of situations that allow one to function as both a researcher and practitioner.

Although opportunities to do both research and practice may be rare, we should not overemphasize the limitations this places on one's ability to integrate science and practice. Psychologists working in an organization may not have the opportunity to do research, but there is nothing to prevent them from basing their practice as a psychologist on others' research findings. Similarly, some academics and employees of research units may have few opportunities to actually practice psychology in organizations. This does not prevent them, however, from doing research on problems that are relevant to the practice of I/O psychology. Although doing both research and practice is desirable, it is not essential for the effective integration of science and practice. Thus, limitations on one's ability to do research or to practice are barriers to their integration, but these barriers are not fatal to the scientist-practitioner model. Recognition of the constraints that are often placed on a psychologist's ability to do research *and* apply this research in organizations may help us to develop more realistic expectations about scientist-practitioners, and may also point toward recommendations for minimizing those constraints.

CHANGING THE CONTEXT

It is clear that the relationship between science and practice has not worked out in the way that the early applied psychologists expected. For example, Munsterberg predicted that . . . "Applied psychology will . . . become an independent experimental science which stands related to ordinary experimental psychology as engineering to physics" [Quoted in Kargon (1986), p. 24]. In I/O psychology, this clearly has not occurred. We believe that this can be partly explained by examining the context in which I/O psychologists work, particularly those in private industry.

As we noted earlier, I/O psychologists working in industry are likely to have job titles such as "manager of human resources," or "director of personnel," and are very unlikely to have job titles that include the term "psychologist." These job titles reflect the underlying reality, that I/O psychologists lose some of their status as psychologists when they take jobs in industry. That is, they are very likely to take jobs in which they do not function solely, or even primarily, as psychologists. As a result, their opportunities to do psychological research, or to keep up with the research of other psychologists are somewhat limited.

The plight of I/O psychologists is not shared by all scientists, scientist-practitioners, or professionals employed by organizations. For example, a microbiologist or chemist who is hired by a large organization is generally able to function as a microbiologist or chemist. This person may be moved into management at some later point in his or her career, but this move is not automatic. Thus, scientists hired in these disciplines (and other natural science disciplines) are able to function, for at least part of their careers, as scientists. That is, they are likely to have opportunities to do research, and the results of their research are likely to be taken seriously by organizations. Similarly, engineers are hired by organizations to work on technical projects, and are not expected to cease functioning as engineers the moment they enter the organization, although this may happen later in their careers (i.e., when they are moved into management). Finally, lawyers employed in organizations have a status closer to that of a semiautonomous professional than to that of a manager working in a legal department. Their legal research and advice is likely to have a substantial impact on the organization.

Why is it that many members of some disciplines retain their status as scientists, engineers, or professionals when working in industry, while many psychologists (and other behavioral scientists) do not? We believe that one explanation is that natural scientists, engineers, lawyers, and so forth are thought by other members of the organization to have at their command a substantial array of specialized information that is critical to the success of the organization, and is not readily available to managers who have not received extensive advanced training in these fields. Psychologists, on the other hand, are not thought by organization members to possess unique specialized knowledge of this sort. This is so for at least two reasons. First, other organization members are likely to feel that they too know a good deal about human behavior; although a manager may never be exposed to chemistry, or to legal research, he or she deals with human behavior every day. Managers might not have any well-developed theories, hunches, or stereotypes about the best way to combine chemicals, but they are very likely to have theories and hunches about the behavior of other organizational members, and they are unlikely to believe that the psychologist's specialized knowledge is in any way unique. Second, the specialized knowledge that *is* possessed by psychologists is unlikely to be perceived as essential for the success of the organization. Although other managers may acknowledge that psychologists possess some knowledge that they do not (e.g., knowledge of psychometrics and experimental design), they are unlikely to value that knowledge.

If I/O psychologists are to have any realistic hope of eventually attaining the status of scientists or scientist-practitioners in organizations, it will be necessary to change both the way we do research and the way we practice psychology in organizations.

Changing Research

Ruback and Innes (1988) noted that psychological research is often viewed as irrelevant by policymakers, and suggested a fourfold classification of psychological research similar to that depicted in Fig. 3.2. This classification is based on two variables: (a) whether the dependent variables are relevant and important to policymakers, and (b) whether the independent variables represent parameters that could be changed by instituting new policies. They make the point that psychological research is useful in forming policies only if it includes dependent variables that are of interest to the decision maker, *and* if it deals with independent variables that can be changed by instituting new policies. Personnel selection is an example of an area of I/O psychology where the dependent variables studied (e.g., job performance, absenteeism, productivity) are thought to be highly relevant, and where decision makers in the organization can institute policies (e.g., adopt a valid test, or improve a method currently used in selection) that are likely to have an impact on the dependent variables. Although some

NUMBER OF POLICY VARIABLES INVESTIGATED

RELEVANCE OF DEPENDENT VARIABLES	NONE	ONE OR MORE
LOW	Irrelevant and unlikely to be useful I	Irrelevant but potentially useful information II
HIGH	III Irrelevant but potentially useful	IV Relevant and useful

FIG. 3.2. Relevance and utility of psychological research to policymakers.

widely used personnel selection practices are not completely consistent with psychological research (e.g., continued reliance on the interview despite negative research findings), personnel selection represents, in general, an area in which science and practice are well-integrated.

Quadrants I, II, and III of Fig. 3.2 represent areas in which science and practice are less likely to mesh. Research on cognitive processes in performance appraisal represent an example of Quadrant I research. This research deals with dependent variables such as memory accuracy and schematic intrusions into encoding and memory; the independent variables in this research often represent manipulations of fairly basic cognitive processes in well-controlled settings (e.g., the amount of information presented can be manipulated to increase or decrease demands on memory). Managers in organizations are not likely to be interested in memory, attention, and other psychological constructs, and even if they are, it is unlikely that they will be willing or able to devise policies that will directly affect basic cognitive processes. As a result, research on cognitive processes in appraisal, while scientifically interesting, is unlikely to have much impact on the way in which performance appraisals are conducted in organizations (Banks & Murphy, 1985).

Our example raises an important point about the relationship between research and application. It is hard to imagine *any* research that does not have some distal relevance to application. Thus, the issue that needs to be considered in assigning different lines of research to quadrants is the extent to which the research has clear implications for fairly immediate application. The cognitive processes studied in performance appraisal research probably *are* related to outcome variables that are of interest to policy makers (e.g., accuracy of evaluations, cost-effectiveness of the appraisal system), but to date, researchers have not articulated these links in a clear or convincing fashion. We are not saying here that the "bottom line" *should be* the ultimate criterion in deciding whether or not to pursue a line of research. Rather, we recognize that it *is* an important consideration, and that scientists who do not pay attention to the policy implications of their work will not be effective in organizations.

Research on job redesign represents an example of Quadrant II research. Here, it is possible to develop policies that are based on research (e.g., job enrichment), but research that deals with the effects of job characteristics on variables such as intrinsic motivation, job commitment, and the like is not likely to be compelling to a manager. Unless dependent variables such as performance, productivity, and other "bottom line" variables are explicitly addressed, research on the effects of job redesign is unlikely to be used by policymakers.

Research on the stresses associated with working night shifts or rotating shifts is an example of Quadrant III research. Although the dependent variables (e.g., absenteeism, productivity) are likely to be relevant, it may be politically and practically impossible to develop policies to reduce the negative effects of unusual working hours. Many factories and other businesses must stay open continuously, and it may not be possible to avoid the problems that people working on odd shifts experience.

The failure to integrate research and practice in I/O psychology has led to many suggestions for changing the way we do and apply research. Boehm (1980) noted that there is often a poor fit between the traditional scientific method and the realities of organizational settings. She suggested modifications of the traditional method that would make it easier to do relevant research and to apply the results of that research to solving problems in the organization. Rubak and Innes (1988) suggested several additional issues that must be considered in determining whether research is likely to be useful in practice. First, as noted earlier, it must address dependent variables that are important to the policymaker, and must suggest some change in policy that would be likely to have a desirable impact on those variables. Second, researchers must carefully consider the unit of analysis of their work. Most psychological research deals with individual reactions to different stimuli or conditions; many policies, however, involve some larger unit of analysis, such as the department or the organization as a whole. Third, researchers must be sensitive to economic issues. The recent emphasis on utility analysis in the I/O literature (Cascio, 1987; Hunter & Hunter, 1984; see Boudreau, in press, and Murphy, 1986, for criticisms of current utility research) suggests that this issue is being dealt with by at least some I/O psychologists. Researchers who do not deal in some way with these issues are unlikely to have a substantial impact on policy.

It is not clear whether all research by applied psychologists *should* be both immediately relevant and useful to practitioners. We do not think that research that falls in Quadrants I, II, and III should be abandoned, but rather that such research should be broadened to *include* the key facets of Quadrant IV. That is, more of the research conducted by I/O psychologists should include dependent variables that are of interest to policymakers. It is neither necessary nor useful to ignore dependent variables that are of scientific, but little immediate practical interest. However, the failure to directly or indirectly address dependent variables that *are* of interest will reduce the impact of research on practice. Similarly, research programs should not concentrate solely on independent variables that can be easily manipulated by organizational decision makers, but rather should give *some* attention to variables that are under policymakers' control.

Levy-Leboyer (1988) noted that applications of psychological research are likely to fail if they require the client to change attitudes, values, norms, or roles. Applications that threaten the existing order, or that require changes in the climate of the organization, are also likely to be resisted. Finally, applications of psychology that require the client to reformulate the problem are likely to fail. It is one of the unique burdens of psychology that the clients are likely to believe that they know the nature and the causes of the problems that they employ psychologists to solve. For example, a manager may contact a psychologist to help solve a productivity problem that he believes is due to low levels of employee motivation. If the psychologist's assessment of the core problem is substantially different than the manager's assessment (e.g., the problem may be poor management rather than unmotivated workers), the psychologist's recommendations are not likely to be followed.

We want to end this section on a cautious note. The argument that psychology should become more concerned with applications is open to challenge, and should not be accepted without criticism. While substantial barriers to the successful application of psychology in organizations do exist, it may be that there should be *more* rather fewer barriers. Levy-Leboyer (1988) noted that there is often a temptation to apply psychological theories that have not been adequately tested. He cited several examples from the I/O literature, including the motivation theories of Maslow and Herzberg, as well as faddish techniques such as T groups, sensitivity training, quality circles, and job enrichment, in which application has occurred before the underlying theory was adequately tested and supported. Subsequent tests of the theories underlying these techniques have been far from encouraging. Unfortunately, practices based on these theories are now ingrained in many organizations, and there is little evidence that the substantial body of literature questioning these applications has led to a decrease in their popularity. These premature applications can only damage the future credibility of psychologists.

Changing Practice

It appears to us that most of the literature dealing with the integration of science and practice in I/O psychology concentrates on ways that science should change to better fit the needs of practice. Perhaps this is a reflection of our own biases; both of us are primarily scientists, and less frequently fill the role of practitioner, and we may pay more attention to suggestions that we change our own behavior than to suggestions that someone else must change theirs. Nevertheless, we believe that it is essential that *both* scientists and practitioners change their ways.

The key to becoming better practitioners is first to become better scientists. For example, many psychologists working in industry have not applied or even attempted to apply research conducted by psychologists outside of their own areas of interest. Research in social psychology, cognitive psychology, perceptual psychology, psychometrics, and judgment is plainly relevant to the problems encountered by I/O psychologists, but is rarely brought to bear on organizational problems. Part of the fault lies with research-oriented psychologists, who often fail to consider the applicability of their findings and recommendations. In addition, it is probably unrealistic to expect any psychologist, particularly those in nonacademic careers, to keep completely up to date in all areas of psychology. Nevertheless, there are many opportunities for continuing education that will expose psychologists to the most important aspects of recent research; many state licensing boards now require periodic updating and continuing education for all psychologists. The Master Lecture series offered by APA is one example; workshops offered at the annual conventions of APA and of Society for Industrial and Organizational Psychology (SIOP) are another.

Practitioners must not only be aware of a broader range of research, they must also concentrate their efforts on developing applications for this research. It should not be the sole responsibility of researchers to identify applications. Practitioners are likely to be highly familiar with the organizational context, and therefore more likely than researchers to identify useful and credible applications.

Finally, practitioners could aid the integration of science and research by helping to identify organizational problems that might be addressed through psychological research. As we noted earlier, one of the ways that practice contributes to science is through the identification and clarification of problems that need to be solved. For example, a substantial body of research on assessment centers was stimulated by the need, during World War II, to quickly identify promising candidates for espionage assignments. This research contributed to our understanding of basic psychological processes (e.g., studies of assessor judgments), of small group behavior (e.g., studies of the development of a consensus), and of psychological measurement. Another example is presented by one of the most widespread and most successful applications of psychology, ability testing. The group tests that made large-scale testing programs possible were developed as a direct result of the need to solve a pressing practical problem (i.e., the screening of recruits and draftees for World War I).

WHAT SHOULD WE EXPECT FROM
SCIENTIST-PRACTITIONERS?

How can one determine whether the scientist-practitioner model is reasonable and viable for a particular area of psychology? As we noted in the preceding section, simply counting the number of people in a field who do research and apply its results in the settings where they work is probably not sufficient. A field that includes a substantial number of members who are primarily research-oriented, and also a substantial number who are primarily practice-oriented could still be characterized by an effective integration of science and practice.

We believe that there are two reasons to be optimistic about the viability of the scientist-practitioner model in applied areas of psychology. First, *psychological* practice is, by definition, based on the results of empirical research. We have highlighted the term *psychological* to help identify an important qualifier that is directly relevant to I/O psychologists. That is, not all activities of applied psychologists working in the field can or should be regarded as the practice of psychology. For example, I/O psychologists employed in large corporations typically have jobs as managers; the term *psychologist* is rarely, if ever, included in their job titles. Thus, the fact that they are psychologists may be irrelevant to much of their day-to-day activity.

A manager might *use* his or her knowledge of psychology to be more effective, but this is not the same thing as practicing as a psychologist in an organization. The practice of psychology implies that the practitioner is recognized and consulted as a psychologist, or an expert in some area of psychology, and that the activities carried out are relevant to the psychologist's expertise. For example, a psychologist in an organization might be asked to evaluate the suitability of a personality inventory as a screening device in hiring entry-level managers. A scientist-practitioner will base his or her evaluation on the available research. A psychologist who bases recommendations on personal preference, on undocumented clinical lore, or on the results of obviously faulty studies is not functioning as a scientist-practitioner; we would not regard such practice as psychological in nature, except in the most trivial sense. In contrast, a psychologist employed as a manager will have many functions that are not unique to psychologists, and that do not draw in any meaningful way on his or her expertise as a psychologist. It does not make sense to require that these activities should be directed by the results of psychological research, although psychological knowledge might indeed be beneficial in carrying them out.

The distinction between psychological practice and the day-to-day activities of individuals who happen to hold degrees in psychology is an important one, particularly for I/O psychologists. Such a psychologist might spend part of his or her time in the role of "manager," and another part in the role of "psychologist." We should not necessarily be concerned if the "manager" activities are not guided by psychological research, as long as the "psychologist" activities are.

The second reason for believing that this model is working is the state of current I/O research. We believe that much of this research is of high quality, and *is* relevant to problems that are encountered in the settings where psychology is applied. We admit that translating this research into specific applications is not an easy or trivial task. However, we find the published research very useful when working on real-world problems in organizations. Unfortunately, determining whether research is relevant for application is no easy matter; there is often room for honest disagreement over the applicability of a specific piece of research. For example, much of the current research on cognitive processes in performance appraisal has been criticized as irrelevant to appraisal in organizations (Banks & Murphy, 1985). Yet, other researchers have pointed out numerous ways in which this research could be applied (Feldman, 1986; Murphy & Cleveland, 1990).

The guideline we can suggest is that the choice of problems to study, and of the methods used to study those problems, must be guided by the researcher's judgment that there is some realistic possibility of using this research to advance our ability to solve applied problems. We expect that there will be disagreements over the long-term implications for practice of research in several areas of psychology, and that one researcher's judgment concerning the relevance of his or her work may not be shared by others. For this reason, we think the "burden of proof" should fall on the researcher, and not on the critics of that research. That is, researchers who accept the goal of doing research designed to improve practice should bear the responsibility of defining and defending the eventual applicability of their research.

In summary, we believe that the scientist-practitioner model can work well, even in situations where most psychologists choose only one role, scientist or practitioner. The viability of the model is not defined in terms of the career choices of psychologists in a particular area, but rather by the relationship between science and practice. This model requires that science should provide a basis for practice, and that both scientists and practitioners must contribute to the effective integration of science and practice. Some of the ways science and practice can be better integrated in I/O psychology are discussed in the remaining chapters of this volume.

REFERENCES

Banks, C. G., & Murphy, K. R. (1985). Toward narrowing the research-practice gap in performance appraisal. *Personnel Psychology, 38,* 335–345.

Bickman, L. (1987). Graduate education in psychology. *American Psychologist, 42,* 1041–1047.

Boehm, V. R. (1980). Research in the 'real world'—A conceptual model. *Personnel Psychology, 33,* 495–503.

Boudreau, J. W. (in press). Utility analysis for decisions in human resource management. In M. Dunnette (Ed.), *Handbook of industrial/organizational psychology.* Palo Alto, CA: Consulting Psychologist Press.

Cascio, W. F. (1987). *Costing human resources: The financial impact of behavior in organizations* (2nd Ed.). Boston: Kent.

Chein, I. (1966). Some sources of divisiveness among psychologists. *American Psychologist, 21,* 333–342.

Feldman, J. M. (1986). Instrumentation and training for performance appraisal: A perceptual-cognitive viewpoint. In K. Rowland & G. Ferris (Eds.), *Research in personnel and human resources management* (Vol. 4). Greenwich, CT: JAI Press.

Frank, G. (1984). The Boulder model: History, rationale, and critique. *Professional Psychology: Research and Practice, 15,* 417–435.

Goldfried, M. R. (1984). Training the clinician as scientist-professional. *Professional Psychology: Research and Practice, 15,* 477–481.

Hoch, E. L., Ross, A. O., & Winder, C. L. (1966, August). Professional preparation of clinical psychologists. *Proceedings of the Conference on the Professional Preparation of Clinical Psychologists.* Chicago Center for Continuing Education.

Howard, A. (1984). I/O careers in industry. *The Industrial-Organizational Psychologist, 21*(4), 46–54.

Howard, A., Pion, G. M., Gottfredson, G. D., Flattau, P. E., Oskamp, S., Bray, D. W., & Burstein, A. G. (1986). The changing face of American psychology: A report of the Committee on Employment and Human Resources. *American Psychologist, 41,* 1311–1327.

Hunter, J. E., & Hunter, R. F. (1984). Validity and utility of alternative predictors of job performance. *Psychological Bulletin, 96,* 72–98.

Levy-Leboyer, C. (1988). Success and failure in applying psychology. *American Psychologist, 43,* 779–785.

Kargon, R. (1986). Expert testimony in historical perspective. *Law and Human Behavior, 10,*(1), 15–27.

Kimble, G. A. (1984). Psychology's two cultures. *American Psychologist, 39,* 833–839.

Kupfersmid, J. (1987). Improving what is published: A model in search of an editor. *American Psychologist, 43,* 635–642.

McGuire, W. J. (1967). Some impending reorientations in social psychology. *Journal of Experimental Social Psychology, 3,* 124–139.

Moses, J. (1986). Long range planning committee: Focus on the future—long range themes. *The Industrial-Organizational Psychologist, 24*(1), 33–35.

Murphy, K. R. (1986). When your top choice turns you down: Effects of rejected offers on the utility of selection tests. *Psychological Bulletin, 99,* 133–138.

Murphy, K. R., & Cleveland, J. N. (1990). *Performance appraisal: An organizational perspective.* Boston: Allyn & Bacon.

Raimy, V. C. (1950). *Training in clinical psychology.* New York: Prentice-Hall.

Ring, K. (1967). Experimental social psychology: Some sober questions about some frivolous values. *Journal of Experimental Social Psychology, 3,* 113–123.

Roe, A., Gustad, J. W., Moore, B. V., Ross, S., & Skodak, M. (1959). *Graduate education in psychology.* Washington, DC: American Psychological Association.

Ruback, R. A., & Innes, C. A. (1988). The relevance and irrelevance of psychological research: The example of prison crowding. *American Psychologist, 43,* 683–693.

Sackett, P. R., Callahan, C., DeMeuse, K., Ford, K. J., & Kozlowski, S. (1986). Changes over time in research involvement by academic and nonacademic psychologists. *The Industrial-Organizational Psychologist, 24*(1), 40–43.

Spence, J. T. (1987). Centrifugal versus centripetal tendencies in psychology: Will the center hold? *American Psychologist, 42,* 1052–1054.

Streufert, S. (1987). Applied social psychology. *Journal of Applied Social Psychology, 17,* 605–608.

Strother, C. R. (1956). *Psychology and mental health.* Washington, DC: American Psychological Association.

II SCIENCE AND PRACTICE IN PERSONNEL PSYCHOLOGY

The first section of this book examined, in a very general way, the problems and prospects of the scientist-practitioner model in I/O psychology. The second and third sections examine this model in the contexts of the two primary subdisciplines within the field. This section focuses on personnel, or human resources psychology.

As it is typically defined, personnel psychology incorporates a variety of topics including (but not limited to) job analysis and evaluation, compensation, recruiting, personnel selection and training, and performance appraisal. To a greater or lesser extent, the foundation of each of these topics rests on two basic psychological processes—assessment and evaluation. Assessment, or measurement, refers to either the *categorization* of stimuli (people, objects, behaviors, events, etc.) according to qualitatively different characteristics (sex, race, religious preference), or to the relative or absolute determination of *how much* of a quantifiable characteristic (height, attendance, productivity) they possess. Evaluation refers to the assignation of subjective value judgments (good/bad, unsatisfactory/excellent) to the results of assessment. Because of their pivotal position in personnel psychology, and because of their obvious impact on people's organizational lives, each of the five chapters in this section focuses explicitly on evaluation and/or assessment. Furthermore, each chapter places assessment or evaluation in the context of a procedure or technique designed to maximize the potential and productivity of an organization's human resources.

In Chapter 4, Kevin Williams and John Lillibridge describe a proactive approach to assessing individuals' potentials to function as effective managers. In Chapter 5, Robert Goldsmith examines a widely accepted approach to assessing and evaluating human resources—assessment centers—and describes how utility analysis can be used to estimate the cost-effectiveness of this method. Chapter 6 is devoted to Jan Cleveland and George Thornton's discussion of simulations, exercises that often play a central role in assessment centers but can also be used by themselves to facilitate personnel selection and development. In the final two chapters of this section, the focus shifts from personnel selection and development to performance appraisal. In Chapter 7, Bill Balzer and Lorne Sulsky propose a new framework for identifying and choosing job performance criteria, a framework that emphasizes the needs and goals of specific organizational constituencies (individuals and groups) over the more traditional statistical and psychometric indices. In Chapter 8, Kevin Murphy concludes this section by focusing on productivity and stressing the need for job performance indices that are relevant and contribute to this very important, "bottom-line" organizational concern.

Consistent with the theme of this volume, each of these authors not only examines a specific topic, but also integrates an analysis of the extent to which the scientist-practitioner model has contributed to the development of that topic, as well as a prediction (often accompanied by specific recommendations) of how the model might contribute in the not-too-distant future. In this way, we hope to provide you, the reader, with sufficient information to allow you to assess for yourself the past, present, and future viability of the scientist-practitioner model in the domain of personnel psychology.

4

The Identification of Managerial Talent: A Proactive View

Kevin J. Williams
The University at Albany, State University of New York

John R. Lillibridge
Wilton Developmental Center

INTRODUCTION

This chapter examines the interface of the science and practice of industrial/ organizational (I/O) psychology in the area of predicting managerial success. Although prediction and selection represent areas in I/O psychology where science and practice have successfully interacted, the exchange has been less successful in the identification of managerial potential. This is unfortunate; both organizational leaders and scientists have labeled managerial talent a critical national resource (Campbell, Dunnette, Lawler, & Weick, 1970). In this chapter we address the science-practice interface by introducing a different theoretical perspective for understanding and predicting the realization of managerial potential.

ASSESSING THE SCIENCE-PRACTICE DIALOGUE

A review of organizational practices led Campbell et al. (1970) to conclude that most methods of identifying managerial talent were bereft of empirical support. Indeed, there was a lack of concern for the psychological processes underlying effective managerial behavior and the relations of various predictors to criterion measures. Science had clearly not contributed to the practices of the organizations surveyed by Campbell et al. (1970), or perhaps practitioners had preferred nonscientific methods. Unfortunately, similar conclusions may be drawn 2 decades later. A survey of the current literature would lead one to conclude that organizations still do not draw on empirical findings in selecting managers and scientists have not yet been able to present a coherent model of the realization of managerial talent. Research findings have lacked both consistency and a strong theoretical base. Recent studies, while appearing to identify a core set of predictors (Hall, 1976), have not met with consistently high levels of predictive success.

Both sides must share responsibility for the absence of a healthy science-practice dialogue in this area. However, rather than affixing specific blame, we concentrate on the roles that the scientist and practitioner must enact in order to facilitate new and mutually beneficial interaction. Scientists must generate theories and methods that confirm or extend the understanding of organizational relationships, processes, and outcomes. In addition, scientists must be prepared to demonstrate the relevancy of their theories and methods to organizations. The practitioner's role in ensuring an effective dialogue involves identifying pressing or unique problems and assessing the validity and feasibility of treatments or methods aimed at addressing those problems. In essence, practitioners can provide stimuli and feedback for theory building and expansion. Some noteworthy examples of this type of involvement exist, such as the Sears and A.T. & T. assessment centers, but additional attempts are needed to provide an impetus to theory building. Presently, it is not clear that organizations are extensively involved in research-based practice (see Howard & Bray, 1988 for an exception) or are receptive to theory.

In our opinion, new theoretical perspectives are needed to improve the science-practice dialogue in this area. The scientist and practitioner both value theory; poorly articulated theories result in inadequate understanding of complex behavior, and atheoretical applications often turn out to be inefficient and costly. Because scientists are free to be speculative, creative, and hypothetical (Quick, Bhagat, Dalton, & Quick, 1987), they are in a prime position to initiate new and better exchanges between science and practice. Constructive propositions and theses would allow for new avenues of exploration. This chapter represents an attempt at theoretical enrichment in the prediction of managerial success.

Novel conceptualizations of managerial talent have been inhibited because researchers continue to search for predictors of managerial success using traditional prediction paradigms and with little consideration of theory generation. Progress has been slow due, in part, to unique problems managerial selection presents for predictive validity models (e.g., one is typically trying to predict behavior over many years) and from problems in measuring managerial effectiveness (Cascio, 1987).[1] However, the nature of the research paradigm employed in most studies may be largely responsible for the stagnation in the field. Two

---

[1] The "criterion problem" in I/O psychology is particularly troublesome for the prediction of managerial success. Different measures have been used as indicators of managerial effectiveness in prediction studies: supervisor evaluations, subordinate satisfaction, promotion rate, salary, department profitability, turnover rates, and behavior-based criteria. There is no clear consensus regarding the best measures of managerial effectiveness (cf. Luthans et al., 1988).

aspects of the prediction paradigm are of particular concern, and form the basis for the present chapter. First, prediction of managerial behavior has seldom been made from a theoretically integrated, multivariate perspective. Studies have often used single predictor domains or have used multiple predictors without concern for the psychological processes underlying the effectiveness and integration of the predictors. Second, the typical predictive validity model fails to adequately consider the *proactive* side of managerial development (Plunkett & Hale, 1982). Studies have tended to be reactive in the sense that individuals are seen as having certain credentials, skills, or aptitudes that enable them to successfully perform certain tasks in a fixed environment. This approach overlooks the ability of individuals to mold and create their environments (Caspi, 1987; Ford & Ford, 1987; Streufert & Swezey, 1986). In the following sections, we introduce a model for research that addresses these two shortcomings. It is argued that a proactive, multivariate approach will enable researchers to improve and understand prediction of successful performance as a manager, and offer practitioners new strategies for identifying and developing managerial talent.

A PROACTIVE VIEW OF MANAGERIAL DEVELOPMENT

Individuals develop skills through interactions with their environments. Both the individual and the environment provide input to these interactions: individual differences represent the individual's input, while situational demands that facilitate or inhibit skill development are provided by the environment. Accordingly, when studying managerial development, researchers should not only be interested in how experiences shape individuals, but also in how individuals act on their environments to take advantage of opportunities they encounter. In this sense, our view is similar to recent views of personality, social, and developmental psychologists (Bandura, 1986; Buss, 1987; Caspi, 1987; Ford, 1987; McClelland, 1985; Scarr & McCartney, 1983; Snyder, 1983). Scarr and McCartney (1983) argued that an individual's genotype plays an active role in personality development by: (a) determining the effect environments have on the individual; and (b) affecting the individual's selection of environments. For example, individuals who are prone to shyness are likely to avoid situations that are likely to bring out this trait.

Buss (1987) hypothesized that three causal mechanisms affect person-environment correspondence. *Selection* refers to the process by which individuals choose and congregate nonrandomly in certain environments. *Evocation* is the process by which individuals elicit responses unintentionally from environments. *Manipulation* is the process by which individuals intentionally create or alter certain environments. These processes may be seen as underlying the realization of managerial talent. Managerial positions may be sought based on one's motives or goals; certain personal characteristics may attract the attention of significant others (e.g., mentors); and, finally, effective managers may openly act on part of their environment to progress toward their goals. Clawson, Kotter, Faux, and McArthur (1985), for example, found that successful managers differed from others in that they proactively took responsibility for their own development and learning. They "seek out role models and mentors . . . they don't wait to be assigned to new projects and jobs by others; they nominate themselves" (p. 370). Similarly, Luthans, Hodgetts, & Rosenkrantz (1988) offered a proactive view of leadership, suggesting that while job and environmental constraints limit personal discretion, leaders vary in their ability to (1) operate effectively within those constraints; and (2) influence the parameters of those constraints.[2]

Research in I/O psychology has typically been concerned with Buss' (1987) selection mechanism. An individual's motive to manage or cognitive abilities, for example, are seen as increasing one's suitability for managerial positions. Much less attention has been paid to variables that affect evocation and manipulation processes. Consideration of these processes will allow researchers and practitioners to understand better how individuals become intrinsically linked with their environments. Assessment center research represents such an attempt at investigating the proactive element of managerial development (Klimoski & Brickner, 1987). By obtaining multiple measures of key behavior domains and deriving indicators of these behaviors from past experiences and personality measures, the typical assessment center is able to examine the ability of individuals to act on their environments. Not surprisingly, assessment centers have been fairly successful in predicting managerial success (Howard & Bray, 1988; Klimoski & Brickner, 1987).

A number of steps must still be taken, however, to more fully understand how managers proactively interact with their environments. First, theoretical models of how individuals respond to and manipulate their environments are needed. Scientists should devote attention to identifying behavioral processes that mediate effective individual-environment interactions. Second, valid predictors of managerial success need to be identified within these theoretical models. Attempts should be made to group predictors of managerial talent by their underlying function. These issues are addressed in the following two sections. We (1) present a model of managerial potential based on recent work by Ford (1987), who has identified an array of behavior functions mediating person-environment interactions; and (2) review empirical research on the prediction of managerial potential, relating predictors of managerial talent to the array of behavior functions posited by Ford (1987).

---

[2]It is important to differentiate leadership studies from managerial studies. Management and leadership are not identical, but share some common processes. For this reason, we have included leadership studies in our review. It is important to note, however, frequent differences in terms of research design: Leadership studies are more apt to be cross-sectional while managerial potential studies tend to be longitudinal. One needs to be careful in extrapolating from cross-sectional to longitudinal research.

FORD'S (1987) PROACTIVE VIEW OF BEHAVIOR
AND DEVELOPMENT

Ford (1987) proposed an open, living-systems model of human behavior and development. Individuals are seen as open systems, using information gathered from their environments to shape or influence their environments. Their action and information-collection capabilities are directed, regulated, and controlled by "behavioral functions." While Ford's (1987) theory is much broader than our immediate concerns, his concept of behavioral functions can be used to structure our review of the empirical literature and highlight variables important for managerial development and success.

Transactional functions allow for information flow necessary to "move around in or to manipulate" one's environment. The effective exchange of information involves both collecting and emitting (i.e., communicating) information. *Arousal functions* allow one to effectively cope with his or her environment by selectively varying the amount, rate, and intensity of behavior. Emotions serve arousal functions in that they are anticipatory in nature; they prepare individuals for different circumstances and signal certain behavior patterns.

The remaining functions to be incorporated in our model are referred to as *governing functions* in that they "organize, transform, store, and use information to produce coordination and control of human behavior" (Ford, 1987, p. 90). They are seen as representing different types of cognitions. *Directive functions* include motives, interests, goals, position of goals in goal hierarchies, purposive thought and intentions. In short, they specify intended states of individuals. *Regulatory functions* specify criteria for selection among options and evaluate progression toward intended states. Included among these processes are one's evaluative thought, self-evaluations, self-monitoring, consideration of consequences, and moral reasoning. *Control functions* relate to what individuals can make sense of or understand: problem-solving, planning, reasoning, and causal attribution processes. These processes combine current perceptual information with one's knowledge base and behavioral repertoire to guide behavior.

It is important to note that psychological variables may fall into more than one of Ford's function categories. Empathy, for example, is seen as having a cognitive as well as an emotional or arousal component (Davis, 1983) and thus may be seen as linking arousal and regulatory functions. In addition, predictors may be successful because they cut across or tap into several behavioral functions. Biographical data, for instance, provide information relevant to a number of functions, such as directive, regulatory, arousal, and control. This may explain their relatively strong predictive power (Neiner & Owens, 1985; Owens & Schoenfeldt, 1979).

Ford's (1987) model also contains a number of subsystems that help coordinate the different functions and facilitate information flow through the system. The information-processing subsystem seems especially relevant for understanding the realization of managerial potential. One's information-processing capabilities will determine approaches to problem solving and the effectiveness of solutions. An individual's ability to project into the future is also tied to this subsystem. Through these processes, the time dimension can be added to prediction models of managerial success. We return to this subsystem in a later section of this chapter that extends current theories of managerial selection and development.

In applying Ford's model to the identification of managerial talent, we follow the lead of Bergin (1987) and McDevitt and Ford (1987), who used the model as a heuristic device to organize a scattered literature and to explicate the processes underlying complexly organized behavior. This model allows us to identify behavioral functions crucial to successful interactions with one's environment, functions that have been overlooked by traditional conceptions of managerial potential.

Our analysis enhances Ford's framework in at least two ways. First, we extend it to a new content area. Most of the research emanating from Ford's model has occurred in social settings (Ford & Ford, 1987). Many organizational theorists view organizational behavior in much the same way as Ford: as multiply determined and multiply intended (Campbell et al., 1970; Naylor, Pritchard, & Ilgen, 1980). Second, while the work discussed by Ford and Ford (1987) deals with a relatively short-time frame, we concentrate on the prediction of behavior over an extended time.

PREDICTORS OF MANAGERIAL SUCCESS

A survey of the applied literature reveals a large set of predictors of managerial behavior and outcomes. Biographical data, cognitive abilities, behavioral simulations, motivational hierarchies, assessment center judgments, values, interests, and personality inventories have all been used to predict managerial success. These predictors, best used in combination (Dunnette, 1971), provide a snapshot of an individual early in, or prior to, his or her career from which future behavior can be predicted. Because our main objective is to raise theoretical and empirical issues by setting the predictors of managerial potential within a framework that links individuals with their environments, we do not exhaustively review the research on each of these areas. Rather, we discuss the research findings as they relate to Ford's (1987) framework.

We have divided the predictors of managerial potential into categories reflecting five of Ford's functions: directive, regulatory, control, arousal, and transactional. Individuals with the potential to be successful managers are likely to have skills and abilities in each of these domains. In the following review, emphasis is placed on general conclusions regarding each predictor, as well as gaps that exist in the literature. For each behavioral function, we distinguish between variables that have been shown to be predictors and correlates of managerial potential and variables that have not been studied in the applied literature but, based on our review, may be considered likely predictors of managerial potential.

Directive Functions

Motives, goals, values, interests, and impression management provide directive functions (Ford & Ford, 1987). Each of these variables may be related to managerial talent or effectiveness.

Motivation to manage.   Social motives have emerged as individual-difference measures predicting managerial success. Studies suggest that managers reveal stronger motives for achievement, power and status, and are more likely to exercise initiative than nonmanagers (Boyatzis, 1982; Campbell et al., 1970). Evidence also suggests that effective managers may initiate interpersonal contact. Sorrentino and Field (1986), for example, found that both high need for achievement and high need for affiliation were related to leader emergence in a longitudinal laboratory study of leaderless groups. Much of the recent research on managerial motives, however, has focused on the role of an individual's need for power. Most representative of this research have been Miner's (1978) and McClelland's (1975, 1985) theories relating personality profiles to managerial success. Both theories view one's motivation to manage as reflecting high strivings for power and dominance, and higher than average self-control.

Miner's hierarchical role-motivation theory (Miner, 1978) predicts that high-level managers will demonstrate strivings for power and domination coupled with a liking for administrative work and high assertiveness (Berman & Miner, 1985). Research testing role-motivation theory has generally supported its propositions (e.g., Berman & Miner, 1985; Cornelius & Lane, 1984; Miner, 1978). McClelland's leadership motive pattern (LMP, McClelland & Burnham, 1976) characterizes effective managers as high in need for power, low in need for affiliation (or at least lower than one's need for power), and able to inhibit or constrain their need to express power ("activity inhibition"). Research relating LMP to managerial effectiveness has also generally supported the theory (McClelland & Boyatzis, 1982). Interestingly, high need for affiliation was found to be important for leader emergence but not for managerial success. This finding may relate to differences between management and leadership (cf. Saal & Knight, 1988). Affiliation motives may influence the occupancy of informal leadership roles, but not one's effectiveness in an assigned or formal, authority position.

The power motive provides a directive function for individuals; it establishes goals and goal hierarchies, and guides purposive thoughts and interactions. Research has indicated, however, that the manner in which need for power is expressed influences effectiveness. The goals of successful managers reflect the desire to lead individuals for a common cause as opposed to the desire to advance one's own personal interests at the expense of others. McClelland's LMP and Miner's role-motivation profile both reflect this socialized power rather than personalized power.

Little is known about how socialized power is established as one's goal instead of personal power. Winter (1988) recently suggested that responsibility training is an important moderator in the expression of the power motive. He presented evidence that differences in profligate or responsible expressions of power are related to the degree to which individuals have had to care for others. Being responsible for others may direct individuals to express their need for power in socially desirable ways rather than for personal gain. In essence, responsibility training may represent preparation for future managerial roles.

Managerial aspirations.   One's career interests, aspirations and values are important for the development of managerial talent. Rynes (1987) examined engineering undergraduate majors who expressed interest in becoming managers and found that those with high levels of aspiration, determination, and initiative were more likely to succeed. Howard (1986) examined how college experiences mold managerial aspirations and performance as part of her longitudinal studies of managerial development at AT&T. One's college major was found to be related to later managerial performance. Humanities and social science majors outperformed science and math majors on many managerial skills, including interpersonal and verbal skills. Bray (1984; cited in Howard, 1986) identified "a formative response, whereby some beginning managers respond to initial job experiences by developing or further developing appropriate motivations, where-as others let motivations weaken or fail to develop. College may have prepared the managerial aspirants with conceptual and dispositional openness that needed a proper role to be brought to fruition" (p. 549). Thus, aspirations, values and dispositions are intrinsically linked to motivations and, indeed, may determine whether these motivations strengthen or weaken.

Nevill and Super (1988) have found that individuals committed to work possess positive attitudes toward career exploration and career planning (aspects of their "career maturity" construct). Career maturity may interact with one's motives or needs to establish a detailed knowledge and understanding of life tasks (Sorrentino & Higgins, 1986). The career development literature in general may be related to understanding managerial effectiveness and success.

Impression management.   The ability of individuals to manage others' perceptions of them is related to goal attainment (Schlenker, 1985; Tedeschi & Melburg, 1984). Impression management has been hypothesized to play a primary role in leadership and social influence tactics in organizations (Tedeschi & Melburg, 1984; Zerbe & Paulhus, 1987). Unfortunately, impression management has not been directly related to managerial potential in the applied literature. It remains a possible predictor that deserves attention, however.

Research in social psychology leads to the hypothesis that individuals who present themselves favorably with respect to organizational and social norms are more likely to influence interpersonal interactions and to attract more mentoring. Self-protective and self-enhancing responses promote effective interactions with others (Wolfe, Lennox, & Cuttler, 1986). Individuals whose behaviors conform to expectations or elicit valued responses are more likely to be accepted and judged favorably by group members (Kaplan, 1986). These impression management tendencies are likely to provide crucial directive functions for managers as well.

Summary. Individual differences in intended states of individuals are related to managerial potential. Our review has identified motivation to manage, values, interests, career aspirations, and college experiences as predictors of managerial success. Strong support was found for the motivational theories of McClelland (1975) and Miner (1978). Expressing one's need for power in socially desirable ways for common interests as opposed to self-interests underlies this effectiveness. The science and practice of I/O psychology are in agreement regarding these predictors; empirical studies have found them to be valid predictors of managerial potential and they have been included in managerial assessment and training programs (McClelland & Burnham, 1976). However, there are other potential predictors, such as responsibility training and impression management skills, that practitioners have largely ignored, and that scientists have failed to incorporate fully into their models. These variables appear to serve important directive functions for individuals and may thus improve prediction of managerial success.

Regulatory Functions

The preceding section describes a link between individuals' intended states and their career goals. Regulatory processes, in turn, help individuals evaluate their goal-attainment efforts and progress. Sorrentino and Higgins (1986) argued that individuals rely on self-knowledge (i.e., self-schemata and strategies of self-protection and self-enhancement) to plan and regulate behavior. Guidance may be obtained from one's environment, as in judging the appropriateness of behavior in certain situations, or from information stored in memory regarding anticipated outcomes. Our discussion of regulatory functions related to managerial potential will focus on critical self-referent thoughts and constructs.

Self-monitoring. Self-monitoring has been related to a wide range of social facilities, including the ability to judge and enact situationally appropriate behavior, the ability to intentionally express and communicate a wide variety of emotions, enhanced self-control of emotional expression, and the ability to modify self-presentation (Snyder, 1974). Sensitivity to situational cues should allow high self-monitors to better evaluate how they are progressing toward intended states than low self-monitors. Boosted by this heightened awareness, high self-monitors should be more likely to gain status and acceptance (Lennox & Wolfe, 1984).

High self-monitors adopt a pragmatic orientation to social interactions and strategically create appropriate patterns of interactions with others (Gangestad & Snyder, 1985). Garland and Beard (1979) found self-monitoring to be positively related to leader emergence in leaderless group tasks. Presumably high self-monitors are able to judge appropriateness of actions and respond accordingly, thereby increasing perceptions of themselves as leaders (perhaps by evocation, Buss, 1987). Lillibridge and Williams (1987) found that self-monitoring was positively related to selection into an early managerial identification program. Self-monitoring ability has also been related to individuals' boundary spanning ability (Caldwell & O'Reilly, 1982). Thus, it appears that self-monitoring skills may enable managers to evaluate their goal progressions and mold their interactions to further enhance their goals. Research directly linking self-monitoring and related social skills to managerial development, however, is still lacking. Recent conceptualizations of social skills (Riggio, 1986) may be particularly useful for expanding the role of self-monitoring in organizations.

Self-evaluations.   Individuals also regulate their behavior through the use of self-knowledge, internal standards, and self-evaluations. Individuals attach great value to self-knowledge elements (e.g., self-efficacy, self-images, and abilities) and are motivated to maintain positive evaluations of themselves (Raynor & Entin, 1982). Higher self-images and levels of self-knowledge, in turn, have been related to greater social functioning (Raynor & Entin, 1982). Self-confidence and positive self-image foster a proactive openness to others (Glauser, 1984) and increased self-disclosure (Derlega & Berg, 1987), which enhance effective communication and goal attainment. Unfortunately, research on the role of these self-referent thoughts and cognitions in the development of managerial potential has been scare. They remain likely predictors of the goal attainment process. Preliminary evidence of their importance was provided by Bentz (1987), who found that confidence to initiate and act without support from others was related to managerial potential.

Summary.   Self-monitoring and positive self-referent thoughts provide regulation functions necessary for organizing complex behavior. Although such constructs should also relate to managerial effectiveness, few scientific attempts have been made to directly link them to managerial behavior. As a result, important variables related to regulatory functions have been excluded from the science-practice dialogue. Important variables, such as the ability to judge the situational appropriateness of behavior, the ability to engage in situation-specific behavior, feelings of competence and perceptions that one will achieve his or her goal, are likely predictors of managerial effectiveness that await future empirical attention.

Control Functions

Control processes affect managerial potential through differences in: (1) cognitive abilities to understand, reason, and know one's environment; and (2) the formulation of behavioral plans. Reasoning processes and behavioral repertoires both have been found to predict managerial potential.

Intelligence. Studies investigating the relationship between cognitive ability and managerial potential have found consistent support for a positive correlation between verbal intelligence and managerial potential, although the strength of the connection has been questioned. The work of Ghiselli (1973), for example, suggested a relatively weak correlation (average $r = .30$). It has been argued, however, that the correlation is actually much higher, once one controls the statistical artifacts that distort many studies (Hunter & Hunter, 1984; Schmidt & Hunter, 1981). Hunter and Hunter (1984) reported correlations in excess of .50 using validity generalization techniques to correct for some of these artifacts (sample size and unreliability of measures).

Other researchers have examined the relation between intelligence and leader performance (Fiedler & Leister, 1977; Simonton, 1985). In his review and synthesis of the literature, Simonton (1985) related verbal intelligence to two dimensions of leadership: (1) capacity to solve problems, and (2) high quality communication skills (fluent, flexible, rich vocabulary). In addition, Simonton (1985) identified a nonlinear relationship between verbal intelligence and leadership. Very high intelligence was found to lower comprehension of leader performance by others and detract from performance. Interestingly, Simonton (1985) found the relation of intelligence to leadership to be mediated by the individual's perceived competence and perceived comprehensibility. This research demonstrates the importance of reasoning, problem solving, and verbal intelligence to managerial effectiveness. It also exemplifies the complex interactions that exist between processes occurring within the individual. In this case, regulatory functions of perceived competence and comprehensibility mediate the effect of reasoning and problem solving (control processes) on managerial potential.

One shortcoming of this research is the relatively narrow view of intelligence that it represents. The prediction research does not reflect changing views and theories of intelligence (e.g., Sternberg, 1986; Sternberg & Wagner, 1986). Sternberg identified different categories of intelligence: problem-solving ability (fluid intelligence), verbal ability (crystallized intelligence), social competence (social intelligence and practical intelligence), and motivation (drive, involvement, and persistence). Both conceptual and practical knowledge are included in this expanded view of intelligence and may affect the ability to alter one's environment to increase his or her task effectiveness (Russell & Wexley, 1988).

Social intelligence is of special concern for our model because it demonstrates the organization of psychological processes or functions within an individual. Social intelligence can be defined as individual differences in the interpretation of, and solutions for, current life tasks (Cantor & Kihlstrom, 1987). Peters (1987) identified three essential components of social intelligence: the ability to assess others' abilities, to empathize with others' feelings and values, and to analyze group processes. Research on social intelligence led Peters (1987) to conclude that effective managers are higher in all three of these abilities than less effective managers.

We were only able to uncover a few studies that reflected this more expanded view of intelligence. The Sears assessment center work (Bentz, 1987) is one research program that has started in this direction. Baltes' (1987) psychological theory of wisdom also promises to tie managerial prediction closer to the practical or pragmatic side of intelligence. Wagner and Sternberg (1985) examined the role that tacit knowledge (a component of social intelligence) plays in organizational settings. They found three categories of tacit knowledge that were related to successful performance: (1) managing self (motivational and organizational knowledge about the self), (2) managing tasks (specific work-related knowledge), and (3) managing others (knowledge about interacting with peers and subordinates). This research points toward a role for practical and social intelligence in the prediction of managerial potential. Much more research, however, needs to be conducted.

Behavioral repertoire.   The more diverse a person's behavioral capabilities are, the easier it is to create, elicit, and maintain behavior plans (Ford, 1987). This behavioral flexibility relates to how sensitive individuals are to the broad meanings and implications of their everyday actions (Vallacher & Wegner, 1985). Individuals who understand the implications of their actions are more likely to have a clearly articulated, trait-like understanding of themselves; those who are not sensitive to the broader meanings of their actions may lack such a coherent self-understanding. The greater one's self-understanding, the greater one's action control (Vallacher & Wegner, 1985).

Potential managers who possess greater behavior flexibility may be better able to mold and shape their environments to achieve their goals (Howard & Bray, 1988). In a longitudinal study of managerial development, Howard (1986) demonstrated that extracurricular activities and grade-point averages of college students (two indicators of diverse capabilities) were positively related to performance on managerial tasks. The success that biographical data in general have shown in predicting career paths (e.g., Childs & Klimoski, 1986; Neiner & Owens, 1985) may reflect the measurement of people's behavioral repertoires.

Summary.   One line of research on control processes has centered on cognitive ability, verbal intelligence, and problem solving. High levels of reasoning and verbal ability have been found to be valid predictors of managerial potential. This line of research is constrained, however, by the narrow view of intelligence that has been adopted by researchers. Future research needs to look more directly at practical and social intelligence as possible predictors of managerial competence. A second line of research on control processes has examined the role of one's behavioral repertoire. Behavioral flexibility, or the ability of an individual to respond in different patterns to situational changes, has emerged as a valid predictor of managerial success.

Arousal Functions

Arousal functions allow individuals to effectively cope with their environments by varying the amount, rate, and intensity of behavior. Emotions and anxiety may be of particular concern here because they provide individuals with information about their environment and signal adaptive or maladaptive behavioral patterns. As we will see, these variables have been largely ignored by the scientific and applied literatures and remain only potential predictors of managerial effectiveness.

Emotion.   The examination of the role of emotions in organizational behavior has been limited to expressed and felt emotions as indicators of employee attitudes and health (Rafaeli & Sutton, 1987). Much of this research revolves around the emotional components of job stress and is discussed later in our review of effective coping skills. Expressed emotions, however, can also be considered part of the work role. Rafaeli and Sutton (1987) proposed that expressed emotions mediate between the sources of role expectations and outcomes. Both organizational and individual outcomes follow from emotions expressed in order to satisfy role expectations. Empirical work is needed to identify individual differences in emotional behavior and their relationship(s) to managerial success.

Empathy.   Empathy has received empirical attention from social psychologists interested in its role in interpersonal relations. Much of this research has shown increased and more effective social functioning among highly empathic individuals. Reviews of empathy research clearly indicate a dual view of the construct: a cognitive and an emotional component. It is because of this dual view that empathy was mentioned earlier as a link between arousal and regulatory functions.

Cognitive components of empathy include perspective-taking ability, "intellectual objectivity" (Peters, 1987), and separation or distancing of one's own reactions from those of others. Accordingly, empathy is related to one's ability to recognize or understand another's reactions to events. Emotional components of empathy include arousal, sensitivity to others, and a positive regard or concern for others. Thus, empathy also refers to the vicarious arousal or emotional reactions of an individual to the (observed) experiences of another. Davis (1983) found that both cognitive and affective components of empathy were positively correlated with indices of social competence, self-esteem, and sensitivity to others. Since these latter measures have already been discussed as linked to managerial success, it can be hypothesized that empathy measures will predict managerial competence.

Although empathy remains a likely predictor of managerial potential, it has received limited attention from applied psychologists. Peters (1987) identified empathy as an important component of managerial effectiveness. Empathy is represented in the core of social and practical intelligence constructs, and is thus related to high social functioning. It is therefore surprising that empathy has to date been left out of the managerial potential prediction equation.

Anxiety and Coping.   Individuals may experience stress in a variety of organizational settings and roles. Anxiety triggers adaptive and maladaptive responses to perceived stressors. The coping skills that individuals develop, especially early in their careers, will determine how successful they are in adjusting to their work environments. Latack (1984) addressed the role of coping skills in career development and career transition. She explored work transitions as a function of coping skills and perceived stress and challenge. Ability to cope well with perceived stress was identified as a key skill for managing successful transitions. More important, coping was related to success over the long term. The "hardiness" personality dimension (Kobasa, 1979) may be a key moderator of one's success in coping with stressful changes. Kobasa's hardiness construct is comprised of a sense of commitment to life, an overall sense of purpose and control, a feeling that one's actions have some impact, a sense of challenge (rather than helplessness) in the face of adversity, and the ability to see change as positive. Such factors may enable potential managers to develop adaptive methods of responding to stressors early in their careers thereby enabling them to successively manage career transitions.

Behavioral Vigor.   Numerous studies that have factor-analyzed personality predictors of management success have found a major factor variously called Activity, Surgency, Ascendency, Energy, or Dominance (e.g., Foundation for Research on Human Behavior, 1968; Hogan, 1982; Schmitt, 1977). The central theme of this predictive dimension is forcefulness and vigor. Research on temperament (Buss & Plomin, 1984) has identified four basic temperaments shared by all social mammals: fearfulness, aggressiveness, affiliativeness, and impulsiveness. Behavior vigor and tempo are emergent traits or attributes derived from combinations of these basic dimensions of temperament. It seems likely that forcefulness or vigor would relate to managerial ambition and advancement (Howard & Bray, 1988).

Summary.   Our discussion of arousal functions reveals many *likely* predictors but few *established* predictors of managerial potential. Coping strategies, perhaps best represented by the hardiness concept, predict managing career transitions. Presumably, such measures should also predict success in one's field. Empathy is related to various indices of social competence, and thus can also be expected to predict success in areas where interpersonal interactions are vital to success (such as management). Both felt emotions and perspective-taking can be expected to facilitate interpersonal interactions. Behavioral vigor has been related to perseverance and success across a wide range of tasks; it is likely to predict managerial success as well. Less is known about the role of expressed emotions.

Transactional Functions

Transactional functions relate to the information flow necessary to manipulate one's environment. Behaviors, actions, and skills related to the exchange of information are discussed. Emphasis is placed on individuals' adeptness in collecting and emitting information.

Communication Skills.   A major portion of a manager's activities depend on communication skills: receiving and disseminating requested information; reading, writing, and summarizing reports; addressing procedural questions, etc. (Campbell et al., 1970; Luthans et al., 1988). Not surprisingly, individuals proficient in communicating with others are likely to be effective managers. Luthans et al. (1988), for example, found that managers with high performing and satisfied work groups displayed higher levels of communication skills than less effective managers.

The importance of oral communication skills in the prediction of managerial success has long been recognized (Campbell et al., 1970). Measures of oral communication skills have routinely been included in assessment center batteries (Bray & Grant, 1966; Wollowick & McNamara, 1969). Although judgments of oral communication skills are often embedded in exercise (e.g., in-basket) ratings in assessment center research, the established validity of these exercises suggests that oral communication skills are predictors of managerial success (Thorton & Byham, 1982).

Persuasiveness is another important managerial skill. Peters and Austin (1985) sketched a picture of the persuasive, effective manager that encompasses actions such as: teaching and reinforcing values, paying attention to important details, believing in one's purpose, eliciting commitment, enabling others to act, demonstrating and coaching, portraying a vision of the goal, and being enthusiastic, dramatic, and exciting. This complex theme of persuasiveness, cited by many as characteristic of effective managers, should find a place in the predictive model for managerial success.

Managerial Opportunities.   The opportunity to engage in managerial activities early in one's life is intuitively related to later success, because individuals obtain hands-on experience in, among other things, controlling information flow. The first investigations of early opportunity as a predictor of managerial success were biodata studies examining extracurricular activities in high school and college (e.g., Ritchie & Boehm, 1977). Unfortunately, managerial activity items were included in total inventory scores in most of these biodata studies and therefore their independent contributions could not be ascertained (Howard, 1986). Recently, Howard (1986) examined the relation between extracurricular leadership activities in college and subsequent managerial performance in two longitudinal studies from the AT&T data base. Weak but significant, positive correlations between the number of leadership positions held in college and assessed administrative skills and general effectiveness ratings emerged. Not surprisingly, holding leadership positions in college was related to managerial effectiveness indices years in the future.

Summary.   Our review has uncovered at least two established predictors of transactional functions. Oral communication skills, such as those measured during in-basket exercises, have consistently predicted managerial success. Leadership activities and managerial opportunities early in one's career (e.g., college experiences) also serve a transactional function in that they help establish ways of controlling information flow in one's environment. These early opportunities facilitate the development of managerial capabilities. In addition, evidence suggests that persuasiveness is a likely predictor of managerial success and should be included in future assessments of managerial potential.

General Conclusions

We have identified a number of variables related to managerial potential. Table 4.1 summarizes these variables according to their function and whether they are established or only likely predictors of managerial talent. It is evident in Table 4.1 that research has identified a relatively large number of predictors in some areas (e.g., directive functions), but few in other areas (e.g., arousal). We have argued that the realization of managerial potential depends on how individuals shape and interact with their environments to take advantage of their abilities and experiences. The living systems model (Ford, 1987) stresses the importance of all five functions to effective environmental interactions. Yet, researchers have not identified predictors from each function domain. Instead, they appear to have sampled heavily from a few domains and overlooked the others.

It is doubtful that practitioners consistently make use of all the known predic-

TABLE 4.1
Known and Likely Predictors of Managerial Potential

Function	Known Predictors	Likely Predictors
Directive	Motivation to manage Need for power (socialized) Managerial aspiration Defined career goals	Impression management Values Responsibility training Career maturity

Regulatory		Self-monitoring
		Self-efficacy
		Strong sense of self
		Insight into situational
		  appropriateness
		Confidence to initiate
		  action

Control	Verbal ability Behavioral repertoire	Social intelligence
Arousal	Behavioral vigor	Hardiness Coping ability Empathy Emotion expressiveness
Transactional	Communication skills Managerial skills	Persuasiveness

tors from each function. We propose that both the prediction and development of managerial potential will improve if variables related to each function are included in a "final" model. Immediate attention should be given to arousal and regulatory functions. Such variables activate and monitor behavior patterns in changing environments, and thus are crucial for fulfilling one's potential. Rather than attending to these variables, research has concentrated on motives, cognitive processes and communication skills.

The middle column of Table 4.1 identifies an array of crucial behavioral functions that are related to managerial success. How managerial competence develops, however, has not been addressed. What is needed is an understanding of how competence evolves over time as individuals move through and across organizational boundaries in their careers. A time dimension that links characteristics of individuals early in their careers with managerial effectiveness some time in the future must be included. An initial attempt to provide such a perspective appears in the following section.

THEORETICAL EXTENSIONS: TEMPORAL CONSIDERATIONS

In this section we seek to conceptually bridge the time span that separates predictor measurement from criterion evaluation in the prediction of managerial potential. The nature of one's organizational environment years in the future cannot be assessed during initial selection procedures. In addition, individuals must often progress across or through organizational boundaries before they can display complex behavior criteria. Given this future perspective, the best approach for I/O psychologists may be to measure variables that facilitate more effective interactions and promote more effective organizational opportunities and support over time (Morrison & Hock, 1986). Research on how individuals approach career junctions and confront life tasks may be useful in extending our knowledge of how the variables identified in the preceding section influence managerial success.

Career Transitions and Life Tasks

Predicting managerial success involves assessing the likelihood that individuals will move across organizational boundaries into higher positions and perform effectively in these positions. Schein (1971, 1987) outlined the processes involved in one's career path across organizational boundaries. From an organizational perspective, career moves may be hierarchical (moving up to another organizational level), inclusionary (moving into a more central social group), or functional (moving around between organizational units). Organizations apply filtering mechanisms such as required attributes and competencies to control boundary passage (Schein, 1971). From the perspective of the manager, his or her career is conceptualized in terms of the construction of social selves to meet new social demands presented by boundary passage. Socialization and learning can mold these social selves in the sense of developing new attitudes and values, new competencies, new self-images, and new ways of relating to social situations. The individual draws upon his or her repertoire of attributes, skills, and knowledge (i.e., behavioral functions) to meet new social demands brought about by career transitions.

While career transitions are a source of opportunity for individuals, they may also create problems or undesirable outcomes. Discrepancies between expectations and actual experiences in the new roles and settings are likely to occur (Louis, 1980). Such discrepancies, in turn, may produce cognitive dissonance, frustration, denial, regret, or a sense of failure. To cope, the manager must make sense of the transition experience. Various personality predispositions, orienting purposes, and memories of past experiences may help during the coping process (Louis, 1980). The task for managers during career transitions, then, is to learn new role requirements and match their competencies, attitudes, and values to those requirements.

Our proactive model of managerial potential suggests ways in which this transition task can be accomplished. Effective managers will be able to mold environments to fit their capabilities. The likelihood of shaping one's environment, and thus successfully passing through organizational boundaries, increases as a manager acquires (1) greater knowledge of what methods work in the particular environment; and (2) greater knowledge of what one is capable of doing in a given environment or situation. As managers accumulate work experiences, they gain tacit knowledge of behavior contingencies in their environment; they learn which strategies or behaviors are effective and what to expect in given situations. This tacit knowledge also includes an understanding of how they can best function in the environment, what skills they should rely on to be effective. Self-efficacy beliefs are likely to combine with tacit knowledge in determining how individuals behave (see earlier discussions of self-efficacy and self-referent thought as providing regulatory functions). Self-efficacy theory involves dual prediction from (1) response-efficacy contingencies (behavior-to-outcome linkages); and self-efficacy, or confidence that oneself can attain the outcome (Scheier & Carver, 1987). That is, prediction of behavior is made from self-statements such as "this response will work" combined with "I can effectively do this response." From this perspective, individuals successful at crossing organizational boundaries are those who have learned about particular environments and have shaped them so that they have confidence in their ability to attain desirable outcomes.

Skills that promote acquisition of tacit knowledge about the self in particular environments are likely to improve the prediction of managerial success. The challenge for researchers is to identify such skills. Our literature review suggests that self-efficacy and self-knowledge are likely to predict transition success. Self-insight and knowledge have been found to predict career success (Schein, 1987), and thus may help facilitate boundary passage. One needs to comprehend his or her own needs and biases in order to communicate clearly and to make intelligent choices. Other predictors of successful career transition may be characteristics that enhance perception of external perspectives, interpretation schemes, social comparisons, and organizational history. Future research should investigate the role of these variables in managers' careers.

Research on how individuals confront major life tasks may be useful in understanding career transition processes over extended time spans. Cantor and Kihlstrom (1987) proposed a model of intentional problem solving that is applicable to how managers confront major tasks, junction points, and transitions during their careers. Individuals' world views (composed of their self-concepts, social concepts, autobiographical memories, and interpretive rules) influence the goals they set in particular contexts. Action strategies are then developed by individuals to work on those task goals. The focus is on the managers' characteristic patterns of problem solving as they use their uniquely organized social intelligence to work on current life tasks (Cantor & Kihlstrom, 1987). Effective problem solving in this sense would require knowledge of how one's capabilities fit a given situation.

Individuals' problem-solving approaches reflect their unique history, values, and needs. While structured life transitions, such as career changes, constrain the nature and timing of one's efforts, they are uniquely shaped by the individual within current constraints as variations on common themes (Cantor & Kihlstrom, 1987). In developing a strategy, the manager draws on concepts and rules (declarative and procedural knowledge) as well as skills concerning when and how to use this knowledge to shape a plan of action consistent with the goals inherent in the current task. He or she engages in a problem-solving cycle of planning, action, and monitoring of outcomes that is conditioned by such factors as beliefs, social comparisons, obstacles encountered, reactions to risk or conflict, actions of others, and attempts to protect or enhance one's self-esteem.

This problem-solving model helps to clarify the role of the information-processing subsystem of individuals identified by Ford's (1987) living systems framework. The information-processing subsystem of individuals is the primary way by which individuals adopt a future orientation. Factors and characteristics involved in the quality of managers' problem-solving approaches and skills, such as flexibility, creativity, persuasiveness, and reactions to conflict, are likely predictors of managerial success.

Summary

This section extends our model of managerial potential by incorporating a future orientation or temporal dimension. This time dimension allows us to better understand why certain variables forecast managerial competence. Successful predictors are those that facilitate tacit knowledge of how one functions best given behavioral contingencies existing in particular environments. Abilities to set goals in changing contexts and to develop action strategies to work toward those goals are likely to be important predictors of managerial success. The ability to cope with career transition experiences will affect the extent to which individuals with managerial aspirations or skills are able to successfully negotiate boundary passages and become successful managers. In addition, predictors may relate to one or more key boundary moves or to critical performance requirements in one or more positions. Skills, attributes, knowledge or life experiences that facilitate a wider range of boundary passages or help performance in several kinds of positions should be strong predictors of success.

Finally, the time gap between predictor assessment and criterion evaluation may be marked by periods of environmental or organizational instability. Prediction of managerial competence over time will likely be affected by such organizational or environmental changes. Shifting environmental situations may tap a different mix of predictors over time and individual differences in traits, skills, and knowledge may make a different mix of predictors salient. Research should attempt to match environmental situations with predictors of ability to negotiate boundary passage and of managerial competence.

IMPLICATIONS FOR THE SCIENCE-PRACTICE DIALOGUE

We began this chapter by noting that the low level of interaction between scientists and practitioners of I/O psychology was due, in part, to stagnation in empirical efforts to predict managerial potential. The confirmed predictors in

Table 4.1 are nearly identical to those cited in Campbell et al. (1970) and Hall (1976). Progress has been slow because researchers have not been successful in explaining *why* different variables predict managerial competence over time (Klimoski & Brickner, 1987). We have attempted to provide a theoretical framework that identifies areas of research which hopefully will stimulate scientist–practitioner interactions. A multivariate prediction model is advocated, one that incorporates predictors that manifest living systems functions (Ford, 1987) and indicates an individual's ability to effectively interact with and create opportunities in environmental situations across organizational boundaries. Scientists may increase their success in predicting managerial competence if they adopt a proactive view of managerial competence and seek to identify variables that facilitate the career transition process and enable individuals to create opportunities in shifting environments. By providing the practitioner with a set of predictors related to managerial competence and career progressions, the scientist will increase the chance that his or her research will be implemented and applied.

Among current research, perhaps the work of Howard and Bray (1988; Bray & Howard, 1983) and Owens and Schoenfeldt (1979) best reflects the approach we are advocating. Both of these lines of research represent attempts to provide a complete picture of an individual's abilities and motivations. Both incorporated multiple domains of behavior in their prediction models and predicted behavior over an extended time period. Neither approach, however, considered all the behavior functions we have identified as relevant for managerial success. In addition, both approaches represent largely empirically driven work; neither fits managerial prediction into a broad theoretical context, as we have done here. Nonetheless, they offer scientists and practitioners relatively strong prediction models and should be used as points of departure for future empirical studies and theory building.

Owens and Schoenfeldt (1979) developed a classification system of persons based on dimensions of past behavior and found that this classification scheme projected into future behaviors. College freshmen responded to a biographical questionnaire and were assigned to subgroups reflecting differences in past behavior. Subsequent college and postcollege experiences were measured. Results revealed that subgroups differing in terms of past behavior continued to behave differently in subsequent studies. Owens and Schoenfeldt (1979) discuss implications of their model for the early identification of managerial talent. The behavioral repertoires of subgroups high in managerial potential may be due to specific experiences in the past. Owens and Schoenfeldt's (1979) model has added value in that it involves prediction from both "human characteristics and environmental context" (p. 570). Such an approach allows us to examine more closely how individuals are linked to their environments.

Howard and Bray (1988) presented a detailed analysis of managers' careers over nearly a 30-year period at the Bell System (AT&T). This work provides a rare examination of changes in motivation, work and life attitudes, personality, and success levels over a manager's career. Much can be learned about the realization of managerial talent from this approach. One of the main objectives of their project was to relate assessment center ratings to managerial success, as defined by level of management attained in the organization. The assessment centers incorporated a variety of tests and exercises that reflected 9 component dimensions of managerial potential: (1) administrative skills; (2) interpersonal skills; (3) stability of performance; (4) intellectual ability; (5) work involvement; (6) advancement motivation; (7) independence of others; (8) nonconformity; and (9) general effectiveness (for a complete description of these dimensions see Howard, 1986; Bray & Howard, 1983; or Howard & Bray, 1988). Managers were rated on each of these 9 dimensions by trained assessors. These nine dimensions of managerial potential relate to many of the predictors listed in Table 4.1. However, arousal and regulatory functions are once again underrepresented.

Assessment center ratings were consistently related to managerial progression in these studies. Bray and Howard (1983), for example, reported a 55% "hit" rate overall (64% for college and 40% for noncollege men) for managers predicted to reach the third (of six) management levels after 8 years. The relationship between assessment center predictions and managerial progress was significant yet the number of false negatives and false positives was considerable. In addition, the question of why assessment centers work (Klimoski & Brickner, 1987) was not fully resolved by Howard and Bray's (1988) research. Future research should examine if accuracy of assessment center predictions is improved by including additional predictors, especially those tapping into regulatory and arousal functions. Attempts should also be made to monitor how individuals progress in organizations in order to discover mediating factors that facilitate passage across organizational boundaries.

A number of findings from the Howard and Bray (1988) studies support the proactive view of managerial development. Prediction of managerial progression was higher when individuals were in "high job-challenge" positions than in "low challenge" positions (Bray & Howard, 1983). Further, a majority of the false negatives (those predicted not to reach middle management but who did) were in high challenge positions. These findings suggest that individuals who have certain skills or abilities are able to take advantage of enriched opportunities given to them.

Conclusion

The intent of this chapter was to suggest a new way of conceptualizing managerial potential and to indicate areas where research should be conducted. Proactive or facilitative measures have been indexed; research aimed at testing the predictive validity of these measures is needed. The relevance of the time span between predictor assessment and criteria evaluation to understanding why predictors predict competence far into the future was discussed. Research is needed to identify predictors of successful career transitions at different stages. The dynamic nature of predictor–environment linkages needs to be examined. Different situations may tap a different mix of predictors. Investigations of this type will help the practitioner in identifying and facilitating managerial potential.

For many of the questions and research directions raised, researchers may have to look to theoretical and empirical studies where the focus has not been managers or prediction but where domains involved may be a source of predictor variables. We have identified a number of such domains for each behavioral function related to managerial potential. Drawing from research in these areas may fill in the gaps identified by the present prediction model. The potential for a strong science–practice interface exists in this area. Research horizons must be broadened and the prediction process reconceptualized to draw science and practice together.

REFERENCES

Baltes, P. B. (1987, August). *Toward a psychological theory of wisdom.* Invited lecture presented at the annual meeting of the American Psychological Association, New York.

Bandura, A. (1986). *Social foundations of thought and action.* Englewood Cliffs, NJ: Prentice-Hall.

Bentz, V. J. (1987, August). *Contextual richness as a criterion consideration in personality research with executives.* Paper presented at the annual meeting of the American Psychological Association, New York.

Bergin, C. A. C. (1987). Prosocial development in toddlers: The patterning of mother-infant interactions, In M. E. Ford & D. H. Fords (Eds.), *Humans as self-constructing living systems: Putting the framework to work.* Hillsdale, NJ: Lawrence Erlbaum Associates.

Berman, R., & Miner, J. B. (1985). Motivation to manage at the top executive level. *Personnel Psychology, 38,* 377–391.

Boyatzis, R. (1982). *The competent manager.* New York: Wiley.

Bray, D. (1984, August). *Assessment centers for research and application.* Psi Chi Distinguished Lecture delivered at the annual convention of the American Psychological Association. Toronto, Canada.

Bray, D. W., & Grant, D. L. (1966). The assessment center in the measurement of potential for business management. *Psychological Monograph, 80* (17, Whole No. 625).

Bray, D. W., & Howard, A. (1983). The AT&T longitudinal studies of managers. In K. W. Schaie (Ed.), *Longitudinal studies of adult psychological development* (pp. 266–312). New York: Guilford.

Buss, D. (1987). Selection, evocation, and manipulation. *Journal of Personality and Social Psychology, 53,* 1214–1221.

Buss, A., & Plomin, R. (1984). *Temperament: Early developing personality traits.* Hillsdale, NJ: Lawrence Erlbaum Associates.

Caldwell, D., & Reilly, C. (1982). Boundary spanning and individual performance: The impact of self-monitoring. *Journal of Applied Psychology, 67,* 124–127.

Campbell, J., Dunnette, M., Lawler, E., & Weick, K. (1970). *Managerial behavior, performance, and effectiveness.* New York: McGraw Hill.

Cantor, N., & Kihlstrom, J. (1987). *Personality and social intelligence.* Englewood Cliffs, NJ: Prentice-Hall.

Cascio, W. F. (1987). *Applied psychology in personnel management* (3rd ed.). Englewood-Cliffs, NJ: Prentice-Hall.

Capsi, A. (1987). Personality in the life course. *Journal of Personality and Social Psychology, 53,* 1203–1213.

Childs, A., & Klimoski, R. (1986). Successfully predicting career success: An application of the biographical inventory. *Journal of Applied Psychology, 71,* 3–8.

Clawson, J., Kotter, J., Faux, V., & McArthur, C. (1985). *Self-assessment and career development* (2nd ed.). Englewood Cliffs, NJ: Prentice-Hall.

Cornelius, E. T. III, & Lane, F. (1984). The power motive and managerial success. *Journal of Applied Psychology, 69,* 32–39.

Davis, M. H. (1983). Measuring individual differences in empathy: Evidence for a multidimensional approach. *Journal of Personality and Social Psychology, 44,* 113–126.

Derlega, V., & Berg, J. (1987). *Self-disclosure: Theory, research, and therapy.* New York: Plenum.

Dunnette, M. (1971). Multiple assessment procedures in identifying and developing managerial talent. In P. McReynolds (Ed.), *Advances in psychological assessment* (Vol. 2). Palo Alto, CA: Science and Behavior Books.

Fielder, F., & Leister, A. (1977). Leader intelligence and task performance: A test of a multiple screen model. *Organizational Behavior and Human Performance, 20,* 11–14.

Ford, D. H. (1987). *Humans as self-constructing living systems: A developmental perspective on behavior and personality.* Hillsdale, NJ: Lawrence Erlbaum Associates.

Ford, M. E., & Ford, D. H. (1987). *Humans as self-constructing living systems: Putting the framework to work.* Hillsdale, NJ: Lawrence Erlbaum Associates.

Foundation for Research on Human Behavior (1968). *Predicting managerial success.* Ann Arbor, MI: F.R.H.B.

Gangestad, S., & Snyder, M. (1985). On the nature of self-monitoring: An examination of latent causal structure. In P. Shaver (Ed.), *Review of Personality and Social Psychology* (Vol. 6, pp. 65–85). Beverly Hills, CA: Sage.

Garland, H., & Beard, J. (1979). Relationship between self-monitoring and leader emergence across two tasks. *Journal of Applied Psychology, 64,* 72–76.

Ghiselli, E. E. (1973). The validity of aptitude tests in personnel selection. *Personnel Psychology, 26,* 461–477.

Glauser, M., (1984). Self-esteem and communication tendencies. *Psychological Record, 34,* 115–131.

Hall, D. (1976). *Careers in organizations.* New York: Goodyear.

Hogan, R. (1982). A socioanalytic theory of personality. In M. Page & R. Dienstbier (Eds.), *Nebraska symposium on motivation* (pp. 55–89). Lincoln: University of Nebraska Press.

Howard, A. (1986). College experiences and managerial performance. *Journal of Applied Psychology, 71,* 530–552.

Howard, A., & Bray, D. W. (1988). *Managerial lives in transition: Advancing age and changing times.* New York: Guilford.

Hunter, J., & Hunter, R. (1984). Validity and utility of alternative predictors of job performance. *Psychological Bulletin, 96,* 72–98.

Kaplan, H. (1986). *Social psychology of self-referent behavior.* New York: Plenum.

Klimoski, R., & Brickner, M. (1987). Why do assessment centers work? *Personnel Psychology, 40,* 243–260.

Kobasa, S. (1979). Stressful live events, personality and health: An inquiry into hardiness. *Journal of Personality and Social Psychology, 37,* 1–11.

Latack, J. (1984). Career transitions within organizations. *Organizational Behavior and Human Performance, 34,* 296–322.

Lennox, R., & Wolfe, R. (1984). Revision of the Self-Monitoring Scale. *Journal of Personality and Social Psychology, 46,* 1349–1364.

Lillibridge, J., & Williams, K. (1987). *Assessment of the five-factor model of personality.* Unpublished manuscript. The University of Albany, State University of New York.

Louis, M. (1980). Career transitions: Varieties and communalities. *Academy of Management Review, 5*, 329–340.

Luthans, F., Hodgetts, R. M., & Rosenkrantz, S. (1988). *Real Managers.* Cambridge, MA: Ballinger.

McClelland, D. C. (1975). *Power: The inner experience.* New York: Scott-Foresman.

McClelland, D. C. (1985). *Human Motivation.* New York: Scott-Foresman.

McClelland, D. C., & Boyatzis, R. E. (1982). Leadership motive pattern and longterm success in management. *Journal of Applied Psychology, 67,* 737–743.

McClelland, D. C., & Burnham, D. H. (1976). Power is the great motivator. *Harvard Business Review,* March-April, 159–166.

McDevitt, T. M., & Ford, M. E. (1987). Processes in young children's communicative functioning and development. In M. E. Ford & D. H. Ford (Eds.), *Humans as self-constructing living systems: Putting the framework to work.* Hillsdale, NJ: Lawrence Erlbaum Associates.

Miner, J. B. (1978). Twenty years of research on role-motivation theory of managerial effectiveness. *Personnel Psychology, 31,* 739–760.

Morrison, R., & Hock, R. (1986). Career building: Learning from cumulative work experience. In D. Hall (Ed.), *Career development in organizations.* New York: Jossey-Bass.

Naylor, J. L., Pritchard, R. D., & Ilgen, D. R. (1980). *A theory of behavior in organizations.* New York: Academic Press.

Neiner, A., & Owens, W. A. (1985). Using biodata to predict job choice among college graduates. *Journal of Applied Psychology, 70,* 127–136.

Nevill, D., & Super, D. (1988). Career maturity and commitment to work in university students. *Journal of Vocational Behavior, 32,* 139–151.

Owens, W. A., & Schoenfeldt, L. F. (1979). Toward a classification of persons. *Journal of Applied Psychology Monograph, 65,* 569–607.

Peters, R. (1987). *Practical intelligence.* New York: Harper & Row.

Peters, T., & Austin, N. (1985). *A passion for excellence.* New York: Random House.

Plunkett, L., & Hale, G. (1982). *The proactive manager.* New York: Wiley.

Quick, J., Bhagat, R., Dalton, J., & Quick, J. (1987). *Work stress: Health care systems in the workplace.* New York: Praeger.

Rafaeli, A., & Sutton, R. (1987). Expression of emotion as part of the work role. *Academy of Management Review, 12,* 23–37.

Raynor, J., & Etnin, R. (1982). *Motivation, career striving and aging.* Washington, DC: Hemisphere.

Riggio, R. (1986). Assessment of basic social skills. *Journal of Personality and Social Psychology, 51,* 649–660.

Ritchie, R. J., & Boehm, V. R. (1977). Biographical data as a predictor of women's and men's management potential. *Journal of Vocational Behavior, 11,* 363–368.

Russell, J. S., & Wexley, K. N. (1988). Improving managerial performance in assessing needs and transferring training. In G. R. Ferris & K. M. Rowland (Eds.), *Research in personnel and human resource management* (Vol. 6, pp. 289–323). Greenwich, CT: JAI.

Rynes, S. L. (1987). Career transitions from engineering to management: Are they predictable among students? *Journal of Vocational Behavior, 30,* 138–154.

Saal, F. E., & Knight, P. A. (1988). *Industrial-organizational psychology: Science and practice.* Monterey, CA: Brooks-Cole.

Scarr, S., & McCartney, K., (1983). How people make their own environments: A theory of genotype-environment effects. *Child Development, 54,* 424–435.

Scheier, M. F., & Carver, C. S. (1987). Dispositional optimism and physical well-being: The influence of generalized outcome expectations on health. *Journal of Personality, 55,* 169–210.

Schein, D. (1971). The individual, the organization and the career. *Journal of Applied Behavioral Science, 7,* 401–426.

Schein, D. (1987). Individuals and careers. In J. Lorsch, (Ed.), *Handbook of organizational behavior.* Englewood Cliffs, NJ: Prentice-Hall.

Schlenker, B. (1985). *The self and social life.* New York: McGraw-Hill.

Schmidt, F. L., & Hunter, J. E. (1981). Employment testing: Old theories and new research findings. *American Psychologist, 36,* 1128–1137.

Schmitt, N. (1977). Interrater agreement in dimensionality and combination of assessment center judgments. *Journal of Applied Psychology, 62,* 171–176.

Simonton, D. (1985). Intelligence and personal influence in groups. *Psychological Review, 92,* 532–547.

Snyder, M. (1974). Self-monitoring of expressive behavior. *Journal of Personality and Social Psychology, 30,* 526–537.

Snyder, M. (1983). The influence of individuals on situations: Links between personality and social behavior. *Journal of Personality, 51,* 497–516.

Sorrentino, R., & Field, N. (1986). Emergent leadership over time: The functional value of positive motivation. *Journal of Personality and Social Psychology, 50,* 1091–1099.

Sorrentino, R. M., & Higgins, E. T. (Eds.). (1986). *The handbook of motivation and cognition: Foundations of social behavior.* New York: Guilford.

Sternberg, R. (1986). *Advances in the psychology of human intelligence* (Vol. 3). Hillsdale, NJ: Lawrence Erlbaum Associates.

Sternberg, R., & Wagner, R. (1986). *Practical intelligence.* New York: Cambridge University Press.

Streufert, S., & Swezey, R. (1986). *Complexity, managers and organizations.* New York: Academic Press.

Tedeschi, J. T., & Melburg, V. (1984). Impression management and influence in the organization. In S. B. Bacharach & E. Lawler (Eds.), *Research in the sociology of organizations* (Vol. 3, pp. 31–58). Greenwich, CT: JAI.

Thorton, G. C., III, & Byham, W. C. (1982). *Assessment centers and management performance.* New York: Academic Press.

Vallacher, R., & Wegner, D. (1985). *A theory of action identification.* Hillsdale, NJ: Lawrence Erlbaum Associates.

Wagner, R., & Sternberg, R. (1985). Practical intelligence in real-world pursuits: The role of tacit knowledge. *Journal of Personality and Social Psychology, 49,* 436–458.

Wagner, R., & Sternberg, R. (1986). Tacit knowledge and intelligence in the everyday world. In R. Sternberg & R. Wagner (Eds.), *Practical intelligence.* New York: Cambridge University Press.

Wolfe, R., Lennox, R., & Cutler, B. (1986). Getting along and getting ahead: Empirical support for a theory of protective and acquisitive self-presentation. *Journal of Personality and Social Psychology, 50,* 356–361.

Wollowick, H. B., & McNamara, W. J. (1969). Relationship of the components of an assessment center to management success. *Journal of Applied Psychology, 53,* 348–352.

Winter, D. (1988). The power motive in women and men. *Journal of Personality and Social Psychology, 54,* 510–519.

Zerbe, W., & Paulhus, D. (1987). Socially desirable responding in organizational behavior. *Academy of Management Review, 12,* 250–264.

5 Utility Analysis and its Application to the Study of the Cost-effectiveness of the Assessment Center Method

Robert F. Goldsmith
Development Dimensions International

One of the many areas in which the scientific study and applied practice of industrial and organizational (I/O) psychology intersect is evaluating the utility of personnel systems in organizations. Utility can be thought of as the cost-effectiveness of a policy, practice, or procedure. Cost-effectiveness, of course, has implications for sound business decisions. Determining the utility of various organizational interventions has become increasingly important for both psychologists and organizations, and affords us a unique opportunity to apply the results of scientific research in helping organizations make decisions about personnel policies and practices, as well as other organizational interventions.

The application of utility analysis to assessment centers is especially appropriate and necessary, considering their high cost vis à vis other selection methods. This chapter presents an example of the use of utility analysis in evaluating a specific assessment center, and shows how the techniques of utility analysis can enhance the integration of science and practice in this area of I/O psychology.

A BRIEF HISTORY OF UTILITY ANALYSIS

As Schmidt, Hunter, McKenzie, and Muldrow (1979) pointed out, I/O psychologists have been interested in evaluating the benefits obtained from organizational interventions since the early days of the discipline. The interventions most often evaluated are personnel selection procedures. In the 1920s, a number of industrial psychologists evaluated the validity of selection tests by comparing the standard error of job performance scores predicted by a given test with the standard error of performance based on random selection. This was known as the "index of forecasting efficiency." It was replaced in the 1930s and 1940s by the "coefficient of determination," which was simply the percentage of job performance variance accounted for by variance in performance on a selection instrument, that is, the validity coefficient squared. Unfortunately, neither the index of forecasting efficiency nor the coefficient of determination proved sufficient because they did not take into account such varying but relevant parameters of selection situations as the selection ratio.

This problem was overcome by Taylor and Russell (1939), who developed a model and corresponding tables that incorporated both the selection ratio and the base rate, or percentage of candidates who would be successful given random selection. They demonstrated that the interaction of validity, selection ratio, and base rate needed to be taken into account to carry out comparisons among selection procedures, or between selection procedures and random selection. Although this was an improvement over the index of forecasting efficiency and the coefficient of determination, the Taylor-Russell method relied on a dichotomous criterion (successful/unsuccessful). It failed to distinguish among multiple levels of performance, and required usually arbitrary designations of "successful" performance.

Brogden (1949) stimulated a major advance in the study of selection utility by using the principles of linear regression, and by directly addressing the dollar value of performance. His utility equation can be expressed as follows:

$$\Delta \bar{U} / \text{selectee} = r_{xy} SD_y \bar{Z}_{xs}$$

U is utility and ΔU is marginal utility. Marginal utility is directly proportional to the correlation between predictor scores and job performance (r_{xy}), to the standard deviation of the dollar value of job performance (SD_y) and to the average standard score on the predictor obtained by the applicant group $(\bar{Z}_x)$. If it is assumed that test scores are normally distributed, the equation can be expressed as follows:

$$\Delta U / \text{selectee} = r_{xy} \phi / p SD_y,$$

where p is the selection ratio and ϕ is the ordinate of the normal curve at a cut-off point corresponding to p.

The next major advance in the study of utility came from Cronbach and Gleser in 1957. They subsequently elaborated their ideas in a 1965 book titled *Psychological Tests and Personnel Decisions*. Cronbach and Gleser applied decision theory principles to the study of utility, and incorporated the cost of information gathering. Their utility model can be expressed as follows:

$$\Delta U = t N_s \, \Delta r \, SD_y \, \lambda / SR - N_s \, \Delta c / SR$$

Where ΔU is the dollar gain in job performance when using the selection procedure of interest rather than the prior or an alternative procedure, t is the average tenure in years of incumbents in the target position, N_s is the number of individuals selected, Δr is the difference in the validity coefficient associated with the two selection procedures being considered, SD_y is the standard deviation of the dollar value of job performance, SR is the selection ratio, λ is the ordinate of the normal curve corresponding to the selection ratio, and Δc is the difference in cost associated with the two procedures being considered. Thus, utility is directly proportional to tenure, number of people to be hired, incremental validity, and variability of on-the-job performance. It is reduced by incremental costs, and is inversely proportional to the selection ratio.

Most of the data needed to use the Cronbach-Gleser model can be obtained, or at least estimated, from personnel records and human resources staffing plans. Obtaining accurate validity information can be difficult, particularly if the purpose of the utility analysis is to determine whether a new selection procedure (for which no data exist) should be implemented. One way to overcome this problem is to estimate the validity of the "new" procedure based on data obtained using the same or similar procedure in a similar setting. Validity generalization techniques are now available for determining the predicted validity of a selection instrument.

As Greer and Cascio (1987) pointed out, the most difficult parameter to estimate when determining utility is SD_y, the standard deviation of the dollar value of job performance. Several different estimation procedures have been developed. Cost-accounting procedures have been used because they are reliable and, for positions to which the dollar value of performance can be easily determined, apparently valid. A drawback to cost-accounting is that many positions do not lend themselves to expressing performance in terms of dollars and cents. It is easier to compute the dollar value of job performance of a manufacturing employee or a salesperson than for a clerk, a manager, or a professional. In addition, there are contributions made by manufacturing employees or salespersons, such as suggestions for productivity improvement or increased customer satisfaction, that are not easily quantifiable and that are not typically considered in cost-accounting procedures. Cascio and Ramos (1986) noted that a cost-accounting approach to estimating SD_y is often not feasible and requires indefensible estimates.

A second method for estimating SD_y, that is far less complex than the cost-accounting approach, was discussed by Schmidt, Hunter, and Pearlman (1982). They asserted that SD_y is usually approximately 40% of wages, and cited the average results of 39 studies to support this assertion. Although easy to use, this approach risks underestimating SD_y when the dollar value of performance takes into account the cost of an error, particularly in a capital-intensive industry. For example, a single mistake by an operator in a chemical plant could result in millions of dollars in property damage and legal costs, yet that operator's compensation does not fully reflect those potential negative consequences. One reason is that job evaluation systems typically incorporate the market values of skills and responsibilities, at least indirectly. In other words, chemical plant operators don't receive million dollar salaries because there are competent people who are willing to do the job for less. Another reason that the 40% method may underestimate SD_y is that in many organizations, particularly those that are capital intensive, employees at all levels are paid only a fraction of their "value," if value is interpreted as the worth of what they *and the capital they are using* is actually worth.

A third method for estimating SD_y is the Cascio-Ramos estimate of performance in dollars, known as CREPID (Cascio, 1982). This procedure utilizes traditional job analysis, performance measurement, and employee wages. It involves determining the job's principle activities, rating each incumbent on those activities, and apportioning salary across those activities to determine each incumbent's total worth. The standard deviation of the distribution of total worth is SD_y. The CREPID method examines ways in which each incumbent contributes to the success of an organization, and it is applicable to any type of job, not merely those for which cost-accounting methods are easily applied. However, it too is susceptible to underestimating SD_y because it relies on wage information (for the same reasons discussed earlier).

A fourth method of computing SD_y was described by Schmidt et al. (1979), and has come to be known as the Global Estimation Method (GEM). They asserted that performance in dollars is normally distributed, and that experienced managers can estimate the dollar value of various levels of performance. The GEM method focuses on the dollar value of job performance at the mean, (50th percentile), the 85th percentile, and the 15th percentile of a normal distribution. These points correspond to the mean and close approximations to one standard deviation above and below the mean, respectively. Schmidt et al. asked managers to estimate the dollar value of employees' performance at the 50th, 85th, and 15th percentiles. They then calculated SD_y by computing the average differences between the mean and both the 85th and 15th percentiles. Schmidt et al. used two sets of instructions to obtain these estimates. One asked for the dollar worth of current employees; the other asked for the cost to hire outside contractors who could perform at the various levels (percentiles).

An advantage of the GEM approach is that managers can take a wide range of factors into account, including cost of errors, when using this method. Thus, the likelihood of underestimating SD_y is not as great as when using the 40% or CREPID approaches. It is also far easier to apply than cost-accounting procedures, and notably easier to apply than CREPID. A disadvantage associated with the GEM approach is that some managers, particularly those who are less experienced, may not provide reliable or valid estimates. However, Bobko, Karen, and Parkington (1983) compared archival data with the GEM method to show that supervisors' estimates of SD_y are quite accurate. Another potential disadvantage concerns the estimates of costs associated with bringing in outside contractors. In industries and organizations where subcontractors are never used, for example to perform manufacturing or sales jobs, such estimates are irrelevant. In others, they are distorted by market or other factors that mitigate the relationship between cost of subcontractors and their actual value, for example, when fees are based more on supply and demand than real value to the organization. As an example, consider the case of a company going through a growth phase and contracting with an outside physician to conduct employment physicals in order to provide relief for an overloaded company doctor. The fee rate for the physician is set by professional committees and prevailing fees in the community, and may not accurately reflect the dollar value of the physician's performance. This is particularly the case when another physician of widely different skill level is required to charge the same fees.

Various studies have compared methods of measuring SD_y in order to explore convergent validity. For example, Weekley, Frank, O'Connor, and Peters (1985) compared the 40% rule, the CREPID procedure, and the GEM procedure. Their results showed convergence between the 40% rule and CREPID procedures, but the GEM procedure yielded a markedly larger value of SD_y. Greer and Cascio (1987) compared CREPID, cost-accounting, and GEM to find that cost-accounting and GEM converged, but the CREPID approach produced a notably smaller value of SD_y. As noted before, Bobko et al. (1983) found that the GEM and the cost-accounting procedures produced similar results. To summarize, CREPID and the 40% rule tend to converge, and GEM and cost-accounting procedures tend to converge, with the former two tending to result in lower estimates of SD_y than the latter two. This is probably due to the central role of actual salary data in the CREPID and 40% rule procedures.

A BRIEF HISTORY OF ASSESSMENT CENTERS

An assessment center is an integrated series of activities and instruments designed to evaluate participants in terms of the requirements of a target job, a family of jobs, or a level of jobs. Assessment centers feature the use of simulations of important aspects of the target job in order to elicit behaviors that reflect the skill level of the participant. Some assessment centers use other sources of information in addition to simulations, such as paper-and-pencil tests or background interviews. Some assessment centers rely solely on simulations. Assessment centers typically involve several observers, or assessors who observe, record, classify, and evaluate assesses' behavior. The assessors reach a consensual evaluation of the competency of each assessee on the different dimensions being evaluated. Participants are typically assessed in groups, although this is only necessary if group exercises are used; otherwise it is done merely for administrative convenience. Assessment centers are used both for selection/promotion and for development purposes.

In his overview of assessment centers, William Byham (1989) traced the history of this method. In 1970, approximately twelve organizations in the

United States used assessment centers. In 1980, the number was about 1000, and in 1990 it is estimated to be 2000. These include businesses, government agencies, and nonprofit institutions across the whole spectrum of American organizations. The growth in assessment centers is not limited to the United States. For example, over 120 organizations in Japan use assessment centers. According to Byham, assessment center methodology can be traced to the early days of this century. During World War I, systematic testing and observation in various exercises was used to evaluate officer candidates for the German air force. Psychologists acted as assessors, who presented their findings to a senior military officer for a final decision.

In 1941 the British Army instituted Officer Selection Boards to evaluate candidates for promotion. Candidates were evaluated through paper-and-pencil tests, as well as a variety of exercises designed to measure skills such as leadership, practical intelligence, and decision-making under fatigue-inducing conditions. At the same time, Henry Murray in the United States was developing techniques at the Harvard Psychological Clinic for integrating data from various sources. These techniques were initially used to diagnosis patients, but they were applicable to evaluating the skills of any individual.

The first large-scale use of assessment centers in the United States occurred in the Office of Strategic Services (OSS), predecessor of the Central Intelligence Agency, which was formed shortly after the U.S. entered the Second World War. The OSS, headed by William Donovan, was charged with conducting covert operations against the Axis nations (Germany, Italy, Japan). Donovan needed to select agents who were highly skilled in a variety of areas. He had learned of Britain's Officer Selection System, and recruited Murray to lead the OSS assessment program. Murray recruited other psychologists and together they created, often with last minute improvisations, a program that included various personality tests and a series of exercises. The exercises were designed to simulate the kind of problem solving, decision making, leadership, cooperation, and stress tolerance required of successful candidates in the field. The original assessment center was located in Virginia, but additional centers were opened in Washington D.C., California, Ceylon, India, and China. Over 7000 candidates were assessed in these programs.

The first civilian application of assessment centers for evaluating job skills was conducted at AT&T by Douglas W. Bray. Bray was familiar with the OSS program, and was hired by AT&T to conduct a longitudinal study of managers. He used a variety of instruments, including paper-and-pencil tests and business-oriented exercises, to evaluate each candidate's skills and make an overall prediction of each candidate's management potential. The original study, begun in 1956, is still going on, as Bray and his colleagues follow candidates' histories and periodically re-assess them as they progress through their careers. This study is documented in *Managerial Lives in Transition* (Bray & Howard, 1988).

By 1958, the methods developed by Bray were being used to assess candidates for managerial positions in many parts of AT&T. Soon other large organizations, such as IBM, Standard Oil of Ohio, and J.C. Penney were using this method. During the 1970s and 1980s, assessment centers rapidly grew in popularity as more and more organizations began to use them, and more research was conducted and published about them. The method has been used to select candidates and identify developmental needs at all levels, from hourly workers to chief executive officers, and in all types of organizations and industries.

A number of reviews have examined the research on assessment centers. For example, Huck (1973) reviewed research published prior to 1973 and drew several conclusions:

1. assessment center procedures have been consistently related to a number of measures of performance effectiveness;

2. simulations make contributions to predictions of managerial performance beyond that of paper-and-pencil tests alone;

3. assessment techniques have adequate reliability, and no differences exist in evaluations when psychologists or trained nonpsychologists serve as the assessors; and

4. there is no differential validity among subgroups of assessees or assessors with regard to sex, race, or job differences.

Thornton and Byham (1982) published one of the most extensive reviews of assessment center research. They stated, " . . . it is our view that the criticism that practice outruns research evidence is incorrect for assessment centers—this technique probably has more research support than any other technique in industrial psychology "(p. 251). Thornton and Byham's review of criterion-related validity studies of assessment centers is particularly interesting. Categorizing studies according to the research designs used, they described five longitudinal studies in which assessment results were not revealed to participants or their managers, and concluded that correlations between assessment center ratings and performance criteria (generally dollar volume of sales or performance ratings made by supervisors) were all significant. They described nine studies that utilized control groups, and found that in seven of these nine studies, individuals promoted as a result of assessment center evaluations performed significantly better than individuals promoted through traditional methods. They reported seven studies in which participants and their managers were informed of assessment center results, and in which assessment center ratings were correlated with a variety of subsequent criteria of progress or performance. These studies supported the predictive validity of the method for several types of criteria: ratings of overall performance and potential, increases in management responsibility (job complexity, financial responsibility, and skill requirements); performance dimension ratings on behavioral scales; measures of reactions to problems on the job;

and measures of personal effectiveness on the job. Criteria information came from a variety of sources. Finally, they reported seven concurrent validity studies that showed mixed results. Thornton and Byham speculated about design flaws that may have resulted in nonsignificant correlations in some of the studies.

The sum of all this information provides strong evidence that assessment centers are valid predictors of performance. This is corroborated by Hunter and Hunter (1984) who performed a meta-analysis on assessment center validity research showing that the average validity of assessment centers is .43. It is certainly appropriate to apply utility analysis to the assessment center method. Assessment centers are relatively expensive and labor-intensive procedures for evaluating the strengths and developmental needs of individuals. They require much more time, and therefore expense, to design, install, administer, and score, than other methods of evaluating candidates, such as paper-and-pencil tests and interviews.

AN EXAMPLE OF UTILITY ANALYSIS APPLIED
TO ASSESSMENT CENTERS

This section offers a "real-world" example of utility analysis. A new selection procedure that utilizes an assessment center as a key screening procedure is compared to the prior method of selection. The prior method, which I label System One, featured a paper-and-pencil test that was designed to predict success in supervision, and that included both judgmental and autobiographical components. The judgmental component presented the respondent with brief descriptions of typical problems confronting a supervisor and provided multiple choices of the best solution; the autobiographical component asked for biographical information such as highest level of education. The new selection procedure, which I call System Two, is a multiple-step process that includes an assessment center, the same paper-and-pencil test used in System One (with the same cut-off score), a behavioral reference check, and two behavioral interviews. Other paper-and-pencil instruments (a problem-solving test, a general intelligence test, and a motivational inventory) were included in System Two for research purposes only. All participants completed the paper-and-pencil tests and the assessment center requirements. Successful participants then participated in the interviews and the reference check.

Assessors for the System Two assessment center were selected through a screening interview, in-basket simulation, and behavioral interview. They completed a 5-day assessor-training program. In addition, a consultant coadministered the first implementation of the assessment center in order to provide coaching and guidance. The assessment center consisted of four simulations: a 25-item in-basket set in an industrial environment, a role-play in which each participant was given background information and then interacted with an assessor who played the part of a problem subordinate, a scheduling exercise in which tasks had to be prioritized and employees scheduled and rescheduled, and a leaderless group discussion in which six participants interacted to reach consensus on four supervisory problems.

The target job was all first-level blue collar supervisor positions in the Nuclear Division of a large public utility in the eastern United States. (Efforts are made here to avoid confusion between the two very different meanings of the word "utility"). With the exception of specific methods used to measure technical skill and departmental differences in licensing requirements, the same procedures were used to evaluate candidates for supervisory positions in all departments (operations, maintenance, security, and various support functions). The purpose of the utility analysis was to determine whether we could justify the high expense of running System Two to top management. The methods and assumptions used to derive or estimate each component of the equation needed to compute ΔU are described below. ΔU was actually computed twice, once to compare System One with System Two, and once to compare System One with the assessment center alone.

COMPUTATION OF ΔU

In order to compute ΔU, it was necessary to make a number of assumptions. These assumptions are specified as the method used to derive each component of the equation is described. The utility model, as previously discussed, is:

$$\Delta U = t N_s \, \Delta r \, SD_y \, \lambda / SR - N_s \, \Delta c / SR$$

t According to the organization's personnel records, the average tenure of a first-level blue collar supervisor in the Nuclear Division was 2.58 years. This number may seem small, but the organization was growing, so promotion to second-level supervision was not rare. Also, moving from one company to another within the nuclear energy industry is not uncommon.

N_s Based on current hiring and turnover information, it was anticipated that, on the average, the organization would need to fill 20 positions within the target job per year for the foreseeable future. If projections were made for a 5-year period, N_s was 100.

Δr In order to determine Δr, the validity of both System One and System Two had to be determined. In the case of System One, the recruiter interviews were used as screening devices. Validity was based entirely on the paper-and-pencil test. This test was developed by Richardson, Bellows and Henry, Inc. for the purpose of predicting performance in first-level supervision positions. It used a multiple choice format. It had both autobiographical and judgment-oriented sections. The test was developed, refined, and validated through the participation of dozens of organizations grouped into several consortia. A concurrent validity model was used. The criteria against which test items and overall scores were correlated were evaluations on duty (task) performance and job ability. Evaluators were the immediate managers of the incumbent supervisors, other individuals knowledgeable of the performance of the incumbent supervisors, and a combination of the two.

Correlations between the test and criteria scores were reported separately for the combined duty evaluation score and the combined ability evaluation score. They were also reported separately for the three groups of evaluators: managers, others, and managers and others combined.

The various consortia in which the test was validated represented different industry groups, different levels of refinement of the test, and different levels of refinement of the criteria. After the first five consortia studies were conducted, a sixth consortium was used to conduct a cross-validation study. This sixth consortium consisted of 25 utility companies, including the organization in the present study. Validities, as described earlier, were reported for the consortium as a whole and for various functions within the companies. One of these groupings was "Nuclear Plants."

A decision had to be made concerning which validity coefficient to use in the present study. There were two criteria (duties and abilities), three rater sources (managers, others, and combined), and a variety of samples (early consortia, utility company consortia, nuclear plants). It seemed unnecessary to compute r for every conceivable use of the test. Instead, the most appropriate r was selected for this analysis.

With regard to criteria, it was appropriate to validate a selection tool or system based on its capacity to predict performance of job tasks or duties, and its capacity to predict levels of abilities important for success on the job. Therefore, I examined r for both duties and abilities. With regard to rater sources, it was most appropriate to use manager rating criteria. These are the most typical criteria in criterion-related validity research. With regard to samples, the nuclear plant sample is most similar to the jobs of interest in the present study. In fact, the organization used in this study was a member of that consortium, and the target job at the organization was included in the nuclear plant sample. Therefore, the validity information for the nuclear plant sample was used. The uncorrected validity coefficients of the test, using managers as raters and the nuclear plant sample, were .30 and .31 for duties and abilities, respectively. The corrected validities were .40 for both duties and abilities.

With the possible exception of estimating SD_y, estimating Δr was the most difficult part of this study because upper management's mandate for justifying System Two ignored the fact that a criterion-related validity study had not been conducted. Thus estimates of the validity of System Two had to be estimated based on the validity of similar programs. As mentioned in the previous section, the validity of assessment centers has been researched extensively. Thornton and Byham (1982) found validities to vary widely, generally ranging from the teens to the 70s, with validities in the upper .30s and .40s more common. Hunter and Hunter (1984) used validity generalization techniques to determine that the mean validity of assessment centers is .43. Therefore, it seemed reasonable to estimate the validity of the assessment center component of System Two as .43.

But System Two involves more than just its assessment center component. The behavioral interviews and reference check, as well as the test from System One, probably all contribute to the predictive validity of System Two. Until further data can be gathered, it is impossible to estimate the contributions of the various components to the overall validity of the system. McDaniel's (1988) recent review of the literature and meta-analyses indicated that behavioral interviews had mean validities of .50 for job performance criteria and .42 for training performance criteria. As noted earlier, typical assessment center validities are in the .30s to .40s, and the validity of the System One supervisor test is .40. Although it cannot yet be demonstrated, it is reasonable to assume that these measures are not perfectly intercorrelated, and that each predicts some unique variance in the criteria. Therefore, as an estimate, and possibly a conservative one at that, the validity of System Two was estimated to be .55 for the purposes of this analysis. Being forced to make "guestimates" of this type is one of the pitfalls of doing research in real world settings. Answers are sometimes required before all the necessary data are available.

Differences between the assessment center and System One, and between System Two and System One validity coefficients were determined by performing Fisher's r to z transformation, computing the difference, and reconverting the difference to r.

Thus two estimates of Δr were used; these are presented in Table 5.1.

SD_y As discussed earlier, there are several methods for estimating SD_y, and no method is conspicuously superior to any of the others. In the present study, it was decided to use the GEM method (Schmidt et al, 1979) because it shows reasonably good convergence with other methods, because it allows estimates that take into account several factors (such as the

TABLE 5.1
Values of Δr

	Assessment Center (r=.43)	System Two (r=.55)
System One (r=.40)	.04	.19

cost of capital and the cost of mistakes), and because data collection is relatively easy. The importance of this last issue should not be underestimated. With the exception of the 40% Rule, GEM is the easiest method to use to estimate SD_y. In "real world" research where the time of many well paid individuals is involved, the simpler, less time consuming, less expensive method is preferred when there is no evidence that it is notably inferior to other methods.

Nineteen managers of first-level blue collar supervisors in a representative sample of departments at the company's Nuclear Division were asked in individual or group interviews to estimate the dollar value to the company of supervisors whose performance fell at the 15th, 50th, and 85th percentiles. SD_y was determined by computing the mean difference between the 50th percentile estimates and the 15th and 85th percentile estimates. Using this method, SD_y was computed as $190,600.

The reader may be surprised at the magnitude of this figure. Keep in mind that an ineffective performer can directly or indirectly be responsible for mistakes that could cost the company millions of dollars. Conversely, a particularly effective performer could anticipate and act to prevent sequences of events that could lead to a catastrophe.

The same nineteen managers were asked to estimate the cost to the company of hiring outside contractors to perform the work of supervisors and who performed at the 15th, 50th, and 85th percentiles. This was not an uncommon practice in this company, particularly in certain departments. Unfortunately, several of the managers were so familiar with the costs and practices of hiring contractors that they did not assign any variability to the costs, stating that they knew the cost of contractors and they were either qualified to do the job or they were not hired. Eight of the 19 respondents indicated the same costs at the 15th, 50th, and 85th percentiles. This lack of variability among almost half of the respondents produced a low estimate of SD_y of $22,100. Due to the lack of variability among so many managers, this estimation method was abandoned.

SR   The company anticipated that 54 candidates would enter System Two annually. It also estimated that 20 openings for first-level blue collar supervisors in the Nuclear Division would occur annually. This results in a selection ratio of .37.

λ The ordinate of the normal curve for a selection ratio of .37 is .38.

Δc Two values of Δc were of interest in the present study. One was the difference between the costs of the System One and the costs of the assessment center portion of System Two. The other was the difference between the costs of System One and the total costs of System Two. In order to determine this information, the unit (candidate) and fixed costs for System One, System Two, and the assessment center alone were computed.

According to data reported by the company, the unit cost for System One was $622. This included $522 for interviewers' and candidates' wages (the vast majority of the candidates were already employed by the company, and they interviewed on company time). The remaining $100 was the cost to purchase, administer, and score the paper-and-pencil test.

Fixed costs of the programs were prorated over the cost of each candidate. A conservative estimate of 5 years was used as an estimate of the time period over which the program would be used without incurring notable additional fixed costs. It should be noted that the job analysis conducted to establish the content validity of System Two took into account anticipated changes in the job, and used the next 5 years as a benchmark for the "foreseeable future." Thus fixed costs were divided by 270 (54 candidates per year for 5 years.)

The fixed cost to install System One in the nuclear division of the company was $14,088. This included the Nuclear Division's portion of the consulting fee for the paper-and-pencil test, job analysis and validation, the wages of managers, engineers, senior supervisors, and supervisors involved in that study, and miscellaneous costs such as coffee for participants. Dividing $14,088 by 270 resulted in an implementation cost of $52.18 per candidate. Thus the total cost per candidate for System One was $674.18.

The fixed cost to install System Two in the Nuclear Division, excluding fixed costs associated with System One, was $79,899. This included the consulting fees and expenses for System Two job analysis and validation, the wages of managers, engineers, senior supervisors, and supervisors involved in that study, recruitment costs for assessors, consultant fees, and expenses for assessors, interviewers, reference checks, and administrator training, and development of an orientation program. Adding the fixed System One cost yielded a total fixed System Two cost of $93,987. Dividing this by 270 yielded a prorated cost of $348.10 per candidate.

The fixed cost of the assessment center portion of System Two was separated from the total fixed cost. These costs were for assessor recruitment, assessor and administrator training including consulting fees, training materials, wages of trainees, facility charges, and consultant administration of the first assessment center. Total fixed costs for the assessment center were $61,100, or $226.30 per candidate. Because I am calculating the costs if the assessment center alone had been implemented, the cost of the job analysis is included in this total.

The unit cost of System Two, including the paper-and-pencil test from System One, was $1,769.42. This included the cost of materials, facilities, and wages for assessors, administrators, reference checkers and interviewers. Due to the labor-intensive nature of the assessment center, unit costs for the assessment center alone were $1,468.00 (Outside contractors were used as assessors.) Thus the total cost per candidate for System Two was $348.10 plus $1,769.42, or $2,117.52. The total cost per candidate for the assessment center portion alone was $226.30 plus $1,468.00, or $1,694.30.

Thus two values of Δc were computed. The per candidate difference in costs between System One and System Two was $1,443.34. The per candidate difference in costs between System One and the assessment center alone was $1,020.12.

The utility analysis compared System One with the assessment enter alone and System One with System Two. Remember that these comparisons necessitated two different estimates of Δr and Δc. All other information was the same for both comparisons.

ΔU By entering all the information described above into the utility equation, the estimated total dollar gain in supervisor performance attained by using System Two instead of System One was $9,205,639.31. The mere fact that this number is positive indicates that it is worth the company's while to implement System Two. The fact that it is so large suggests that even if certain assumptions were somewhat optimistic (e.g., a validity coefficient of .55), the program is still justified in terms of costs. The ΔU for the assessment center portion of System Two alone compared to System One was $1,744,445.84, a substantial sum.

DISCUSSION

The foregoing analysis allows one to conclude that an integrated selection system built around an assessment center was worth over nine million dollars when promoting employees to the position of first-line blue collar supervisors in the Nuclear Division of the public utility being studied. Of course, the assessment center portion alone was worth nearly two million dollars. These conclusions are warranted only if the stated assumptions are reasonable. Every attempt will be made to verify these assumptions through future data collection. A brief discussion of each follows.

The tenure estimate (2.58 years) seems low, and was computed at a time of moderate growth in the Nuclear Division. As the organization's size and structure stabilize, tenure may increase, resulting in a larger ΔU because any increase in performance due to more valid selection procedures is realized over a longer period of time. It should also be noted that improved selection for first level supervision may provide additional benefits to the organization as these selectees advance to second-level supervision and beyond. As an organization stabilizes and matures, N, the number of positions to be filled, may decrease. This would result in lower utility. Decreasing the selection ratio would, however, raise ΔU.

As discussed earlier, the validity coefficients used in this application were estimated. The validity of the System One test seems to be a very good estimate because the consortium that developed it was very similar to the Nuclear Division. The validity coefficient of the assessment center was based on validity generalization, and should be verified when criterion data in the company can be gathered. This may be said even more strongly for the estimated validity of System Two, which was nothing more than a "best guess." Examining the intercorrelations of components, as well as measuring criteria, is necessary to have a high degree of confidence in the estimates of ΔU.

The method of estimating SD_y was discussed as well. Further research should be conducted to examine the reliability and validity of the GEM method. The research to date suggests that it is a reasonable and feasible approach.

Assumptions about costs will also affect ΔU. If efficiencies can be developed, such as reducing time through eliminating a source of redundant information (e.g., an assessment center exercise), then costs will be lower, and ΔU will increase. If the fixed costs are prorated over a longer period of time, ΔU will also increase. However, increased fixed costs, such as the training of additional assessors or periodic updating of the job analysis, will result in a lower ΔU.

SUMMARY

The purpose of this chapter was to discuss utility analysis and illustrate how it can be used to evaluate the cost-effectiveness of assessment centers and related selection procedures. The analysis revealed some of the difficulties associated with obtaining precise information in the *real world,* but showed that estimates may be used to derive the dollar value of alternate selection methods.

Utility analysis of the sort reported here represents an effective combination of science and practice. Estimates of the validity coefficient, as well as methods of estimating SD_y, were obtained from the research literature. These data were combined with other data provided by the organization and the consultant to estimate utilities. These scientific estimates were used, in turn, to make an applied decision—whether to use System One or System Two. There are two reasons why science and practice seem to fit well together in this context. First, utility researchers have taken care to translate somewhat complex formulas into terms that can be understood by a nontechnical audience i.e., the dollar value of productivity gains. Second, practitioners have been willing and able to incorporate scientific research (e.g., validity studies) into their work.

The example presented here also illustrates some of the problems in integrating science and practice. First, applications sometimes demand answers to questions that have not yet been addressed by researchers. For example, the decision to implement System Two was made prior to any validity study. Second, practical problems are often too specific to provide useful guidance to researchers. The comparison of two specific selection systems is of great interest to the client, but may be of less interest to assessment center researchers. Taking these problems into account, it still seems reasonable to regard utility estimation in assessment centers as an effective marriage of science and practice.

REFERENCES

Bobko, P., Karen, R., & Parkington, J. J. (1983). Estimation of standard deviations in utility analysis: An empirical test. *Journal of Applied Psychology, 68,* 170–176.

Bray, D. W., & Howard, A. (1988). *Managerial lives in transition.* New York: Guilford.

Brogden, H. E. (1949). When testing pays off. *Personnel Psychology, 2,* 171–183.

Byham, W. C. (1989). *The Assessment Center Method in Perspective* (Video). Pittsburgh, PA: Development Dimensions International, Inc.

Cascio, W. F. (1982). *Costing human resources: The financial impact of behavior in organizations.* Boston, MA: Kent.

Cascio, W. F., & Ramos, R. A. (1986). Development and application of a new method for assessing job performance in behavioral/economic terms. *Journal of Applied Psychology, 71,* 20–28.

Cronbach, L. J., & Gleser, G. C. (1965). *Psychological tests and personnel decisions.* Urbana: University of Illinois Press.

Greer, O. L., & Cascio, W. F. (1987). Is cost accounting the answer? Comparison of two behaviorally based methods for estimating the standard deviation of job performance in dollars with a cost-accounting based approach. *Journal of Applied Psychology, 72,* 588–595.

Huck, J. R. (1973). Assessment centers: A review of the external and internal validities, *Personnel Psychology, 26,* 191–212.

Hunter, J. E., & Hunter, R. F. (1984). Validity and utility of alternative predictors of job performance, *Psychological Bulletin, 96,* 72–98.

McDaniel, M. A. (1988, September). *The validity of the employment interview.* Paper presented at the Personnel Testing Council of Southern California, Newport Beach, CA.

Schmidt, F. L., Hunter, J. E., McKenzie, R. C., & Muldrow, T. W. (1979). Impact of valid selection procedures on work-force productivity. *Journal of Applied Psychology, 64,* 609–626.

Schmidt, F. L., Hunter, J. E., & Pearlman, K. (1982). Assessing the economic impact of personnel programs on work-force productivity, *Personnel Psychology, 35,* 333–347.

Taylor, H. C., & Russell, J. T. (1939). The relationship of validity coefficients to the practical effectiveness of tests in selection: Discussion and tables. *Journal of Applied Psychology, 23,* 565–578.

Thornton, G. C., III, & Byham, W. C. (1982). *Assessment centers and managerial performance.* Orlando, FL: Academic Press.

Weekley, J. A., Frank, B., O'Connor, E. J., & Peters, L. H. (1985). A comparison of three methods of estimating the standard deviation of performance in dollars. *Journal of Applied Psychology, 70,* 122–126.

6

Use of Simulations in Management Development: Reciprocity Between Science and Practice

Jeanette N. Cleveland
George C. Thornton, III
Colorado State University

One significant contribution of Industrial and Organization Psychology to management development in the United States is the use of simulations in managerial research, assessment, and training. In this chapter, we discuss the history, uses, theory, and types of simulations as an example of the scientist/practitioner model operating in exemplary form. Specifically, we provide examples where there has been and continues to be a healthy interchange between scientists and practitioners in the use of simulations for managerial development. Although the interchange has been extensive, there are opportunities for further collaboration. Therefore, the chapter also includes a discussion of questions and contributions that scientists and practitioners have ignored or have not communicated to each other.

RECIPROCITY OF SCIENCE AND PRACTICE: HISTORY OF SIMULATIONS

A simulation usually refers to a "complex performance test carried out in realistic or lifelike settings" (Thornton & Byham, 1982). This definition epitomizes the integration of science and practice. The history of performance testing began with the civil service examinations in China in 2200 B. C. (DuBois, 1970). The earliest direct antecedents of psychological testing were the efforts of Galton and Cattell to measure human ability and intelligence through psychomotor tasks (DuBois, 1970). Binet advanced and redirected this work when he attempted to diagnose retardation among children (an application) by assessing judgment and learning skills through test items that required overt, complex behavioral responses (Cronbach, 1970). Our understanding of intelligence has evolved as psychologists have worked with the tasks that are a part of the Stanford-Binet test. In the early 1900s, guided by advances in psychological testing, Woodworth, Knox, and Pintner and Patterson (DuBois, 1970) used performance tests to study race differences, assess mental deficiency among immigrants, and aid general clinical practice. Prior to World War I, performance tests and simulations including Thurstone's work on auditory testing for telegrapher selection and Henmon's work predicting flying ability (Thornton & Byham, 1982) were used to assess an individual's aptitudes for jobs.

During World War I and into the 1920s, research on performance testing decreased while efforts to develop valid paper-and-pencil tests increased through the efforts of such scientists as Otis, Yerkes, and Bingham (Thornton & Byham, 1982). The re-emergence of more complex simulations can be seen in several places in the 1930s. In Germany, the early application of multiple assessment techniques to evaluate military officers was based on techniques developed in psychological laboratories (Thornton & Byham, 1982). In England, the War Office Selection Boards used simulations to identify and select officers for military services. After World War II, the British Civil Service Selection Board (Vernon, 1953) modified situational tests to assess managerial and administrative responsibilities.

Murray's (1938) research at the Harvard Psychological Clinic using multiple assessment techniques (including performance tests) to assess personality represents another scientific advancement that was later incorporated in practice. Murray believed that in order to measure an individual's personality one must conduct a complete analysis of the total person using a variety of methods: interviews, paper–and-pencil tests, projective tests, and simulations. Further, Murray believed that the situation or job demands must be analyzed. Murray incorporated many of these evaluation procedures in the assessment strategy devised by the Office of Strategic Services (OSS) during the late stages of World War II (OSS, 1948). At the OSS, the evaluation procedures were used for the purpose of evaluating the total personalities of candidates for a variety of espionage jobs around the world. A more comprehensive theory of multiform assessment emerged from this applied work.

The procedures developed for the OSS were later used to study many basic psychological processes. The Institute for Personality Assessment and Research (IPAR) used situational tests including the leaderless group discussion (LGD), simulations and group performance tests to study the personality structure and functioning of normal adults. Much of this and earlier research (Stern, Stern, & Bloom, 1956) was incorporated into the first industrial application of performance tests and the multiple assessment method. During the 1950s at AT&T, the Management Progress Study, a long-range psychological study of adult development, was instituted to identify and understand the individual and organizational characteristics that lead to success as a manager.

The next significant work on simulations was the in-basket, developed by a research team at the Educational Testing Service. The in-basket was first developed for the United States Air Force in 1957 to measure curriculum effectiveness in teaching officers to organize information, to discover problems in a complex situation, to anticipate events, and to arrive at decisions based on many types of considerations or constraints. The outcomes of these studies have included not only practical methods for assessing and training administrative skills but also a better understanding of the composition of these constructs.

The AT&T Management Progress study, which represented a large-scale, long-term study of the validity of a number of assessment methods, including simulations, is an important milestone in the history of this method of assessment. Partly as a result of AT&T's experiences with simulations, the use of individual simulations for diverse purposes grew in the 1960s and spread throughout industry in the 1970s and 1980s. In 1986, Ralphs and Stephen reported that among 280 Fortune 500 companies, 22% were using complex simulations (such as Looking Glass, Inc.) and 44% were using role-plays as training methods. More recently, approximately 55% of the large organizations in the United States were using simulations or business games in management training (Faria, 1987). The popularity of simulations is revealed by the fact that there is a journal, *Simulations and Games,* devoted exclusively to educational and training uses.

USES OF SIMULATIONS

In this chapter, we discuss what is formally called gaming simulation (Jones, 1972). A game involves one or more players who are given background information to study, rules and conditions to follow, and roles to play. The players are then asked to take actions and make decisions to see how the system reacts. The essential feature of a game is the interactive process of players and the system. Nongaming simulations, such as computer models of economic conditions, are not useful for studying managerial behavior and will not be emphasized in this chapter. A simulation is a model or representation of real-world events in which elements are depicted by symbols, numbers, or in physical form. Simulations used for management development may model something as simple as the interactions of a manager and subordinate dealing with a performance problem on the job, or something as complex as an island nation faced with multiple economic and political crises (Streufert, Pogash, & Piasecki, 1988).

We have grouped the uses of simulations in the management development process into three areas: research to study managerial and organizational behavior, assessment of managerial abilities, and training managerial skills.

First, simulations provide an effective method of studying managerial behavior. Prior to the development of simulations, our knowledge of leadership and managerial behavior was based on direct observational methods or questionnaire surveys of managers (Mintzberg, 1971, 1973). Unlike direct observation of managers, simulations allow greater control and opportunity for manipulating an event and understanding subsequent behavior. Unlike questionnaires, simulations involve overt behaviors of participants that reflect complex skills such as communication, decision-making, and interpersonal interactions. The use of simulations in research is important because an understanding of complex managerial skills is enhanced using multiple methods of data collection.

Second, simulations provide a rich medium for the assessment of managerial competence. Complex settings that resemble actual organizational demands can be presented and complex, overt responses resembling on-the-job behavior can be elicited. Simulations provide observers and participants with an opportunity to evaluate skills such as conflict resolution or feedback to employees regarding negative or poor performance that cannot be attained with paper-and-pencil instruments. Simulations such as the leaderless group discussion, the in-basket, and complex organizational simulations provide a setting for generating peer and observer feedback and self-assessment. They also allow the individual participant to experience a segment of organizational life in a relatively safe environment.

Simulations can be used to predict managerial potential (Thornton & Byham, 1982). They provide a standardized method for observing behavior often lacking in evaluations of on-the-job performance. Simulations have also been employed as a criterion for evaluating the effectiveness of other assessment techniques and training devices. For example, the assessment center has been used to evaluate skill acquisition from behavioral-modeling training (King & Arlinghaus, 1976; Moses & Ritchie, 1975).

Finally, managerial skills can be developed in simulations. Participation in a simulation that diagnoses weaknesses often makes the manager ready to engage in training. Such readiness increases when other contingencies (such as potential pay raises or promotions) increase one's desire to overcome these weaknesses. Simulations such as the one-on-one interview or role-plays can be used to acquire or enhance skills through practice. One advantage of the simulation for skill development is that it is likely to yield greater transfer of training because actual behaviors are practiced in the context of other managerial activities and responsibilities.

Groups that work regularly together can participate and be observed under realistic conditions. Once problems with team interactions are identified, the simulation can be replayed to explore alternative strategies (Kaplan, Lombardo, & Mazique, 1985; McCall & Lombardo, 1978). For potential or new employees, a simulation is a useful method for providing realistic information about the job. Because simulations are designed to model a given job or work situation, an applicant or new employee has the opportunity to develop realistic job expectations and, in turn, may be less likely to leave the organization (Wanous, 1977).

For current employees, a simulation can be used to provide concrete examples of how the organization's values and culture are reflected in problem solving and decision making. Further, once the values or culture that guide decisions and behavior are identified, the simulation provides a method for reinforcing or changing those values.

A HIERARCHY OF SIMULATIONS WITH INCREASING COMPLEXITY

Simulations can be viewed along a continuum of complexity that reflects the levels and types of involvement of the participant. Complexity of both the stimulus conditions and the response requirements in the simulation is relevant here. Stimulus conditions consist of background information, organizational descriptions, variety in the content of problems, number of people to interact with, and stress created by the instructions. Response requirements can also vary. For example, simple simulations may call for a demonstration of communication skills in discussing a specific work habit or problem with an employee, whereas complex simulations may require numerous administrative actions to deal with multiple inputs, unpredictable events, or diverse and competing groups. We recognize that complexity could be viewed as a two-dimensional construct, reflecting both stimulus and response characteristics. However, we believe that both stimulus and response complexity in simulations are highly correlated rather than orthogonal. Therefore, we have represented simulations in Fig. 6.1 along a unidimensional continuum of complexity as the more general case.

Figure 6.1 depicts examples of simulations along a continuum of complexity. One-on-one interview simulations, often called role-plays, are short-term simulations of specific interpersonal interactions. They may simulate interactions between the manager and a subordinate, a peer professional, or a customer. The participant is given time to read background information and prepare for the interaction, which usually lasts only 8 to 10 minutes. The leaderless group discussion simulates numerous ad hoc committee situations in organizations where problem analysis and decision making take place. Four to eight participants, with no designated leader, are given an hour to solve one or more written problems. The situation may be a cooperative discussion to formulate a new policy or a competitive allocation of funds among departments of a city government. The in-basket exercise is a simulation of the paper work on a manager's desk. Participants are given information about the position they are to assume, the organizational structure, personnel, regulations, union contracts, etc. An in-basket usually contains letters, memos, and reports that require action, and also considerable information that may not be useful. The participant is given 3 or 4 hours to study the material and make decisions, request more information, direct others to action, schedule meetings, and write letters to outsiders.

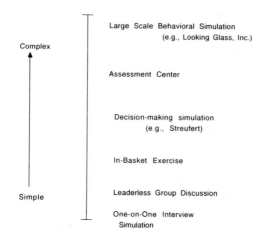

FIG. 6.1.   A continuum of simple to complex simulations.

The remaining simulations reflect a substantial increase in the level of complexity, because they encompass several simpler simulations and they take a longer period of time to conduct. Streufert (1986) has developed two elaborate, computer-driven, 6-hour simulations to study managerial decision making. In one, the participant assumes the position of Disaster Control Coordinator of Woodline County, potential flood victim from a broken dam. The participant can give directions to public and civil personnel to prepare for the crisis. In the second simulation, the participant is the governor of a developing country beset with economic and social problems. An assessment center is a complex procedure using multiple simulations, which may be unrelated to each other (e.g., the group discussion and the in-basket may be set in different organizations) or may be totally integrated (e.g., the in-basket may provide information that is useful in a later discussion with a problem employee). Examples of a large scale behavioral simulation include Looking Glass, Inc. (McCall & Lombardo, 1978), Metrobank, Investcorp, Norwood Arts Center, Foodcorp International, Globalcorp, and Landmark Insurance (Stumpf, 1988a, 1988b). Looking Glass, Inc., the oldest and most researched simulation of its kind, involves twenty positions in three divisions across four levels of a glass manufacturing company with $200 million in sales. The simulation is 6 hours in length, includes telephone and written communication systems, and is often conducted in several hotel rooms.

Both simple and complex simulations can have content validity. The stimulus material and the response requirements in the simulation can be representative of a small or large portion of the actual job situation. For example, in a one-on-one simulation, the participant may be asked to discuss only a single performance problem, yet one that is frequently encountered on the job. By contrast, in more complex organizational simulations, the employee's performance problem is embedded in structural, financial, and environmental crises, and the participant must simultaneously deal with personnel matters in conjunction with decisions about payroll, purchases, and external demands.

It is important to note that a simple simulation may be quite useful; a high level of complexity need not be present to provide the opportunity to assess managerial competence or to learn a managerial skill. In fact, in some instances there are clear advantages to isolating a set of behaviors in order to provide focused assessment or training. For example, a simple presentation exercise allows the participant to demonstrate and practice skills of organizing and communicating material without the pressures of a large and hostile audience.

RECIPROCAL RELATIONSHIP BETWEEN SCIENCE AND PRACTICE

The traditional notion (Bass, 1973; Blood, 1983; Byham, 1983; Campbell, 1983; Owens, 1983) that science contributes to practice or practice contributes to science implies a one-way influence that might be depicted by: Science → Practice or Practice → Science. These unidirectional links suggest that the scientist works in one setting to develop a basic understanding of general phenomena and then the practitioner applies such knowledge in another setting. Or, the practitioner observes problems in organizational settings and the scientist then comes up with solutions in the laboratory. We believe that a more accurate and helpful model of the relationship between science and practice in the domain of management simulations can be depicted as Science ↔ Practice. This model implies a reciprocal relationship between the two endeavors, which is mutually reinforcing and continuous. Neither of the two are predominant or more important. Rather, each is seen as necessary to the other's effectiveness. This model may be more accurate in depicting the multiple scientific and practical activities of individuals who have used simulations to study, assess, and train managers. The model also suggests that the distinctions between laboratory and field settings and between scientist and practitioner roles are blurred in the area of complex simulations.

In the development of performance tests and simulations, a common pattern is discernable: science is studying a topic, and concurrently, a practical problem is being faced. A request for assistance is addressed to the scientific community. Both the scientist and practitioner work together to apply the technique or procedure developed in the laboratories. By applying the simulation in the context of the organization, further advances in understanding the phenomena are made, and thus a contribution to science ensues. The cyclical relationship continues as better applications emerge from the enhanced science or understanding.

In summary, we see instances where a practical problem is being faced and science is studying a related topic. The Science ↔ Practice model implies that these two realms of knowledge are often simultaneously examining the same or similar issues as a result of extensive interactions. As a result, when we discuss the reciprocal relationship between the two, there is an inherent difficulty in clearly identifying instances where the sequence reflects science explicitly contributing to practice or practice to science. Several examples of the reciprocal relationship between scientists and practitioners in the use of simulations for managerial development are presented next. In each case, we discuss a scientific principle, theory or research area that has contributed to our understanding of simulations, show how the theory is incorporated into the practice of simulations in organizations, and indicate subsequent changes in the basic theoretical understanding. Although the scientific contribution is presented first, we are not suggesting a unidirectional influence. We are simply presenting instances where the activities of science and practice are consistent and contribute to each other. Theoretical perspectives and key practical developments for each of the three uses of simulations for management development (research, assessment and diagnosis, and training) are discussed.

Managerial Research

There are a number of explanations for simulations' contributions to managerial research. A simulation is a special kind of model for expressing a theory that attempts to identify and duplicate the most central components of a real-life situation (Coppard, 1976; Raser, 1968). The model or simulation is *valid* to the extent that it results in outcomes that are the same as those outcomes occurring in the referent system (i.e., reality). That is, a manager in a simulation should behave in ways that are similar to the ways he or she would behave under similar circumstances in the organization (McCall & Lombardo, 1979). For example, Looking Glass, Inc., was designed to preserve as much of the contextual reality of organizational life as possible in order to study leadership behavior (McCall & Lombardo, 1979). Consistent with Raser's (1968) definition of a simulation, a key concern for Looking Glass designers was to include examples of typical problems managers encounter in organizations so that simulation behavior is representative of organizational behavior. The 6-hour Looking Glass, Inc. simulation was designed, developed, and tested over 3 years through the joint efforts of the Center for Creative Leadership (McCall & Lombardo, 1979) and the Office of Naval Research. It was initially designed as a research tool to study managerial and organizational behavior in a realistic setting. Three divisions of the simulated corporation vary along two environmental dimensions: stability and uncertainty. The Looking Glass, Inc. developers drew heavily from the knowledge and expertise of behavioral scientists. On the other hand, for over 10 years now, this complex simulation has provided scientists with an opportunity to study the relationships among executives in various functions and at various organizational levels while working cooperatively in a complex, high-pressure situation.

Simulations can be used to test theories of organizational behavior. Research on conflict resolution indicates that individuals who respond to surveys show that they would take a harsher, less cooperative approach to negotiating or problem solving through bargaining than is observed in face-to-face interactions in a simulation (Baron, 1988; Bottger, 1984; Williams, Haskins, & Latane, 1981). Questionnaires measure knowledge and beliefs about social interactions, whereas simulations may be necessary to engage social processes and to measure the application of social skills. Theories of social interaction may be more effectively tested in simulations than with paper-and-pencil surveys. For example, the in-basket technique was originally developed as a simulation to study administrative skills among military officers (Frederickson, 1962, 1966) and school officials (Hemphill, Griffiths, & Fredericksen, 1962). Later, in-baskets were used as assessment and training devices. Subsequent research by the scientific community geared toward enhancing our knowledge about managers indicated that the technique contributed unique information to the evaluation of such dimensions of managerial competency as planning and organizing, decision making, and administrative control (Thornton & Byham, 1982).

Simulations provide a means of controlling and manipulating stimulus variables in the study of behavior. Planned variations can be introduced into the simulation and participants' responses can be observed. For example, Streufert (1986), a social psychologist, argued that his quasi-experimental simulations provide the best, and possibly only, feasible medium for studying managerial decision making under conditions of uncertainty. They are called "quasi-experimental" because inputs to the participants are more controlled than in a free simulation such as a leaderless group discussion. Throughout the simulation, the administrator (researcher) can inject information or changes in conditions to present the participant with predetermined crises. These simulations include the use of computers, both as a source of information and as an interactive recording device. When a crisis episode is introduced in Streufert's simulations, the decision-making activities and behaviors of individual managers and groups of managers can be recorded and compared with previous noncrisis behaviors. Streufert's simulation of crisis situations is based on his theoretical research on decision making. However, the simulations have been used extensively to train managers in industry to react and make decisions under emergency conditions.

The process of building a simulation and observing practicing managers interact with each other in the context of that simulation has led to a better understanding of the basic concepts that simulations were designed to depict. The increasing use of complex simulations has led to an opportunity for scientists to study the constructs that simulations measure and develop. For example, Stumpf (1988a) has identified components of strategic planning using simulation information collected from managers.

Assessment and Diagnosis

Simulations are used to make assessments about competence, strengths and weaknesses, and potential. There are a number of psychometric principles underlying the design and use of simulations that contribute to their effectiveness as evaluation devices. First, simulations are more standardized than observations and evaluations occurring in the real organization. All individuals are observed in the same situation and all evaluators use the same standards. Advantages of standardized measures over unstandardized judgments include enhanced objectivity, control of extraneous variables, quantification, enhanced communication, and scientific generalization (Murphy & Davidshofer, 1988).

Second, reliability of assessment can be enhanced by repeated observations of individuals in similar situations. For example, multiple leaderless group discussions can be conducted to assess whether participants consistently emerge as leaders. Additionally, an essential ingredient of the assessment center method is the use of multiple, situation exercises (Task Force on Assessment Center Standards, 1980).

Perhaps the most central psychometric feature underlying simulations as an evaluation device is content validity. Simulations can be built to realistically portray essential features of managerial jobs and organizational processes and can satisfy requirements for content valid measures (Guion, 1977). First, simulations portray reasonably standardized stimulus conditions. Second, well-built simulations are constructed to model well-defined domains, either narrowly defined specific task-related skills or more broadly defined complex skills such as decision making. Third, simulations can be built to elicit a sample of behavior representative of a larger domain. A set of one-on-one simulations can represent the types of employee problems a supervisor must deal with; a complex organizational simulation can cover problems dealt with by an executive. Sackett (1987) points out that the content validation approach to the development of simulations such as assessment centers requires careful attention not only to stimulus and response compatibility, but also to many other aspects of the test procedure, such as the instructions. However, if carefully constructed, simulations can be built to have just as much content validity as more traditional paper-and-pencil tests.

An assessment center is a complex procedure using some combination of simulations such as one-on-one interviews, role-plays, in-basket exercises, and so forth. The use of multiple measures emerged from the tradition of Murray (1938), described earlier, and from the practitioner's belief that a manager's job is a complex one requiring multiple measures to adequately assess it. Multiple, trained assessors, who are usually higher level managers, observe behavior, classify behaviors into performance dimensions, rate these dimensions across exercises, and make ratings regarding overall performance and potential. For example, at middle and higher levels of management, the results of an assessment center are frequently used for diagnostic purposes. At Kodak's Colorado Division, assessment ratings of strengths and weaknesses on managerial competencies are used in conjunction with self-evaluations and input from subordinates and the manager to identify a small number of developmental needs. For each weak dimension, the specific area to be developed is specified. Developmental follow-up steps are written down, along with the goal to be achieved, measurable indicators of improvement, and dates for completion. The developmental plan then becomes a contract between the manager and his or her boss regarding future actions for improvement.

Related to the issue of content validity is the relationship between the features of a measurement device and the nature of the targeted construct domain. Some managerial skills are more appropriately and adequately assessed through simulation than through paper-and-pencil tests. For example, conflict resolution by a manager would be more adequately observed and assessed in a one-on-one exercise than by presenting written scenarios of conflicts at work and having the examinee respond with written descriptions of action. Further, some constructs cannot be assessed by techniques other than a simulation. For example, leaderless group discussions tap the emergence of a leader, which would be difficult to assess outside of the context of an actual group interaction. Through the work of Stumpf and his colleagues, large-scale behavioral simulations, such as the Investcorp (Stumpf & Dunbar, 1988), Metrobank, Landmark Insurance and Northwood Arts Center, are being used for both research and applied purposes simultaneously. Using information from managerial participants, Stumpf has identified components of strategic planning. Each of these simulations has been designed to correspond to complexities in the managerial position and the organizational environment. Stumpf's work on strategic planning represents an attempt to identify and diagnose the constructs that large-scale simulations measure and develop.

Finally, Wernimont and Campbell (1968) and others (Asher & Sciarrino, 1974; Howard, 1983) suggested that samples of behavior should be more predictive of future performance than signs of aptitudes or predispositions to behave (as indicated by traditional tests). According to the behavioral consistency approach, simulations should have higher predictive validity coefficients because both the work sample or simulation and future performance are two parallel measures of job performance (Wernimont & Campbell, 1968). Asher and Sciarrino (1974) echoed this view by stating that the more points in common between the predictor (simulation) and the criterion, the higher the validity coefficient. Simulations, which use the logic of the behavioral consistency approach, have been shown to have predictive validity. For example, hundreds of organizations use assessment centers to provide information for selection, promotion, and developmental purposes (Byham, 1983). Far more research has been conducted on the assessment center method than any alternative (e.g., tests or large-scale behavioral simulations) for evaluating managerial potential (Thornton & Byham, 1982). Further, much of this research was conducted using managers in organizations with ongoing assessment centers.

From the extensive application of simulations for assessment purposes, a well-articulated set of measurement principles has emerged. This theory of multiple-behavioral assessment emphasizes the careful observation of overt behaviors in situational tests by multiple, trained observers who judgmentally integrate information from several sources.

Simulations as Training Techniques

Simulations employ many of the principles of adult (Knowles, 1970) and social learning theories (Bandura, 1977, 1986; Cooper, 1982; Goldstein & Sorcher, 1974; House, 1982). Active participation in the learning process, particularly important for adults (Mehta, 1978), allows the manager to experiment with alternative styles of behavior (Gagne, 1970; Kolb, 1984). Practice is particularly effective if done in several different contexts soon after learning. Mere experience and exposure is not sufficient, however; learning is enhanced with guidance, feedback, and reinforcement (Gagne, 1970; Lippitt, 1969), especially if provided by multiple sources (Kolb, 1984). Many of the adult learning principles have been integrated in the one-on-one simulations at General Electric (Goldstein & Sorcher, 1974). These simulations are an integral part of a management development program designed to teach supervisory skills. The training is structured around problems the manager faces, such as poor performance of a subordinate, tardiness, or dealing with discrimination complaints. Participants are given opportunities to practice and watch others practice the skills in simulations, supportive feedback is given, and participants practice with increasingly difficult scenarios. In this context, the simulations are called skill practice sessions to emphasize that the participant should behave as he or she would on the job.

Another example is the use of an in-basket as a method to practice administrative skills. The Medical Group Management Association has conducted training programs in which participants complete an in-basket after a series of lectures and discussion about skills such as planning and organizing, delegating, and controlling. In group discussions, guided by the trainer, colleagues review the strengths and weaknesses of actions taken by each participant and generate alternative courses of action. Participants are given a "scoring sheet" to keep track of effective actions and missed opportunities related to the administrative skills. This record is used later in developmental planning.

Participation with other managers allows the manager to learn vicariously by observing and modeling the successful behaviors of others (Bandura, 1986). Knowles (1970) has argued convincingly that adults learn most effectively through interactions with other adults. Simulations such as role plays and in-basket encourage careful observations of others and introspection about one's own beliefs and behaviors (House, 1982). Managers can then internalize those behaviors that lead to successful outcomes for themselves and for others, and discard those behaviors that do not (Cooper, 1982; Kolb, 1984).

The theory of adult learning and education emerged, in part, from practitioners' disenchantment with applying traditional learning principles to adult training. Although successful with children and young adults, traditional lecture presentations, for example, tend to be less effective with managers. Based on input from adult trainees such as engineers participating in up-dating activities (Farr, Dubin, Enscore, Kozlowski, & Cleveland, 1980), both scientists and practitioners simultaneously developed more experienced-based training techniques through interactions with each other.

Simulations that utilize realistic organizational problems allow managers to draw from their reservoir of experience and relate training to significant life roles (Knowles, 1970). Lesgold (1984) has shown that learning varies according to the type and amount of prior experience and the level of expertise the learner brings to the learning situation. For example, nearly all simulations draw their content from actual organizational problems. However, there is evidence suggesting that simulations should be used in a planned and purposeful manner, progressing from less to more complex. This is based on the concept of managerial readiness to develop, which is analogous to the concept of readiness to learn (Craig, 1983). Norris (1986) has argued that increasing realism in training procedures is beneficial up to a point, then serves as a detriment to learning because the learner may miss the underlying relationships in complex simulations. Similarly, Keys (1987) warned that in highly active situations the learner has little time for reflection. Thornton and Cleveland (in press) extend this thinking by asserting that there are individual differences among managers in the levels of simulation complexity that they are ready to handle in the development process. The rationale for this notion is based, in part, on anecdotal evidence from managers that an employee may be ineffective in new jobs or more challenging activities because they were not sufficiently ready for the job rather than insufficiently skilled.

Consistent with the notion of readiness to learn and develop, Logan (1985) has articulated a distinction between a skill and automaticity which may be helpful in deciding when and what type of simulation should be employed. The term *skill* applies to performance on a complex task, whereas *automaticity* refers to specific properties of performance on tasks which can be performed effortlessly. Skilled performance can be viewed as a collection of automatic processes. Both skill and automaticity are acquired with practice. In management training, automatic processes would be accomplished best through more simple simulations such as role-play exercises; then an individual may be ready to participate in more complex simulations where a full set of skills is necessary. Furthermore, the appropriate use of simple vs. complex simulations may depend on the individual's developmental stage of skill acquisition. For example, in practice, participants in large-scale behavioral simulations such as Metrobank or Investcorp (Stumpf, 1988a) are almost exclusively middle and upper level managers and executives.

Simulations provide a significant opportunity for transfer of training because many of the conditions which foster transfer are present. Of most relevance to our discussion is the training design. Training tends to transfer when there are identical stimulus and response elements in the training program and the job situation, when the training covers general principles rather than rote practice of behaviors, when there is variability in the types of problems covered in the content of training, and when there are several different conditions and situations for practice (Baldwin & Ford, 1988). When considering simulations with differing levels of complexity, the training designer faces a clear dilemma. Simple and shorter-term simulations provide opportunities for practice and thus actual skill development with a wider range of problem situations. Longer simulations, requiring several hours to execute, assume one-trial learning from one scenario. On the other hand, the more complex simulations maximize the number of identical elements and may convey general principles rather than narrow, specific facts. For example, experienced executives may need to be involved in one of the large-scale behavioral simulations in order to accept as meaningful any feedback about their decision making or leadership style.

Our theories of adult learning and education and social learning are enhanced by practitioners' observations that managers express a preference to learn by doing, to learn from peers who are similar to them, and to work on realistic activities rather than tasks tangential or not related to problems encountered at work. That is, the science of training is enhanced through the work of practitioners who emphasize the more subjective, yet important, factors involved in successful training, trainee readiness and motivation, and trainee acceptance of training, etc. (Goldstein, 1986).

SCIENCE AND PRACTICE: WHEN THEY TRAVEL IN DIFFERENT DIRECTIONS

Science and practice have worked hand in hand to develop simulations that further our basic understanding of management processes and our identification and enhancement of management skills. This is not to say that the relationship is complete or symmetric. Both parties have missed opportunities.

Science Ignores Practice

Too little attention has been paid in the development of simulations to the contextual variables that influence behavior in organizations. Quite appropriately, much emphasis has been placed on matching the tasks, activities, and behaviors of the simulation with analogous job requirements. The result has been a high degree of content validity for the responses in the better simulations. What has not been represented as well in simulations are many of the surrounding stimulus variables such as group, organizational, and environmental influences. Behavior in organizations is a function of social relations that build up over time and have consequences for the future. Simulations have not captured these dynamics as well as they might. The background for such advances exists: The major features of organization climate (Schneider, 1975) and culture (Smircich, 1983) have been studied and could be built into simulations. An example of how this can be done is seen in Looking Glass, Inc. (McCall & Lombardo, 1979) in which environmental uncertainty and instability are varied in the four major divisions comprising the glass manufacturing company.

Until recently, industrial/organizational psychogists have emphasized the study of selection procedures from the point of view of the organization and neglected the point of view of the individual. Porter, Lawler, and Hackman (1975) described processes by which individuals and organizations attract and select each other. What needs more attention is the effect of assessment and selection procedures, designed to give the organization valid information about the individual, on the applicants' perceptions of the organization. There is probably some tradeoff of benefits from detailed evaluation information and negative effects on applicants from gathering intrusive data. Some studies along these lines have been conducted and theoretical integrations have been proposed (Rynes, 1988). More research is clearly needed. For example, simulations can be used as the medium for manipulating the stringency of applicant evaluation procedures and measuring responses among simulated applicants.

As we have argued elsewhere (Thornton & Cleveland, in press), when simulations are used for management training, there is a need to match the level of complexity of the simulation with the level of readiness to develop in the manager. Unfortunately, there are no systematic means available to assess the manager's readiness to benefit from a complex organizational simulation experience. Thus, managers are sometimes put into developmental experiences that are far above their capabilities. It is our observation that not only does the manager not learn, but he or she can become discouraged by the experience. Furthermore, the manager often reacts negatively toward the simulation, which probably would have been an effective technique if appropriately applied. Two lines of research might be pursued to advance our capabilities to assess readiness to develop. One would entail the identification of basic personality correlates, such as optimism (Seligman, 1975) or locus of control (Lefcourt, 1982). A second approach would be to assess managers' reactions to mini-simulations in a manner analogous to trainability testing (Robertson & Downs, 1979).

Practice Ignores Science

In choosing selection instruments, practitioners have shown too little concern with the overall utility of procedures and too much concern with one factor in utility equations—cost (Cascio, 1987). The search for quick, easy solutions is understandable in today's cost-conscious organizations, but cost is only one factor to consider. Studies have shown that even the more elaborate procedures, such as assessment centers, more than pay for themselves in terms of improvements in productivity (Cascio & Ramos, 1986).

Practitioners also have paid too little attention to the utility of training procedures. Simulation techniques require more time and staff to use, but they are essential for skill-building. Lectures, presentations, demonstrations, and other didactic methods are appropriate for disseminating information, but not very effective in changing behavior. The science side of our camp has shown that simulations employ sound learning principles that foster behavior change and transfer of such learning to the job situation. There is a need to look at the magnitude of change in the implementation or demonstration of skills rather than simply the acquisition of knowledge. Practitioners need to apply simulations more frequently, but also more judiciously. Unfortunately, the training field continues to demonstrate much faddish behavior, adopting the latest new procedure that comes along. This happened with assessment centers in the late 1970s and early 1980s, and it may be happening today with the large-scale, total organizational simulations. The danger of unquestioned use is that procedures with proven effectiveness are used in inappropriate ways. They may receive an unfavorable reputation, not because of inherent weaknesses, but because of poor applications.

Related to the utility issue, practitioners continue to fail to evaluate the effectiveness of development procedures. In light of the enormous amounts of money spent on training and development each year, it is unfortunate that better studies are not conducted on a regular basis to determine what effects training has on job performance. We are not the first to point out this departure of science and practice (Latham, 1988). Certainly the statistical, psychometric, and research design techniques for evaluation exist (Cook & Campbell, 1979). And where they have been used, they provide valuable insight into program effectiveness. At the present time, some evaluation of managerial development has been reported for the large-scale behavioral simulations, although the initial evaluation efforts have focused on enhancing our understanding of strategic decision making (Stumpf & Dunbar, 1988) rather than assessing the effect of the simulation on the effectiveness of the organization. As we point out in the following section, we are optimistic that more research of this kind will be carried out, and we predict both practical and theoretical payoffs from such efforts.

CURRENT STATUS OF THE USE OF SIMULATIONS
FOR MANAGERIAL DEVELOPMENT

Managerial talent will continue to be important in the future as organizations respond to critical national and international demands. In particular, the ability of a person to respond to difficult, complex, and frequently changing situational conditions is becoming increasingly important. The need for the managerial skill to deal with and make decisions in such situations suggests that simulations should vary environmental conditions, present more complex stimuli, and require complex responses from managers. Further, organizations in the United States appear to be feeling pressure to **develop,** not just identify and select, managers. With increasing competition at home and abroad, organizations cannot wait for experienced, committed, and capable managers to naturally develop and progress in the organization. There is a need to identify and develop lower level managers so they will remain with the organization and more quickly become productive at higher levels.

There is additional reason to believe that simulations will be used more extensively in the future. First, simulations are gaining popularity in executive development. Both simple and complex simulations often are embedded in week-long executive development programs. Participants respond positively to such methods for development even months after the training or diagnostic program. Second, there is evidence of more extensive marketing of simulations, especially large-scale behavioral simulations (Stump, 1988a, 1988b; Stumpf & Dunbar, 1988). We expect more organizations will become aware of such methods and will utilize them. Related to this, there are currently consulting firms and individual consultants who specialize or have expertise in simulations (e.g., Hay, Levanthal, & Horwoth, New York University Management Simulation Program, Development Dimensions International, Personnel Decisions, Inc., and so forth). Therefore, when an organization contacts a consulting firm for assistance in addressing a research, assessment and/or a training problem, such firms will present simulations as part of their repetoire of approaches. Third, there now seems to exist a *critical mass* of large-scale behavioral simulations; in comparison, 10 years ago there appeared to be only the Looking Glass, Inc. simulation. This critical mass provides a basis for other researchers and practitioners to build on and develop additional and improved simulations more quickly. Fourth, simulations are heavily utilized as educational devices in MBA and advanced management programs (Cooper, 1982; Stumpf, 1988a). Further, participants seem to like them. It is likely, then, that these future managers will have a positive attitude toward simulations and will use them in their organizations. Finally, simulations have demonstrated effectiveness. There is abundant evidence that they are a class of methods that have substantial validity in predicting managerial success (Thornton & Byham, 1982) and developing managerial talent (Thornton & Cleveland, in press).

We also anticipate some factors that may inhibit the increased use of simulations for managerial development. First, some simulations, especially assessment centers and large-scale behavior simulations, are time-consuming and expensive. Second, many organizations do not have a climate for formal, off-the-job managerial development. Development programs for managers require a long-term investment and often entail few short-term returns. Third, there is a great affinity within management for on-the-job training for middle- and high-level managers.

At these levels, there may be resistance to the use of simulations. Fourth, assessment and training with simulations is labor intensive and requires skilled administrators. Organizations may not want or be able to invest in such methods. Finally, if the use of simulations increases dramatically without careful consideration of where they should be appropriately used, they may be used faddishly, misused, or produce negative results.

Will the reciprocal relationship between science and practice that simulations have enjoyed in the past continue and flourish in the future or will it wither? There are a number of encouraging signs that this relationship will flourish. First, the historical development and implementation of simulations and the contribution such work has made to the understanding of managerial talent represent the essence of the science-pratitioner model. The reciprocity of science and practice in this area has been successful in the distant and the recent past, and it currently exists. There seems to be a self-perpetuating quality to the research and application in this area that we believe will continue. Second, collaboration between scientists and practitioners interested in simulations is being recognized and rewarded. Academic institutions and professional societies have rewarded psychologists for their professional contribution to the areas of managerial assessment and training. For example, Melvin Sorcher has been recognized for applying the behavioral modeling theory of social learning to training managers, and Douglas Bray has been noted for his contribution in the area of adult development and assessment centers. Finally, with more Industrial/Organizational psychologists and management faculty working together in business schools, there is more awareness and opportunity for collaboration.

There are barriers, however, that may inhibit the healthy interchange between scientists and practitioners in improving the effectiveness and understanding of simulations for managerial development. With shrinking profit margins, competition from other nations, and restructuring (including mergers/take-overs, downsizing and fewer staff positions), organizations may not support basic research. For example, with the breakup of AT&T, basic research support has virtually disappeared. Further, these external pressures may motivate organizations toward more short-term marketing gains, and away from more long-term investments in the development of research, products, and people. Second, disincentives for collaboration may outweigh incentives. Scientists in academic institutions often are rewarded for studying more basic, psychological questions. Practical applications may not be the primary objective and may not eminate from such basic research at least in the short run. On the other hand, practitioners are rewarded for solving problems quickly and for attaining business or organizational objectives. Scientists and practitioners may have different and inconsistent goals, and may be rewarded for different behaviors and outcomes (see Lapointe's chapter in this volume).

Finally, for those individuals and organizations that value and embrace the scientist-practitioner model in understanding and solving problems, it is very difficult to be both a good scientist and an effective practitioner. On the other hand, our review of the use of simulations for developing managerial talent shows clearly that both scientific and practical benefits accrue when the scientist–practitioner model is followed.

REFERENCES

Asher, J. J., & Sciarrino, J. A. (1974). Realistic work sample tests: A review. *Personnel Psychology, 27,* 519–533.

Baldwin, T. T., & Ford, J. D. (1988). Transfer of training: A review and directions for future research. *Personnel Psychology, 41,* 63–105.

Bandura, A. (1977). *Social learning theory.* Englewood Cliffs, N.J.: Prentice-Hall.

Bandura, A. (1986). *Social foundations of thought and action.* Englewood Cliffs, NJ: Prentice Hall.

Baron, R. A. (1988). Attributes and organizational conflict: The mediating role of apparent sincerity. *Organizational Behavior and Human Decision Processes, 41,* 11–127.

Bass, B. M. (1973). *The substance and the shadow* (Technical Report no. 68). Management Research Center, University Rochester.

Blood, M. R. (1983). *Science and practice: Vive la difference.* Paper presented at symposium, "Advancing I/O Psychology as a Science" (R. A. Katzell, Chair). American Psychological Association, Anaheim, CA.

Bottger, P. C. (1984). Expertise and air time as bases of actual and perceived influence in problem-solving groups. *Journal of Applied Psychology, 69,* 214–221.

Byham, W. C. (1983). *Are academic models appropriate for the I/O psychologist practicing in industry?* Paper presented at symposium, "Advancing I/O Psychology as a Science" (R. A. Katzell, Chair). American Psychological Association, Anaheim, CA.

Campbell, J. P. (1983). *The science of I/O psychology: Can we change ourselves?* Paper presented at a symposium, "Advancing I/O psychology as a Science" (R. A. Katzell, Chair). American Psychological Association, Anaheim, CA.

Cascio, W. F. (1987). *Applied psychology in personnel management* (3rd Ed.). Englewood Cliffs, NJ: Prentice Hall.

Cascio, W. F., & Ramos, R. A. (1986). Development and application of a new method for assessing job performance in behavioral/economic terms. *Journal of Applied Psychology, 71,* 20–28.

Cook, T. D., & Campbell, D. T. (1979). *Quasi-experimentation: Design & Analysis Issues for field setting.* Boston, MA: Houghton Mifflin.

Cooper, C. L. (1982). A theory of management learning: It's implications for management education. In R. D. Freedman, C. L. Cooper, & S. Stumpf (Eds.), *Management education: Issues in theory research and practice.* New York: Wiley.

Coppard, L. C. (1976). Gaming and simulation and the training process. In R. L. Craig (Ed.), *Training and development handbook.* New York: Harper & Row.

Craig, G. J. (1983). *Human development* (3rd ed). Englewood Cliffs, NJ: Prentice-Hall.

Cronbach, L. J. (1970). *Essentials of psychological testing.* New York: Harper & Row.

DuBois, P. H. (1970). *A history of psychological testing.* Boston: Allyn & Bacon.

Faria, A. J. (1987). A survey of the use of business games in academia and business. *Simulation and Games, 18,* 192–206.

Farr, J. L., Dubin, S., Enscore, E. E., Kozlowski, S., & Cleveland, J. N. (1980). *The relationship among individual motivation, work environment and updating in engineers* (NSF Grant # SED78-21940). Department of Psychology, Pennsylvania State University.

Fredericksen, N. (1962). Factors in in-basket performance. *Psychological Monographs, 76,* (22, Whole No. 541).

Fredericksen, N. (1966). Validation of a simulation technique. *Organizational Behavior and Human Performance, 1,* 87–109.

Freedman, R. D., Cooper, C. L., & Stumpf, S. A. (1982). *Management education: Issues in theory, research, and practice.* New York: Wiley.

Gagne, R. M. (1970). *The conditions for learning* (2nd ed.). New York: Holt, Rinehart & Winston.

Goldstein, A. P., & Sorcher, M. (1974). *Changing managerial behavior.* New York: Pergamon Press.

Goldstein, I. L. (1986). *Training in organizations: Needs, assessment, development and evaluation.* Monterey, CA: Brooks/Cole.

Guion, R. M. (1977). Content validity: The source of my discontent. *Applied Psychological Measurement, 1,* 1–10.

Hemphill, J. K., Griffiths, D. E., & Fredericksen, N. (1962). *Administrative performance and personality: A study of the principal in a simulated elementary school.* New York: Teachers College Bureau of Publications, Columbia.

House, R. S. (1982). Experiental learning: A social learning theory analysis. In R. D. Freedman, C. L. Cooper, & S. A. Stumpf (Eds.), *Management education: Issues in theory, research and practice.* New York: Wiley.

Howard, A. (1983). Work samples and simulations in competency evaluation. *Professional Psychology, 14,* 780–796.

Jones, G. T. (1972). *Simulations and business decisions.* Middlesex, England: Penguin.

Kaplan, R. E., Lombardo, M. M., & Mazique, M. S. (1985). A mirror for managers: Using simulations to develop management teams. *Journal of Applied Behavioral Sciences, 21,* 241–253.

Keys, B. (1987). Total enterprise business games. *Simulation and Games, 18,* 225–241.

King, H. D., & Arlinghaus, L. G. (1976). Interaction management validated in the steel industry. *Assessment and Development, 3,* 1–2.

Knowles, M. S. (1970). *The modern practice of adult education: Andragogy versus pedagogy.* New York: Association Press.

Kolb, D. A. (1984). *Experiential learning: Experience as a source of learning and development.* Englewood Cliffs, NJ: Prentice-Hall.

Latham, G. P. (1988). Human resource training and development. In M. R. Rosenzweig & L. W. Porter (Eds.), *Annual review of psychology* (vol. 39). Palo Alto, CA: Annual Reviews.

Lefcourt, H. M. (1982). *Locus of control: Current trends in theory and research* (2nd ed.). Hillside, NJ: Lawrence Erlbaum Associates.

Lesgold, A. M. (1984). Human skill in a computerized society: Complex skills and their acquisitions. *Behavior, Research Methods, Instruments and Computers, 16,* 79–87.

Lippitt, G. L. (1969). Conditions for adult learning. *Training and Development Journal, 23,* 2.

Logan, G. D. (1985). Skill and automaticity: Relations, implications and future directions. *Canadian Journal of Psychology, 39,* 367–386.

McCall, M. W., & Lombardo, M. M. (1978). *Looking Glass, Inc.: An organizational simulation* (Technical Report No. 12). Center for Creative Leadership, Greensboro, North Carolina.

McCall, M. W., & Lombardo, M. M. (1979). *Looking Glass, Inc.: The first three years* (Technical Report no. 13). Center for Creative Leadership, Greensboro, North Carolina.

Mehta, P. (1978). Dynamics of adult learning and development. *Convergence, 11,* 36–43.

Mintzberg, H. (1971). Managerial work: Analyses from observation. *Management Science, 18,* 97–110.

Mintzberg, H. (1973). *The nature of managerial work.* New York: Harper & Row.

Moses, J., & Ritchie, R. (1975). Assessment center used to evaluate an interaction modeling program. *Assessment and Development, 2,* 1–2.

Murphy, K. R., & Davidshofer, C. O. (1988). *Psychological testing: Principles and applications.* Englewood Cliffs, NJ: Prentice-Hall.

Murray, H. (1938). *Explorations in personality.* Cambridge, England: Oxford University Press.

Norris, D. R. (1986). External validity of business games. *Simulation and Games, 17,* 447–459.

Office of Strategic Services Assessment Staff (1948). *Assessment of men: Selection of personnel for the office of the strategic services.* New York: Rinehart.

Owens, W. A. (1983). *Some major barriers to scientific progress in personnel psychology.* Paper presented at a symposium, "Advancing I/O Psychology as a Science" (R. A. Katzell, Chair). American Psychological Association, Anaheim, CA.

Porter, L. W., Lawler, E. E., & Hackman, J. R. (1975). *Behavior in organizations.* New York: McGraw-Hill.

Ralphs, L., & Stephen, E. (1986). HRD in the Fortune 500. *Training and Development Journal, 40* (Oct.), 69–76.

Raser, J. R. (1968). *Simulation and society.* Boston, MA: Allyn and Bacon.

Robertson, I. T., & Downs, S. (1979). Learning and prediction of performance: Development of trainability testing in the United Kingdom. *Journal of Applied Psychology, 64,* 42–50.

Rynes, S. L. (1988). The employment interview as a recruitment device. In R. W. Eden & G. R. Ferris (Eds.), *The employment interview.* Beverly Hills, CA: Sage Publications.

Sackett, P. R. (1987). Assessment centers and content validity: Some neglected issues. *Personnel Psychology, 40,* 13–25.

Schneider, B. (1975). Organizational climates: An essay. *Personnel Psychology, 28,* 447–479.

Seligman, M. E. (1975). *Helplessness.* San Francisco: Freeman.

Smircich, L. (1983). Concepts of culture and organizational analysis. *Administrative Science Quarterly, 28,* 339–358.

Stern, G. G., Stein, M. I., & Bloom, B. S. (1956). *Methods in personality assessment.* Glencoe, IL.: Free Press.

Streufert, S. (1986). *Assessment of task performance via a quasi-experimental simulation technology.* Unpublished report, College of Medicine, Pennsylvania State University.

Streufert, S., Pogash, R., & Piasecki, M. (1988). Simulation based assessment of managerial competence: Reliability and validity. *Personnel Psychology, 41,* 537–557.

Stumpf, S. A. (1988a). Business simulations for skill diagnosis and development. In M. London & E. M. Mone (Eds.), *Career growth and human research strategies.* New York: Quorum Books.

Stumpf, S. A. (1988b). Leadership and beyond: The need for strategic management skills. In R. Lamb *Advances in strategic management, Vol. 5.* Greenwich, CT: JAI Press.

Stumpf, S. A., & Dunbar, R. L. M. (1988, July). *Using behavioral simulations in teaching strategy implementation.* Paper presented at the meeting of the National Academy of Management, Anaheim, CA.

Task Force on Assessment Center Standards (1980). Standards and ethical considerations for assessment center operations. *The Personnel Administration, 25(2),* 35–38.

Thornton, G. C., III, & Byham, W. C. (1982). *Assessment centers and managerial performance.* New York: Academic Press.

Thornton, G. C. III, & Cleveland, J. N. (in press). Developing managerial talent through simulation. *American Psychologist.*

Vernon, P. E. (1953). *Personality tests and assessment.* London: Methuen.

Wanous, J. D. (1977). Organizational entry: The individual's viewpoint. In J. R. Hackman, E. E. Lawler, & L. W. Porter (Eds.), *Perspectives on behavior in organizations.* New York: McGraw Hill.

Wernimont, P. F., & Campbell, J. P. (1968). Signs, samples and criteria. *Journal of Applied Psychology, 52,* 372–376.

Williams, K., Harkins, S., & Latane, B. (1981). Identifiability as a determinant to social loafing: Two cheering experiments. *Journal of Personality and Social Psychology, 40,* 303–311.

7 Performance Appraisal Effectiveness

William K. Balzer
Bowling Green State University

Lorne M. Sulsky
Louisiana State University

The identification and choice of criteria for evaluating the quality of performance ratings (i.e., rating effectiveness) has been recognized as a central problem for researchers and practitioners since the early work of Weitz (1961), Wallace (1965), and Smith (1976). A large number of criteria have been suggested (e.g., several rating error indices and rating accuracy indices) with no rationale for choosing among them. Recent research has been highly critical of these available criteria, but has not yet proposed a solution to the criterion problem (Guion & Gibson, 1987; Murphy & Balzer, 1989; Sulsky & Balzer, 1988; Wexley, 1987). As we prepared this chapter, it became quite clear that, despite admonitions by Weitz (1961), Wallace (1965), and Smith (1976), we still have not come to grips with problems in evaluating and choosing performance appraisal criteria.

In the first section of this chapter, we draw three general conclusions that may not be new, but merit repetition:

1. Some of our most popular measures of performance appraisal effectiveness, namely rating error and rating accuracy indices, have serious conceptual and methodological flaws. Thus, it is questionable whether research using these measures to evaluate performance appraisal systems tells us much about performance appraisal effectiveness.

2. Most of our measures of performance appraisal effectiveness are those that are of interest to performance appraisal researchers, but *not* to other constituents of the performance rating process such as company executives, personnel managers, raters, and ratees.

3. Researchers and practitioners have not adequately investigated how (or whether) performance appraisal effectiveness contributes to more distal indices of organizational effectiveness, such as productivity or profitability.

133

In light of these problems, we will attempt to expand our conceptualization of appraisal effectiveness to encompass a broader range of effectiveness criteria, including measures that may reflect the principal interests of organizations—whether employee productivity improved and whether personnel programs are cost-effective? Furthermore, we will attempt to show that the "correct" measures of performance appraisal effectiveness differ depending on whether the individual making that determination is a researcher (who might concentrate on the pattern or distribution of performance ratings), a company executive (who might concentrate on the correctness of promotion or firing decisions), a personnel manager (who might concentrate on the acceptance and use of the appraisal system by members of the organization), an employee's supervisor (who might concentrate on the ease of use of the rating system), or a person being evaluated by the system (who might concentrate on the accuracy and representativeness of critical incidents provided during the performance appraisal interview). Finally, given the variety of criteria that could be used to evaluate performance appraisal effectiveness, we propose a framework for formalizing the selection of criteria for evaluating appraisal systems.

APPRAISAL CRITERIA: A BRIEF,
BUT CRITICAL, REVIEW

Many excellent papers have catalogued large numbers of measures for evaluating performance appraisal effectiveness (Bernardin & Beatty, 1984; Jacobs, Kafry, & Zedeck, 1980; Kane, 1980; Smith, 1976). But forgetting for the moment the number of criteria that are available, which criteria are we *using?* In preparing this chapter, we reviewed the major industrial/organizational (I/O) psychology journals (*Journal of Applied Psychology, Personnel Psychology, Organizational Behavior & Human Decision Processes,* and *Academy of Management Journal*) for the years 1976 and 1986 to identify the performance appraisal criteria reported during this period.[1] The results of our review are shown in Table 7.1. The three most common types of criteria used in 1976 were rater error measures (54%), reliability and validity of ratings (31%), and rater/ratee attitudes (8%). In 1986, the use of rater/ratee attitudes increased (to 25%), while studies employing rater error measures and reliability and validity measures decreased (to 30% and 10%, respectively). In addition, rater accuracy measures became the third most common criteria used in performance appraisal studies. Evidence continues to mount, however, that seriously questions the use of each of these criteria.

---

[1]We wish to thank Lance E. Anderson for his help in reviewing this literature.

TABLE 7.1
Dependent Measures in Performance Appraisal
(1976 and 1986)

	1976	1986
Total Studies	N=13	N=20
Setting:		
Laboratory	69%	60%
Field	31%	40%
Dependent Measures:		
Rater error	54%	30%
Reliability/Validity	31%	10%
Attitude	8%	25%
Rater accuracy	0%	15%
Recall/Recognition	0%	10%
Attributions	0%	10%
Feedback issues	0%	10%
Other (e.g., Rating mean comparisons, Goodness of fit indices, Factor loadings)	8%	25%

Rater Error Measures

Rater error measures, including halo, leniency/severity, central tendency, and similar-to-me error, are frequently used to investigate the quality of judgmental ratings of performance. A number of theoretical and methodological concerns have been raised regarding the use of rater error measures (Saal, Downey, & Lahey, 1980; Murphy & Balzer, 1989). Saal et al.'s (1980) review pointed out that the various conceptual and operational definitions for rater error measures have been inconsistent, thereby creating some confusion. For example, the different conceptual definitions of leniency/severity error (e.g., the assignment of ratings higher or lower than warranted given some external criterion; a shift in mean ratings from the scale midpoint) found in the studies reviewed are based on different underlying assumptions (i.e., the former requires "true" performance scores for comparison purposes, while the latter assumes that ratings which deviate from the scale midpoint are necessarily in error). And even where conceptual confusion was of less concern, multiple operational definitions make it difficult to compare and integrate research findings. For example, Fig. 7.1 presents seven different operational definitions of halo error, identified by Saal et al. (1980) and Fisicaro (1988), that have been used by various researchers and practitioners.

Saal et al. (1980) also provided some empirical evidence that both the choice of rater error measures and the operational definitions of those measures can lead to different conclusions regarding the evaluation of alternative rating scale formats. Finally, the authors noted that different approaches for collecting appropri-

Intercorrelations among ratee dimension ratings collapsed across raters

Factor analysis/principal component analysis of ratee dimension intercorrelation matrix

Variance of a rater's ratings of a particular ratee across all dimension ratings

Rater x ratee interaction in a rater x ratee x dimension analysis of variance design

Median intercorrelation among ratee dimension ratings for a single rater

Sum (across dimensions and ratees) of the absolute value of illusory halo minus true halo

Sum (across dimensions and ratees) of the squared deviation of illusory halo minus true halo

FIG. 7.1.   Operational definitions of halo (based on Saal, Downey, & Lahey, 1980, and Fisicaro, 1988).

ate rating data were necessary to compute different rater error measures. Overall, Saal et al.'s (1980) thorough review raises serious questions regarding the usefulness of rater error measures as meaningful measures of rating effectiveness. But the paper ends on a positive note, suggesting that "the increased precision at both the conceptual and operational levels that is available through [a multivariate approach to evaluating ratings and a revised typology of rating characteristics] will facilitate psychology's quest for a better understanding of the complex phenomena of rating behavior" (p. 426).

A second, more pessimistic conclusion on the usefulness of rater error indices was provided by Murphy and Balzer (1989). They pointed out that rater error measures are typically used to provide indirect measures of rating accuracy when direct measures of accuracy are unavailable or difficult to obtain. But what if direct measures of accuracy are available? Are rater error measures related to direct measures of rating accuracy? Murphy and Balzer examined relationships between rater error and rater accuracy indices in ten separate data sets. Four measures of rating accuracy (elevation, differential elevation, stereotype accuracy, and differential accuracy; Cronbach, 1955) were computed for each subject. In addition, six rater error measures (two each for halo, leniency, and central tendency) discussed by Saal et al. (1980) were also computed. The average correlations among rater error and rating accuracy measures, weighting correlations from each study according to the study's sample size, are shown in Table 7.2. Their major conclusion was that *none* of the rater error measures showed consistent correlations with *any* of the accuracy measures. Furthermore, alternative measures of halo, leniency, and range restriction showed little equivalence (this was also suggested by Saal et al., 1980). Murphy and Balzer (1989) concluded that error

TABLE 7.2
Average Estimated Intercorrelations Among Error and Accuracy Measures

	1	2	3	4	5	6
1. Halo (median correlations between performance dimensions, over rates)	–					
2. Halo (variance of the ratings assigned to each ratee, averaged across ratees)	.25	–				
3. Leniency (absolute value of the difference between mean rating, over ratees and dimensions, and the scale midpoint)	-.03	-.09	–			
4. Leniency (skew of the distribution of ratings, over ratees and dimensions)	.15	-.01	-.47	–		
5. Range restriction (standard deviation of the rating distribution over ratees and dimensions)	-.37	.35	-.09	-.18	–	
6. Range restriction (kurtosis of the rating distribution, over ratees and dimensions)	-.24	-.02	.13	-.09	.26	–
7. Elevation accuracy	-.05	-.02	-.10	.13	.02	.10
8. Differential elevation accuracy	-.06	.01	.00	.14	-.12	-.14
9. Stereotype accuracy	-.12	-.28	.00	-.01	-.07	-.08
10. Differential accuracy	-.30	-.50	.05	.00	-.10	-.10

Based on Murphy and Balzer (1989). Meta-analysis (N = 1096, analysis includes 10 studies).

measures provide little information about accuracy, and may in fact reflect real group differences in the pattern and level of performance. They also concluded that the validity of rater error measures is questionable, and that great caution should be exercised in their use.

Conclusions.   Although rater error measures have been used widely by researchers to evaluate the effectiveness of different rating scale formats and rater training programs, both theory and empirical evidence casts doubt on the validity of the conclusions drawn in this research. Perhaps many of the "mixed" patterns of findings reported in the performance appraisal literature (for a review, see Landy & Farr, 1983) are due largely to the use of different rater-error criteria across studies. Although reanalysis of earlier studies' data using consistent operational definitions of rater error measures may generate consistent results across studies, the issue of validity would remain unexamined.

Rater Accuracy Measures

Accuracy scores are typically computed by comparing a rater's performance evaluations for n ratees on k performance dimensions with corresponding evaluations provided by "expert" raters. The closer the rater's ratings are to the experts' ratings, the more accurate those ratings are thought to be (Borman, 1977). The primary advantage to using accuracy scores is that they provide a direct, rather than indirect, measure of accuracy. Furthermore, whereas rater error scores are often computed under the assumptions that performance ratings are normally distributed and correlations among rating dimensions are essentially zero, accuracy scores require no assumptions about the actual distribution of ratee performance or the "true" intercorrelations among rating dimensions.

As we have seen earlier, accuracy scores are becoming more popular in performance rating research (Sulsky & Balzer, 1988; for applications of accuracy scores in research on the selection interview and job evaluation, see Dipboye, Stramler, & Fontenelle, 1984; Hahn & Dipboye, 1988; Vance, Kuhnert, & Farr, 1978). In addition, halo and leniency have been reconceptualized to allow computation of "illusory halo" and "illusory leniency" based on comparisons between raters' and experts' ratings (Bingham, 1939; Cooper, 1981; Murphy & Balzer, 1989). But rater accuracy measures are also characterized by conceptual and methodological problems. A recent paper by Sulsky and Balzer (1988) provides a critical analysis of the accuracy measures used in performance appraisal research. Four distinct criticisms are raised.

1. *Current measures of rating accuracy are based on different conceptualizations of accuracy.*

Sulsky and Balzer (1988) identified a variety of conceptualizations of accuracy. For example, Borman (1977) conceptualized rating accuracy as the *relationship* between the ratings and a second set of ratings considered to be an acceptable standard for comparison. This second set of ratings is usually gathered from expert raters and has been termed "true score" ratings. Alternately, Cronbach (1955) conceptualized accuracy as the *distance* between the ratings and corresponding true score ratings. This latter conceptualization of accuracy is more consistent with other psychometric definitions of accuracy (e.g., Guion, 1965), while the former might more appropriately be labeled an indicator of rater validity.

2. *Different operational definitions of accuracy exist and result in a variety of measures that do not show evidence of convergence.*

To illustrate the importance of different operationalizations of accuracy measures, data from two studies were used to compute eight different accuracy scores. These accuracy scores were then correlated to assess whether their interrelationships were strong and positive. These correlations, shown in Table 7.3, show weak relationships among the various measures, with an average correlation of .19. Taken together, these findings suggest that different accuracy mea-

TABLE 7.3
Average Intercorrelations Among Accuracy Measures

Measure	1	2	3	4	5	6	7	8
1. Elevation	–							
2. Differential Elevation	.04	–						
3. Stereotype Accuracy	.11	.00	–					
4. Differential Accuracy	.12	.04	.23	–				
5. Borman's Differential Accuracy	.18	.41	.16	.22	–			
6. Distance Accuracy	*	*	*	*	.47	–		
7. Halo Accuracy	*	*	*	*	*	*	–	
8. Leniency Accuracy	1.00	-.04	.09	.12	.18	.66	.07	–

*Correlations not computed because relationships are data dependent.
Adapted from Sulsky and Balzer (1988).

sures may tap different facets of rating ability (e.g., different facets of rating accuracy and different facets of rating validity). These findings also support Cronbach's (1955) view that accuracy is not a unitary construct and that theory and research on the meaning of accuracy is needed. In general, the data suggest that we should be careful when choosing accuracy measures; a given study may yield different conclusions depending on the particular accuracy measure(s) used.

3. *Procedures for estimating true scores have been inconsistent.*

Despite the importance of true scores as a standard for comparison, procedures for estimating true scores vary considerably, ranging from simply averaging ratings from undergraduate raters (Bernardin & Pence, 1980) to elaborately training experts and formally examining their ratings for interrater reliability and discrimination among ratees and rating dimensions (Borman, 1977). Clearly, averaging scores from nonexperts should not imply agreement among raters on the true level of ratee performance, because the dispersion around this average score can be quite large. Also, asking experts who disagree to reach consensus on a final score may result in artificial agreement. In sum, the quality of the resulting estimates may be highly questionable, notwithstanding the use of experts.

4. *Accuracy scores have limited usefulness.*

Although accuracy may be an important criterion for evaluating the effectiveness of performance appraisal ratings, it is by no means the ultimate criterion. Sulsky and Balzer (1988) argued that accuracy should not be the only performance appraisal criterion of interest to researchers and practitioners. Validity and reliability, as discussed in the next section, can be useful criteria when decisions require only that raters correctly rank order ratees for organizational decisions (e.g., promotions, deciding who should receive first access to training, etc.). Alternatively, accuracy may be important for decisions based on a cutoff score (requiring correspondence with some "real-world" state of affairs). In other words, we need to establish the purposes or objectives for performance appraisal, and choose criteria that will tell us whether we are meeting those objectives.

Conclusions.   Despite the growing popularity of accuracy scores, theoretical and methodological limitations are as serious for these measures as for rater error scores. Adoption of accuracy measures as substitutes for error measures only replaces one set of theoretical and methodological concerns with another. Hence, while useful, accuracy scores must be viewed in light of their potential limitations, and as only one of many criteria that may be used to evaluate the effectiveness of performance ratings.

Reliability and Validity Measures

Two concerns are noted regarding the use of reliability and validity of performance ratings as criteria for rating effectiveness: (a) they are underused, and (b) they have been confused with accuracy. Our own impression (Sulsky & Balzer, 1988) is that in the excitement over the prospect of directly computing performance raters' accuracy, researchers neglected reliability and validity criteria. Perhaps it was because reliability and validity were necessary but not sufficient conditions for accuracy (i.e., they provide information on the *strength* of the relationship between a set of scores and a corresponding set of true scores, whereas accuracy also includes information about the *nature* of the relationship between the two score distributions; Gordon, 1970). Thus, accuracy scores seemed to be more important. Or perhaps it was because the relationship between reliability, validity, and accuracy is unclear. Borman's (1977) measure of differential accuracy, for example, is more precisely (using Gordon's, 1970, and Guion's, 1965, definition of accuracy) a measure of rating validity.

For whatever reason, reliability and validity have been less prominent measures of rating effectiveness than error and accuracy measures. This is unfortunate because the information provided by reliability and validity can be important effectiveness criteria. When consistent and correct rank ordering of ratees is important for the purpose at hand, reliability and validity should be the criteria of choice.

As a final point, it is worth noting that several authors (e.g., James, 1973; Smith, 1976) have called for research on the construct validity of ratings. Unfortunately, research in this vein has been rather difficult to do, in part because the "performance" construct is still not well-defined (Campbell, 1983; Guion, 1983; Hunter, 1983; Naylor, 1983). Nevertheless, some interesting work has been completed in this area (Nathan & Alexander, 1988; Pulakos, Borman, & Hough, 1988; Vance, MacCallum, Coovert, & Hedge, 1988).

Rater/Ratee Attitudes and Perceptions

A number of rater/ratee attitudes toward, and perceptions of, performance appraisal have been investigated, including satisfaction with appraisal ratings, perceptions of fairness, feedback, and appraisal interviews, rating format ease of use and objectivity, meaningfulness and accuracy of feedback, and perceptions of appraisal system operation and organizational impact (Bannister, 1986; Barr, Brief, & Fulk, 1981; Dipboye & DePontbriand, 1981; Dorfman, Steven, & Loveland, 1986; Landy, Barnes, & Murphy, 1978; Pearce & Porter, 1986; Wiersma & Latham, 1986). For example, Landy et al. (1978) found that appraisal system characteristics (e.g., the frequency of performance evaluations, the opportunity for ratees to express their opinions during the evaluation process) influenced perceptions of fairness in performance evaluations. Dipboye and DePontbriand (1981) found that employee satisfaction with the appraisal process was related to employee participation during the performance feedback process, to discussion of plans or objectives for future performance, and to perceptions that evaluations were based on relevant work factors.

Many of the attitudinal scales used in this research appear to be well constructed, and information on scale development and psychometric properties (predominantly internal consistency reliability) is available. A number of attitudinal measures are questionable, however; some use single-item scales with no evidence of reliability or validity, some adapt previously existing scales (and thereby potentially affect their psychometric properties), and some fail to provide any evidence of scale validity. Thus, a careful methodological analysis of reported rater/ratee attitudinal measures, particularly their validity, should be conducted prior to accepting a study's conclusions.

Summary

No performance appraisal criterion measure is perfect. Each can, however, provide useful information given an adequate understanding of the conceptual and methodological issues underlying the measure. Most important, careful consideration should be given to the choice of performance appraisal criteria. Criteria must be chosen that address the issue (or issues) one is interested in, whether it be rating distributions, correct rank-ordering of performance, or distance from some true level of performance.

CHOOSING CRITERIA FOR EVALUATING PERFORMANCE APPRAISAL EFFECTIVENESS

In a recent paper, Banks and Murphy (1985) pointed to a widening gap between researchers' and consumers' (i.e., organizations') activities and needs in the area of performance appraisal. For example, Banks and Murphy noted that current investigations of raters' cognitive processes may not be useful to practitioners in terms of suggesting ways to improve performance appraisal procedures. Although Banks and Murphy focused primarily on the independent variables in performance appraisal research, we believe the argument should also be extended to the dependent variables used. Specifically, we argue in the remainder of this chapter that the dependent variables (or criteria) traditionally measured by performance appraisal researchers may be of little or no interest to practitioners. Alternatively, certain criteria of performance appraisal effectiveness that might be of interest to practitioners have been either largely or completely ignored in performance appraisal research.

Perhaps at the core of this apparent "criterion gap" is a failure to appreciate the inherent complexity of the meaning of performance appraisal effectiveness. Researchers appear to have equated performance appraisal effectiveness with the psychometric quality of ratings; thus, error-free ratings are effective ratings, and effective ratings imply an effective performance appraisal system. Practitioners, however, may be concerned with other criteria of performance appraisal effectiveness (e.g., Do the employees accept their ratings? Do ratings influence future levels of performance?). Ultimately, however, the concept of performance appraisal effectiveness is perhaps best characterized as a larger, multidimensional construct; it will include a variety of specific criteria (e.g., rater error indices, employee attitudes toward appraisal, etc.) that collectively comprise the construct of performance appraisal effectiveness.

If we accept the premise that a researcher-practitioner gap exists in terms of measuring performance appraisal effectiveness, this will diminish the useful contributions of science to practice and practice to science in performance appraisal. Published performance appraisal research may be viewed by practitioners as an academic exercise of limited value to organizations struggling with the task of appraisal (e.g., Dossett, Feldman, Timmreck, & Vandaveer, 1989), and practitioners' contributions to the area may be ignored by researchers (perhaps due to the lack of experimental controls in field research), or more seriously, not submitted to professional meetings or scholarly journals (Guion, 1988).

Although the source(s) of this gap may be difficult to trace, we believe part of the difficulty can be explained by the fact that researchers have not shown enough concern for the *process* of choosing criteria used to define performance appraisal. In a laboratory situation where a researcher is investigating raters' conceptual similarity error, the choice of a halo measure as a criterion is clearly appropriate. In some laboratory and field research, however, it is less clear what rating criterion (or criteria) should be used. For example, when evaluating a new rater training program, what properties should be included as criteria: amount of rater halo, accuracy of ratings, satisfaction with training program, and so forth? Components of the performance appraisal system can be evaluated on a number of conceptually and methodologically different criteria, but we have no clear procedure for choosing which criteria to use in specific situations.

We believe that researchers too often choose criteria on the basis of inappropriate considerations, including: (a) they are familiar criteria that have been used in the past; (b) they are newly discovered criteria that are thought to be the wave of the future; or (c) they are readily available criteria that are easy and inexpensive to gather. Weitz (1961) made a similar point when he pointed out that criteria are not chosen because of some careful understanding of the construct "performance," but rather are chosen because the criteria are thought to be relevant, have been used by other investigators, or are readily available (see also Guion, 1961). Thus, we see laboratory studies with videotapes of ratee behavior that use rater accuracy scores (given their relative ease of computation and their use in other lab studies), and field studies using rater error measures (because estimating true scores in the field is extremely difficult). Although these choices are understandable, these are *not* sufficient reasons for choosing criteria. Criteria may seem sensible and interesting to the researcher, but they may be of no interest or relevance to other constituents of the performance appraisal system (Strasser & Bateman, 1984). Clearly, both scientists and practitioners need a more systematic rationale for choosing criteria to evaluate the effectiveness of performance appraisal systems.

Performance Appraisal Criteria: Constituencies and Goals

In choosing criteria to evaluate a performance appraisal system, it is important to consider the goal(s) and purpose(s) of appraisal in the organization. We believe that any framework for choosing criteria should emphasize that the choice of criteria depends on the *goals* of the performance appraisal system; others have made similar suggestions in the past (e.g., Smith, 1976; Sulsky & Balzer, 1988; Weitz, 1961). Furthermore, the framework should recognize that different individuals or constituencies involved in the performance appraisal system may have similar, overlapping, or different goals when evaluating the effectiveness of a system. Different goals may lead to different choices of what aspects of the performance appraisal system should be examined, and which criteria should be chosen to examine those aspects.

As an example, four different constituencies can be identified who have some interest in evaluating the effectiveness of a performance appraisal system: (a) the organization that sponsors and supports the performance appraisal system; (b) raters responsible for conducting performance appraisals; (c) ratees who are evaluated by the appraisal system; and (d) researchers internal (e.g., individuals from the company's human resource department) or external (e.g., academicians) to the organization. Other constituencies may also be identified (e.g., personnel technicians responsible for administering and compiling performance appraisal information), but these four interest groups represent most of the individuals with vested interests in the performance appraisal system. Within each constituent interest group, different individuals or subgroups may also have different interests and goals when evaluating the performance appraisal system. For example, raters responsible for evaluating many ratees may have different notions of the effectiveness of the performance appraisal system than do raters who are required to evaluate only one ratee.

Each constituent interest group can have a number of goals for the performance appraisal system. For example, an organization's goals for the performance appraisal system may include increased employee productivity, higher company profits, defensibility in court against charges of discrimination, and compatibility with other organizational functions (e.g., compensation or production). They may also have different goals for the performance appraisal system. Raters may focus on how easy the system is to use, on positive ratee attitudes toward the performance appraisal system, on improvements in ratee work motivation, and/or on the absence of role conflict or role overload for the raters (e.g., the performance appraisal system's workload does not interfere with the performance of other responsibilities). Ratee goals may include a performance appraisal system that can be trusted, that clarifies instrumentalities between job performance and organizational rewards, that provides fair access to rewards, and that provides accurate and detailed feedback that can be used to direct future performance. Finally, researchers' goals may include ratings that are highly accurate and free from traditional rater errors, that allow for evaluation of performance appraisal system components (e.g., rating format, rater training, etc.), that lead to an understanding of raters' underlying psychological processes, and rater/ratee attitudes toward performance appraisal and their relationship to other work attitudes (e.g., job satisfaction) and behaviors (e.g., turnover).

In summary, a wide variety of goals can be identified for different groups of individuals interested in evaluating performance appraisal systems. Two additional points can also be made. First, different individuals within a constituent interest group may have unique performance appraisal system goals. For example, some researchers may be interested solely in the psychometric qualities of ratings, whereas other researchers may be interested in information processing capabilities (recallability of performance appraisal information, strategies for integrating appraisal information). Second, it is possible that the goals of different constituencies may overlap. For example, both rater and ratee constituencies may require an effective performance appraisal system to provide accurate feedback information during the performance appraisal interview. In general, however, it appears much more likely that each constituency will be interested in a narrower range of goals that are particularly relevant for that group.

Constituencies and goals: Choosing criteria.   Specific categories of goals for evaluating performance appraisal effectiveness are proposed to direct attention toward certain features of the performance appraisal system. The performance appraisal system can be broken down into three components: (a) inputs to the performance appraisal system, the components in place prior to the evaluation of performance (e.g., rating purpose, rater selection, rating instrument, rater training, etc.); (b) throughputs of the performance appraisal process, the components involved in the appraisal of performance (e.g., feedback, performance monitoring, completing the rating instrument, etc.); and (c) outputs of the performance appraisal system, the components that result from the appraisal of performance (e.g., performance ratings, personnel decisions based on these ratings, characteristics of feedback, etc.). These aspects of the performance appraisal system provide sources of information for evaluating performance appraisal effectiveness.

The goals of a constituent of the performance appraisal system should direct the investigator's attention toward particular outcomes or products of the performance appraisal system, and this should in turn influence the choice of criteria. As shown in Fig. 7.2, if the goal is compatibility with other systems, a number of components of the appraisal system may be of interest: rating purpose (i.e., is performance appraisal providing information necessary for compensation, planning, etc.), selecting raters, rating schedule, performance monitoring (i.e., is performance appraisal interfering with rater/ratee abilities to fulfill other organizational roles), and goals (i.e., are performance appraisal goals contributing to all required areas of job performance). If the goal is the rater's ease of use, an investigator might instead investigate only input and throughput characteristics (e.g., How much training is required? How much time will performance monitoring take? Is the rating instrument easy to complete? Does the feedback meeting take too much time, and is it difficult to conduct?).

Our model for selecting criteria for evaluating the effectiveness of performance appraisal systems proposes that effectiveness is determined by the goals of particular constituents of the performance appraisal system, and that these goals may lead investigators to focus on a subset of information regarding the performance appraisal system. It is this information that should determine the actual criteria chosen. The use of this framework leads to a number of conclusions regarding research on performance appraisal effectiveness.

First, as noted earlier, performance appraisal effectiveness should be viewed as a multidimensional construct. Multiple constituencies and goals imply that a single criterion of effectiveness will be deficient for measuring the complex construct of performance appraisal effectiveness. Thus, multiple criteria would appear to be critical for evaluating performance appraisal effectiveness.

Second, the selection of criteria for evaluating performance appraisal effectiveness should recognize that "effectiveness" means different things to different people. Different groups of individuals involved in the appraisal process have particular and unique goals for evaluating effectiveness. Thus, effectiveness criteria should be carefully reviewed to determine whether they reflect the goals of all constituents of the performance appraisal system.

Third, our review suggests that past research has focused on a limited number of criteria such as the psychometric qualities of ratings, rater/ratee attitudes, and

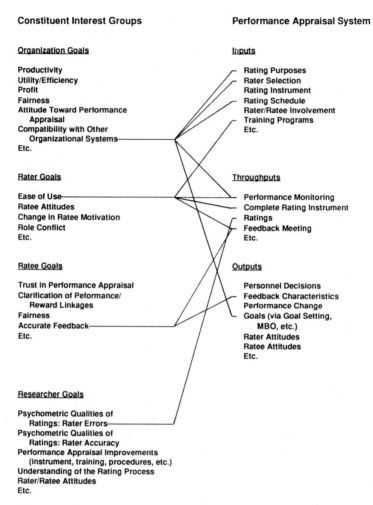

Constituent Interest Groups

Performance Appraisal System

Organization Goals

Inputs

Productivity
Utility/Efficiency
Profit
Fairness
Attitude Toward Performance
    Appraisal
Compatibility with Other
    Organizational Systems
Etc.

Rating Purposes
Rater Selection
Rating Instrument
Rating Schedule
Rater/Ratee Involvement
Training Programs
Etc.

Rater Goals

Throughputs

Ease of Use
Ratee Attitudes
Change in Ratee Motivation
Role Conflict
Etc.

Performance Monitoring
Complete Rating Instrument
Ratings
Feedback Meeting
Etc.

Ratee Goals

Outputs

Trust in Performance Appraisal
Clarification of Peformance/
    Reward Linkages
Fairness
Accurate Feedback
Etc.

Personnel Decisions
Feedback Characteristics
Performance Change
Goals (via Goal Setting,
    MBO, etc.)
Rater Attitudes
Ratee Attitudes
Etc.

Researcher Goals

Psychometric Qualities of
    Ratings: Rater Errors
Psychometric Qualities of
    Ratings: Rater Accuracy
Performance Appraisal Improvements
    (instrument, training, procedures, etc.)
Understanding of the Rating Process
Rater/Ratee Attitudes
Etc.

FIG. 7.2.   A framework with examples for selecting criteria for performance appraisal effectiveness.

raters' information processing of ratee performance. All of these criteria, while important to the goals of performance appraisal researchers (i.e., scientists), may be of little or no interest to other constituents of the performance appraisal system. Past research has apparently ignored (or at least failed to stress) criteria of interest to raters, ratees, and management (i.e., practitioners). As Barber (1988) pointed out, practitioners provide important perspectives on the applications of scientific theories and methods to the evaluation of practical problems such as evaluating performance appraisal effectiveness. For example, practitioners can identify prominent, everyday problems facing members of the organization, provide a practitioners' perspective on problems or solutions identified by their scientist counterparts, help restructure research designs, instruments, tasks, and so on to reflect the real-world task in a real-world environment; in addition, they can help interpret and communicate findings to organizational members and decision makers. Thus, the perspectives and insights of organizational members (including industrial/organizational psychologists employed by organizations) involved in performance appraisal can help guide the direction of research on performance appraisal effectiveness. It is this last point we address in the remainder of this chapter.

PERFORMANCE APPRAISAL EFFECTIVENESS AND ORGANIZATIONAL GOALS

Given that researchers and practitioners have often neglected to consider criteria that might be of interest to other constituencies, what can we do to increase their awareness to a broader set of criteria for effectiveness? One solution is a comprehensive framework to guide the choice of effectiveness criteria; such a framework would serve to close the existing gap between scientists, practitioners, and other constituencies. Here, we propose such a framework and describe how it can help us identify and choose criteria of interest to one constituency—the organization. We focus our example on how one might identify organizationally relevant criteria that can be used to evaluate a performance appraisal system. Our decision to use the organization as the constituency was not an arbitrary one; published research that addresses the impact of performance appraisal systems on organizational goals such as productivity and profit, goals that have been seen as "the ultimate effectiveness criteria" for many organizations (Katz & Kahn, 1978), is relatively scarce.

Clearly, organizations may have interests that overlap with those of other constituents of the performance appraisal process. All constituent groups may have an interest, for example, in the attitudes expressed toward the performance appraisal process or the correctness of the rankings of individuals in line for promotion. But what about those goals that may be more specific to the organization such as increased performance and productivity? To be sure, reviews of research on appraisal feedback (Guzzo & Bondy, 1983; Kopelman, 1986) and goal setting (Guzzo & Bondy, 1983; Latham & Baldes, 1975) suggest that characteristics of the performance appraisal system do affect "bottom-line" measures of performance (i.e., the quantity and quality of performance) and productivity; recent applications of utility measurement (Cascio, 1987) may enhance our ability to estimate dollar savings to an organization due to certain aspects (e.g., feedback, rater training, etc.) of the performance appraisal system (Landy, Farr, & Jacobs, 1982). But as Smith (1976) pointed out, measuring the impact of appraisal systems on organizational goals remains elusive because these criteria do not easily lend themselves to measurement, because the financial costs associated with measuring them are often prohibitive, and because of the distal relationship of these criteria to the characteristics of the appraisal system. Difficulties inherent in conducting rigorous and internally valid studies using such criteria may also be responsible for the de-emphasis on organizational goals and the emphasis instead on researcher goals by methodologically rigorous researchers. In any event, given real world constraints, measuring organizational goals may prove to be extremely difficult.

Organizational Objectives: Measures for Realizing Organizational Goals

It is very difficult to determine whether an appraisal system is influencing the attainment of organizational goals such as profit and productivity. It may, however, be easier to evaluate whether the appraisal system is meeting organizational *objectives*. Our use of the term is not simply semantic. Objectives differ from goals in terms of scope, specificity, and proximity to performance appraisal system characteristics. Thus, an objective is more narrow than a goal, and suggests a specific measure of the goal of interest. For example, if the organizational goal is productivity, specific objectives that must be reached to obtain this goal include: (a) promote the best worker (who should be the most productive); (b) provide valid appraisal feedback to ratees (thereby enhancing work performance); and (c) develop performance goals (because goals have been found to lead to increased performance, e.g., Latham & Kinne, 1974). If the organizational goal is an appraisal system that permits fair access of minorities to upper-level positions, objectives may be: (a) rating distributions that yield similar distributions for minority and majority employees; (b) personnel decisions that promote a certain proportion of minorities; or (c) that minority ratees who perceive the appraisal system as fair.

It should be noted that achieving objectives does *not* guarantee goal attainment, although achieving objectives should help in this regard. Thus, forced promotion of a proportion of minorities before some are adequately prepared may lead to voluntary and involuntary turnover that inhibits goal achievement. Similarly, even if we promote the most qualified workers, productivity may suffer due to a host of factors unrelated to worker qualifications (e.g., downturn in the economy, aging equipment, etc; Landy & Farr, 1983). But even if we cannot be certain whether, or to what extent, the appraisal system is having a positive impact upon distal organizational goals, evaluating objectives related to these goals provides useful information regarding the quality of the system outputs. That is, even if we cannot guarantee that correct personnel decisions lead to increased performance, we are in a position to evaluate whether correct decisions were made. If we cannot guarantee that workers are using feedback to improve performance, we can at least evaluate the quality of the feedback given.

Changing the focus from organizational goals to specific objectives related to those goals has implications for the choice of criteria. If organizational objectives are considered important, criteria should be chosen based on careful consideration of the degree to which they correspond to those organizational objectives.

An example may help clarify our point. Consider a situation where an appraisal system is being used to make promotion decisions. Two possible organizational goals may be to: (a) promote the best employees to improve productivity and, given affirmative action goals, (b) increase the proportion of minority promotions (perhaps giving little weight to differences in minority and majority performance ratings). One objective for reaching the goal of increased productivity is to promote only the most qualified individuals in the work force. This would prescribe that one criterion for evaluating the appraisal decision should focus on whether, in fact, the "best" performers (based on previous performance) were selected. A number of psychometrically oriented criterion measures could be used to examine the ratings used for promotional decisions. The choice of criterion, however, will depend on the particular decision to be made (i.e., the specific objective). If the rating system is used to promote the top n employees, our criterion need only examine the degree to which employees were correctly ranked in terms of performance levels. On the other hand, if all qualified ratees (based on some cut-off performance score) are to be promoted, rating accuracy is the more important criterion, because accuracy measures evaluate the degree of correspondence between ratees' performance rating levels and true levels of performance.

Focusing on the organization's goal to improve minority representation in management, one objective might be the promotion of a certain proportion of minorities into upper level positions. In this case, the criterion of interest regarding the appraisal decision is not the validity or accuracy of ratings, but rather some fairness criterion (Hunter & Schmidt, 1976). If employees' perceptions of the fairness of the personnel decisions is the organization's objective, the criterion would most likely be some attitudinal measure.

A Final Note: Identification of Organizational Goals and Objectives

The use of organizational goals and objectives as a framework for selecting criterion variables implies some agreement on what those goals and objectives are. Unfortunately, identifying agreed upon organizational goals and objectives is extremely difficult (Cameron & Whetten, 1983; Landy & Farr, 1983; Smith, 1976). As Katz and Kahn (1978) pointed out, decisions made in defining performance in organizations are not made rationally, but rather reflect bargaining and negotiation on the part of representatives of various organizational sectors or constituencies. Schein (1980) acknowledged that it may not be possible to satisfy the objectives of one constituency without adversely affecting those of another.

Thus, we are left with the basic, yet potentially impossible, challenge of specifying organizational goals and objectives in order to choose appropriate criteria. Without a clear specification of goals and objectives, the contribution of the appraisal system to the organization (if any) will remain unclear. Although we cannot adequately deal with this issue in the present chapter, we can make several recommendations.

One method for identifying what the organization considers important is to ask those organizational members responsible for developing organizational policy and strategy. One can presume that such a system-wide perspective would help prevent subgoals from particular sectors of the organization from replacing organizational goals. Or perhaps the goals of the direct users of the performance appraisal system should take precedence, particularly if the outcomes of the performance appraisal system have only distal relationships to organizational goals such as market share or profitability. In contrast, perhaps allowing key individuals who represent various areas of the organization develop organizational goals and objectives would be preferred; multiple perspectives on work processes and organizational constraints may lead to more realistic goals and objectives.

As Cameron and Whetten (1981) warned, organizational goals and objectives: (a) are often difficult to recognize or articulate, (b) differ widely among individual organizational members, and (c) change over time. Points (a) and (b) may be resolved by using judgment analytic techniques such as cognitive feedback for reducing conflicting values (e.g., Balke, Hammond, & Meyer, 1973; Balzer, Doherty, & O'Connor, 1989; Hammond & Adelman, 1976; see also Baron's chapter in this volume). Point (c) may pose a more difficult obstacle to establishing goals and objectives, but strategies to monitor or predict changes in goals and objectives as organizations mature through their life cycles may be promising (Cameron & Whetten, 1981; Quinn & Cameron, 1983). Once goals and their accompanying objectives are defined, we can begin to identify and choose specific criterion measures for evaluating the appraisal system based on those objectives.

AN APPLICATION OF THE FRAMEWORK
FOR SELECTING CRITERIA

The proposed framework for selecting criteria based on considerations of organizational goals and objectives can be extended to other constituents of the performance appraisal process—raters, ratees, or researchers. Because each of these "interest groups" may have their own goals and more specific objectives, a framework for selecting criterion measures should be useful when conceptualizing performance appraisal studies. Such a framework, including several distinct and formal steps for selecting the appropriate criteria for evaluating performance appraisal system effectiveness, is illustrated in Fig. 7.3.

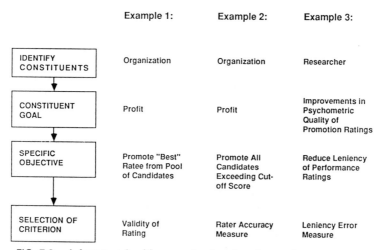

FIG. 7.3. A framework with examples for choosing performance appraisal criteria.

Identification of constituent group(s).   As we have suggested, an appraisal system's effectiveness can be evaluated by a number of different constituent groups. Although each of these groups may share common goals for the appraisal process, some goals are likely to be unique to each group. If researchers ignore this important step, they may inadvertently choose criterion measures that are of peripheral value or of no interest to the practitioner, organization, or other constituencies. This is one factor that can contribute to the present researcher/practitioner gap in performance appraisal research (Banks & Murphy, 1985). Clearly identifying the constituent group will help to identify the specific goal(s) for evaluating appraisal system effectiveness (Edwards & Newman, 1982).[2] Brief guidelines for identifying constituent groups and selecting participants from these groups were suggested by Delbecq, Van de Ven, & Gustafson (1975).

Identification of constituent goal(s).   As discussed earlier, each constituent group can have a number of different goals. Each goal can lead to different decisions regarding how to evaluate appraisal effectiveness, which implies that it is important to clarify which goal will be the focus of the study. The decision-making literature (e.g., Delbecq et al., 1975; Edwards & Newman, 1982; Ham-

---

[2]Edwards and Newman (1982) distinguished between two general categories of constituents: *actors,* individuals who make decisions about programs and have the ability to modify programs; and *stakeholders,* individuals who are either directly or indirectly affected by a program. In the present context, this distinction between actors (e.g., researchers, upper-level management, personnel officers) and stakeholders (e.g., raters and ratees) may lead to hypotheses about the subsequent goals and objectives of these constituent groups.

mond & Adelman, 1976) offers some direction for identifying and prioritizing goals from various constituencies.

Identification of specific objective(s).   Given the distal nature and vagueness of many goals, specific objectives associated with the constituent group's goal(s) should be clearly identified. This step provides the investigator with one (of many possible) specific measure of the goal of interest that can be used to evaluate the appraisal system's effectiveness.

Selection of criterion.   Finally, available criteria should be reviewed, and the criterion measure(s) that assess(es) whether objectives have been met should be chosen and used to evaluate the appraisal system effectiveness.

Figure 7.3 presents three examples in which this framework is used to choose an appropriate criterion for evaluating the effectiveness of a performance appraisal system. It can be seen that differences in constituent groups, goals, and objectives all affect the characteristics required of a criterion, thereby helping us to identify the most relevant criterion for evaluating performance appraisal effectiveness. Of course, the model simplifies a very complex process. There are often many constituencies to satisfy, and multiple goals and objectives to meet. But the framework provides a strategy for allowing identifiable goals and objectives, rather than our personal biases or convictions, to guide our choice of criteria for judging the effectiveness of performance appraisal systems.

CONCLUSIONS

In this chapter, we have explored criterion measures currently used in performance appraisal research, and have highlighted some of the methodological and theoretical limitations associated with these measures. Our primary purpose, however, has been to argue that a "criterion gap" exists in performance appraisal research, and to help close this gap by providing a framework for the informed choice of criterion measures. To that end, we conceptualized performance appraisal as a process of inputs, throughputs, and outputs. We highlighted the fact that we might be interested in any of a number of different components of the overall process. Furthermore, we pointed out that a number of different constituencies or interest groups may have partially overlapping as well as distinctly different interests. Because constituents may have different interests, it is not surprising that they may choose different criterion measures for evaluating effectiveness.

We believe that the lack of communication between researchers and practitioners, and the lack of communication of both these groups with organizational members affected by the performance appraisal system, has contributed to "gaps" separating these different individuals; however, these gaps may partially reflect the fact that these individuals simply have different interests. It would appear, then, that establishing or improving communication among these groups of individuals may help close the gaps. Raters and ratees must be surveyed, interviewed, and so on to determine their views on the characteristics of an effective performance appraisal system, and these concerns should be seen as no less important than those identified by researchers and practitioners. Practitioners need to communicate with researchers, sharing problems and concerns they face when attempting to implement performance appraisal systems, and providing constructive feedback on the perceived applicability of performance appraisal research programs. This is one way in which practitioners can make an important contribution to science. Researchers, of course, must also share advances in theory, method, and so on with practitioners and other organizational members; perhaps this could be accomplished by providing informal "continuing education" for practitioners. Finally, if researchers can be more attentive to the concerns of organizations, new and previously unresearched criterion measures may evolve and become a focus of interest, and studies may be designed to examine the effects of various appraisal system-factors on these criteria, thereby providing important contributions to practice (Dossett et al., 1989).

This latter point raises an important issue that we have thus far ignored: the process of choosing criterion measures may be useful for generating hypotheses and designs for specific studies. That is, rather than designing a study and then searching for criteria to test hypotheses, the choice of criteria could actually guide the researcher during hypothesis and research design generation. Thus, for example, if satisfaction with performance feedback is deemed to be an important criterion, we might attempt to develop and test models that explain and predict satisfaction with appraisal feedback. Criterion measures may help us to ask the right questions, and may be more than simply vehicles used to provide solutions.

ACKNOWLEDGMENTS

We thank Kevin Murphy and Skip Saal for their helpful comments and criticisms on an earlier draft of this paper.

REFERENCES

Balke, W. M., Hammond, K. R., & Meyer, G. D. (1973). An alternative approach to labor-management negotiations. *Administrative Science Quarterly, 18,* 311–327.

Balzer, W. K., Doherty, M. E., & O'Connor, R., Jr. (1989). The effects of cognitive feedback on performance. *Psychological Bulletin, 106,* 410–433.

Banks, C. G., & Murphy, K. R. (1985). Toward narrowing the research-practice gap in performance appraisal. *Personnel Psychology, 38,* 335–345.

Bannister, B. D. (1986). Performance outcome feedback and attributional feedback: Interactive effects on recipient responses. *Journal of Applied Psychology, 71,* 203–210.

Barber, P. (1988). *Applied cognitive psychology*. New York: Methuen.

Barr, S. H., Brief, A. P., & Fulk, J. L. (1981, August). Correlates of perceived fairness and accuracy of performance. *Proceedings of the 41st Academy of Management Meeting*, Las Vegas, pp. 156–160.

Bernardin, H. J., & Beatty, R. W. (1984). *Performance appraisal: Assessing human behavior at work*. Boston, MA: Kent Publishing Company.

Bernardin, H. J., & Pence, E. C. (1980). Rater training: Creating new response sets and decreasing accuracy. *Journal of Applied Psychology, 65*, 60–66.

Borman, W. C. (1977). Consistency of rating accuracy and rating error in the judgment of human performance. *Organizational Behavior & Human Performance, 20*, 238–252.

Cameron, K. S., & Whetten, D. A. (1981). Perceptions of organizational effectiveness across organizational life cycles. *Administrative Science Quarterly, 26*, 525–544.

Cameron, K. S., & Whetten, D. A. (1983). Some conclusions about organizational effectiveness. In K. S. Cameron & D. A. Whetten (Eds.), *Organizational effectiveness: A comparison of multiple models*. New York: Academic Press.

Campbell, J. P. (1983). Some possible implications of "modeling" for the conceptualization of measurement. In F. Landy, S. Zedeck, & J. Cleveland (Eds.), *Performance measurement and theory*. Hillsdale, NJ: Lawrence Erlbaum Associates.

Cascio, W. F. (1987). *Costing human resources: The financial impact of behavior in organizations* (2nd Ed.). Boston, MA: PWS-Kent Publishing Company.

Cooper, W. H. (1981). Ubiquitous halo. *Psychological Bulletin, 90*, 218–244.

Cronbach, L. J. (1955). Processes affecting scores on "understanding of others" and "assumed similarity". *Psychological Bulletin, 52*, 177–193.

Delbecq, A., Van de Ven, A., & Gustafson, D. (1975). *Group techniques for program planning: A guide to nominal group and delphi processes*. Glenview, IL: Scott, Foresman.

Dipboye, R. L., & DePontbriand, R. (1981). Correlates of employee reactions to performance appraisals and appraisal systems. *Journal of Applied Psychology, 66*, 248–251.

Dipboye, R. L., Stramler, C. S., & Fontenelle, G. A. (1984). The effects of the application on recall of information from the interview. *Academy of Management Journal, 27*, 561–575.

Dorfman, P. W., Stephan, W. G., & Loveland, J. (1986). Performance appraisal behaviors: Supervisor perceptions and subordinate reactions. *Personnel Psychology, 39*, 579–597.

Dossett, D. L., Feldman, J., Timmreck, C. W., & Vandaveer, V. V. (1989, May). *Real world performance appraisal: What do scientists have to offer?* Symposium conducted at the Fourth Annual Conference of the Society of Industrial and Organizational Psychology, Boston.

Edwards, W., & Newman, J. R. (1982). *Multiattribute evaluation*. Beverly Hills, CA: Sage.

Fisicaro, S. A. (1988). A reexamination of the relation between halo error and accuracy. *Journal of Applied Psychology, 73*, 239–244.

Gordon, M. E. (1970). The effect of correctness of the behavior observed on the accuracy of ratings. *Organizational Behavior & Human Performance, 5*, 366–377.

Guion, R. M. (1961). Criterion measurement and personnel judgments. *Personnel Psychology, 14*, 141–149.

Guion, R. M. (1965). *Personnel testing*. New York: McGraw-Hill.

Guion, R. M. (1983). Comments on Hunter. In F. Landy, S. Zedeck, & J. Cleveland (Eds.), *Performance measurement and theory*. Hillsdale, NJ: Lawrence Erlbaum Associates.

Guion, R. M. (1988). Special section: From psychologists in organizations (Editorial). *Journal of Applied Psychology, 73*, 693–694.

Guion, R. M., & Gibson, W. M. (1987, August). Discussion with the authors of the 1988 *Annual Review of Psychology* chapter at the Annual Meeting of the American Psychological Association, New York City.

Guzzo, R. A., & Bondy, J. S. (1983). *A guide to worker productivity experiments in the United States 1976–1981*. Elmsford, NY: Pergamon Press.

Hahn, D. C., & Dipboye, R. L. (1988). Effects of training and information on the accuracy and reliability of job evaluations. *Journal of Applied Psychology, 73,* 146–153.

Hammond, K. R., & Adelman, L. (1976). Science, values, and judgment. *Science, 194,* 389–396.

Hunter, J. E. (1983). A causal analysis of cognitive ability, job knowledge, job performance, and supervisor ratings. In F. Landy, S. Zedeck, & J. Cleveland (Eds.), *Performance measurement and theory.* Hillsdale, NJ: Lawrence Erlbaum Associates.

Hunter, J. E., & Schmidt, F. L. (1976). Critical analysis of the statistical and ethical implications of various definitions of test bias. *Psychological Bulletin, 83,* 1053–1059.

Jacobs, R., Kafry, D., & Zedeck, S. (1980). Expectations of behaviorally anchored rating scales. *Personnel Psychology, 33,* 595–640.

James, L. R. (1973). Criterion models and construct validity for criteria. *Psychological Bulletin, 80,* 75–83.

Kane, J. S. (1982). *Evaluating the effectiveness of performance appraisal systems.* Unpublished manuscript.

Katz, D., & Kahn, R. L. (1978). *The social psychology of organizations.* (2nd Ed.), New York: Wiley.

Kopelman, R. E. (1986). Objective feedback. In E. A. Locke (Ed.), *Generalizing from laboratory to field settings.* Lexington, MA: Lexington Books.

Landy, F. J., Barnes, J. L., & Murphy, K. R. (1978). Correlates of perceived fairness and accuracy of performance evaluation. *Journal of Applied Psychology, 63,* 751–754.

Landy, F. J., & Farr, J. L. (1983). *The measurement of work performance: Methods, theory, and applications.* New York: Academic Press.

Landy, F. J., Farr, J. L., & Jacobs, R. R. (1982). Utility concepts in performance measurement. *Organizational Behavior & Human Performance, 30,* 15–40.

Latham, G. P., & Baldes, J. J. (1975). The "practical significance" of Locke's theory of goal setting. *Journal of Applied Psychology, 60,* 122–124.

Latham, G. P., & Kinne, S. B. III. (1974). Improving job performance through training in goal setting. *Journal of Applied Psychology, 59,* 187–191.

Murphy, K. R., & Balzer, W. K. (1989). Rater errors and rating accuracy. *Journal of Applied Psychology, 74,* 619–624.

Nathan, B. R., & Alexander, R. A. (1988). A comparison of criteria for test validation: A meta-analytic investigation. *Personnel Psychology, 41,* 517–535.

Naylor, J. C. (1983). Modeling performance. In F. Landy, S. Zedeck, & J. Cleveland (Eds.), *Performance measurement and theory.* Hillsdale, NJ: Lawrence Erlbaum Associates.

Pearce, J. L., & Porter, L. W. (1986). Employee responses to formal performance appraisal feedback. *Journal of Applied Psychology, 71,* 211–218.

Pulakos, E. D., Borman, W. C., & Hough, L. M. (1988). Test validation for scientific understanding: Two demonstrations of an approach to studying predictor-criterion linkages. *Personnel Psychology, 41,* 703–716.

Quinn, R. E., & Cameron, K. S. (1983). Life cycles and shifting criteria of effectiveness: Some preliminary evidence. *Management Science, 29,* 33–51.

Saal, F. E., Downey, R. G., & Lahey, M. A. (1980). Rating the ratings: Assessing the psychometric quality of rating data. *Psychological Bulletin, 88,* 413–428.

Schein, E. H. (1980). *Organizational psychology* (3rd Ed.). Englewood Cliffs, NJ: Prentice-Hall.

Smith, P. C. (1976). Behaviors, results, and organizational effectiveness: The problem of criteria. In M. D. Dunnette (Ed.), *Handbook of Industrial and Organizational Psychology.* Chicago: Rand McNally.

Strasser, S., & Bateman, T. (1984). What we should study, problems we should solve: Perspectives of two constituencies. *Personnel Psychology, 37,* 77–92.

Sulsky, L. M., & Balzer, W. K. (1988). The meaning and measurement of performance rating accuracy: Some methodological and theoretical concerns. *Journal of Applied Psychology, 73,* 497–506.

Vance, R. J., Kuhnert, K. W., & Farr, J. L. (1978). Interview judgments: Using external criteria to compare behavioral and graphic scale ratings. *Organizational Behavior and Human Performance, 22,* 279–294.

Vance, R. J., MacCallum, R. C., Coovert, M. D., & Hedge, J. W. (1988). Construct validity of multiple job performance measures using confirmatory factor analysis. *Journal of Applied Psychology, 73,* 74–80.

Wallace, S. R. (1965). Criteria for what? *American Psychologist, 20,* 411–417.

Weitz, J. (1961). Criteria for criteria. *American Psychologist, 16,* 228–231.

Wexley, K. (1987, August). Panel discussant in K. R. Murphy (Chair), *Cognitive research in performance appraisal: Prospects for application.* Presented at the Annual Meeting of the American Psychological Association, New York City.

Wiersma, U., & Latham, G. P. (1986). The practicality of behavioral observation scales, behavioral expectation scales, and trait scales. *Personnel Psychology, 39,* 619–628.

8 Job Performance and Productivity

Kevin R. Murphy
Colorado State University

Productivity has become a national concern, and for good reason. Productivity growth in this country has slowed considerably since the late 1970s (Tuttle, 1983); in 1984, productivity grew nearly three times as quickly in Japan as in the United States. Low productivity will eventually affect our standard of living, and could lead to substantial hardships for future generations (Perloff & Nelson, 1983). The possibility that psychology can be applied to increase productivity in organizations has therefore become an increasingly important concern; productivity-oriented research has, as a result, become increasingly common in the social and behavioral sciences (Brief, 1984; Campbell & Campbell, 1988a; Kopelman, 1986).

Prior to 1980, psychologists and managers were generally pessimistic about the impact of psychologically based interventions, ranging from ability testing to goal setting, on productivity. Although researchers were aware of scattered studies demonstrating the benefits of different interventions, there was widespread doubt, both among practitioners and organizations, that these interventions were economically worthwhile. Recent research has suggested that the impact of psychologically based interventions is in fact substantial. For example, Schmidt, Hunter, McKenzie, and Muldrow (1979) estimated that the federal government could save $376 million over 10 years by using cognitive ability tests to select computer programmers. Hunter and Hunter (1984) estimated that the use of ability tests in selection for federal entry-level jobs could lead to a productivity gain of over $15 billion per year. Finally, Hunter and Schmidt (1982) estimated that the nationwide productivity gain associated with the use of valid tests in personnel selection could exceed $80 billion per year. Although Murphy (1986)

157

cautioned that these estimates may be inflated by 30–80%, the sizes of potential productivity gains are probably substantial.

The aim of most psychologically based interventions in organizations is to increase the performance of workers, work groups, or organizational units. The assumption of the research cited earlier is that increases in performance or efficiency lead directly to increases in productivity. This chapter critically examines the assumption that interventions targeted at increasing job performance are optimal, or even appropriate means of increasing productivity in organizations.

Note that the terms "performance," "productivity," and "efficiency" have not been defined in the preceding paragraphs. This is not unusual. Landy and his colleagues reviewed research on performance rating and suggested several innovative directions for further research and application (Landy & Farr, 1980, 1983; Landy, Zedeck, Cleveland, 1983). In the area of prediction, Schmidt, Hunter and their colleagues reviewed hundreds of studies which suggest that ability tests provide valid predictions of job performance (Hunter & Hunter, 1984; Pearlman, Schmidt, & Hunter, 1980; Schmidt & Hunter, 1977, 1981). Both of these literatures are notable for the fact that performance, which is the central concern of the research reviewed, is rarely, if ever, defined. As a result, we know a great deal about predicting future performance, and we know a great deal about measuring past performance, but we know little about *what* we have predicted or measured. Campbell (1983) noted that we have been quite successful in modeling and defining different parts or aspects of performance, but that we have expended little effort on defining the overall performance domain. In this chapter, I argue that the precise definition of these terms, especially the term "performance," is crucial to understanding the links between psychology-based interventions and productivity.

Does Performance Equal Productivity?

Although research by Schmidt, Hunter, and their colleagues suggests that increasing job performance is synonymous with increasing productivity, the performance-productivity link is, in fact, complex and uncertain. First, neither productivity nor performance are well-defined constructs. We know surprisingly little about the dimensions of performance and productivity, or about the organization of these dimensions. For example, there is relatively little research on whether or not performance can be meaningfully viewed as a unidimensional construct (Campbell & Campbell, 1988a; See Schmidt & Kaplan, 1971 for a discussion of composite vs. multiple criteria). If not, the phrase "increasing job performance" may be hopelessly ambiguous. Second, most definitions of productivity refer to both the value of goods and services produced (output) and the cost of producing those goods and services (input) (Guzzo, 1988; Mahoney, 1988). Performance is usually defined by psychologists as an output variable (Schmidt & Hunter, 1983), but recent research suggests that performance may be an input variable, an output variable, or both (Murphy, in press). Finally, the human influence on input and output variables is rarely equal. Depending on whether an industry is labor intensive or capital intensive, the optimal strategy for increasing productivity may focus on increasing the number and the quality of goods and services produced or on decreasing the costs of production.

In examining the relationship between performance and productivity, six questions must be addressed:

a. What is meant by productivity and productivity enhancement?
b. What behaviors does "job performance" encompass?
c. Is the underlying model linking performance and productivity reasonable?
d. What kinds of interventions are most appropriate for increasing productivity?
e. Is productivity worth pursuing? and
f. What are the implications for the science and practice of psychology in organizations?

PRODUCTIVITY

There are many different definitions of productivity (Campbell & Campbell, 1988b; Muckler, 1982; National Academy of Science, 1979; Sutermeister, 1976). For example, the Bureau of Labor Statistics defines productivity in terms of goods produced per worker-hour in the private sector (Alluisi & Meigs, 1983). Economists define productivity as a function of production volume, labor, capital, intermediate products purchased, and time, whereas accountants define productivity in terms of ratios of sales or profits to capital or assets (Tuttle, 1983). Although there is no single definition of productivity, there is consensus that productivity must be defined in terms of a ratio of output variables to input variables (Cascio, 1987a; Mahoney, 1988). Output variables include the value of both goods and services produced by an organization. Input variables include the costs of capital, labor, equipment, and materials.

Definitional issues are important, because different productivity improvement programs may be aimed at different input and output variables. Different interventions might be used if the aim is to identify or encourage employees who are most likely to produce a large number of products (output) than if the program's goal is to minimize avoidable costs (input). Personnel selection programs are typically designed to achieve the former,[1] whereas programs designed to reduce absenteeism are targeted toward the latter.

---

[1]Some recruitment (e.g., realistic job previews) and selection (e.g., biodata) programs are designed to reduce absenteeism.

The definition of productivity as a ratio of output value to input costs has a variety of important implications. First, the metric employed in most of the productivity research published in psychological journals (i.e., dollar value of goods produced) is inappropriate or incomplete. Because productivity is best expressed as a ratio (e.g., the value of goods and services produced is 1.7 times the cost of production), research that focuses solely on output value without considering input costs does not deal directly with productivity. Second, the gains or losses associated with changes in productivity are uncertain; it is not always clear who benefits and who loses as a result of efforts to increase productivity. The easiest way to increase productivity is to drastically cut wages, which clearly does not benefit workers. Productivity researchers must consider the perspectives of several different constituencies (e.g., workers, management, customers) when evaluating productivity improvement programs.

Increasing Productivity

Applied psychologists have developed a number of programs designed to increase productivity. These include ability testing, training, performance feedback, goal setting, worker participation programs, job previews, flextime, and stress management programs (Cascio, 1987a; Latham & Naiper, 1984). Application of cognitive ability tests in personnel selection has been the focus of a significant body of research, and is regarded by many [e.g., Hunter and Hunter (1984)] as the specific application of psychology that is most likely to have a sizeable effect on productivity.

Methods of estimating the economic gain associated with testing have long been available (cf. Brogden & Taylor, 1950: Cronbach & Gleser, 1965; Sands, 1973), but were rarely applied prior to 1979. It is important to note that for most methods in this research literature, economic gain is equated with productivity. All of these represent straightforward applications of linear regression, in which increases in the cognitive ability of those hired using tests (as opposed to random selection) can be directly translated into expected increases in job performance. Since the correlation between test scores and performance is typically substantial (Hunter & Hunter, 1984), the impact of selection tests on performance is also substantial.

In recent years, a variety of methods for estimating productivity gains have been developed (Cascio, 1987b; Cascio & Ramos, 1986; Schmidt & Hunter, 1983; Schmidt et al., 1979), and the accuracy of these methods has been examined (Bobko, Karren, & Parkington, 1983). These methods have been applied in examining the productivity gains associated with selection testing (Hunter & Hunter, 1984; Hunter & Schmidt, 1983; Schmidt, Mack, & Hunter, 1984) and with the use of tests in placement (Hunter & Schmidt, 1982). These methods have also been generalized to contexts such as performance appraisal (Landy, Farr, & Jacobs, 1982) and training (Mathieu & Leonard, 1987). Finally, more sophisticated models that take into account the principles of accounting and work force flow variables have been developed (Boudreau, 1983a, 1983b; Boudreau & Berger, 1985; Cronshaw & Alexander, 1985).

Although productivity researchers are rarely explicit in defining the precise meaning of job performance (cf. Murphy, in press), applications of the Cronbach-Gleser utility model appear to concentrate on increasing outputs, and pay little attention to decreasing input costs. Two lines of evidence support this interpretation. First, the causal model presented by Schmidt, Hunter, and Outerbridge (1986) to explain the link between cognitive ability and job performance suggests that job knowledge (i.e., knowledge of how to perform major tasks) is the major direct cause of individual differences in job performance. It is reasonable to infer that an individual with greater job knowledge will produce more and better products in a given period than one with limited job knowledge. Second, in one of the few instances in this literature that deals explicitly with input costs, Schmidt and Hunter (1983) noted that increases in job performance would lead to lower labor costs, since a given quantity of goods could be produced with fewer workers if each worker was a high performer.

DIMENSIONS OF JOB PERFORMANCE

It is often assumed that job performance can be adequately defined in terms of the job incumbent's success in carrying out the tasks that are included in a formal job description. Unfortunately, things are not that simple. There are several reasons to believe that job performance *cannot* be equated with task performance.

First, most observations of work behavior confirm the common perception that workers spend relatively little time performing job-related tasks. For example, Bialek, Zapf, and McGuire (1977) reported that enlisted infantrymen spent less than half their work time performing the technical tasks for which they had been trained; in many cases, only a small proportion of their time was in any way devoted to accomplishing the tasks specified in their job description. Campbell, Dunnette, Lawler, and Weick (1970) noted similar patterns for managers. The fact that most peoples' work time is not devoted solely to work tasks has serious implications for several aspects of criterion development. For example, many methods of job analysis are based explicitly on the assumption that most, if not all, of a worker's time is spent working on identifiable tasks (e.g., the Air Force's task analysis system; see Christal, 1974). As much of the work day is spent doing something outside of the typical domain of tasks, indices of the percentage of time spent on different tasks present a warped view of the activities actually carried out by workers. Unless we are willing to ignore much of what a person does at work, it is difficult to equate job performance with task performance.

Second, many of the performance evaluation systems currently in use include specific measures or indices that are only tangentially related to task performance. Examples include measures of absenteeism and turnover, as well as supervisory ratings of broad traits such as dependability or motivation. Admittedly, the use of such measures does not prove that the job performance domain is broader than the task performance domain; it is possible that these measures, although widely used, are inappropriate and therefore invalid. Nevertheless, the widespread use of measures that do not relate directly or solely to the accomplishment of tasks does suggest that the job performance domain is *perceived* by researchers and practitioners to be broader than the domain of task performance.

A third argument for assuming that job performance cannot be defined solely in terms of task performance is that job performance must be defined over longer time periods and in relation to more organizational units than is true for task performance. This can be seen most clearly by considering the case of a plant manager who successfully meets a first-quarter production quota by depleting all available reserves of material and by diverting resources from other parts of the organization. Although this manager has successfully achieved his main task, the long-term implications of such task performance are clearly not favorable. In many jobs, it would not be difficult to provide examples of individuals who successfully completed most tasks, but whose performance was judged to be low. Rather than defining job performance solely in terms of task accomplishment, several authors have suggested defining job performance in terms of a wider array of work behaviors (James, 1973; Smith, 1976). The question is how to define this performance domain.

Defining the Performance Domain

Astin (1964) noted that in developing criteria, we must identify the relevant goals of the organization, or of the measurer. In the context of work, the relevant goals of the organization would include both short-term goals, such as the successful completion of specific tasks, and long-term goals, such as the maintenance of effective relations among work groups, departments, etc. According to Astin (1964), the construct "performance" is nothing more than a verbal abstraction of the relevant goals or the outcomes desired; the set of possible criterion measures would include any observable index or state which is judged relevant to the construct. Thus, it is possible to define the domain of performance and to indicate the set of behaviors that are included in that domain. *The performance domain is defined here as the set of behaviors that are relevant to the goals of the organization or the organizational unit in which a person works.*

In order to specify the range of behaviors that define performance, one would have to know the relevant goals of the organization. Note here that the global set of goals that define the overall effectiveness of the organization (e.g., maximize after-tax profits) are not as relevant as the set of goals which are defined for an incumbent in a specific position within the organization. That is, the organization defines a set of goals to be met by incumbents in each job, and these goals may vary considerably from job to job, or across different levels in the organization. This is particularly true when specific task goals are considered, but it is also true for several nontask goals. For example, one goal that is likely to be broadly relevant, but which is not tied to any specific task, is that incumbents must maintain effective interpersonal relations with their coworkers and with other organizational members with whom they interact. The type and extent of these interpersonal contacts will vary across departments and across levels of management. One might infer that the skills and behaviors that contribute to successful maintenance of interpersonal relations will vary from job to job. Nevertheless, for the great majority of jobs, this general class of behaviors is likely to represent one aspect of effective performance.

As the relevant goals of organizations and of organizational units differ, it may not be possible to draw up a *completely* general definition of the dimensions of job performance. Nevertheless, there are enough broad similarities in organizational goals and in job demands to justify a framework that is relevant for defining performance in a large class of jobs. For example, the performance dimensions that are relevant for describing skilled craft jobs (e.g., electrician, plumber) would vary in some of their specifics, but would probably show considerable communality.

The framework developed by Murphy (in press) suggests that the performance domain for most jobs contains at least four clusters of behaviors: (a) task-oriented behaviors, (b) interpersonally oriented behaviors, (c) down-time behaviors (e.g., absenteeism), and (d) destructive/hazardous behaviors. The performance domain for specific jobs may include other clusters of behaviors, but the four defined here will always be represented in a complete definition of performance. This fact has two clear implications. First, performance includes output variables (task-oriented behaviors), input variables (down-time and destructive/hazardous behaviors), and variables that cannot be clearly classified as inputs or outputs (interpersonal relations). Second, there are many strategies that might be used to increase performance. Some interventions, such as financial incentives, are likely to increase the time and effort spent on essential job tasks. Others, such as work rescheduling, are likely to reduce down-time behaviors. Interventions such as sociotechnical system redesign may primarily affect interpersonal relations on the job.

Interventions that concentrate solely on one part of the performance domain (e.g., using incentives to increase time spent producing goods and services) may run the risk of *lowering* overall performance by adversely affecting other aspects of performance. For example, some organizations use computers to monitor the time spent on specific tasks by clerical and production workers. Workers find this sort of monitoring stressful and aversive. Although this system may lead to short-term gains in output, it is also possible that it will lead to strained relations between workers and management, absenteeism, turnover, grievances, and stress-related illness in the workforce. Similarly, using ability tests in selection may result in hiring workers whose output is higher, but who are more likely to be dissatisfied with jobs that are not challenging, more likely to leave the organization, or more difficult to supervise than their less able colleagues.

Relating Performance to Productivity

The question of *how* psychological interventions affect productivity (increasing output, decreasing input, or both) is critical, but has not been examined in depth (Feldman, 1983). Research on the utility (productivity gains) associated with selection tests has barely considered the problem. The underlying model—that ability leads to performance, which leads to productivity—begs the question of what is meant by increased performance. If we accept the widely-held assumption that job performance is multidimensional, (Bass, 1982; Dunnette, 1963; Pickle & Friedlander, 1967; Roman & Prien, 1966: Schmidt & Kaplan, 1971; Seashore, 1975), there are many ways that performance could be increased, not all of which have the same implications for productivity. Is performance synonymous with task accomplishment (output), with reduced absenteeism (input), or with fewer mistakes (both input and output)? It would be very useful to know precisely what a good performer does that a poor performer fails to do. Without answering this question (which will be taken up later), it is unlikely that we will ever understand the nature of the link between an intervention such as selection testing and productivity.

If performance *is* multidimensional, it is likely that an intervention will have simultaneous effects on different aspects of job performance. Little attention has been given to the problem of integrating these multiple effects in a way that meaningfully relates to the definition of productivity. For example, Guzzo et al. (1985) examined the effects of psychological interventions on both inputs and outputs, but failed to fully consider how these effects are combined to affect productivity. In their analysis, the effects of interventions on output, withdrawals, and disruptions were averaged to estimate the aggregate effect of each intervention on productivity. The problem with this approach can be illustrated by considering the effect of an intervention that leads to a 20% increase in output and a 30% decrease in input costs. An averaging model would incorrectly indicate that such an intervention would lead to a 25% productivity increase. Because the typical definition of productivity implies a multiplicative model rather than an averaging model, the best estimate of the effects of that intervention is that it will lead to a 58% increase in productivity. (i.e., if output increases by 20% and input costs increase by 30%, input/output will increase by 58%).

Understanding precisely how the characteristics and the behaviors of individuals in organizations change when an intervention such as selection testing, goal setting, or sociotechnical system redesign is introduced is important for both theoretical and practical reasons. The theoretical importance is fairly obvious; we need to clearly understand central concepts such as performance and productivity before we can understand their relationship. The question is also practically important, since the design and evaluation of intervention efforts might depend greatly on whether the intervention is targeted toward reducing input costs or increasing the value of outputs. The question of which intervention works best might depend on the degree to which the organizational context favors changing inputs or changing outputs. The most widely researched intervention (i.e., ability tests) are designed to increase output, but this strategy is unlikely to work in a setting such as an assembly line, since the pace of production is not determined by individual output levels. A better strategy here would be to develop interventions that reduce output costs (e.g., absenteeism).

The key to understanding productivity interventions is to develop a clear understanding of the construct "job performance." At the most fundamental level, all of the interventions discussed earlier can be viewed as programmatic efforts to increase the performance of workers and managers. Performance is not, however, a unitary variable. Performance is multifaceted, includes both input and output variables, and may be defined differently depending on the context in which an individual works. Thus, the statement "job performance will increase if you apply intervention X" refers to a complexly determined outcome. There are many ways in which performance on a given job could increase or decrease. To understand the precise impact of programs designed to increase performance and productivity, it is necessary to examine in some detail the domain we refer to under the heading of "job performance."

DESIGNING EFFECTIVE INTERVENTIONS

The effectiveness of an intervention depends on its impact on the entire array of behaviors that comprise the performance domain. The definition of productivity suggests that the traditional univariate approach to assessing economic gains (i.e. the Cronbach-Gleser model) is insufficient. Assessment must be multivariate, and at a minimum must consider the impact of any intervention on both input costs and output value. The design of an effective intervention must also consider both of these variables. First, examples are presented of ways that input costs and output values might be considered in assessing interventions. Second, strategies for designing optimally effective interventions are discussed.

Guzzo, Jette, and Katzell's (1985) analysis provides estimates of the effects of several interventions on outputs and on two input variables (withdrawals and disruptions); the results of this analysis are shown in Table 8.1. In order to translate these effect size estimates into productivity estimates, both the numerator and the denominator of the productivity ratio must be expressed in comparable units. This is most easily done by estimating the standard deviation (SD) of each of the three dependent variables employed by Guzzo et al. (1985). Since d

TABLE 8.1
Effective Size (d) for Eleven Psychological Interventions

	Output	Withdrawal	Disruptions	Composite
Selection/placement	$-^a$	-.03	--	-.03
Training	.85	.63	.56	.78
Appraisal and feedback	.41	.18	1.43	.35
Management by objective	.45	-.01	-.31	.12
Goal setting	.65	.10	1.68	.75
Financial incentives	2.12	.34	--	.57
Work redesign	.52	.28	--	.42
Decision making	.70	--	--	.70
Supervisory methods	.51	.11	--	.13
Work rescheduling	.30	.10	--	.21
Socio-technical systems	.66	.19	--	.62
Overall	.63	.13	.82	.44

^{a}Insufficient data for effect size estimation.

measures the size of effects in standard deviation units, expressing all *SD*s in comparable units allows us to meaningfully combine and compare these effects. For the purpose of illustration, assume that an average worker produces goods and services valued at $25,000 in a year, and that the total cost of production averages $22,000 per worker per year. Using the 40% rule (Schmidt & Hunter, 1983), it would be reasonable to estimate the standard deviation of output to be $10,000 per year. No simple methods exist for estimating the *SD* of withdrawal or disruptions. Note, however, that absenteeism, lateness, accidents, etc. are low base-rate behaviors. The *SD* for these variables should therefore be considerably smaller than for output. I have arbitrarily chosen figures of $2,200 and $1,100 per year for the *SD* of withdrawal and disruptions, respectively. These figures represent 10% and 5% (respectively) of the average cost of output. If there is no intervention, productivity is defined by the ratio of output value to input costs, which in this example is equal to 1.13 ($25,000/$22,000). The effects of interventions on productivity must be evaluated in reference to this figure.

Using these figures, together with data from Guzzo et al. (1985), the effects of four productivity improvement programs are estimated: (a) selection, using cognitive ability tests, (b) training, (c) appraisal and feedback, and (d) goal setting. The set of field experiments reviewed by Guzzo et al. (1985) did not provide sufficient data for estimating the effect of selection testing on output, and provided limited evidence regarding the effect of testing on withdrawal. Drawing on data presented in Hunter and Hunter (1984) and in Mowday, Porter, and Steers (1982), *d* values for the effect of selection testing on output, withdrawal and disruptions were estimated to be 1.0, .10, and .00, respectively.

Table 8.2 illustrates the way in which these four interventions would affect productivity. To illustrate how these figures are derived, consider the case of selection. Personnel selection is likely to lead to an increase in output of $10,000 per worker; in this case, the increase is equal to the value of one standard

TABLE 8.2
Effects of Interventions on Productivity

Assume: Average worker produces $25,000 in goods
Average cost per worker is $22,000
S.D. of output value is $10,000
S.D. of withdrawal costs is $2,200
S.D of disruption costs is $1,100

Therefore, without interventions, output/input = 1.13

		Effect Sizes			
	Output	Withdrawal	Disruptions	Output/ Input	Percent Increases
Selection	1.00	.10	.00	1.60	41%
Training	.85	.63	.56	1.67	47%
Appraisal and feedback	.41	.18	1.43	1.45	28%
Goal setting	.65	.10	1.68	1.57	39%

deviation unit (i.e., $d = 1.00$). Selection will result in a decrease in withdrawal equivalent to $1/10$ of a standard deviation (i.e., $d = .10$). Since the standard deviation of withdrawal costs is $2,200, the average decrease in costs per person is $220. Because selection has no effect on disruptions (i.e., $d = 0.00$), we do not need to consider costs associated with this variable. Thus, we expect the value of output to go from $25,000 to $35,000 per person as the result of selection. We also expect costs to go from $22,000 to $21,780 (i.e., $22,000–$220). The ratio of costs to outputs is therefore $35,000/$21,780, or 1.60.

The figures shown in Table 8.2 suggest that selection, training, feedback, and goal setting are all effective, and would lead to productivity increases of 41%, 47%, 28%, and 39%, respectively. It is useful to note that the specific effects of these interventions were quite different. Feedback resulted in a very substantial drop in disruptions ($d = 1.43$) and a somewhat modest rise in output ($d = .41$). Selection testing resulted in a substantial rise in output ($d = 1.00$), and a somewhat trivial drop in input costs. Training, which was estimated here (given the assumptions made about SD values) to be the most effective intervention, had moderate to large effects on input costs *and* on output.

Throughout this paper, I have noted that the optimal intervention may be one that increases output *and* decreases input costs; the analyses discussed earlier illustrate how this might come about. It is useful, then, to speculate on the type of intervention that is most likely to reach this goal.

Interventions that increase workers' commitment to and identification with the job and the organization would seem particularly promising. It could be argued that workers who identify with the job will have lower levels of absenteeism and other disruptions *and* higher levels of output (Mowday et al., 1982). The hypothesis that this sort of intervention will be highly effective is difficult to test, since effective programs for increasing worker commitment are hard to institute. However, it is useful to note that the popular literature on corporate culture clearly reflects the belief that employee identification with the organization is one of the keys to high productivity.

An alternative strategy for designing effective interventions is to use several interventions together, each of which is targeted toward a specific outcome variable of interest. For example, the use of cognitive ability tests in selection or placement is quite likely to increase output in almost all jobs (Hunter & Hunter, 1984). Combining ability tests with other interventions that reduce input costs might be a particularly effective strategy for increasing productivity. For example, a program that combined testing, training, and goal setting might be highly effective in increasing outputs, reducing withdrawal, *and* reducing disruptions (see Table 8.1).

Guzzo et al.'s (1985) analysis points to some clear directions for future research in constructing composite programs (e.g., testing, plus training, plus goal setting) designed to enhance productivity. Many interventions are quite effective in increasing outputs and decreasing disruptions (Table 8.1 shows mean d values of .63 and .82, respectively), but few methods have been shown to be effective in reducing withdrawal behaviors (mean $d = 13$). The development of effective programs to reduce withdrawal behaviors might be one of the keys to future progress in enhancing productivity in organizations. Some of the issues involved in this effort can be illustrated by considering the history of attempts to reduce absenteeism.

Reducing Absenteeism

Absenteeism is recognized as a major drain on the productivity of organizations, one that has increased steadily since World War II (Chadwick-Jones, Nicholson, & Brown, 1982). According to some estimates, approximately 2–4% of the American workforce is absent on a given day. Steers and Rhodes (1978) estimated the cost of absenteeism at $24.6 billion per year. This estimate is nearly 10 years old; the current figure is undoubtably higher.

Research on the prevention of absenteeism has been disorganized and disappointing. In part, this is because there are well over 40 definitions of absenteeism in the literature (Gaudet, 1963), and different measures of absenteeism show little, if any, correlation (Landy & Farr, 1983). The conceptual model that has guided most efforts to reduce absenteeism has also been criticized. This model suggests that absenteeism is a function of the individual worker's motivation to attend and his or her ability to attend (Mowday et al., 1982). Nicholson, Brown, and Chadwick-Jones (1976, 1977) have shown that the central prediction of this model, that absenteeism is negatively correlated with job satisfaction, is not correct. Rather, it appears that individual attitudes have little effect on absenteeism. It is no wonder that programs designed to increase job satisfaction and work motivation have failed to reduce absenteeism.

Chadwick-Jones et al. (1982) suggested that absenteeism is governed primarily by the norms of the workgroup and the organization, rather than by the attitudes or motives of the individual (see also Steers & Rhodes, 1984). Their research suggests that absenteeism is a complex form of social exchange between work groups and management. Viewed from this framework, the most effective interventions for decreasing absenteeism will likely involve redefining the absence culture or renegotiating absence norms.

It is worth noting that efforts to decrease absenteeism involve a variety of costs, some of which may be hard to express in dollar terms. For example, shop floor workers may use absenteeism to restore equity with executives and managers, who have highly flexible work schedules (Chadwick-Jones et al., 1982). An organization that wishes to reduce absenteeism on the shop floor may find it necessary to restrict the flexibility of the schedules of managers and executives. Programs designed to increase output have typically ignored costs, which are often trivial. Programs designed to reduce absenteeism may involve such fundamental changes in the organization that top management does not regard the productivity gain associated with reducing absenteeism as worthwhile.

IS PRODUCTIVITY WORTHWHILE?

Since 1979 there has been a steady stream of research documenting the cost effectiveness of psychological interventions in organizations, and suggesting that the savings associated with these programs could run into billions of dollars (e.g., Hunter & Hunter, 1984; Hunter & Schmidt, 1982). Given the nationwide obsession with productivity improvement and the documented effectiveness of a wide variety of interventions, it is somewhat surprising that industry is *not* beating a path to psychologists' doors.

The preceding discussion on absenteeism highlights an aspect of productivity improvement programs that is often ignored. These programs may have negative side effects or may involve costs that the organization is unwilling to incur. These costs are not necessarily financial; many interventions might involve a change in fundamental aspects of the organization, such as the amount of time discretion that is available at different levels in the hierarchy. The question of whether the gains associated with productivity improvement programs are likely to exceed their costs deserves serious consideration.

The financial benefits of productivity improvement programs are likely to exceed the dollar value of the time and resources invested in those programs (Hunter & Hunter, 1984). In part, this is because the costs per person of productivity improvement programs are typically low, and decrease further as the number of persons involved increases (output, on the other hand, increases as N increases). It is not clear whether the nonfinancial costs of productivity improvement programs are so easily offset by productivity gains.

Nonfinancial costs can be grouped into three categories: (a) changes in the worker, (b) changes in work methods, and (c) changes in the relationships between organizational levels. For example, selecting workers on the basis of cognitive ability and training them in complex technologies may result in a pool of smart, highly skilled workers who are more difficult to manage and more susceptible to dissatisfaction and turnover than would occur without testing and training. Redesigning jobs to add responsibility, variety, and autonomy may result in difficulty in forecasting, scheduling, and coordinating the work of different individuals or departments. Changes in relationships among organizational levels may represent an important source of nonfinancial costs that prevent many organizations from implementing productivity improvement programs.

In the 1960s and 70s, there was considerable interest in behavioral science interventions designed to increase workplace democracy and the quality of working life (Davis & Cherns, 1975; Hill, 1971). Two features of this literature are noteworthy. First, these interventions appeared to increase productivity. Second, these interventions involved power sharing. That is, they typically involved increasing the power and discretion of lower levels of the organization at the expense of higher levels in the organization. Interest in these sorts of interventions has declined dramatically in the last 10–15 years. One possible explanation for this decline is that management does not feel that a *probable* gain in productivity is worth a *certain* loss in power and discretion.

The marked asymmetry between the probable causes of and the proposed cures for low productivity may reflect the role of nonfinancial costs in choosing among productivity improvement programs. It is likely that the low productivity of American industry is largely the fault of inept management (Schmidt, 1983); yet, most productivity improvement programs are aimed at changing the behavior of labor (Tuttle, 1983). One hypothesis that would account for this discrepancy is that nonfinancial costs of programs that may change the way in which top management behaves are highly salient to those individuals who decide what programs to implement or cancel.

Prospect theory (Kahneman & Tversky, 1979) provides a powerful tool for understanding the potential impact of costs (financial and nonfinancial) on decisions regarding productivity improvement programs. The theory suggests that: (a) people undervalue gains and overvalue losses; and (b) *certain* gains and losses receive more extreme values than corresponding probable gains or losses. Thus, a loss of $10 is more negative than a gain of $10 is positive. A certain loss of $10 is worse than a 50% chance of losing $20. This theory suggests that management might decide not to implement a productivity improvement program even if the expected benefits exceed the costs. In fact, the expected value of uncertain benefits must exceed certain costs by a substantial amount before management is likely to adopt the program. Because benefits are largely financial, the differential between expected benefits and financial costs of a program (adjusted for certainty effects and differences in slopes of the cost and gain curves) provides an index of the costs associated with nonfinancial outcomes. Thus, if management adopts a program for which the adjusted annual gains are $200,000 more than financial costs, it is reasonable to assume that nonfinancial costs (e.g., loss of power and discretion of managers) are judged to be worth less than $200,000.

THE SCIENCE AND PRACTICE OF
PRODUCTIVITY ENHANCEMENT

At first glance, research on the effects of psychology-based interventions on productivity seems like a perfect marriage of science and practice. That is, practitioners' concerns over demonstrating the financial impact of different personnel practices contributed to scientists' interest in assessing financial gains. Scientists, in turn, were able to produce data that suggest that psychological interventions are highly practical, and can have a marked influence on productivity. I will argue for the opposite point of view, that productivity research represents one of the outstanding *failures* to effectively combine science and practice.

One complaint that can be directed at much of this research is that it is bad science. This is apparent if the hallmarks of rigorous science are considered. These would include clear specification of the constructs involved, good operational measures of these constructs, and a well-developed theory linking these constructs. None of these characteristics are present in the body of research on job performance and productivity. Although many studies of productivity have been published, there has been little attempt to understand the constructs involved or the processes that link them. As I noted earlier, the question of which behaviors change as a result of productivity-improvement programs has rarely, if ever, been addressed in a serious way. Thus, there has been a great deal of research on *what* happens as the result of interventions, but little research on *why* it happens.

The second complaint that can be directed at this research is that it is bad practice. This research has led researchers and practitioners to make statements about the benefits of psychology-based interventions that are either incorrect or incomplete. For example, Murphy's (1986) research suggests that the most widely quoted estimates of productivity gain are inflated by 30–80% as the result of a failure to fully consider the decisions of job applicants and incumbents. Formulas that are used to predict the effects of interventions on the financial state of the firm rarely take into account even the rudiments of accounting (Boudreau, 1983a; Cronshaw & Alexander, 1985; see, however, Hunter, Schmidt, & Coggin, 1988). Murphy and Cleveland (1990) suggested that the current rush to estimate the financial impact of psychological interventions may even *reduce* the credibility of these estimates. The psychologist who claims that an intervention will lead to savings in the millions of dollars, but who has clearly failed to take into account such obvious issues as the time value of money, the tax rate, the potential return on alternative investments, or the frequency with which interventions do not go exactly as planned will not be credible. Inaccurate estimates of productivity gain are likely to be seen by managers as self-serving guesswork, and the failure to deliver the promised millions could set back the cause of applied psychology in that organization for some time to come.

What steps can be taken to better integrate science and practice in this area? Guzzo (1988) suggested that, first, we need more theory development. Researchers must specify in much more detail what they mean by performance and productivity, and how their interventions are linked to these two constructs. Second, organizations need to take a different perspective toward productivity research. A myopic focus on the bottom line clearly does the science of applied psychology no good; psychology is the science of behavior, not the science of profit. One can argue that in the long run, a myopic focus on the bottom line does the *organization* no good. The bottom line frequently implies a focus on short-term gains, but many productivity improvement programs are designed for long-term changes in the organization. What we need is organizations that are willing to ask not only *what* works, but also *why* and *under what circumstances* it works. Guzzo suggested that productivity researchers will have to be concerned simultaneously with science and practice, and must balance academic and managerial roles to be truly effective.

Guzzo also suggested several directions that we should *not* pursue if our goal is to unify science and practice. First, the temptation to form an overarching, multidisciplinary theory of productivity is to be avoided. Different disciplines have different things to offer in this area, and we should not be reluctant to stick to our psychological roots. Second, we must not get sidetracked in discussions of what is the *real* definition of either performance or productivity. The psychologist who works with those constructs should certainly specify what he or she means by them, but there is no single definition of either that is clearly preferable to all others.

Although the present link between science and practice in this area is weak and tenuous, there *are* reasons for optimism. First, I/O researchers are paying more attention to theory development, which is likely to increase the scientific value of productivity research. Second, there have been rapid developments in the sophistication of models used to predict the extent and value of the productivity increase that is likely to result from an intervention (Boudreau, 1983b; Boudreau & Berger, 1985; Boudreau & Ryncs, 1985; Cronshaw & Alexander, 1985). Future estimates of productivity gains are likely to be more accurate than the estimates that dominate the current literature in applied psychology. Third, it is now apparent that many interventions designed to improve productivity work, and that they can result in substantial gains for the organization. Organizations may become increasingly willing to apply what productivity researchers have learned.

ACKNOWLEDGMENTS

Preparation of this chapter was partially supported by U.S. Army Research Office and Battelle Laboratories contract DAAG 29-81-D-0100. The author thanks George Thornton, Jeanette Cleveland, and Theresa Philbin for their comments.

REFERENCES

Alluisi, E. A., & Meigs, D. K. (1983). Potentials for productivity enhancement from psychological research and development. *American Psychologist, 38,* 487–493.

Astin, A. (1964). Criterion-centered research. *Educational and Psychological Measurement, 24,* 807–822.

Bass, B. (1982). Individual capability, team performance, and team productivity. In M. Dunnette & E. Fleishman (Eds.), *Human performance and productivity: Human capability assessment.* Hillsdale, NJ: Lawrence Erlbaum Associates.

Bialek, H., Zapf, D., & McGuire, W. (1977, June). *Personnel turbulence and time utilization in an infantry division* (Hum RRO FR-WD-CA 77-11). Alexandria, VA: Human Resources Research Organization.

Bobko, P., Karren, R., & Parkington, J. J. (1983). The estimation of standard deviations in utility analyses: An empirical test. *Journal of Applied Psychology, 68,* 170–176.

Boudreau, J. W. (1983a). Economic considerations in estimating the utility of human resource productivity improvement programs. *Personnel Psychology, 36,* 551–576.

Boudreau, J. W. (1983b). Effects of employee flows on utility analysis of human resource productivity improvement programs. *Journal of Applied Psychology, 68,* 396–406.

Boudreau, J. W., & Berger, C. J. (1985). Decision-Theoretic utility analysis applied to employee separations and acquisitions. *Journal of Applied Psychology, 70,* 581–612.

Boudreau, J. W., & Rynes, S. L. (1985). Role of recruitment in staffing utility analysis. *Journal of Applied Psychology, 70,* 354–366.

Brief, A. P. (1984). *Productivity research in the behavioral and social sciences.* New York: Praeger.

Brogden, H. E., & Taylor, E. K. (1950). The dollar criterion-applying the cost accounting concept to criterion construction. *Personnel Psychology, 3,* 133–154.

Campbell, J. (1983). Some possible implications of "modeling" for the conceptualization of measurement. In F. Landy, S. Zedeck, & J. Cleveland (Eds.), *Performance measurement and theory.* Hillsdale, NJ: Lawrence Erlbaum Associates.

Campbell, J., & Campbell, R. (1988a). Industrial organizational psychology and productivity: The goodness of fit. In J. Campbell & R. Campbell (Eds.), *Productivity in organizations.* San Francisco: Jossey-Bass.

Campbell, J., & Campbell, R. (1988b). *Productivity in organizations.* San Francisco: Jossey-Bass.

Campbell, J., Dunnette, M., Lawler, E., & Weick, K. (1970). *Managerial behavior, performance and effectiveness.* New York: McGraw-Hill.

Cascio, W. F. (1987a). *Applied psychology in personnel management* (3rd ed.). Englewood Cliffs, NJ: Prentice-Hall.

Cascio, W. F. (1987b). *Costing human resources: The financial impact of behavior in organizations* (2nd ed.). Boston: Kent.

Cascio, W. F., & Ramos, R. A. (1986). Development and application of a new method for assessing job performance in behavioral/economic terms. *Journal of Applied Psychology, 71,* 20–28.

Chadwick-Jones, J. K., Nicholson, N., & Brown, C. (1982). *Social psychology of absenteeism.* New York: Praeger.

Christal, R. E. (1974). *The United States Air Force occupational research project.* (AFHRL-TR-73-75). Lackland AFB, TX: USAF, AFHRL, Occupational Research Division.

Cronbach, L. J., & Gleser, G. C. (1965). *Psychological tests and personnel decisions* (2nd ed.). Urbana: University of Illinois Press.

Cronshaw, S. F., & Alexander, R. A. (1985). One answer to the demand for accountability: Selection utility as an investment decision. *Organizational Behavior and Human Decision Processes, 35,* 102–118.

Davis, L. E., & Cherns, A. B. (1975). *The quality of working life. Vol. 2.* New York: The Free Press.

Dunnette, M. (1963). A note on the criterion. *Journal of Applied Psychology, 47,* 251–254.

Feldman, J. M. (1983). Problems and prospects of organizational interventions. In K. Rowland & G. Ferris (Eds.), *Research in personnel and human resources management. Vol. 1.* Greenwich, CT: JAI Press.

Gaudet, F. J. (1963). *Solving the problems of employee absence.* New York: American Management Association.

Guzzo, R. A. (1988). Productivity research in review. In J. Campbell & R. Campbell (Eds.), *Productivity in organizations.* San Francisco: Jossey-Bass.

Guzzo, R. A., Jette, R. D., & Katzell, R. A. (1985). The effects of psychologically-based intervention programs on worker productivity. *Personnel Psychology, 38,* 275–293.

Hill, P. (1971). *Towards a new philosophy of management.* New York: Harper & Row.

Hunter, J. E., & Hunter, R. F. (1984). Validity and utility of alternative predictors of job performance. *Psychological Bulletin, 96,* 72–98.

Hunter, J. E., & Schmidt, F. L. (1982). Fitting people to jobs: The impact of personnel selection on national productivity. In M. Dunnette & E. Fleishman (Eds.), *Human performance and productivity: Human capability assessment.* Hillsdale, NJ: Lawrence Erlbaum Associates.

Hunter, J. E., & Schmidt, F. L. (1983). Quantifying the effects of psychological intervention on employee job performance and work-force productivity. *American Psychologist, 38,* 473–478.

Hunter, J. E., Schmidt, F. L. & Coggin, T. (1988). Problems and pitfalls of using capital budgeting and financial accounting techniques in assessing the utility of personnel programs. *Journal of Applied Psychology, 73,* 522–528.

James, L. (1973). Criterion models and construct validity for criteria. *Psychological Bulletin, 87,* 72–107.

Kahneman, D., & Tversky, A. (1979). Prospect theory: An analysis of decision under risk. *Econometrica, 47,* 263–291.

Katzell, R. A., & Guzzo, R. A. (1983). Psychological approaches to productivity improvement. *American Psychologist, 38,* 468–472.

Kopelman, R. A. (1986). *Managing productivity in organizations: A practical, people-oriented perspective.* New York: McGraw-Hill.

Landy, F. J., & Farr, J. L. (1980). Performance rating. *Psychological Bulletin, 87,* 72–107.

Landy, F. J., & Farr, J. L. (1983). *The measurement of work performance: Methods, theory and applications.* New York: Academic Press.

Landy, F. J., Farr, J. L., & Jacobs, R. (1982). Utility concepts in performance measurement. *Organizational Behavior and Human Performance, 30,* 15–40.

Landy, F. J., Zedeck, S., & Cleveland, J. N. (1983). *Performance measurement and theory.* Hillsdale, NJ: Lawrence Erlbaum Associates.

Latham, G. P., & Napier, N. K. (1984). Practical ways to increase employee attendance. In P. Goodman, R. Atkin, & Associates (Eds.). *Absenteeism.* San Francisco: Jossey-Bass.

Mahoney, T. (1988). Productivity defined: The relativity of efficiency, effectiveness, and change. In J. Campbell & R. Campbell (Eds.), *Productivity in organizations.* San Francisco: Jossey-Bass.

Mathieu, J. E., & Leonard, R. L., Jr. (1987). Applying utility concepts to a training program in supervisory skills: A time-based approach. *Academy of Management Journal, 30,* 316–335.

Mowday, R. T., Porter, L. W., & Steers, R. M. (1982). *Employee-Organization linkages: The psychology of committment, absenteeism, and turnover.* New York: Academic Press.

Muckler, F. A. (1982). Evaluating productivity. In M. Dunnette & E. Fleishman (Eds.), *Human performance and productivity: Human capability assessment.* Hillsdale, NJ: Lawrence Erlbaum Associates.

Murphy, K. R. (1986). When your top choice turns you down: Effect of rejected offers on the utility of selection tests. *Psychological Bulletin, 99,* 133–138.

Murphy, K. R. (in Press). Dimensions of job performance. In R. Dillon (Ed.), *Progress in testing and training. Vol. 1.* New York: Academic Press.

Murphy, K. R., & Cleveland, J. N. (1990). *Performance appraisal: An organizational perspective.* Boston: Allyn & Bacon.

National Academy of Science (1979). *Measurement and interpretation of productivity.* Washington, D.C.: Author.

Nicholson, N., Brown, C. A., & Chadwick-Jones (1976). Absence from work and job satisfaction. *Journal of Applied Psychology, 61,* 728–737.

Nicholson, N., Brown, C. A., & Chadwick-Jones (1977). Absence from work and personal characteristics. *Journal of Applied Psychology, 62,* 319–327.

Pearlman, K., Schmidt, F. L., & Hunter, J. E. (1980). Validity generalization results for tests used to predict job proficiency and training success in clerical occupations. *Journal of Applied Psychology, 65,* 373–406.

Perloff, R., & Nelson, S. D. (1983). Economic productivity and the behavioral sciences. *American Psychologist, 38,* 451–453.

Pickle, H., & Freidlander, F. (1967). Seven societal criteria of organizational success. *Personnel Psychology, 20,* 165–178.

Ronan, W. W., & Prien, E. P. (1966). *Toward a criterion theory: A review and analysis of research and opinion.* Greensboro, NC: The Richardson Foundation.

Sands, W. A. (1973). A method for evaluating alternative recruiting—selection strategies. The CAPER model, *Journal of Applied Psychology, 57,* 222–227.

Schmidt, F. L. (1983). Alternative theories: A reply to Goldman. In F. Landy, S. Zedeck, & J. Cleveland (Eds.), *Performance measurement and theory.* Hillsdale, NJ: Lawrence Erlbaum Associates.

Schmidt, F. L., & Hunter, J. E. (1977). Development of a general solution to the problem of validity generalization. *Journal of Applied Psychology, 62,* 529–540.

Schmidt, F. L., & Hunter, J. E. (1981). Employment testing: Old theories and new research findings. *American Psychologist, 36,* 1128–1137.

Schmidt, F. L., & Hunter, J. E. (1983). Individual differences in productivity. An empirical test of the estimate derived from studies of selection procedure utility. *Journal of Applied Psychology, 68,* 407–414.

Schmidt, F. L., Hunter, J. E., McKenzie, R. C., & Muldrow, T. W. (1979). Impact of valid selection procedures on work-force productivity. *Journal of Applied Psychology, 64,* 609–626.

Schmidt, F. L., & Hunter, J. E., & Outerbridge, A. N. (1986). Impact of job experience and ability on job knowledge, work sample performance, and supervisory ratings of job performance. *Journal of Applied Psychology, 71,* 432–439.

Schmidt, F. L., & Kaplan, L. B. (1971). Composite vs. multiple criteria: A review and resolution of the controversy. *Personnel Psychology, 24,* 419–434.

Schmidt, F. L., Mack, M. J., & Hunter, J. E. (1984). Selection utility in the occupation of U.S. park ranger for three modes of test use. *Journal of Applied Psychology, 69,* 490–497.

Seashore, S. (1975). Defining and measuring the quality of working life. In L. Davis & A. Cherns (Eds.), *The quality of working life* (Vol. 1). New York: The Free Press.

Smith, P. C. (1976). Behaviors, results, and organizational effectiveness: The problem of criteria. In M. Dunnette (Ed.), *Handbook of industrial and organizational psychology.* Chicago: Rand McNally.

Staw, B. M. (1980). The consequences of turnover. *Journal of Occupational Behavior, 1*, 253–273.

Steers, R. M., & Rhodes, S. R. (1978). Major influences on employee attendance: A process model. *Journal of Applied Psychology, 63*, 391–407.

Sutermeister, R. A. (1976). *People and productivity.* New York: McGraw-Hill.

Tuttle, T. C. (1983). Organizational productivity: A challenge for psychologists. *American Psychologist, 38*, 479–486.

III

SCIENCE AND PRACTICE IN ORGANIZATIONAL PSYCHOLOGY

This section focuses on the second major subdiscipline of I/O psychology, often referred to simply as organizational psychology. Unlike personnel psychology, which relies on specific, human resources procedures and techniques and is still relatively devoid of theory, organizational psychology encompasses topics that are broader, more abstract, and (so far, at least) more amenable to theoretical development. In addition to such obviously relevant topics as organizational design, change and theory, organizational psychology addresses work motivation and satisfaction, job involvement, organizational commitment, and leadership. This subfield of I/O psychology also concerns itself with issues that pertain to the psychological environments that characterize organizations—their climates and cultures. Because of its pervasiveness and enormous potential to affect workers' behaviors, the psychological environment within organizations is the common thread that connects the four chapters in this section.

In Chapter 9, Walt Freytag takes a detailed look at the construct we now label "organizational culture," paying particular attention to how such culture evolves, the nature and some of the manifestations of its content, and some of the strategies for assessing the culture of an organization. In Chapter 10, Robert Baron examines a phenomenon that can influence and be influenced by an organization's culture—organizational conflict—and focuses on the major causes of and some of the dominant strategies for managing this challenging organizational phenomenon. Chapter 11 deals with another issue that almost certainly has a reciprocal relationship with organizational culture and climate—sexual harassment; Frank Saal's program of research suggests that interpersonal misperceptions may play an important role in some of the more common forms of sexual harassment in organizations. Finally, Chapter 12 is devoted to another highly salient and controversial organizational topic—drug abuse and drug testing in the workplace; Larry Reid, Kevin Murphy and Douglas Reynolds examine drug addiction and screening, and the implications of these phenomena for organizational (and individual) well-being.

As in Section II, each of these chapters deals not only with a specific issue that pertains to an organization's psychological environment, but also includes an analysis of the contributions of the scientist-practitioner model to our present understanding of that issue (or lack of such contributions), and some prognostication concerning the potential of the model to contribute to future understanding. Such analyses speak directly to the viability of the scientist-practitioner model as a guide for the science and practice of I/O psychology.

Before we move on to the chapters of this section, we'd like to point out similarities and contrasts between the chapters in Section II and Section III. First the contrasts. As we already noted, the topics covered in Section III are broader, more abstract, and more highly developed in a theoretical sense than those included in Section II. Because they are more abstract, their influence on individuals in organizations is less immediate, and therefore less clearly recognizable. A worker participates in an assessment center or a performance appraisal process, and some of the results are readily discernible—one is or is not hired, promoted, awarded a salary increase. The ways in which one is affected by the culture or climate of an organization, however, are far more diffuse and less immediate; many workers may never consciously consider the psychological climate that characterizes the organization in which they work. So, there are differences . . .

But, more importantly, there are basic similarities, too. Direct or indirect, obvious or obscure, the fact is that all of the topics discussed in these two sections are known to have profound effects on workers' feelings about their jobs and the levels at which they perform those jobs. Further, and of particular relevance to this book, we believe the scientist-practitioner model has played, and will continue to play a vital role in our quest to understand all of these diverse organizational phenomena.

9 Organizational Culture

Walter R. Freytag
Advanced Technology Laboratories

The concept of organizational culture is certainly not new. Indeed, in a recent article in *Fortune,* Clemens (1986) traced the concept back to a speech made by Pericles in 431 B.C. at the funeral of an Athenian soldier. Yet, the concept of organizational culture did not receive much attention from organizational researchers or practitioners until the 1980s. Now, however, one can hardly pick up a business periodical without seeing an article devoted to the subject. For example, a recent article in the *Wall Street Journal* discussed the "rigid" culture at IBM but praised it for the loyalty it breeds (Kneale, 1986). Another report stated that a key element of the turnaround strategy of Scott Paper's CEO is to ensure that the company's culture is aligned with its strategy (Milne, 1988). The problems encountered by Johnson & Johnson as it attempts to go "from Band-Aids to high tech" have also been reported (Changing a Corporate Culture, 1984). There are numerous additional examples that could be cited; clearly the topic of organizational culture is an important one in the business news today.

But the interest in this topic goes beyond mere reporting. Indeed, organizations are systematically studying their cultures and actively attempting to modify them. For example, Hewlett-Packard is attempting to align its organizational culture with its business objectives, and it is trying to use its human resource management strategy to shape its culture (Harris, 1984). Both Simplot Company, a major producer of french fries for McDonald's, and BankAmerica Corp. are attempting to modify their cultures to increase the entrepreneurial spirit exhibited by their employees (Wilkins & Patterson, 1985).

There are various reasons for this relatively newfound interest in organizational culture. Practitioners assume that organizational culture is important because it has an impact upon the organization's ability to achieve its objectives.

179

This is especially important in today's business environment, which is characterized by the necessity to respond to rapid changes in the organizational environment. In Tichy's (1983a) view, "Organizations' cultures are perhaps the most complex and subtle yet most pervasive influence on their effectiveness" (p. 45). Researchers assume that organizational culture is important because the concept enhances our understanding of individual behavior and organizational effectiveness. As Smirich (1983) pointed out, the concept of culture provides the academician with a link between the micro and macro levels of analysis. Concomitantly, the ability to predict individual and organizational outcomes should be enhanced. This chapter discusses ways in which both scientists and practitioners use the concept of organizational culture, and suggests ways in which the interaction between science and practice in this area can be enhanced.

NATURE OF ORGANIZATIONAL CULTURE

The construct of organizational culture itself has not been well defined by either researchers or practitioners. As Sathe (1983) noted, "Different people think of different slices of reality when they talk of culture" (p. 6). This is not surprising when one considers that the broad concept of culture has been borrowed from anthropology and that, although the concept has been in use in this field since the late 19th century, anthropologists have not yet reached consensus on how it should be defined. While early anthropologists focused on observable behaviors exhibited by members of a society, including customs and habits, during the last 30 or 40 years most anthropologists who study culture have focused more on the assumptions, values, and beliefs that are used by a society's members to interpret their experiences and to generate behaviors. These two approaches, which have been respectively called the "cultural adaptationist" and "ideational schools" (Sathe, 1983), have influenced writers in the field of organizational culture.

A review of the literature shows that definitions of corporate culture run the gamut from the very broad to the very narrow. For example, Louis (1985) simply stated that culture is "shared tacit knowledge" (p. 126). Schwartz and Davis (1981) defined culture as "a pattern of beliefs and expectations shared by the organization's members" (p. 33). Similarly, Cooke and Rousseau (1988) defined it as the "shared beliefs and values guiding the thinking and behavioral styles of [organizational] members" (p. 245). On the more narrow side, Lorsch (1985) defined culture as "the beliefs top managers in a company share about how they should manage themselves and their employees and how they should conduct their business" (p. 84). This definition is more narrow than the others in that it restricts consideration to the beliefs of top managers.

Wilkins' (1983) definition of culture as the "taken-for-granted and shared assumptions that people make about how work is to be done and evaluated and how people relate to one another" (p. 26) is broader in scope than those cited earlier. In a later article, Wilkins wrote that "Culture consists of the conclusions a group of people draws from its experience. An organization's culture consists largely of what people believe about what works and what does not" (Wilkins & Patterson, 1985, p. 267). Although these two definitions are not in direct conflict, it is clear that even the same author sometimes sees different "slices of reality" when defining culture.

Although other definitions of organizational culture have been proposed, those cited give a good overview of what can be found in the current literature. Clearly, there are a number of commonalities, with most writers basing their definitions on shared assumptions, beliefs, or values that guide organizational members' behavior.

It should be noted that some writers have pointed out that the components of culture mentioned earlier—behaviors, values and assumptions—are actually distinct levels of culture. For instance, Schein (1985) cited three levels: On the first level are artifacts, such as art, technology, and behaviors. On the second level are values, which are the group members' conceptions of what ought to be. On the third level are assumptions about reality. Sathe (1983) also posited three levels that are very similar to Schein's: (1) organizational behavior patterns; (2) justifications of behavior (i.e., the ways in which people explain and justify what they do); and (3) assumptions that govern people's justifications and behavior. While all three levels are clearly interrelated, both Schein and Sathe noted that combining them leads to conceptual and analytical difficulties. Both authors also indicated that because the third level is the most basic and influences the other two, it is the most appropriate level for examination. Although I agree with the first proposition, I do not agree with the latter. While investigators must get to the deepest level to truly capture an organization's culture, in later sections of this chapter I show that a great deal of information useful to both practitioners and researchers can be generated by including the other two levels in their examination.

With all this in mind, I propose the following definition: Organizational culture is a distinct and shared set of conscious and unconscious assumptions and values that binds organizational members together and prescribes appropriate patterns of behavior.

ORGANIZATIONAL CULTURE FORMATION

To understand how organizational cultures form, one must first review some obvious facts about organizations themselves. First, an organization exists in order to achieve objectives, and these objectives center on the satisfaction of some need in the organization's environment. Second, organizations consist of a group of people brought together to achieve these objectives. Third, the objectives must be such that they cannot be achieved by one person acting alone.

While these facts have several implications, one of the primary implications is that the behaviors of certain group members will be interdependent. For example, in a manufacturing facility, production workers may depend on those in procurement for raw materials, while the sales force may depend on employees in production. Of course, the nature of the dependencies will vary depending on the complexity of the organization, but even in a small organization, once particular jobs are defined with a scope narrower than achievement of the organizational objective itself, interdependencies are created. Devising ways to handle these interdependencies presents the grist for problems that all organizations must face.

A second implication is that organizations must interact with their environments. From the open-systems perspective (Katz & Kahn, 1978), organizations input raw materials and human resources from their environments, engage in transformation processes, and then output the transformed product or service to the environment. To remain viable the organization must produce a product or service for which there is an environmental need. Therefore, one reason that organizations must interact with their environments is that they must obtain information about whether they are satisfying needs. The other reason is that they must obtain human and material inputs. Devising ways to handle interactions with the environment presents a second source of problems for organizations.

During the early stages of an organization's development, each problem it encounters in dealing with the external and internal environment is new. Thus, to solve a particular problem, organizational members must engage in some behaviors based on beliefs or values that have been formed in other situations. If the solution is satisfactory, the behavior is positively reinforced and, in the presence of a similar stimulus situation, it is more likely to be repeated than alternative responses. During this formative stage, the beliefs and values of the organization's founder and other organizational leaders exert the greatest influence on how the problem is solved.

At this point in an organization's development, the behaviors are probably still executed consciously. Over time, however, some of the behaviors begin to be executed unconsciously (i.e., habits are formed), and an assumption develops that when faced with a particular problem situation that has been encountered in the past, a particular behavior that has been used in the past is still most appropriate. The set of assumptions, both conscious and unconscious, and values that are used to define appropriate responses to the many problem situations that the organization encounters are a central component of culture.

Inherent in these statements is the implication that organizational culture evolves over time. One mechanism for cultural evolution is that when new problem situations are encountered—and this is an important feature of culture for the organizational practitioner—the culture itself defines the response. This feature of culture may sometimes be positive, in that direct managerial action is unnecessary to solve each and every problem. On the other hand, it may sometimes be negative, such as when the behavior specified is not optimal, but the optimal solution is not considered because of cultural constraints. Another mechanism for cultural evolution is that, due to changes in the internal or external environment, extant solutions are rendered ineffective responses to particular problems. Here again, one sees that culture may have either a positive or negative effect. Nonetheless, it is apparent that if adaptations to environmental changes cannot be made, the organization's long-term survival will be in jeopardy.

CONTENT OF ORGANIZATIONAL CULTURE

Even when culture is defined (e.g., Cooke & Rousseau, 1988), the dimensions of the construct are usually not specified. To do so is not an easy task, given the complexity of the construct. However, both the theoretician and the practitioner need to know the dimensions on which culture is based in order to assess it.

The most detailed description of the content of culture is given by Schein (1985). He identified dimensions based on a comparative study of several Southwestern cultures by Kluckholn and Strodtbeck (1961), together with observations gathered in the course of his own work within organizations.

It is important to recall that Schein believes the true nature of culture lies in the assumptions that underlie behavior. Schein delineated five dimensions or categories around which an organization's assumptions are formed. The first category, the relationship to the environment, consists of assumptions about the appropriate behavior of the organization vis-à-vis the environment. The second category, the nature of reality and truth, consists of assumptions that are primarily concerned with the way that truth is discovered. For example, does truth come from a leader, from the scientific method, or from some other source? Schein also included the organization's conceptions of time and space in this category. The third category consists of assumptions about the nature of human nature. In this category, we find assumptions concerning the way that employees must be motivated, whether or not they can be developed, and so forth. The fourth category, assumptions on the nature of human activity, concerns the correct behaviors derived from assumptions in the first three categories. The last category, the nature of human relationships, centers on assumptions concerning the way(s) that people should relate to one another.

Schein's framework for identifying the basic assumptions operating in an organization can be useful for investigators attempting to get to the deepest level of culture. For example, researchers may find it useful as a starting point from which to build a model of culture. On the other hand, specification of all of the assumptions operating within these categories may not be appropriate for the practitioner. As Schein pointed out, to attempt to get to this level of culture will be very difficult and time consuming. Given the time constraints that usually confront practitioners, another way to address the content of culture would be useful.

An alternative approach is to directly examine the manifestations of culture. However, because there are many possible manifestations of an organization's culture, here again one needs a framework to guide the examination; this framework must ensure that the investigator will capture the major elements of the content itself. One way to do this is to examine the major systems within an organization. For example, Galbraith's (1973) five organizational design elements (viz., task, structure, information and decision-making processes, reward systems, and people systems) provide a possible framework. Although there are many other frameworks that could be used, Katz and Kahn's (1978) organizational subsystems seem to be most suitable for two reasons. First, the subsystems are derived from an examination of the way in which all organizations develop. Second, it is a comprehensive framework that allows the investigator to capture the major relevant content of an organization's culture.

As mentioned before, Katz and Kahn's subsystems are derived from an examination of the etiology of organizations, and the first problems that confront organizations relate to satisfaction of an environmental need. Hence, the production and technical subsystem is the first to be established. Also, early in an organization's development, decisions and rules concerning how tasks are to be performed and integrated must be made. Thus, an authority structure evolves that is the basis for the later development of a structured managerial subsystem. In addition, a maintenance subsystem develops that serves to keep track of the rules, administer rewards, and perform similar functions. A fourth major subsystem, the boundary subsystem, is concerned with the importation of both material and human inputs into the system, disposal of the outputs, and relations of the organization with other organizations such as governmental regulatory agencies. Finally, the fifth subsystem, the adaptive subsystem, is concerned with ensuring that the organization is responsive to changing conditions in the external environment. Using this framework, the investigator of organizational culture can examine each of the five subsystems, the factors that led to their formation, and the assumptions that underlie each.

When examining the production subsystem, the primary element of concern is the organization's mission or its reason for existence. The organization's approach to task specification or the creation of jobs and organizational roles must also be examined.

Because the maintenance subsystem is concerned primarily with providing stability to other organizational subsystems, especially the production subsystem, a wealth of cultural data will surface when examining this subsystem. It is this subsystem that is concerned with recruitment, selection, socialization, allocation of rewards and punishments, and employee morale. Therefore, examination of these processes and the reasons for their development will yield much information on the organization's culture.

The adaptive subsystem can also yield much cultural information. As is the case with the maintenance subsystem, this subsystem is concerned with organizational survival. However, its primary focus is outward in that it attempts to ensure survival in the face of changing environmental conditions, whether these be driven by sociocultural, political, competitive, or other forces. Thus, research and development and/or corporate planning units will be formed. The strategies and tactics these units formulate and the assumptions on which they are based help define the culture of an organization.

Examination of the managerial subsystem can also yield data about an organization's culture. This subsystem is mainly concerned with coordinating the behavior of organizational members, especially through the classical managerial functions of direction and control. Here factors such as the formal authority structures and regulatory mechanisms extant in the organization, as well as the degree of centralization of decision making, are examined. As with the other subsystems, the initial task for the investigator is to identify the elements themselves; the historical reasons for their existence and the assumptions on which they are based can then be identified.

The final subsystem, the support subsystem, may produce less cultural information than the others. This subsystem is outwardly focused and is concerned primarily with input of materials and the disposition of output. Nonetheless, examination of the elements in this system might provide some valuable information on how the organization relates to its environment.

These subsystems are mainly concerned with the work flow of the organization and, hence, Katz and Kahn classified them as belonging to the *horizontal* dimension of organizations. They pointed out that one must also be concerned with the *vertical* dimension of organizations related to the status, power, and prestige associated with an organizational member's position in the hierarchy. The vertical dimension is important because it shapes members' attitudes and perceptions and, hence, also needs to be considered when defining the content of an organization's culture.

It should be apparent that the investigator who proceeds from Katz and Kahn's framework will uncover many of the same assumptions that can be found using Schein's framework as a starting point. For instance, Schein's assumptions on the nature of human nature will be uncovered when examining Katz and Kahn's maintenance and managerial subsystems. I believe, however, that using the Katz and Kahn framework as a starting point will better facilitate the identification of cultural information for two reasons. First, Schein's categories are highly abstract; starting with more concrete categories should make the identification of assumptions less difficult. Second, by proceeding from subsystems to assumptions, the link between cultural information and variables of interest to organizational researchers or practitioners is more immediately obvious.

ASSESSMENT OF ORGANIZATIONAL CULTURE

A review of the literature revealed seven methods that have been used to assess organizational culture: (1) individual interviews, (2) group interviews, (3) researcher's observations and interpretations of artifacts, (4) insider's descriptions (i.e. ethnography), (5) questionnaires, (6) critical incidents, and (7) field simulations. Each of these techniques is examined briefly and evaluated using the following criteria: (a) time to perform the assessment, (b) the number of people who can be included within reasonable time constraints, (c) organizational disruption, (d) quantifiability of results, and (e) variety of content that can be covered.

The first method for assessing organizational culture is the individual interview. Using this method, key individuals are interviewed using a structured or semistructured format. Key individuals might include the senior management of the organization, a cross-section of current employees, ex-employees, and even customers or suppliers. The disadvantages of this method are that it is time consuming, does not reasonably permit large numbers of people to be included, is organizationally disruptive, and is not easily quantified. However, the variety of content covered can be quite wide.

A second assessment technique based on interview procedures is the group interview. Although different investigators have used slightly different strategies in structuring group interviews, there seem to be three main commonalities. First, members of the organization are interviewed in groups of three to ten people. Second, the interview is structured. Third, there is discussion among group members until consensus is reached. This last point is important. If culture is defined as a set of shared assumptions, then consensus-seeking discussions are an essential way to determine what is really shared. As Wilkins and Patterson (1985) pointed out, this seems to be a good starting point in defining culture, because key actors are given an opportunity to talk about "what is unique and valuable about the company" (p. 200). Individual and group interviews have the same advantages and disadvantages, except that the latter technique permits a larger number of participants to be included.

A third method involves observation and interpretation of symbols, policies, procedures, and other observable cultural artifacts. Using this method, the investigator obtains as many artifacts as possible. These might include annual reports, memos from executives, and policy and procedure manuals as well as observations of the decor, characteristics of the building and office space, and so forth. The investigator then interprets what has been observed as indicators of the organization's culture. Clearly, this method is time consuming, relatively unquantifiable, and the range of topics covered will be rather narrow. It is not, however, disruptive to the organization. A major problem with the method is that researchers must infer the cultural assumptions from their observations. I would, therefore, not recommend that this be the only method used; however, it may be useful as a supplement to one or more of the other methods that do not rely so heavily on observer inferences.

Another technique for assessing culture, insider's description or ethnography, is borrowed from cultural anthropology. In this case, the investigator becomes a participant-observer in the culture under study. This method is time consuming, and the information generated cannot be easily quantified. As with researcher's observation, it also has the drawback of requiring observer inferences, and these inferences may be less or more reliable and valid because of the insider's (often unconscious) emotional involvement with the individuals under study. The advantages of this method are that organizational disruption is minimal, a large number of people can be observed, and a wide variety of content areas can be included.

The questionnaire is probably the most widely used assessment technique. Questions can be objective or open-ended, or a combination of both. Advantages of this method are that it allows large numbers of people to be included without too much disruption to the organization, and investigator time is held to a minimum (except during questionnaire development). In addition, objective items are easily quantified, and narrative items can be quantified through content analysis. The variety of content that can be covered using this technique is greater than is generally permitted by any of the other techniques described in this section. There are no major disadvantages to this method using the criteria enumerated above.

The sixth technique for assessing organizational culture is the critical incidents method. Using this technique, individuals are interviewed and asked to recall some critical event in the history of the company that influenced its direction. A number of key individuals are interviewed, and the investigator then interprets what has been told to him or her. In addition to reliance on observer interpretation, this method has a number of significant disadvantages. It is time consuming and, concomitantly, few people can be included. In addition, it is organizationally disruptive and the results are not easily quantified. It is not possible to predict the range of content that might emerge using this technique.

The final method for assessing culture was discussed by Louis (1985), who called it "field simulation." She defined field simulations as "artificially created instances in which tacit knowledge may be made explicit" (p. 134). Examples included group productions and guided reflections. In a group production, a group of organizational members works together on some task, and work on the task reveals shared understandings. For instance, the group might create a montage, and it is videotaped while doing so. Upon task completion, the tape is reviewed for discussion. In guided reflection, a cross-section of organizational members are interviewed concerning their experiences in the various organizational subunits from which they come, and they are then asked to identify commonalities in their experiences. Although this technique is similar to the group interview, the guided reflection is unstructured. Of course, field simulations have a number of disadvantages associated with them. In fact, they receive negative evaluations on all of the criteria except variety of topics covered, although one cannot be certain what the coverage will be.

Given the complexity of organizational culture, a multiple-stage assessment technique including many of the methods described above would seem to be appropriate. In the first stage, the investigator must become familiar with the organization. Given the framework proposed earlier, the main task is to become familiar with the production, maintenance, adaptive, managerial, and supportive subsystems, as well as with the organization's vertical dimension. This can be done using two sources of information. The first would employ researcher's observations, where the investigator examines the available artifacts that provide information concerning the subsystems. Based on information generated from these observations, interview protocols can be developed to gain in-depth knowledge of the subsystems from each of the organization's principal executives. The focus of the interviews need not necessarily be identical for each executive, but might depend on their primary responsibilities. For example, in a functional organization, an interview with the head of manufacturing might be primarily focused on the production subsystems; an interview with the head of sales could be primarily focused on the support subsystems; and an interview with the head of human resources would focus primarily on the maintenance subsystems. In each interview, the various procedures in use are discussed, and the interviewer attempts to determine the major organizational events that caused these procedures to be formulated and the assumptions on which they are based.

Although the primary focus would be on the subsystems related to the executive's major responsibilities, these executives can also be expected to have relevant information about other subsystems. For instance, although the head of sales would be primarily concerned with the supportive subsystem, he or she might also be aware of information concerning the production subsystem. In addition, all executives would have information concerning the managerial subsystem.

Once this information has been collected, the investigator can organize what has been learned and describe each major subsystem, as well as its procedures and the assumptions on which they are based. At this point, the investigator can proceed to the next step, a group interview. In this case, the major functional executives are gathered in a group, and the investigator reports preliminary findings. The primary task during this step is to explain any inconsistencies the investigator uncovered, and to achieve consensus concerning the assumptions that underlie operations of the primary organizational subsystems.

Because one purpose of this investigation is to ensure that the organization's culture is aligned with its strategic mission, this is the appropriate point in the investigation to discuss whether this is the case. First, the assumptions themselves should be examined with an eye toward determining whether there are any that are no longer valid given the organization's current mission and its internal and external environments. In addition, the degree to which the assumptions fit together must be examined. For instance, if the organization's strategic mission is to expand through new product innovations, and it is assumed that the way to do this is through team effort on the part of the research and development staff, then one must examine the reward structures for these employees to ensure that the emphasis is on team effort rather than individual effort.

Up to this point in my description of culture assessments only the assumptions of the organization's executives have been examined. However, given the definition of the construct of culture, the investigator must determine whether these assumptions are shared by other organizational members. Because one objective of culture assessment is to determine the assumptions of as many organization members as possible, the questionnaire becomes the technique of choice. For each of the major assumptions identified in the previous step, a short scenario can be developed that describes a manifestation of the assumption. For example, if there is an assumption that employees are resources and should therefore be developed from within the organization, then a scenario might describe a situation in which there are two candidates for a job—one from inside the company who has the primary skills but needs some further development that could be accomplished in a reasonable period of time, and one from outside the company who has all of the necessary skills. Two or more alternative responses concerning the outcome of the situation would be listed and, in this case, possible responses would be to select either the internal or the external candidate. Prior to distribution of this questionnaire, the key executives who participated in the previous stage of the investigation would complete the questionnaire, and only items on which there is a high percentage of agreement concerning the outcome would be retained. Although the actual percentage would vary somewhat with the number of executives participating, less than 80% agreement would generally not indicate a sufficient degree of consensus.

A number of positive outcomes can accrue from proceeding in this fashion. First, the degree to which the organization members agree with the executives' perceptions of culture will be determined. This is important because unshared assumptions will not have the desired effects on behavior. Second, by soliciting demographic information such as department from the respondents, subcultures within the organization can be identified. Third, if the organization attempts a culture-change program, readministration of the questionnaire can indicate the degree to which progress has been made.

ORGANIZATIONAL CULTURE CHANGE AND MANAGEMENT

Given what we know about organizational culture, an important question is whether or not it can be changed. Some writers in the field say that it cannot. Schein (1986), for instance, stated that an organization's culture "may be dysfunctional or functional, but you don't really have a choice of what kind of culture you want to have, short of creating a new group altogether" (p. 14). Instead, he believes that knowledge of the culture is important in order to ensure that cultural strengths and weaknesses are taken into account in the strategic decision-making process.

Other authors think that the process of cultural change may be difficult, but that it is not impossible. W. Brooke Turnstall, Chairman of AT&T's Restructure Implementation Board, has been deeply involved in that corporation's divestiture. He stated: "Unquestionably, culture within the corporation is difficult to pin down, nearly impossible to quantify or measure, and remarkably resistant to change. However, the culture can be positively influenced by consistent, thoughtful managerial action" (Turnstall, 1983, p. 17).

Other writers suggest that cultural change is unlikely unless certain conditions are present. Lundberg (1985) cited a set of external enabling conditions, internal permitting conditions, precipitating pressures, and environmental triggering events, and stated that when these are present, the probability is increased that cultural change in response to a planned intervention will take place.

Finally, others have indicated that culture can be managed only indirectly. Stringer and Uchenick (1986) suggested that the way to manage culture is by managing the organizational climate, and offered the following five climinate dimensions: structure, standards, responsibility, recognition, and support. Schneider and Rentsch (1988) also stated that a major component of culture management is climate management, and they defined climate as the reward and routines of the organization.

If culture is indeed a learned set of assumptions about the appropriate ways to behave, then cultural change should result from managerial processes that promote learning. With this in mind, let us now turn to the subject of management development.

MANAGEMENT DEVELOPMENT

Although much has been written on management development, Wexley and Baldwin (1986) stated that it "may still be one of the most ill-defined and variously interpreted concepts in the management literature" (p. 277). They pointed out that some researchers think of it broadly as formalized education, whereas others define it narrowly as specific managerial skill development. Still others look at it as an activity, such as job rotation or coaching. Wexley and Baldwin, however, defined it as "the whole, complex process by which individuals learn, grow, and improve their abilities to perform professional management tasks" (p. 277). London (1985) also took a broad view, but pointed out that management development can be considered from both the individual's perspective and the organization's perspective. London defined management development from the individual's perspective in a way very similar to Wexley and Baldwin. However, he stated that when considering management development from the organization's perspective, it "refers to building the management team needed to run the business successfully. This task involves appropriate policies and procedures for recruitment, selection, training, supervision, promotion, transfer, and related issues" (p. 2). Given that culture is an organizational phenomenon, it is the latter definition that is appropriate for the purposes of this chapter.

Recruitment and selection are related areas within the management development function that can have an impact on the organization's culture. From the standpoint of culture, the main task is to ensure that there is a fit between the organization's assumptions and values and those of prospective new employees. In the area of recruitment, one of the primary things an organization can do is ensure that the candidate has a thorough understanding of the organization and its culture. Realistic job previews have been used to familiarize prospective employees with the job content, but they can also be used to familiarize them with the culture of the company. For example, Sears informs candidates about factors such as the long hours, fast pace, and frequent transfers. Although fewer candidates accept positions, those who do accept know what to expect (Schultz, 1982) and, therefore, these new employees should fit better within the organizational culture.

The selection process also provides an opportunity for organizational members to make their own judgments as to whether the candidate will fit within the culture. Although it is feasible to use personality measures to help identify individuals who either fit or fail to fit within an organization's culture, companies such as IBM and Exxon use extensive interviewing to predict individual-organizational fit (Tichy, 1983b). Important factors that contribute to the success of the interview for assessing the degree of cultural match include not only the depth of the interview, but also the participation of a wide variety of current employees in the selection process.

Another area of management development that has a significant impact on organizational culture is the socialization process. Organizational socialization is the process by which "an individual is taught and learns what behaviors and perspectives are customary and desirable within the work setting as well as what ones are not" (Van Maanen & Schein, 1979, pp. 213–214). Thus, socialization is essentially a process of enculturation. Organizational socialization experiences can be either formal or informal, and formal socialization includes training. At IBM, which has a complete training curriculum that all managers complete, certain modules are focussed on the values and philosophy of IBM; similarly, DEC orients new employees to its management's philosophy and culture (Tichy, 1983b). AT&T also attempts to support cultural values through the Bell Advanced Management Program for high potential managers (Turnstall, 1983).

Informal socialization processes also play an important role in culture transmission. Several writers have pointed out that failure to transfer training from the classroom to the job may frequently be attributable to informal socialization, wherein incumbents or supervisors let the new employee know, either directly or indirectly, that things are not actually done "by the book" (e.g., Schneider & Rentsch, 1988; Van Maanen & Schein, 1979). Although the organization cannot control all socialization activities, in some cases informal socialization processes can be influenced. Admittedly, further research needs to be done concerning the effectiveness of mentorship programs but, by its nature, mentorship is a socialization process. Thus, assuming that mentors are aware of the major cultural beliefs and values, and that they are committed to them, mentorship can potentially be a highly effective informal socialization strategy.

Many authors have stressed the role of the organization's leadership in culture management and change. Although Bennis and Nanus (1985) used the term "social architecture" instead of organizational culture, these authors concluded, based on their interviews with 90 leaders from a wide variety of organizations, that one of the primary functions of a leader is to manage and change the organization's culture. Indeed, one writer put it directly when he said, "culture and leadership . . . are two sides of the same coin . . . In fact, there is a possibility—underemphasized in leadership research—that the *only thing of real importance that leaders do is create and manage culture*" (Schein, 1985, p. 2). Because management development is concerned with succession planning within an organization, wherein future leaders are identified, promotion criteria that include the demonstration of culture management and enhancement must be designed and implemented.

SCIENCE-PRACTICE INTERACTION

Examination of the literature reveals that there has not been much research conducted in the area of organizational culture. Instead, most of the literature in this area is based upon experiences authors have had within organizations, and many of these experiences have involved interventions to modify organizational cultures. In short, the literature is dominated by reports of practitioners, and it cannot be said that there has been a significant degree of interaction between science and practice to date. There are several possible reasons that this subject has not generated more research.

One reason for the lack of research in this area may be associated with the concept itself. As we have seen in the previous pages, the concept of organizational culture is highly complex. An adequate model of organizational culture from which researchers can derive testable propositions would be concomitantly complex. Therefore, perhaps theory building has not been undertaken in this area because the difficulties in definition seem, to most theorists, to be insurmountable.

A second, and perhaps more likely, explanation for the fact that this subject has failed to generate more research may pertain to the difficulties associated with quantifying variables that would be included in a model of organizational culture. Recall that many culture assessment techniques do not allow investigators' observations to be easily quantified. Because one of the key elements of the scientific method is generation and analysis of quantitative data, subject matter that does not produce such data tends to be ignored by scientists.

One additional possibility for the lack of research on this topic comes from Boehm's (1980) article on applied research, where she pointed out that research that is conducted in the "real world" is frequently not disseminated within the scientific community. The model of the scientific method generally accepted by psychologists is frequently unsuitable for performing research in ongoing organizations. Instead, a different model is required and, because this model is scientifically "messy in terms of methodology, complexity, statistical analysis, and the conclusions that can be drawn" (Boehm, 1980, p. 497), research conducted following this "real world" model is viewed as methodologically inadequate. Hence, this research is not published in journals read by members of the scientific community.

Although there has not been much interaction to date between scientists and practitioners in the area of organizational culture, there are several possible science-practice interfaces. Looking first at the ways in which practice can inform science, an obvious potential interface between scientists and practitioners exists in the theory-construction process. In the first three stages of this process, scientists define the variables to be included in the model, delineate the expected interactions among variables, and decide upon the boundaries within which the theory will operate (Dubin, 1976). Given their familiarity with the organizations within which they work, practitioners' observations can be expected to provide valuable insights to theorists engaged in all three of these stages of theory construction. Indeed, discussions about organizational culture among theorists and practitioners are the logical starting point for this process, for as Dubin pointed out, "it is exceedingly difficult to say something meaningful about the real world without starting in the real world" (p. 18).

Practitioners can also inform theorists by specifying organizational problems or issues that they believe are related to the subject of interest, in this case, organizational culture. Here theorists can examine the reasons that practitioners are concerned with organizational culture. As Cooke and Rousseau (1988) pointed out, "culture has been accepted as an organizational fact of life by managers" (p. 246). However, this does not seem to be the case for theorists, given the limited attention that they have devoted to the topic. Through discussions with practitioners, theorists can identify organizational outcomes that practitioners believe to be associated with organizational culture. This dialogue will prove fruitful to researchers designing culture studies.

While it has been shown that practice can inform science, in attempting to understand organizational culture, the converse is also true. Clearly, industrial-organizational psychologists' expertise in measurement can be applied to enhance understanding in this area. Although organizational culture is a complex construct, in order to understand culture and its effects on individual and organizational behavior, the variables of interest must be operationally defined. This process is central to all scientific endeavors, and it is applicable to the study of culture.

A second way that science can inform practice is through research itself.

Studies must be designed to examine organizational culture from a variety of perspectives. First, culture variables can be examined as dependent variables. From this perspective, researchers can identify the factors in organizations and their environments that affect culture variables, including those associated with culture formation and change. Second, culture variables can be examined as independent variables. From this perspective, researchers can examine the effects of culture variables, such as the degree to which the culture is shared (i.e., its strength), on individual behaviors and organizational effectiveness. Finally, culture variables may be viewed as moderator variables. From this perspective, researchers can examine the way in which culture variables influence relationships between other variables. For example, cultural assumptions concerning individual autonomy may affect the relationship between goal setting and goal attainment.

Science can also inform practice through the particular types of studies performed. Research designs that include multiple organizations would be particularly helpful in studying culture. For example, comparisons of highly successful organizations with those that are relatively less successful within a particular industry can determine whether certain culture variables are associated with success. In addition, longitudinal studies to determine factors associated with culture change over time would contribute to our understanding. Because scientists usually have positions within academic institutions, they are likely to have contact with the variety of organizations necessary to conduct comparative studies. Academicians' freedom from time pressures that practitioners usually face (i.e., the need to produce immediate results) permits them to conduct longitudinal studies.

Science can also inform practice when scientists apply general knowledge from other areas of their field. Industrial-organizational psychologists are well schooled in social psychology and in other areas of psychology relevant to behavior in organizations, and this knowledge can be fruitfully applied to the study of organizational culture. Considering the discussion in previous sections of this chapter, areas within psychology that will provide applicable knowledge include group formation, newcomer socialization, group problem solving, and value formation.

CONCLUSION

In this chapter we have seen that organizational culture consists of assumptions and values that prescribe appropriate behavior patterns within an organization and that culture forms as a result of organizational members' problem-solving activities. We have also seen that, although there are several methods to approach the specification of the content of culture, a method that should allow accomplishment of both theorists' and practitioners' objectives is to study the major organizational subsystems that form during the development of all organizations. Techniques for assessing culture were also discussed, and it was concluded that, due to the complexity of the concept, multiple methods must be used. Finally, it was shown that, although there is some disagreement as to whether organizational culture can be changed, one possible approach to culture management and change is through management-development activities.

There has not been much communication between theorists and practitioners in examining organizational culture. Although the reasons for this are unclear, it is clear that practitioners believe that organizational culture is an area to which they must devote their attention as they attempt to create more effective organizations. As Guion (1988) pointed out in his summary statement as editor of the *Journal of Applied Psychology,* "Practice should be informed by the research and theory of the academics, but so also the focus of at least some theory and research should be correspondingly informed by the problems faced, and the methods used, by practitioners" (p. 693). Given the current interest of practitioners in organizational culture, it can be safely assumed that they would respond positively to theorists' work in this area.

Of course, practitioner interest is not a sufficient reason for pursuing a line of scholarly research. For industrial-organizational psychologists, the primary criterion for deciding whether or not an area of research is worth pursuing requires an assessment of whether the knowledge generated enhances our understanding of individual and organizational behavior. I hope that this chapter will stimulate further interest in this area, especially on the part of researchers, and that the research conducted will indeed enhance our understanding.

REFERENCES

Bennis, W., & Nanus, B. (1985). *Leaders: The strategies for taking charge.* New York: Harper & Row.

Boehm, V. R. (1980). Research in the "real world"—A conceptual model. *Personnel Psychology, 33,* 495–503.

Changing a corporate culture. (1984, May 14). *Business Week,* pp. 130–138.

Clemens, J. K. (1986, Oct. 13). A lesson from 431 B.C. *Fortune,* pp. 161–162.

Cooke, R. A., & Rousseau, D. M. (1988). Behavioral norms and expectations: A quantitative approach to the assessment of organizational culture. *Group & Organization Studies, 13,* 245–273.

Dubin, R. (1976). Theory building in applied areas. In M. D. Dunnette (Ed.), *Handbook of industrial and organizational psychology* (pp. 17–40). Chicago: Rand McNally.

Galbraith, J. R. (1973). *Designing complex organizations.* Reading, MA: Addison Wesley.

Guion, R. M. (1988). Editorial. *Journal of Applied Psychology, 73,* 693–694.

Harris, S. (1984). Hewlett-Packard: Shaping the corporate culture. In C. J. Fombrun, N. M. Tichy, & M. A. Devanna (Eds.), *Strategic human resource management* (pp. 217–234). New York: Wiley.

Katz, D., & Kahn, R. L. (1978). *The social psychology of organizations.* New York: Wiley.

Kluckholn, F. R., & Stodtbeck, F. L. (1961). *Variations in value orientation.* New York: Harper and Row.

Kneale, D. (1986, April 7). Working at IBM: Intense loyalty in a rigid culture. *Wall Street Journal,* pp. 21–22.

London, M. (1985). *Developing managers: A guide to motivating and preparing people for successful managerial careers.* San Francisco, CA: Jossey-Bass.

Lorsch, J. W. (1985). Strategic myopia. Culture as an invisible barrier to change. In R. H. Kilmann, M. J. Saxton, R. Serpa, & Associates (Eds.), *Gaining control of the corporate culture* (pp. 84–102). San Francisco, CA: Jossey-Bass.

Louis, M. R. (1985). Sourcing workplace cultures: Why, when, and how. In R. H. Kilmann, M. J. Saxton, R. Serpa, & Associates (Eds.), *Gaining control of the corporate culture* (pp. 126–136). San Francisco, CA: Jossey-Bass.

Lundberg, C. C. (1985). On the feasibility of cultural intervention in organizations. In P. J. Frost, L. F. Moore, M. R. Louis, C. C. Lundberg, & J. Martin (Eds.), *Organizational culture* (pp. 169–185). Beverly Hills, CA: Sage.

Milne, M. (1988). Scott Paper is on a roll. *Management Review, 77*(3), 37–42.

Sathe, V. (1983, Autumn). Implications of corporate culture: A manager's guide to action. *Organizational Dynamics, 12,* 5–23.

Schein, E. H. (1985). *Organizational culture and leadership.* San Francisco, CA: Jossey-Bass.

Schein, E. H. (1986). Deep culture. In J. C. Glidwell (Ed.), *Corporate cultures: Research implications for human resource development* (pp. 7–20). Alexandria, VA: American Society for Training and Development.

Schneider, B., & Rentsch, J. (1988). Managing climates and cultures: A futures perspective. In J. Hage (Ed.), *Futures of organizations: Innovating to adapt strategy and human resources to rapid technological change* (pp. 181–200). Lexington, MA: D. C. Heath.

Schwartz, H., & Davis, S. M. (1981, Summer). Matching corporate culture and business strategy. *Organizational Dynamics, 10,* 30–49.

Schultz, D. P. (1982). *Psychology and industry today* (3rd ed.). New York: Macmillan

Smirich, L. (1983). Concepts of culture and organizational analysis. *Administrative Science Quarterly, 28,* 339–358.

Stringer, R. A., & Uchenick, J. (1986). *Strategy traps and how to avoid them.* Lexington, MA: D. C. Heath.

Tichy, N. M. (1983a). Managing organizational transformations. *Human Resource Management, 22*(1/2), 45–60.

Tichy, N. M. (1983b). *Managing strategic change: Technical, political, and cultural dynamics.* New York: Wiley.

Turnstall, W. B. (1983). Cultural transition at AT&T. *Sloan Management Review, 25*(1), 1–12.

Van Maanen, J., & Schein, E. H. (1979). Toward a theory of organization socialization. In B. Staw (Ed.), *Research in organizational behavior* (Vol 1., pp. 209–264). Greenwich, CT: JAI Press.

Wexley, K. N., & Baldwin, T. T. (1986). Management development. *Journal of Management, 12,* 277–294.

Wilkins, A. L. (1983). The culture audit: A tool for understanding organizations. *Organizational Dynamics, 12,* 24–38.

Wilkins, A. L., & Patterson, K. J. (1985). You can't get there from here: What will make culture-change projects fail. In R. H. Kilmann, M. J. Saxton, R. Serpa, & Associates (Eds.), *Gaining control of the corporate culture* (pp. 262–291). San Francisco, CA: Jossey-Bass.

10 Conflict in Organizations

Robert A. Baron
Rensselaer Polytechnic Institute

Consider the following incidents:

1. In order to close an important deal, a sales representative from one company provides a potential customer with strongly disparaging—and largely inaccurate—information about the products of a competitor.

2. A budget meeting between the heads of various departments in a large government agency degenerates into an angry shouting match as each person attempts to gain the largest share possible for his or her unit.

3. During complex negotiations, the representatives of each side employ various bluffs, maneuvers, and strategies to confuse or demoralize their opponent.

4. Because of a long-standing grudge against its originator, an executive vetos a strategic plan that might, in fact, be helpful to the company in significant ways.

5. Two rising young stars in a large corporation engage in complex political maneuvers designed to win support and expand their own power base within the organization, primarily at each other's expense.

Do these incidents have anything in common? Although they are diverse in scope and background, they are related in one basic respect: all involve instances of *organizational conflict*. In short, all involve conflict between individuals or groups within larger organizational systems (Thomas, in press). Unfortunately, such conflict, in one form or another, is extremely common in work settings. Indeed, practicing managers report that they spend approximately twenty percent of their time dealing with conflict and its impact (Thomas & Schmidt, 1976). Moreover, organizational conflict seems indifferent to international boundaries: it occurs with a high frequency around the globe, in organizations operating in a wide range of different cultures (Habib, 1987).

In view of these facts, it seems clear that organizational conflict is an important topic for both managers and for scientists interested in understanding the nature of organizational behavior and organizational processes. The present chapter, therefore, focuses directly on such conflict. To provide a useful summary of current knowledge about organizational conflict, the following outline is adopted. First, the nature of such conflict is considered and a working definition of it is proposed. Second, the major causes of organizational conflict are examined. These include factors relating to the structure and functioning of organizations (Daft, 1986), as well as factors linked to interpersonal relations between specific individuals (Baron & Greenberg, 1990). Third, several techniques for the effective *management* of conflict are described. Finally, we offer commentary concerning the interplay between science and practice with respect to this important topic.

ORGANIZATIONAL CONFLICT: ITS BASIC NATURE

Because it is so clearly an important issue in work settings, organizational conflict has been the focus of careful study for several decades (Lewicki & Litterer, 1985; Thomas, 1976). One result of this sustained interest has been the formulation of many contrasting definitions and models of such conflict. Although it would certainly be impossible to review all these models here, I will attempt to integrate several popular approaches into a single unified definition. Correspondingly, I describe several contrasting models of conflict, and suggest that most (if not all) are encompassed within a sophisticated, general model proposed recently by Thomas (in press).

Definitions of Conflict.   A sample of influential definitions of conflict includes the following views:

1. Conflict is a perceived divergence of interest between individuals or groups—a belief on the part of these entities that their current aspirations cannot be achieved simultaneously (Pruitt & Rubin, 1986).

2. Organizational (interface) conflict involves an erosion of trust in a relationship in which neither group has the authority to control the other and neither can appeal to a higher level to resolve their differences (Blake & Mouton, 1984).

3. Conflict is a process that begins when one party perceives that the other has negatively affected or is about to negatively affect something he or she cares about (Thomas, in press).

Careful analysis of these and related definitions suggests that while they are far from identical, they do overlap to a considerable extent with respect to several basic elements or concepts. First, taken together, they suggest that conflict includes *opposing interests* between individuals or groups involved in a zero-sum situation: If one attains its major goals, the other will, of necessity, be prevented from obtaining *its* major goals. Second, these definitions all suggest (either implicitly or explicitly) that such opposed interests must be *recognized* for conflict to exist; if such recognition fails to develop, conflict, too, is unlikely to emerge. It may be implicit in the situation, but it is not a current fact. Third, these definitions suggest that conflict involves beliefs, by each side, that the other will *thwart* (or has already thwarted) its interests. Fourth, they suggest that conflict is a *process;* it develops out of existing relationships between individuals or groups, and reflects their past interactions and the contexts in which these took place. Finally, the foregoing definitions imply *actions* by one or both sides that do, in fact, produce thwarting of others' goals.

These definitions are both useful and informative. However, they appear to be lacking in one respect: They do not specify the classes of variables that may serve as antecedents for organizational conflict. Recent research on this topic has been quite revealing, so it seems both appropriate and timely to consider such variables in any useful, working definition of conflict. The definition that is adopted in this chapter, therefore, is as follows:

Conflict is a process in which various antecedent conditions, possibly but not necessarily including (1) opposed interests, (2) negative affect (e.g., anger, dislike), (3) negative cognitions (e.g., stereotypes, real or imagined past wrongs), and (4) actual or anticipated thwarting, result in an individual or group taking actions that are incompatible with the interests of other individuals or groups. In short, conflict is defined as an ongoing process involving not only opposed interests, but also, in at least some instances, negative feelings and negative thoughts about one's adversary.

Models of Conflict

Over the years, many models of organizational conflict have been proposed (cf. Pondy, 1967; Thomas, in press). However, most of these frameworks can be described as falling into one of two major categories: *structural models of conflict* and *process models of conflict.* Structural models (see Thomas, 1976) focus primarily on identifying the conditions that initiate or terminate conflict. Their major goal is that of specifying those factors that are most important in the occurrence of conflict in work settings. In contrast, process models are concerned with the development of conflict over time. They attempt to specify the stages or phases in ongoing conflicts, and to determine the influence of each upon the phases that follow. In a sense, structural models seek to paint a still picture of conflict, identifying its key causes or components; process models seek to represent it as an active, time-linked sequence of events.

Perhaps the most sophisticated and useful model of conflict presented to date is one offered recently by Thomas (in press). This model incorporates elements of both the structural and process perspectives, and offers a broader view of organizational conflict than any other currently know to the author. According to Thomas, conflict, as an organizational process, reflects external conditions (i.e., stems from various antecedents), and affects such conditions in turn. In other words, Thomas argues that conflict should be construed as part of a continuing relationship between the parties involved, *not* as an isolated event that can be understood apart from such historical context. Within this general framework, Thomas calls attention to several elements that play key roles in the development and resolution of conflict.

The first of these elements is *awareness of the conflict*. Unless conflicts are recognized as such by the parties involved, it may fail to emerge. In other words, conflict is very much in the eye of the beholders—unless the parties involved recognize the existence of opposing interests, it remains merely a potentiality and may never actually develop.

Second, the *emotional reactions* of the parties to a conflict must be considered. Once a conflict is recognized as such, the persons involved think about it and experience various emotions. These emotions play a crucial role in shaping the course of a developing conflict. If anger or resentment over real or imagined injustice is strong, conflict is likely to be intense. If other emotions (e.g., Fear over potential retaliation) predominate, the conflict may be of lower intensity.

Third, and closely related, are the *cognitions* of the two sides. Thoughts and reasoning concerning the nature of a conflict can, and often do, play a key role in shaping its development. For example, both sides often map their strategies and plan overt actions on the basis of careful analysis of the potential costs and benefits involved. Similarly, both take account of such factors as how various actions on their part will be viewed by others and to what extent they may received censure (or approval) for adopting a particular stance. Memory, too, plays a key role at this point, as adversaries draw upon past experience in similar situations and knowledge of their past relations with present opponents.

Fourth, both the *intentions* formulated by parties to a conflict, and their overt actions are of major importance. A large body of evidence suggests that overt actions can often be predicted quite effectively from knowledge of *behavioral intentions* (Ajzen, 1986; Ajzen & Fishbein, 1980). Thus, understanding these intentions may shed considerable light on the actions likely to be adopted by conflict adversaries.

As should be readily apparent, Thomas's model is highly consistent with the definition of conflict offered on p. 199. Indeed, it takes specific account of several of the key variables included in this definition (e.g., opposing interests, negative affect, negative cognitions), and directs careful attention to the overt actions of both sides during conflict episodes. For this reason, plus the fact that it reflects the findings of a growing body of empirical research, it appears to represent a useful framework for understanding many aspects of organizational conflict.

MAJOR CAUSES OF ORGANIZATIONAL CONFLICT

To paraphrase our working definition: conflict is a process in which various antecedent conditions lead individuals or groups to engage in actions that are incompatible with the interests or goals of others. But what, precisely, are these antecedent conditions? In short, what factors play an important role in the advent and persistence of costly organizational conflicts? Many of these antecedents exist, but most can be classified as relating either to organizational structure or function— *organizational causes of conflict*, or to personal relations between individuals—*interpersonal causes of conflict*.

Organizational Causes of Conflict

The most obvious cause of conflict relating to organizational structure or design is what can reasonably be termed *competition over scarce resources*. Most organizations have limited resources. As a result, they must somehow determine how to allocate these between individuals, departments, or divisions. As a result, conflicts often arise over the distributions of such valued outcomes as money, space, equipment, personnel, and even various "perks" (e.g., assigned spots in the company parking lot, better furnishings for one's office). Unfortunately, such conflicts are often intensified or exacerbated by various errors in social perception (Wyer & Srull, 1986). For example, individuals tend to overestimate the magnitude of their own contributions to various joint projects, while underestimating those of other contributors (one form of the *self-serving bias*). As a result, each side assumes that it deserves more of the available rewards than the other feels is fair, and intense conflict can follow.

Another important organizational cause of conflict is *ambiguity over jurisdiction*. To the extent uncertainty exists concerning the limits of formal authority, each unit or group involved tends to expand the scope of its own jurisdiction, while limiting that of others. The friction and disputes that arise when these contrasting perceptions collide can be devastating from the point of view of coordination between the individuals or units involved.

A third organizational factor that contributes to many instances of conflict is *interdependence* between various persons or groups. In many work settings, such interdependence is quite high. The persons or groups involved receive input from other organizational members and cannot proceed in its absence. When such input is delayed or delivered in an unsatisfactory form (e.g., it is incomplete, poorly assembled), strong conflict may result. In this case, recipients of such input may perceive that their major work-related goals are being thwarted, and this may lead them to adopt reciprocal actions. The final result may be an upward, costly spiral that interferes with normal operations.

A fourth and final organizational cause of conflict involves the specific *reward* or *compensation systems* adopted by an organization. Such systems can take many different forms, and include many different factors in their operations. However, in Western nations, most compensation systems are designed to pit individuals or groups against one another with respect to the distribution of various rewards. In many compensation plans, raises, budget increases, additional positions, increased power and status go primarily (and sometimes exclusively) to the winners. They are distributed largely to those units or persons whose performance is highest. While this in itself does not guarantee the occurrence of conflict, it is often the case that the "also rans" (i.e., those who did not receive the reward) in such contests perceive a degree of slippage in the system. They may feel that they labored under some important handicap, or that the systems used for evaluating their performance were inaccurate or incomplete. To the extent such perceptions exist in an organization, the groups or persons who do not receive various rewards may conclude that they were somehow cheated (Greenberg, in press). Such beliefs, in turn, may set the stage for actions designed to redress these "wrongs," and so lead to overt conflict.

Needless to add, many additional factors pertaining to the structure or operation of organizations also contribute to the initiation of costly conflicts (e.g., ambiguity over responsibility, growing internal complexity, which makes it increasingly difficult for different groups within the organization to communicate directly or clearly with one another). In the interests of brevity, these factors are not considered in detail here.

Interpersonal Causes of Conflict

Until recently, a large proportion of research dealing with organizational conflict focused primarily on the structural factors noted earlier. In the past few years, however, more attention has been paid to the possibility that in many cases, costly organizational conflicts stem, at least in part, from interpersonal factors, aspects of relationships between specific persons. A wide range of factors seem to play a role in this regard. For example, consider the impact of lasting *grudges*. When individuals are angered by others, and especially when they are then made to lose face (to appear foolish in public), they may develop strong negative attitudes toward those responsible for such outcomes. One result is that they then devote considerable time and effort to the task of planning or actually seeking revenge for these real or imagined wrongs. Such grudges can persist for years (Baron & Richardson, in press), with obvious negative effects for the organizations or work groups in question.

The role of attributions.   Another interpersonal factor that often plays an important role in organizational conflict might be termed *faulty attributions.* These involve errors in individuals' conclusions about the causes behind others' behavior—misconceptions about *why* they behave as they have (Ross & Fletcher, 1985). Such errors seem especially relevant to situations in which the interests of an individual or group have been thwarted in some manner by the actions of another person or group. In such cases, the thwarted party attempts to determine *why* their adversary acted in this manner. Did these actions stem mainly from malevolence—a desire to harm them in some fashion? Was it simply a misunderstanding—the party or group who performed the thwarting was not fully aware of the harmful impact of the actions performed? Did the thwarting agent's actions stem mainly from factors beyond his or her control (e.g., orders from a superior, or situational factors that dictated this course of action)?

As is readily apparent, the attributions formed by individuals in such situations can exert strong effects upon their subsequent behavior. If they conclude that thwarting by others was enacted purposely, with the express purpose of interfering with their goals, considerable anger may be generated and ensuing conflict may be intense. In contrast, if persons whose interests have been thwarted conclude that these outcomes were unintended or unavoidable, the likelihood of overt conflict may be considerably reduced (Baron, 1988a). Clear evidence for such effects has recently been reported by Bies and his colleagues in a series of related studies concerned with *causal accounts* (Bies & Shapiro, 1988).

In one of these investigations, Bies, Shapiro, and Cummings (1988) asked a diverse sample of employed persons to describe a recent situation in which they had made a request or proposal to their boss which was then rejected. After providing this information, participants rated the extent to which their boss had offered a causal account for his or her actions (i.e., an explanation suggesting that he or she had no choice in the decision), the adequacy of the reasoning in support of this claim, and the boss' apparent sincerity. In addition, participants in the study rated the extent to which they became angry after the refusal, the extent to which they felt they were treated unfairly, their disapproval of their boss, and the extent to which they complained about the decision to persons higher up in the company.

Bies, Shapiro, and Cummings hypothesized that merely providing a causal account (such as attributing the negative decision to external causes) would not, by itself, lessen negative reactions among subordinates. However, the more adequate the reasoning provided in support of this claim and the greater its apparent sincerity, the more favorably would participants react. Their results offered support for this reasoning. The more adequate the reasoning behind the boss' causal accounts and the more sincere such explanations appeared to be, the lower participants' feelings of anger and unfairness, and the lower their disapproval of the boss and their tendency to complain to higher-ups.

Other findings from the same project indicated that in offering explanations for their refusals, supervisors most frequently cited subordinates' own behavior (e.g., insufficient preparation, competence), budget constraints, upper management, the political environment in the organization, formal company policy, and company norms. These were not viewed as equally adequate explanations by recipients, however. Participants rated accounts based on company norms, budget constraints, and formal company policy as more adequate than those that emphasized the subordinate's own behavior (perhaps still another reflection of the self-serving bias), upper management, or organizational politics.

Additional evidence for the importance of attributions as a potential interpersonal cause of conflict has been obtained by Baron in several related studies (Baron, 1985, 1988a). In the most recent of these, male and female students played the roles of representatives from different departments in a large organization, and participated in a simulated negotiation with another person (actually an accomplice). These negotiations focused on the allocation of a hypothetical budgetary surplus ($1,000,000). The accomplice adopted a confrontational stance, demanding $800,000 for his or her department, while making only two small concessions during an exchange of eight offers and counter-offers. Statements by this person during negotiations suggested that the accomplice had been instructed to adopt a "tough" stance by his or her constituents (e.g, "I've got firm instructions to get as much as possible . . . I really have no choice—I have to do the best I can.") The apparent sincerity of these statements was one of the key variables in the study. Prior to the start of negotiations, participants were provided with a copy of the accomplice's instructions from his or her department. In one condition (the external attribution-sincere group), these instructions did tell the accomplice to be tough and unyielding. In another (the external attribution-insincere group), however, they instructed the accomplice to be conciliatory and yielding. Thus, in the first condition subjects received information suggesting that the accomplice's attributional statements were sincere, while in the second, they received information suggesting that these statements were insincere.

An additional variable was the pressure on the negotiators to reach an agreement. This factor was included in order to examine the possibility, suggested by research findings (Hansen, 1980), that individuals pay closer attention to attributional statements by others when their behavior is unexpected or unusual. To vary this factor, half of the participants were told that if they did not reach an agreement during this session, they could meet again to discuss the same issue (low time pressure). The remainder were told that if they did not reach an agreement, the funds would be divided among two other departments.

It was hypothesized that participants would react more negatively to the accomplice's tough, unyielding behavior when he or she appeared to be insincere than when he appeared to be sincere with respect to statements about the causes of these actions. Moreover, it was expected that such effects would be larger in the context of high time pressure (when subjects would pay careful attention to such attributional statements) than in the context of low time pressure. All these predictions were confirmed. When asked how they would handle future conflicts with the same person, both males and females reported stronger tendencies to do so through avoidance and competition in the external attribution-insincere condition than in the external attribution-sincere conditions. Further, these differences emerged primarily in the context of high time pressure.

In sum, participants in this study reacted quite negatively to statements attributing confrontational actions to external causes when these statements appeared to be false. Highly similar results were obtained in a follow-up field investigation conducted with officers in a large urban fire department (Baron, 1988a). These individuals, too, reported strong negative reactions to statements that attributed confrontational actions to external causes, but which appeared to be false.

Together, these findings and those of other investigations suggest that the strategy of attributing actions that thwart others' outcomes to external causes may succeed in blunting subsequent anger and conflict, but only if such statements are believed. If they are rejected as false, anger, resentment, and subsequent conflict may all be intensified by the "my hands are tied" strategy and related tactics.

Faulty communication.   In two recent surveys, employees were asked to rate the importance of a wide range of factors as potential causes of conflict in their workgroups (Baron, 1988b; Baron & Bingley, 1989). Results were consistent in identifying *faulty communication* as foremost of these many factors. Communication is a complex process, and can fail in numerous ways (Tracy, Van Dusen, & Robinson, 1987). In work settings, however, the key problem seems to be that individuals communicate with others in ways that anger, irritate, or annoy them, even though this is not their intention.

Such faulty communication often involves a lack of clarity. For example, in assigning a new task to a subordinate, a manager may provide what she believes to be clear and explicit instructions. This person, however, may actually be quite confused about such issues as the nature of the task itself, why it is being assigned, how she or he is supposed to proceed, and the desired end product.

In many cases, failures of communication center around inappropriate forms of *criticism*—negative feedback that is delivered to recipients in a manner that angers or upsets them rather than helping them to do a better job. The negative effects of inappropriate criticism (sometimes labeled *destructive criticism*) have been apparent to managers and management consultants for decades. Indeed, one recent book on this subject (Heldmann, 1988) described numerous incidents in which destructive criticism adversely affected working and personal relationships. Systematic evidence on the nature and scope of such effects, however, has only begun to accumulate within the past few years. One project that provides clear evidence for the negative effects of destructive criticism in work settings was conducted by Baron (1988b).

In an initial investigation, participants (male and female students) were asked to prepare an ad campaign for an imaginary product (a new shampoo); they then received feedback on their work from an accomplice. In one condition (*constructive criticism*) this feedback was negative, but was consistent with established principles for providing such feedback in an effective manner. It was considerate in tone, specific in content, contained no threats, and did not assign poor performance to lasting, internal causes (e.g., a lack of ability). In a second condition (*destructive criticism*), feedback on participants' ad campaign was also negative (the numerical ratings were identical to those in the constructive criticism group). However, in this case, it also violated basic principles of effective feedback. The criticism was harsh in tone, general rather than specific in content, contained threats, and attributed poor performance to internal causes.

After receiving one of these two types of criticism, participants rated their current feelings (e.g., anger, tension), and their likelihood of resolving future conflicts with the accomplice in each of five basic ways (through avoidance, competition, compromise, accommodation, or collaboration; Thomas, 1976). Results indicated that participants who received destructive criticism reported being angrier and more upset than those who received constructive criticism. In addition, those who received destructive criticism reported being more likely to deal with future conflicts through avoidance or competition, and less likely to deal with them through collaboration.

In a follow-up study (Baron, 1988b), participants were asked to work on two different tasks (proof-reading and clerical coding) after receiving either constructive, destructive, or no feedback on their work on a different task. Before performing the proof-reading or clerical task, they indicated their self-set goals for each task (how many lines they would proof; how many instances of clerical coding they would complete). Results indicated that on both tasks, participants who received destructive criticism reported lower self-set goals and lower self-efficacy than those who received constructive criticism. In addition, it was also noted that constructive criticism did not reduce self-set goals below that of the no feedback control condition. This latter finding suggests that it is not negative feedback per se that produces adverse effects. Rather, it is negative feedback that violates the basic principles described earlier (i.e., *destructive* criticism).

Personality and organizational conflict.   Informal observation suggests that some individuals are far more likely to become involved in organizational conflict than others. A growing body of research evidence suggests that this is indeed the case, and that specific personal characteristics do in fact seem to delineate conflict-prone individuals. Jones and Melcher (1982) noted that among a sample of MBA students, the need for affiliation (close, friendly relations with others) was positively related to a preference for handling conflicts through accommodation, but negatively related to a preference for dealing with conflict through competition.

Similarly, in a recent study also conducted with MBA students, Kabanoff (1987) found that individuals high in the need for control were rated by their classmates as more competitive and less willing to compromise than persons low in the need for control. Such persons also scored high on the competitive dimension of the Thomas-Kilmann MODE instrument—a test which measures individual preferences for various modes of resolving interpersonal conflict (Thomas & Kilmann, 1974).

Two additional aspects of personality that might play a role in conflict are the *Type A Behavior Pattern* (Glass, 1977) and *self-monitoring* (Snyder, 1987). Type A persons have been found to be impatient, highly competitive, and hostile in their dealings with others. It seems reasonable to expect that such persons might become involved in conflict more frequently than Type B individuals, who do not demonstrate these trends. Correspondingly, high self-monitors are individuals who are sensitive to their effects on others, and who are readily able to adjust their behavior to each situation that they encounter. Together, such sensitivity and flexibility might make it less likely that such persons will become involved in conflict.

To investigate these and other possibilities, Baron (1989) asked 108 managers at a large food-processing plant to complete questionnaires containing measures of both the Type A behavior pattern and self-monitoring, plus numerous items dealing with the occurrence of conflict in their work units. Results indicated that as predicted, Type A individuals did in fact report a higher incidence of conflict with peers and subordinates than Type B persons. (No difference in reported frequency of conflict was noted for Type A and Type B persons with respect to supervisors.) In addition, Type A persons reported being less likely than Type B individuals to handle conflicts with other organization members through accommodation.

With respect to self-monitoring, persons high and low on this dimension did not differ in terms of overall rate of conflict with others. However, high self-monitors reported a greater likelihood than low self-monitors of resolving conflicts with others through collaboration and compromise. Together with the findings of previous studies, these results suggest that several personality dimensions are indeed linked to the occurrence and resolution of organizational conflict.

Additional interpersonal causes of conflict.   It would be remiss to conclude this discussion without briefly noting that several additional aspects of interpersonal relations can play a role in organizational conflict. These include feelings of *inequity* (the belief that one has been treated unfairly; Greenberg & Folger, 1983); *prejudice*—negative views of others based primarily on their racial, sexual, or ethnic identity; and *dissimilarity* with respect to attitudes, personality, or style, and the dislike that is often based on such perceived differences (Byrne, 1971).

In sum, conflict in work settings often stems from relations between individuals and from their personal characteristics, as well as from underlying structural (organization-based) factors. Although this contention might, at first, appear to offer pessimistic implications for the control or management of organizational conflict, the opposite is actually true. Changing the basic structure of an organization, its long-established policies, or its carefully developed strategies, is a difficult task, to say the least. For example, it is one thing to note that compensation plans that pit units or individuals against one another are contributing to conflict. It is quite another to actually replace such plans with ones that do not generate these effects; after all, human resource systems that reward individual efforts and accomplishment may contribute, substantially, to employee motivation and productivity.

In contrast, it may often be somewhat easier to produce changes in interpersonal behavior and even in many personal characteristics. Numerous techniques for encouraging such change exist, and have been used effectively in a wide range of contexts (Hollin & Trower, 1986). At least some of these procedures seem applicable to the task of countering the impact of interpersonal causes of conflict (cf. Baron, 1984). To the extent that organizational conflict stems from such causes, it may be possible to reduce its occurrence or intensity by using these procedures. We should hasten to add that at present, actual application of such psychological techniques to the management of organizational conflict remains limited. However, interest in such interdisciplinary transfer of knowledge has increased in recent years, and this, in turn, provides the basis for at least a degree of cautious optimism.

MANAGING ORGANIZATIONAL CONFLICT

Because the negative effects of conflict are obvious, it is often assumed that the ultimate goal, with respect to this process, is its total elimination from work settings. This view overlooks an important fact: While conflict certainly *can* disrupt communication and coordination, and divert attention away from major tasks, it is by no means totally negative in its impact. Conflict serves to bring problems that have previously been ignored out into the open, and so enhances the likelihood of innovation and change. It can enhance within-group loyalty, and so improve performance within the units that are party to a conflict. And, conflict frequently encourages both sides to carefully monitor one another's performance—a process that can enhance motivation and performance on both sides.

Because conflict can have such benefits as well as its more obvious costs, the key task with respect to this process appears to be that of *managing* its occurrence. In sum, the major goal is not its total elimination from work settings; rather, it is that of developing procedures that maximize the potential benefits of conflict while minimizing its potential costs. A number of techniques for attaining this goal exist and are currently in frequent use.

Bargaining

By far the most common strategy for resolving organizational disputes, and thus for managing conflict, is *bargaining* (Lewicki & Litterer, 1985). In this process, opposing sides exchange offers, counteroffers, and (it is hoped) concessions, either directly or through representatives. If the process succeeds, an agreement acceptable to both sides is reached. Alternatively, if unsuccessful, deadlock may result, and conflict is intensified. Many different factors shape the course of bargaining and play a role in determining whether, and to what extent, it succeeds. Next, I review several of the most important of these factors.

Bargaining tactics. One group of variables that affects the outcome of bargaining involves specific tactics employed by negotiators. Many of these are designed to reduce opponents' aspirations, or convince them that they have little chance of reaching their goals. For example, one side can suggest (perhaps falsely) that it has other potential partners and will withdraw from the current negotiations if its proposals are not accepted. Similarly, one party to a dispute can claim that its break-even point is much higher (or lower) than it really is. If the other side accepts such information as true, it may be led to make sizable concessions. Third, negotiations are often strongly affected by the nature of initial offers. Relatively extreme offers seem to place considerable pressure on opponents to make concessions (Chertkoff & Conley, 1967).

Cognitive factors. A second group of factors that exerts strong effects upon the nature and outcome of bargaining involves the cognitive set or focus adopted by negotiators. When bargainers focus on the potential benefits of negotiations (they adopt a *positive frame*), the likelihood of an agreement is enhanced. In contrast, when they concentrate on the potential costs (they adopt a negative frame), the likelihood of a settlement is reduced (Neale & Bazerman, 1985).

Perhaps the single most important factor determining the success of negotiations in resolving conflicts, however, involves participants' overall orientation toward this process. As noted by Walton and McKersie (1965), persons taking part in negotiations can approach such exchanges from either of two distinct perspectives. On the one hand, they can view them as "win-lose" (distributive) situations in which gains by one side are necessarily linked with losses for the other. On the other hand, they can approach negotiations as potential "win-win" situations, in which the interests of the two sides are not necessarily incompatible. Not all situations offer this option, of course, but many do. If participants are willing to explore this possibility, and to consider all potential solutions, they can often attain *integrative agreements*—ones that offer greater joint benefits than simple compromise (splitting all differences down the middle).

Several techniques have proven useful in encouraging such agreements. In one, known as *nonspecific compensation,* one side gets what it wants on a specific issue, and the other is compensated on some other, unrelated specific issue (or issues). The question of whether the benefits obtained by each side are precisely equal in size is ignored. In another technique, *logrolling,* each side makes concessions on issues of relatively minor importance to it in order to obtain concessions from the opponent on issues it views as more central to its needs. In a third tactic, *cost cutting,* one side gets what it wants with respect to some issue, and any costs to the other party for granting such concessions are eliminated.

Research findings indicate that when parties to a dispute strive for integrative agreements through such tactics, joint outcomes do indeed increase (Pruitt & Rubin, 1986). Moreover, the nature of their discussions changes too. Contentious tactics such as making threats or taking unyielding positions decrease, and the open exchange of accurate information increases. Thus, not only do the two sides obtain more favorable outcomes, the quality of their relationship, too, may be enhanced. In view of such benefits, it seems clear that encouraging an integrative approach to negotiations can be a highly effective strategy for managing conflict in many work settings.

Third party intervention.   Despite the best efforts of both sides, negotiations sometimes reach a point at which no further progress seems possible. When this occurs, the aid of a third party who is not directly involved in the dispute can be extremely helpful (Lewicki & Litterer, 1985; Sheppard, 1984). Such persons can play the role of a *mediator* or that of an *arbitrator.* In the former case, the third party attempts, through various tactics, to facilitate voluntary agreements between the two sides. Mediators have no formal power and cannot impose an agreement. Instead, they seek to clarify the issues involved and enhance communication.

In contrast, arbitrators do have the power to impose the terms of an agreement. In binding arbitration, the two sides agree, in advance, to accept these terms. In voluntary arbitration, however, they remain free to reject the recommended agreement. In *conventional* arbitration, the arbitrator can offer any package of terms he or she wishes. In *final offer* arbitration, this person must choose between the final offers made by the disputants.

Both mediation and arbitration can be helpful in resolving organizational conflicts. However, both suffer from certain drawbacks. Because it requires voluntary compliance by the parties involved, mediation often proves ineffective. In fact, it may simply serve to emphasize the size of the gap separating the two sides. Arbitration suffers from other potential disadvantages. Sometimes, it exerts a *chilling effect* on negotiations. Because both sides know that the arbitrator will ultimately resolve the dispute for them, they see little point in engaging in meaningful bargaining. Second, one or both sides may come to suspect that the arbitrator is biased. If they do, they may refuse to accept the arbitrator's decisions. Third, commitment to arbitrator-imposed settlements tends to be weaker than that to directly negotiated ones. Despite these drawbacks, however, third-party intervention is often the only means of getting stalled negotiations back on track, so it is certainly a very useful technique in many contexts.

The Induction of Superordinate Goals

Human beings have a strong tendency to divide the world into two basic categories: *us* and *them*. Further, differential attitudes are often linked to this division. Members of one's own group are viewed more favorably, and are seen as being unique individuals. Members of other groups, however, are seen in a more negative light, and are often the subject of stereotyping—they are all viewed as being very much alike in their traits and characteristics (Linville, 1982).

This tendency to divide the social world into two basic categories is quite powerful, and is as common in work settings as in other contexts. Indeed, it often plays an important role in conflicts between various departments and divisions, or between members of various occupational groups. How can such reactions be countered? One effective approach involves the induction of *superordinate goals*—goals that tie the interests of the various groups together. The basic idea behind this tactic is simple: By inducing the parties to a conflict to focus on and work toward common objectives, their tendencies to perceive each other as belonging to the "them" category is reduced. Then, tendencies toward reciprocal stereotyping are thereby reduced, and communication and coordination may be improved.

The induction of superordinate goals to reduce internal conflict is implicit in compensation systems that offer to share profits with employees in some manner. Although it may not be stated explicitly, such systems encourage individuals to identify with their entire organization, and to view it as involved in direct competition with other organizations. To the extent employees adopt the view that "we're all in this together," internal conflicts may recede in perceived importance. Even such traditional adversaries as management and labor may choose to join forces to attain the common goal of overcoming foreign competition that threatens their mutual livelihood. In such cases, the recognition of shared superordinate goals can yield important benefits with respect to motivation and morale, as well as gains stemming mainly from reduced internal conflict.

The Interface Conflict-Solving Model

Several of the tactics and principles discussed previously in this section were combined by Blake and Mouton (1984) into a practical procedure for managing organizational conflict. Their approach is known as the *interface conflict-solving model,* and focuses primarily on conflicts between departments or units within a single organization. The model contends that many conflicts at such organizational interfaces occur because each party to such disputes perceives itself more favorably than its opponent, emphasizes group loyalty over other considerations, and focuses on its own goals while losing sight of broader organizational objectives. In order to counteract such tendencies, Blake and Mouton recommended the following steps.

First, representatives of each side formulate independent descriptions of what *ideal* relations between the groups would be like. Next, these persons meet and attempt to reach agreement on these descriptions. In other words, they try to formulate a description of ideal relations between the two groups that is acceptable to both sides. In a third step, the representatives of each side, again working separately, formulate descriptions of the actual relations between the group. They then meet with their counterparts to compare these perceptions. Not surprisingly, sizable gaps between the views of the two sides often emerge at this time. In a fifth step, the two sides work together to develop a detailed plan for getting from the current situation to the ideal one they have previously described. Finally, times for follow-up discussion are selected, so that progress toward the desired end state can be assessed, and changes in current strategies for getting there can be implemented.

The interface conflict-solving model has already been employed in a wide range of settings (e.g., to resolve conflicts between various departments within a single organization, union-management disputes, and conflicts between parent and subsidiary organizations). In each case, it has provided beneficial results, and ones that seem to persist over time. Clearly, then, this model represents an approach with much potential for widespread use in the years ahead.

ORGANIZATIONAL CONFLICT: ONE PLACE WHERE SCIENCE AND PRACTICE ACTUALLY MEET

Much to the chagrin of both groups, a sizable gap often exists between science and practice in industrial/organizational psychology. Findings uncovered in systematic research do not readily move from the pages of professional journals, where they are initially reported, into actual use by practitioners. Indeed, a gap of several years often exists between their appearance in print and their incorporation into popular textbooks in the field. Conversely, basic researchers often overlook important questions and problems faced by practitioners, or ignore the solutions practitioners formulate on the basis of long experience. The result, of course, is a degree of intellectual impoverishment in both quarters, and unsettling problems of communication between them.

Fortunately, the magnitude of such gaps seem relatively small with respect to organizational conflict. This appears to be one area in which the findings of basic research have attained ready application, and one in which the problems—and insights—of practitioners have found their way, in turn, into the hypotheses and theories of basic researchers. It will be most informative to comment on each of these directions of information flow in turn.

From Science to Practice

As knowledge about the nature of organizational conflict and techniques for its effective management has grown, this information has often been put to practical use. Although numerous examples of such practical applications exist, it will suffice, in this discussion, to mention just a few.

One of the clearest of these techniques involves the finding, in basic research, that most individuals attempt to deal with conflict in one of five distinct ways: compromise, avoidance, collaboration, accommodation, or competition (Rahim, 1983; Thomas, 1976). These five patterns are well known to many practicing managers, and are recognized in actual use. Further, many practitioners are also well acquainted with the basic dimensions underlying these conflict-handling tactics—concerns about one's own and others' outcomes. Familiarity with this framework is useful to managers who must deal with conflict in their jobs. It helps them to understand what is happening in many conflict situations—why the parties involved are acting in specific ways. And it aids them in selecting the approach that is most useful in a given context. In any case, this is certainly one way in which basic knowledge obtained in systematic research has entered into the thinking and planning of many practitioners.

Another illustration of the same principle is provided by broad recognition of the distinction between distributive (win-lose) and integrative (win-win) approaches to bargaining. Prior to widespread reference to this distinction in textbooks, popular volumes, and even many magazines and newspapers, most practitioners assumed that a win-lose approach was the only effective strategy in negotiations. Now many, if not most, practitioners recognize that a win-win approach is often better, and may yield a higher joint outcome for both sides. This principle is often incorporated into actual negotiations, and has yielded positive outcomes in many cases.

Finally, additional information about various tactics of bargaining and their effects has found its way into numerous popular books about the nature of the bargaining process. While the advice in such books is not always sound, and frequently ignores the complex interplay between various bargaining tactics, there can be little doubt that many thousands of practitioners are now much better informed about the basic nature of negotiations and the options available to negotiators during various phases of this process. On the whole, the benefits of this information to practitioners more than offset the potential costs.

At this point, it should be noted that although the flow of information from basic research to informed practice has been quite vigorous, it has certainly not been uniform across all areas. One aspect of practice that might benefit from additional communication in this respect is that of community-based dispute resolution. Thousands of such centers have sprung up across the U.S. and in several other nations as well. Some of the persons who provide services in these centers are quite familiar with the findings of basic research on conflict and negotiation and are, accordingly, well-prepared for the sensitive roles they play. Others, however, are not. Indeed, such individuals, while well-intentioned and highly motivated, must often fall back on their own "common sense" and informal experience when planning their actions as mediators or arbitrators. It seems clear that additional efforts to acquaint these persons with the findings of systematic research would contribute their understanding of the disputes with which they deal, and enhance their effectiveness in bringing them to a satisfactory resolution.

From Practice to Science

Turning to the other side of the coin, have the insights, knowledge, and experience of practitioners contributed in any manner to scientific knowledge about conflict or conflict management? Again, an affirmative answer seems justified.

First, it should be noted that in recent years, interest in conflict and conflict management has increased substantially among I/O psychologists and the members of closely related fields. Two new professional societies devoted to the study of conflict have been formed (the Power, Negotiation, and Conflict Management Interest Group of the Academy of Management, and the International Association for Conflict Management). In addition, a new journal devoted entirely to the topic of conflict management has been organized (the *International Journal of Conflict Management*). The roots of this expanded volume of research on conflict are complex, but one important factor appears to be the repeated requests of practitioners for more information on this topic. During the 1970s and 1980s, the U.S. and many other nations seem to have experienced a rise in the incidence of costly organizational conflicts. This, in turn, reflects the growing litigation-proneness of society generally, and the pressures produced by the internationalization of commerce. In any case, much basic research concerned with conflict and conflict management does appear to represent an attempt by industrial-organizational psychologists to provide added insight into these important topics, and hence improved techniques for resolving costly conflict.

Second, the methods employed in this research have expanded in scope, and are now designed to invite direct input from practitioners. In the past, industrial-organizational psychologists concerned with organizational conflict relied quite heavily on laboratory simulations as a research method. Although such work continues, an increasing proportion of the literature in this area is now based on survey data obtained from practicing managers (e.g., Baron, 1989), or from descriptions of critical conflict incidents provided by persons who have been directly involved (e.g., Bies, Shapiro, & Cummings, 1988).

Third, there is a growing level of collaboration between researchers and practitioners in this area. For example, I noted earlier my basic research on destructive criticism as a cause of organizational conflict. Recently, I have entered a collaborative relationship with a practicing management consultant who is interested in developing a practical program for training managers in the effective delivery of negative feedback to subordinates. Initial data useful in the formulation of this program are now being collected, and it is anticipated that the program, once formulated, will be subject to careful, systematic review after it is put to actual use. In short, basic research findings are being used to construct a practical program for managing one aspect of conflict, and this program, in turn, will yield valuable data concerning this aspect of conflict once it is put to practical use.

It is my view that collaborations of this type are extremely fruitful and are, indeed, the wave of the future in this area of I/O psychology. Through such cooperative arrangements the needs of practitioners for effective conflict management techniques will be met, and at the same time, added scientific insight into this important organizational process will be acquired. Life rarely offers researchers the luxury of meeting both goals at once, so it is gratifying to be working in an area in which such cooperative arrangements between science and practice can flourish.

REFERENCES

Ajzen, I. (1986). From intentions to actions: A theory of planned behavior. In J. Kuhl & J. Beckman (Eds.), *Actions-control: From cognition to behavior*. New York: Springer.

Ajzen, I., & Fishbein, M. (1980). *Understanding attitudes and predicting social behavior*. Englewood Cliffs, NJ: Prentice-Hall.

Baron, R. A. (1984). Reducing organizational conflict: An incompatible response approach. *Journal of Applied Psychology, 69*, 272–279.

Baron, R. A. (1985). Reducing organizational conflict: The role of attributions. *Journal of Applied Psychology, 70*, 434—441.

Baron, R. A. (1988a). Attributions and organizational conflict: The mediating role of apparent sincerity. *Organizational Behavior and Human Decision Processes, 41*, 111–127.

Baron, R. A. (1988b). Negative effects of destructive criticism: Impact on conflict, self-efficacy, and task performance. *Journal of Applied Psychology, 73*, 199–207.

Baron, R. A. (1989). Personality and organizational conflict: Effects of the Type A behavior pattern and self-monitoring. *Organizational Behavior and Human Decision Processes, 44*, 281—296.

Baron, R. A., & Bingley, J. (1989). *Perceived conflict in merging health organizations*. Unpublished manuscript, Rensselaer Polytechnic Institute.

Baron, R. A., & Greenberg, J. (1990). *Behavior in organizations*, 3rd ed. Boston: Allyn & Bacon.

Baron, R. A., & Richardson, D. (in press). *Human aggression*, 2nd ed. New York: Plenum.

Bies, R. J., & Shapiro, D. L. (1988). voice and justification: Their influence on procedural fairness judgments. *Academy of Management Journal, 13*, 676–685.

Bies, R. J., Shapiro, D. L., & Cummings, L. L. (1988). Causal accounts and managing organizational conflict: is it enough to say it's not my fault? *Communication Research, 15*, 381–399.

Blake, R. A., & Mouton, J. S. (1984). *Solving costly organizational conflicts*. San Francisco: Jossey-Bass.

Byrne, D. (1971). *The attraction paradigm*. New York: Academic Press.

Daft, R. L. (1986). *Organizational theory and design*, 2nd ed. St. Paul, MN: West.

Greenberg, J. (in Press). Looking fair vs. being fair: Managing impressions of organizational justice. In B. M. Staw & L. L. Cummings (Eds.), *Research in organizational behavior, Vol. 12*. Greenwich, CT: JAI Press.

Greenberg, J., & Folger, R. (1983). Procedural Justice, participation, and the fair process effect in groups and organizations. In P. B. Paulus (Ed.), *Basic group processes* (pp. 235–256). New York: Springer-Verlag.

Habib, G. W. (1987). Measures of manifest conflict in international joint ventures. *Academy of Management Journal, 30*, 808–816.

Hansen, R. D. (1980). Commonsense attribution. *Journal of Personality and Social Psychology, 39*, 996–1009.

Heldman, M. L. (1988). *When words hurt*. New York: New Chapter Press.

Hollin, C., & Trower, P. (1986). *Handbook of social skills training*. New York: Pergamon Press.

Jones, R. E., & Melcher, B. H. (1982). Personality and the preference for modes of conflict resolution. *Human Relations, 35*, 649–658.

Kabanoff, B. (1987). Predictive validity of the MODE conflict instrument. *Journal of Applied Psychology, 72*, 160–164.

Lewicki, R. J., & Litterer, J. A. (1985). *Negotiation*. Homewood, IL: Irwin.

Linville, P. W. (1982). The complexity-extremity effect and age-based stereotypes. *Journal of Personality and Social Psychology, 42*, 183–211.

Neale, M. A., & Bazerman, M. H. (1985). The effects of framing and negotiator overconfidence on bargaining behaviors and outcomes. *Academy of Management Journal, 28*, 34–49.

Pondy, L. R. (1967). Organizational conflict: Concepts and models. *Administrative Science Quarterly, 12*, 296–320.

Pruitt, D. G., & Rubin, J. Z. (1986). *Social conflict*. New York: Random House.

Rahim, M. A. (1983). A measure of styles of handling interpersonal conflict. *Academy of Management Journal, 26*, 368–376.

Ross, M., & Fletcher, G. J. O. (1985). *Attribution and social perception*. In G. Lindzey & E. Aronson (Eds.), *Handbook of social psychology*. New York: Random House.

Sheppard, B. H. (1984). Third party conflict intervention: A procedural framework. In B. M. Staw & L. L. Cummings (Eds.), *Research in Organizational Behavior* (Vol. 6, pp. 141–190). Greenwich, CT: JAI Press.

Thomas, K. W. (1976). Conflict and conflict management. In M. Dunnette (Ed.), *Handbook of industrial and organizational psychology* (pp. 889–935). Chicago: Rand McNally.

Thomas, K. W. (in press). Conflict and negotiation processes in organizations. In M. D. Dunnette (Ed.), *Handbook of industrial and organizational psychology*, 2nd ed. Chicago: Rand McNally.

Thomas, K. W., & Kilmann, R. H. (1974). *Thomas-Kilmann conflict mode instrument*. Tuxedo, NY: Xicom.

Thomas, K. W., & Schmidt, W. H. (1976). A survey of managerial interests with respect to conflict. *Academy of Management Journal, 19*, 315–318.

Tracy, K., Van Dusen, D., & Robinson, S. (1987). "Good" AND "bad" criticism: A descriptive analysis. *Journal of Communication, 37*, 46–59.

Walton, R. E., & McKersie, R. B. (1965). *A behavioral theory of labor negotiations: An analysis of a social interacting system*. New York: McGraw-Hill.

Wyer, R. S., & Srull, T. K. (1986). Human cognition in its social context. *Psychological Review, 93*. 322–359.

11 Sexual Harassment in Organizations

Frank E. Saal
Kansas State University

Broadly defined, sexual harassment is unsolicited and nonreciprocal male behavior that emphasizes women's sex roles over their roles as organizational members[1] (Farley, 1978; Meyer, Berchtold, Oestrich, & Collins, 1981). Because women's traditional sex roles prescribe a wide variety of behavioral expectations, some of which are more sexual in nature than others, most definitions of sexual harassment focus explicitly on sexually oriented behaviors. The Alliance Against Sexual Coercion (AASC), for example, described sexual harassment as "any sexually oriented practice that endangers a woman's job, that undermines her job performance and threatens her economic livelihood" (Backhouse & Cohen, 1981).

Others have been even more specific. Working Women United Institute (WWUI) defined sexual harassment as "any repeated and unwanted sexual comments, looks, suggestions, or physical contact" that one finds objectionable or offensive and that causes one discomfort on the job (Backhouse & Cohen, 1981). Somers and Clementson-Mohr's (1979) list of specific sexual-harassment behaviors left even less to the imagination: sexually oriented verbal abuse; sexist remarks regarding a woman's clothing or body; patting, pinching, or brushing up against a woman's body; leering or ogling; demands for sexual favors in return for hiring, promotion, or tenure; and physical assault of a sexual nature, up to and including rape.

A common thread running through all these definitions is the relevance and

---

[1]Because reported incidents involving female harassers and male victims are relatively rare, and because we know so little about homosexual harassment, this chapter deals with sexual harassment that involves male perpetrators and female victims.

importance of people's perceptions. The question of whether one person is asserting another person's sex role over their organizational role cannot always be answered objectively. There are no hard and fast criteria for determining when a sexually oriented practice is responsible for undermining a woman's work performance and thereby threatening her professional or financial well-being. Sexual comments or physical contact that one woman finds offensive or objectionable may not cause another woman any discomfort on her job at all. And finally, at what point does a well-intended compliment on one's appearance become a sexist remark or an example of verbal abuse? Who is to distinguish between a leer or an ogle and a friendly, appreciative glance?

In 1980 the Equal Employment Opportunity Commission (EEOC) amended its "Guidelines on Discrimination Because of Sex" in a way that clarified its position on the issue of sexual harassment. That revised document highlighted and legitimized the role of individuals' admittedly subjective perceptions. According to Section 1604.11, sexual harassment involves

> unwelcome sexual advances, request for sexual favors, and other verbal or physical conduct of a sexual nature . . . when (1) submission to such conduct is made either explicitly or implicitly a term or condition of an individual's employment, (2) submission to or rejection of such conduct by an individual is used as the basis for employment decisions affecting such individual, or (3) such conduct has the purpose or effect of substantially interfering with an individual's work performance or creating an intimidating, hostile, or offensive working environment.

The subjectivity inherent in determining when or if certain conduct on the part of others is responsible for interfering with a woman's job performance has already been noted. Similarly, intimidating, hostile, or offensive work environments lie in the eye of the beholder. It seems clear, therefore, that those who would understand the antecedents and dynamics of sexual harassment in organizations must attend to individual workers' perceptions. How do men and women interpret each other's behaviors in organizational contexts, and how do those interpretations and attributions facilitate or promote sexual harassment?

Following a brief summary of selected survey data that suggest the pervasiveness and seriousness of sexual harassment in various types of organizations, and an even briefer summary of existing models or theories of sexual harassment, the remainder of this chapter describes an ongoing program of research designed to illuminate the role(s) of interpersonal perceptions in facilitating or inhibiting harassment behaviors. In keeping with the theme of this book, actual and potential interactions between science and practice will be discussed. I will examine how science has (mis)informed practice, and how practice has (mis)informed science, as scientists and practitioners have attempted to understand and ultimately eliminate sexual harassment in organizations.

SURVEYS AND MODELS

Survey Data

Perhaps the first questionnaire devoted exclusively to the topic of sexual harassment was developed at Cornell University and administered to 155 women in upstate New York in May, 1975. Seventy percent of those women reported personal experience with some form of sexual harassment, and 92% considered it to be a serious problem (Farley, 1978). In November, 1976, *Redbook* published results obtained from a sexual harassment questionnaire that had appeared in the January, 1976, issue of that magazine. Eighty-eight percent of the women who responded ($N > 9000$) reported personal experience with some form of sexual harassment on the job, and (once again) 92% considered it to be a problem (Safran, 1976). A naval officer who used the *Redbook* questionnaire to collect data from the women on his base in Monterey, California, found that 81% of those who responded had experienced some form of sexual harassment (Backhouse & Cohen, 1981; MacKinnon, 1979).

At about the same time an *ad hoc* group from the Equal Rights for Women Committee at the United Nations surveyed 875 women in clerical and professional positions (before U. N. officials confiscated the questionnaire!). Approximately 50% reported personal experience with sexual pressures, or that they knew that such pressures existed within the organization (Farley, 1978). Carey, a sociologist at the University of Texas at San Antonio, surveyed 481 working women in 1977. *All* of them indicated that they had personally experienced some form of sexual harassment (Backhouse & Cohen, 1981). Finally, *Glamour* magazine published the results of a study in which 1000 women had been contacted in 1977 and again in 1979. Thirty and 39 percent, respectively, indicated that sexual harassment was a problem (Meyer et al., 1981).

As Meyer et al. (1981) correctly noted, most of these survey data are seriously flawed. Typically, a self-selected sample of individuals (readers of *Redbook* who take the trouble to complete a questionnaire and mail it back to the magazine's offices, for example) responded to questions about a phenomenon (sexual harassment) that had been defined either ambiguously or not at all. Fortunately, data are available from three more recent surveys that are less vulnerable to such criticisms.

In testimony before a House Judiciary Committee of the State of Illinois in March, 1980, Hayler described the results of a survey conducted by Sangamon State University and the Illinois Task Force on Sexual Harassment in the Workplace. Those results were based on "a scientifically selected sample drawn from a larger population of women employed in 50 . . . departments, agencies, boards, and commissions, and representative of that population. Surveys were sent to 4859 women ranging in age from 18 to 70, approximately 15% of the targeted work force" (State of Illinois, 1980). Of the 1495 women who returned complete questionnaires (a 31% response rate), 59% "reported experiencing one or more incidents of sexual harassment in their present place of employment, ranging from suggestive looks and sexual remarks to propositions and coercive sex." More specifically, "52% had been subjected to sexual remarks or teasing, 41% had been the target of suggestive looks or leers, 26% had experienced subtle sexual hints and pressure, 25% had been physically touched or grabbed, 20% had been sexually propositioned, 14% had been repeatedly pressured to engage in personal relationships, 9% reported other miscellaneous forms of unwanted sexual attention, and 2% had experienced some form of coercive sex" (State of Illinois, 1980).

In 1981 the U. S. federal government published the results of a large-scale survey distributed to a random sample of workers in the executive branch (U. S. Merit Systems Protection Board, 1981). Usable questionnaires were obtained from 10,648 women (representing an 86% response rate) with diverse levels of education, age, marital status, job classifications, and racial and ethnic backgrounds. Those data indicated that, within a 2-year period (May 1978 to May 1980), 33% of the women had been subjected to sexual remarks, 28% had received suggestive looks, 26% had been deliberately touched, 15% had been pressured for dates, 9% had been pressured for sexual favors, 9% had received letters or telephone calls of a sexual nature, and 1% had experienced actual or attempted rape or sexual assault. Although these percentages are smaller than those from the State of Illinois (1980) survey, they are still impressive—and they are based on a sample that is almost ten times larger.

More recently, Gutek (1985) reported relevant data based on telephone interviews with 827 women living in Los Angeles County, California. Selected randomly (using a random-digit dialing method), these women were "all eighteen or older, employed outside the home twenty hours a week or more, and [were] regularly in contact with members of the opposite sex at work as coworkers, supervisors, customers, or clients." They included professional, managerial, clerical, skilled, semiskilled, unskilled, and service workers. When asked if they had ever experienced sexual harassment, 53% of these women said "yes." More specifically, 23% said they had been the target of insulting comments, 20% reported insulting looks or gestures, 33% experienced sexual touching, 12% said they had been expected to socialize as part of their jobs, and almost 8% indicated that they had been expected to engage in sexual activity as part of their jobs.

Further evidence supporting the pervasiveness of the problem is that it is not restricted to business or industrial organizations. Sexual harassment occurs within academic institutions ("Coed Complaint," 1982; Dziech & Weiner, 1984; "Fighting Lechery on Campus," 1980; Pope, Levenson, & Schover, 1979), and apparently inside political and governmental agencies ("Fighting Its Image Problem," 1982; Ray, 1976), military units (Meyer et al., 1981; Rogan, 1981;

"Woman Demoted for Sex Overture," 1980), and even religious organizations (Meyer et al., 1981; "Sexual Harassment Charged," 1980).

Models/Theories of Sexual Harassment

Based on their review of court cases, legal defenses, and prior research, Tangri, Burt, and Johnson (1982) described three explanatory models of sexual harassment in organizations: a Natural/Biological Model, an Organizational Model, and a Socio-Cultural Model. The first of these asserts that it is "natural" for women and men to be attracted to each other, but that men have a stronger sex drive and sexual harassment represents idiosyncratic, "sick" behavior on the part of some men who are unable or unwilling to control their sex drive. A key characteristic of this Natural/Biological Model is the *absence* of any discriminatory intent on the part of male harassers.

The Organizational Model shifts the spotlight away from the individual (and his drives) and focuses instead on the organizational contexts in which men and women work. Its basic contention is that the differential power inherent in different positions within an organizational hierarchy, the numerical ratios of males to females within those positions, the norms and social climate that characterize an organization, and the (un)availability of formal or informal grievance procedures will combine to determine the frequency with which sexual harassment occurs. The Socio-Cultural Model takes the unequal distribution of power and status among and between men and women one step further. According to this model, sexual harassment results from these disparities, and serves as a vehicle for preserving men's dominance over women in the workplace and throughout the general economy.

Using data from the U. S. Merit Systems Protection Board (1981) study, Tangri et al. (1982) reported stronger empirical support for the Organizational and Socio-Cultural Models—both of which view sexual harassment as a function of power and status disparities—than for the Natural/Biological Model. None of the models received clear-cut support, however, and Zedeck and Cascio (1984) subsequently concluded that "we need a better specification of the hypothetical linkages that will cast [sexual harassment] into a testable theoretical framework."

Gutek (1985) is similarly dubious about the adequacy of these three models. She believes instead that her "sex-role spillover" model of sexual harassment (Gutek & Morasch, 1982) is a more promising response to Zedeck and Cascio's (1984) challenge. The basic premise of this model is "the carryover into the workplace of gender-based expectations about behavior." Sex-role spillover is thought to occur whenever the ratio of males to females in particular jobs, occupations, or work groups is skewed in either direction. Women in work situations dominated by other women, sometimes referred to as "pink-collar jobs" (Howe, 1977)—clerical workers or elementary school teachers, for example—are victimized by sex-role spillover because the job itself has assumed feminine sex-role characteristics (helpful, supportive, nurturing, etc.). Men's expectations concerning the behavior of women who hold such jobs mirror their beliefs about the way women "in general" should behave. On the other hand, women who are outnumbered by men in their work situation (construction workers and upper-level managers, for example) tend to be seen as "women" first and "workers" second because their gender is so salient, and sex-role spillover ensues. Of course, one very important and relevant component of the female sex role is being sexually attractive and (at least potentially) available to men. Gutek's confidence in this model was bolstered by the results of her Los Angeles County survey described earlier. Sexual harassment behaviors, ranging from comments to coerced sexual encounters, were more common when jobs were dominated by either women or men than when the ratio of males and females was closer to unity (1 : 1).

Relationships between Science and Practice

Based on these brief reviews of sexual-harassment surveys and models, what can be said about the interface between science and practice? Do these reviews include or imply any information that addresses the viability or relevance of the scientist-practitioner model? I believe they do.

First, there simply were no surveys, scientific or otherwise, of people's experiences with sexual harassment until working women (and, to a much lesser extent, working men) informed researchers that harassment existed in the workplace, and that it was a serious problem in many different types of organizations. Although these women were not practicing industrial/organizational (I/O) psychologists, their success in bringing sexual harassment to the attention of organizational researchers constitutes a typical example of "practice informing science" about the *existence* of an applied problem. The existence of such problems in work organizations is a basic rationale for the existence of the field of I/O psychology, and working men and women are in the best positions to recognize those problems and bring them to the attention of the scientific community. The women who attended a "speakout" on sexual harassment in the mid-1970s in Ithaca, New York, and those who belonged to the Civil Service Employees Association in Binghamton, New York, and who provided information to the Human Affairs Program at Cornell University (Farley, 1978), effectively performed this function.

As I noted in the opening paragraphs of this chapter, numerous definitions of sexual harassment have emerged since that label was created in the mid-1970s to refer to certain male behaviors (Farley, 1978). Although those definitions shared some commonalities, they were neither identical nor interchangeable. This lack of consistency led to diverse operational definitions of sexual harassment in subsequent surveys, and ultimately to measurement errors. A second notable example of "practice informing science," then, was the EEOC's revision of its "Guidelines on Discrimination Because of Sex" in 1980. This document provided researchers with a standard definition of sexual harassment that is applicable throughout the United States and is supported by the authority of Title VII of the 1964 Civil Rights Act. Further, it provided scientists with a definition that explicitly acknowledges the importance of people's perceptions of other's behaviors. Similar to the first example, this was not a case of practicing I/O psychologists offering guidance to their research-scientist colleagues. It is, however, an example of legislation influencing the practice of a variety of professionals in employment-related contexts (managers, affirmative action officers, and yes, I/O psychologists, too), which in turn has influenced the scientific research activities of I/O psychologists who study sexual harassment.

The review of surveys and models in the first part of this chapter also offers several examples of science (mis)informing practice. The results of early surveys concerning sexual harassment were flawed by inappropriate sampling strategies and vague or nonexistent definitions of what was to be measured. Data obtained from self-selected respondents led to overestimates of the percentages of women who had experienced harassment. The effects of confusing or absent definitions were less clear. Respondents who had experienced various sexual abuses, but who considered such treatment to be "normal" or "just part of the job," probably indicated that they had *not* been sexually harassed, and thereby contributed to underestimates of the problem. Alternatively, respondents with unusually broad and inclusive definitions of sexual harassment (including, for example, instances of sex-based discrimination that are not sexual in nature) may have contributed to overestimates of its pervasiveness. The point is that scientists versed in appropriate sampling strategies and sound survey-construction principles were able to identify the flaws in early survey procedures and results, and suggest specific remedies. Although subsequent estimates of the magnitude of sexual-harassment problems within organizations were somewhat smaller, those figures still suggested that a very serious problem existed; and, those subsequent estimates were probably more credible to skeptical (male?) organizational leaders. Thus, science informed practice.

Scientists' contributions to practitioners in the form of explanatory models or theories of sexual harassment are more ambiguous. Practitioners who accept the Natural/Biological Model (despite its relatively weak empirical support) are likely to be frustrated in their efforts to derive organizational interventions for reducing and eliminating sexual harassment. They can either "fold their tents and go home" because sexual attraction between men and women is inevitable and some men are bound to "go too far," or they can embrace Margaret Mead's (1980) proposal that we make "sex" (presumably in any form, including flirtation as well as assault) *taboo* in the workplace (just as we forbid the use of alcohol or other "controlled substances" on the job). Because neither of these alternatives is particularly palatable or constructive, and because this model remains unsubstantiated by empirical data (Tangri et al., 1982), it seems safe to say that practitioners who have adopted it have not been served very well by their model-building colleagues.

Tangri et al.'s (1982) analyses of data obtained from federal employees (U.S. Merit Systems Protection Board, 1981) suggest that practitioners who adopt either the Organizational or the Socio-Cultural Model of sexual harassment have been somewhat better informed. Nevertheless, neither of these models is easily translated into workable organizational interventions because each attributes sexual harassment to firmly entrenched power disparities between men and women that are supported by either organizational or society-wide hierarchies. According to both of these models, sexual harassment is facilitated by and is an expression of differences in women's and men's power. Dismantling the organizational and societal hierarchies that are responsible for these sex differences is simply not a realistic (or perhaps even a desirable) goal for most organizational practitioners.

Rather than eliminating these hierarchies, a more reasonable goal is to achieve an equitable (re)distribution of power among women and men within them. This particular organizational intervention can be derived directly from Gutek's (1985; Gutek & Morasch, 1982) sex-role spillover model of sexual harassment. Recall that this model stipulates that sexual harassment is inhibited when the ratio of women to men in jobs or occupations is more balanced. Because model-based interventions (affirmative action plans, for example) are *relatively* feasible, and because the model has received some impressive empirical support (Gutek, 1985), the sex-role spillover model may be the best example of theoretical organizational scientists informing their practicing colleagues concerning the dynamics of sexual harassment in the workplace.

And yet, scientists can still do better. Affirmative action and other programs for equitably redistributing hierarchical power among men and women cannot be expected to produce results "overnight," and may result in dysfunctional "backlash" among men (Rosen & Mericle, 1979) *and women* (Chacko,1982; Heilman & Herlihy, 1984) who react negatively to favorable treatment of one group at the expense of another group. The remainder of this chapter is therefore devoted to describing a program of research based on a hypothesis that has implications for reducing sexual harassment through organizational interventions that should require less time to implement and may be less vulnerable to destructive backlash. This program of research is, on the one hand, an I/O psychologist's attempt to generate scientific information that can be used by him and his practicing colleagues as they attempt to reduce (and ultimately to eliminate) sexual harassment in organizations. On the other hand, it represents an effort to conduct scientific research that is firmly guided by the "real-world" concerns of those practitioners and the organizations they serve.

PERCEPTIONS AND SEXUAL HARASSMENT

A False Start

Recall that the EEOC's 1980 amendment to its "Guidelines on Discrimination Because of Sex" defined sexual harassment as "conduct of a sexual nature . . . [that] has the purpose or effect of . . . creating an intimidating, hostile, or offensive working environment." Shortly before the publication of that amendment, Vogelmann-Sine, Ervin, Christensen, Warmsun, and Ullmann (1979) reported data that suggested an interesting and relevant hypothesis. Although their study focused on rape, these researchers concluded that there were systematic differences between men and women who were asked to empathize with a woman's feelings in a variety of situations involving coercion and/or sexual advances. Specifically, men tended to *over*estimate the psychological impact (feelings of weakness, threat, humiliation, hostility, etc.) of relatively *less* intense sexual incidents, but they *under*estimated the impact on women of *more* intense incidents.

If these feelings could be generalized to incidents involving sexual harassment, we would be in a position to make specific predictions about men's sexual harassment behaviors. Men who *over*estimate the negative impact of relatively *less* severe forms of sexual harassment might be *less* likely to engage in these behaviors than men who do not misperceive women's reactions in this manner. Men who *over*estimate women's negative reactions may be more likely to assume that women so affronted will be more likely to retaliate through personal, organizational, or legal channels. Alternatively, men who *under*estimate the negative impact of relatively *more* severe forms of sexual harassment (and thus the probability of retaliation) may be *more* likely to engage in such behaviors than men who do not. Of course, it is quite possible that the same men might overestimate the effects of less severe harassment *and* underestimate the effects of more severe harassment.

With these hypotheses in mind, I designed and conducted a study to determine whether Vogelmann-Sine et al.'s (1979) findings could indeed be generalized to the sexual harassment domain by searching for systematic differences between women's and men's abilities to empathize with a woman who has experienced various forms of sexual harassment. If a group (sex) difference can be documented, the next step would entail searching for individual differences among men that would enable us to predict who might be more apt to engage in particular varieties of harassment.

Subjects and Procedures.   Subjects were 194 female and 188 male undergraduate General Psychology students. Each subject read and responded to one of four different versions of a questionnaire. Each version contained 16 different descriptions of interpersonal encounters that involved at least one woman and one man. Three examples of those descriptions are as follows:

225

1. A manager makes his secretary listen while he explains graphically what he would like to do to her in bed.

2. A female student is walking down the hall in the university. As she passes a male professor, she notices that he is surveying her body from head to toe.

3. A female employee's boss threatens to fire her if she does not engage in sexual intercourse with him.

In the actual questionnaires, each description was followed by the phrase "This woman feels . . . " (or "These women feel . . . " if two or more women were involved), which prompted subjects to empathize with the emotional reactions of the woman/women involved.

Some of the descriptions were adapted from Vogelmann-Sine et al.'s (1979) vignettes that depicted various kinds of violent and/or sexual encounters. Others evolved from informal discussions and reviews of both academic and popular sexual-harassment literature (Backhouse & Cohen, 1981; "Coed Complaint," 1982; Dziech & Weiner, 1984; Farley, 1978; "Fighting Lechery on Campus," 1980; MacKinnon, 1979; Meyer et al., 1981). Following Vogelmann-Sine et al.'s lead, a few of the descriptions portrayed coercive encounters that do not involve any overtly sexual behaviors. These were included to assess the *relative* (in)accuracy of men's perceptions of women's reactions to two different kinds of encounters—those involving an element of sexuality and those devoid of any obvious sexual content.

One half of the descriptions in each questionnaire specified a "work" environment, while the other half specified an "academic/school" environment. Each description appeared on a separate page of the questionnaire, and each was followed by the same set of 17 semantic differential scales that allowed subjects to record their estimates of the portrayed woman's/women's emotional reactions. These 17 scales were identical to those used by Vogelmann-Sine et al. (1979), and included dominant/submissive, threatened/safe, flattered/humiliated, interested/uninterested, weak/strong, friendly/hostile, devastated/capable, good/bad, meek/assertive, wise/foolish, aroused/repulsed, angry/pleased, confident/frightened, annoyed/glad, secure/anxious, powerful/powerless, and passive/ active.

Results.   Before pursuing more sophisticated analyses of the data, I decided simply to examine and compare male and female subjects' mean responses to each of the semantic differential scales for each of the descriptions in the four different versions of the questionnaire. The most striking result of these comparisons was the *in*frequency with which men's average responses differed significantly from women's average responses. A total of 1088 comparisons[2] of men's

---

[2]Comparisons were based on Student's *t*-tests for independent means.

and women's mean responses (17 semantic differential scales × 16 descriptions/questionnaire × 4 different versions of the questionnaire) yielded only 171 differences (less than 16%) that were statistically significant at the $p < .05$ level. Given the danger of spuriously obtaining significant differences when conducting large numbers of statistical tests (Kirk, 1982), a more conservative approach is to accept only those differences that satisfy a more stringent criterion of significance. A re-examination of the 1088 comparisons revealed a mere 69 (slightly more than 6%) that were significantly different at the $p < .01$ level. Men's misperceptions of women's reactions to the variety of interpersonal encounters described in the questionnaires definitely seemed to be "the exception" rather than "the rule." Thus, further analyses did not appear to be warranted.

Discussion. This study assessed the congruence between male and female college students' perceptions or expectations of how women react to a variety of interpersonal encounters, many of which are commonly construed as different degrees and forms of sexual harassment in work and academic settings. Statistically significant sex differences were rare. Those that did emerge could be attributed to inflated levels of experimentwise alpha (Type I) error.

If we make the very reasonable assumption that female subjects responded to the semantic differentials according to how *they, themselves,* would react if confronted with the situations described in the questionnaires, these data suggest that men are quite capable of predicting (and, thus, potentially understanding) women's reactions to various kinds of sexual harassment at work and at school. The data, therefore, do *not* support the hypothesis that men's misperceptions of women's reactions to sexual harassment might be an important factor in facilitating or precipitating sexual-harassment behaviors. The general accuracy of men's assessments of women's reactions suggests a different interpretation of the expression "Ignorance is no excuse." Ignorance is probably no excuse here because these data suggest that men are generally *not* ignorant of the emotional effects of sexual harassment on women.

Although these findings cannot be deemed conclusive for a number of reasons (they are based on a sample of college students and may not generalize to men and women who are employed full-time; failure to reject the null hypothesis does not constitute "proof" of that hypothesis, etc.), they are not encouraging. If, in fact, men do not misperceive the *consequences* of sexual harassment for women, where and how else might men's (mis)perceptions contribute to sexual harassment at work or at school? Recent work by Abbey (1982) suggests that men's misperceptions of women's *intentions* and *behaviors* might merit further study.

A Review of Abbey's Findings and Conclusions

Abbey (1982) conducted a laboratory experiment in which unacquainted male–female pairs of subjects engaged in brief conversations while other men and women unobtrusively viewed and overheard those conversations. Data obtained from questionnaires administered following these conversations indicated that there were sex differences in subjects' ratings of the actors (discussants):

> Male actors and observers rated the female actor as being more promiscuous and seductive than female actors and observers rated her. Males were also more sexually attracted to the opposite-sex actor than females were. Furthermore, males also rated the male actor in a more sexualized fashion than females did. (p. 830)

Abbey interpreted these results

> as indicating that men are more likely to perceive the world in sexual terms and to make sexual judgments than women are. Males do seem to perceive friendliness from females as seduction, but this appears to be merely one manifestation of a broader male sexual orientation. (p. 830)

If Abbey's (1982) findings are generalizable and her conclusions sound, if men do tend to perceive "sexy" behavior where women see (or intend to project) only friendliness, these different perceptions may provide a clue to understanding some forms of sexual harassment. That is, women in work or academic environments who strive to create pleasant interpersonal relationships by behaving in a friendly manner may be (mis)perceived by some of their male colleagues (supervisors, coworkers, teachers, etc.) to be sending signals of sexual interest or availability. Repeated requests for dates, staring or ogling, sexual innuendoes, and/or unnecessary touching may result if these men act on their (mis)perceptions. Because men believe that such behaviors are more "normal" and more acceptable in the workplace than women do (Gutek, Morasch, & Cohen, 1983), such responses may not be entirely unpredictable.

These implications of Abbey's (1982) conclusions prompted our series of studies. Our first goals were to replicate the sex differences in perceptions reported by Abbey, and to extend those results to settings where sexual harassment often occurs—the workplace and academia. Next, we wished to investigate the empirical relationships between individual differences among men in the extent to which they (mis)perceive friendliness as "sexiness" and individual differences in the extent to which they endorse or condone typical sexual-harassment behaviors. Demonstration of such connections would have implications for theories or models of sexual harassment, and constitute an important first step toward the development of feasible, potentially effective intervention programs to reduce and eventually eliminate sexual harassment in organizations.

Study 1: Replication of Abbey (1982)[3]

Subjects and Procedures.   Subjects were 110 female and 97 male undergraduate students who participated in this research as part of a class requirement.

---

[3]Studies 1, 2, and 3 are described in greater detail in Saal, Johnson, and Weber (1989).

Because the research was (mis)represented as a study of the "getting acquainted" process, subjects reported to the experiment in groups of four to six such that none of the subjects in any group was previously acquainted with any other student in that group, and each group included at least two women and two men. Upon reporting to the research site, one woman and one man were (randomly) assigned the role of "discussant," while the remainder of the subjects were assigned the role of "observer"; discussants were not informed, however, that their getting-acquainted session would be overheard or observed. Discussants then engaged in short (approximately 10 minutes) getting-acquainted conversations, while observers watched them through a one-way mirror and overheard them over a simple sound system. At the conclusion of the discussion, discussants and observers were asked to complete questionnaires that supposedly asked for their opinions about the getting-acquainted session. Finally, they were debriefed concerning the actual purpose of the study. These procedures were followed with 49 groups of subjects.

The questionnaires did include items that asked about the getting-acquainted process in order to prevent the subjects from becoming suspicious. Also included, however, were the same items that Abbey (1982) used to tap subjects' opinions concerning the discussants' motives or behavioral intentions during the conversation. Using 7-point scales (1 = "not at all . . . "; 7 = "very . . . "), subjects reported the extent to which they thought discussants had tried to be cheerful, friendly, assertive, flirtatious, considerate, enthusiastic, likeable, seductive, attractive, warm, intelligent, promiscuous, and sincere. Half the subjects rated the intentions of the same-sex discussant first, while the remainder assessed the intentions of the opposite-sex discussant first. Discussants, of course, reported their *own* intentions during the preceding discussion when they were asked to evaluate the intentions of the "same-sex discussant."

Results.   Data were analyzed with a 2 × 2 × 2 (Sex of Subject × Role of Subject × Sex of Discussant) multivariate analysis of variance (MANOVA), followed by univariate analyses of variance (ANOVAs) to determine the specific perceptions that were responsible for statistically significant ($p < .05$) MANOVA effects. Although a variety of significant MANOVA effects emerged, the Sex-of-Subject effect is particularly germane to this chapter. Subsequent ANOVAs revealed that men perceived significantly more flirtatiousness, more promiscuity, and more seductiveness, but less friendliness in the female discussants' behaviors than did the women.

These results are highly consistent with Abbey's (1982) earlier findings, thereby essentially replicating her work. Studies 2 and 3 were conducted to examine the robustness of this sex difference in perceptions of women's behaviors and intentions, as well as the extent to which that difference can be generalized to organizational contexts in which sexual harassment is often reported—the workplace and academia.

Study 2: The Workplace

Subjects and Procedures. Subjects were 88 female and 75 male undergraduate students. They reported to the research site in groups of 10 to 15, where they were (mis)informed that the videotape they were about to see had been produced by a group of local retail stores for the purpose of training recently hired clerks and cashiers, and that the purpose of the research was to gather their impressions of the quality of the videotape and its potential usefulness as a training device. In fact, the videotape had been recorded at a check-out counter in a local discount store, but the male assistant store manager and the female cashier were portrayed by drama students who based their interaction on a script written by the experimenters. The script portrayed a typical "orientation session" between two employees who appeared to be trying to establish a pleasant, yet entirely proper working relationship. The "manager" and the "cashier" were reasonably friendly and outgoing toward each other, but neither said or did anything that was overtly seductive of flirtatious.

After viewing the short (approximately 7 minutes) videotape, subjects completed questionnaires. Once again, the questionnaires included distractor items dealing with the apparent utility of the videotape as a training vehicle. The key questions, however, solicited subjects' opinions concerning the intentions and behaviors of the manager and the cashier. Subjects responded using the same 7-point scales described in Study 1, except that an additional item was included for Study 2—"sexy." Half the subjects answered questions about the female cashier first, while the other half evaluated the intentions of the male manager first. Once again, subjects were debriefed after completing the questionnaire.

Results. Data were analyzed with a 2 × 2 (Sex of Subject × Role/Sex of Employee) MANOVA, followed by univariate ANOVAs to identify the specific items that were responsible for statistically significant MANOVA effects. (Role and sex of employees portrayed in the videotape were completely confounded—the manager was male and the cashier was female. This confound is addressed below in Study 4.) Although the MANOVA main effect for Sex of Subject was significant ($p < .05$), only three of the fourteen subsequent ANOVAs revealed significant sex differences in perceptions. Two of these were sexual in nature: Men thought the female cashier was trying to be more promiscuous and more sexy than did the women.

These results effectively extend the replication of Abbey's (1982) findings. Using a different method (videotaped rather than live, face-to-face interactions) and focusing on a specific organizational context (the workplace), we demonstrated once again that men tend to perceive greater levels of "sexuality" in a woman's normal behavior. Study 3 retained the videotape method, but returned the male-female interaction to an academic context, one in which sexual harassment is also common (Dziech & Weiner, 1984).

Study 3: Academia

Subjects and Procedures. Subjects were 102 female and 98 male undergraduates. The procedure was identical to that used in Study 2. The only variation involved (mis)informing subjects that the videotape they were about to see was part of a research program concerning the effectiveness of nonverbal communication in social exchanges, and showing them a different videotape. This tape was also based on a script written by the experimenters, and depicted a meeting involving a male professor and a female student who was requesting an extension of the deadline for her term paper. The female student was portrayed by a drama student and the male professor was played by a professor in the theater department at Kansas State University. The actors were friendly and outgoing, but neither the student nor the professor said or did anything overtly "sexy"; it was a rather ordinary professor-student interaction.

Following the short videotape (approximately 10 minutes), subjects were asked to complete questionnaires that included a sufficient number of items pertaining to nonverbal communication to reinforce the stated purpose of the study. The key items, of course, asked for subjects' opinions concerning the behaviors and intentions of the student and professor. These items were identical to those used in Study 2, and used the same set of 7-point response scales. Half the subjects evaluated the intentions of the professor first, while the remainder assessed the intentions of the female student first. As in the previous studies, subjects were totally debriefed after handing their completed questionnaires to the experimenter.

Results. Data were again analyzed using a 2 × 2 (Sex of Subject × Role/Sex of "Target") MANOVA, followed by univariate ANOVAs to determine the specific perceptions that were responsible for any significant MANOVA effects. (As in Study 2, the role and sex of the target person were completely confounded—the professor was male and the student was female. See Study 4.) Once again, a statistically significant ($p < .05$) MANOVA main effect for Sex of Subject emerged. Univariate ANOVAs revealed that men saw the female student trying to be more flirtatious, more promiscuous, more seductive, more sexy, but less friendly than did the women. These findings further extend the replication of Abbey (1982).

Discussion of Studies 1, 2, and 3

Men do seem to attribute more "sexuality" (flirtatiousness, seductiveness, etc.) to women's behaviors than do other women. These attributions do not appear to be dependent on any specific research method, or limited to any specific social setting. Two caveats merit our attention, however.

First, as Saal, Johnson, and Weber (1989) acknowledged, the absolute levels of sexuality that men reported using the 7-point scales were not large. Although significant sex differences emerged, both men's and women's average ratings of how "sexy" the women (in the discussions or the videotapes) were trying to behave fell below the midpoint (4.00) of the scales. (Abbey's [1982] data were quite similar.) A more accurate interpretation, then, is that men appear to perceive women as behaving in *less un*seductive, *less un*promiscuous, *less un*flirtatious, and *less un*sexy ways than do other women (or the "target" women themselves, as revealed in Study 1; see Saal et al.). Thus, men do *not* see blatantly flirtatious seductresses when confronted with friendly, outgoing women. The data from Studies 1, 2, and 3 *do* suggest, however, that men have a more "sensitive" threshold for perceiving sexy behavior on the part of women. As Saal et al. explained, these data suggest that

> as a woman's interpersonal behavior varies along a continuum ranging from very unfriendly and distant to very friendly and outgoing (as well it might, as a woman becomes more familiar with and comfortable in a given social setting), . . . men will be quicker than women to label that increasingly friendly behavior as "sexy." They *might* then respond in a variety of ways that the woman in question may construe as sexual harassment.

Second, this series of studies focused only on situations where the woman occupied a position in the organizational hierarchy that was either equal to the man's (the original replication of Abbey (1982) based on two undergraduate students) or inferior to the man's (the cashier who was subordinate to the manager, and the student who was subordinate to the professor). These data tell us nothing about the generality of this sex difference in perceptions of women's "sexiness" to situations where the woman is in an organizationally superior position. Study 4 (Johnson, Stockdale, & Saal, 1987) was designed and conducted to fill this gap.

Study 4: Role Reversal: A More Powerful Woman and a Less Powerful Man

Subjects and Procedures.   Subjects were 187 female and 165 male undergraduate students. The procedure was the same as that used in Study 3. Subjects were (mis)informed that they would view a videotape as part of a study concerned with nonverbal communication, and the videotape each student saw was a variation of the professor-student exchange used in Study 3. In this study, however, each subject viewed only one of twelve different versions of a videotaped scenario depicting a student requesting a deadline extension from a professor. Six of these versions portrayed a male professor interacting with a female student (identical to Study 3), but six portrayed a female professor interacting with a male student. An additional variation on the basic procedures followed in Study 3 involved the endings of the different versions of the videotape. In each tape the professor demonstrated one of three different levels of "suggestive" behavior: (a) no suggestive behavior—the professor simply offered several reference books to the student; (b) mildly suggestive behavior—the professor invited the student to return to his/her office later that evening, at which time the professor would be able to "help" the student with the term paper; and (c) moderately suggestive behavior—the professor invited the student to his/her home that evening, where they could "work on the term paper." In this last condition, the professor also made it clear that they would be alone, and that a fine bottle of wine and an excellent collection of jazz records were available. Further, for each of these three conditions, the student either accepted the professor's offer or politely declined it. Thus, the twelve versions of the videotape were created by completely crossing three different offers of "help" from the professor with two different responses from the student (along with the two different conditions created by having the male actor and the female actor play each of the two roles). The same actors appeared in all twelve versions of the videotape.

After viewing one of the twelve versions of the videotape, subjects completed questionnaires that were identical to those used in Study 3. As before, subjects were completely debriefed as to the true purpose of the study after they had submitted their opinions (using 7-point scales) concerning the ways in which the student and the professor were trying to behave during their interchange.

Results.   Data were analyzed separately by videotape condition (male professor/female student or female professor/male student) and separately according to the role (professor or student) of the actor whose behaviors and intentions were being evaluated. Thus, all analyses were 2 × 3 × 2 (Sex of Subject × Level of Suggestiveness × Response of Student) MANOVAs, followed by univariate ANOVAs to determine the specific perceptions responsible for any significant multivariate effects.

In all of the twelve different conditions (versions of the videotape), men perceived greater levels of sexuality in the behaviors of the female actor than did women. Consistent with the results of Study 3, men perceived the female student trying to be significantly more promiscuous, more seductive, and more sexy than did the women. Men also saw the female professor trying to be significantly more promiscuous, more seductive, more flirtatious, and more sexy than did the women. The only unusual finding involved subjects' perceptions of the *male* professors' intentions. When the male professor behaved in a moderately suggestive fashion (an invitation to his home, wine, jazz . . .), the women saw *him* as trying to be more seductive, more flirtatious, and more sexy than did the men.

Discussion.   Study 4 suggests, then, that the sex difference in perceptions of women's intentions in various organizational settings is *not* limited to situations where the woman is in an organizationally inferior position to the man. Whether the woman was presented in the role of student or professor, she was still perceived by male subjects as trying to be more "sexual" than she was perceived by female subjects. Study 4 also suggests that these different perceptions of women's intentions are not influenced by either the level of "suggestiveness" portrayed in a male-female exchange or by the response of the woman to the man's suggestive behavior. It would appear, therefore, that Abbey's (1982) original findings and conclusions regarding sex differences in perceptions of women's intentions and behaviors are extremely robust and can be generalized to a variety of different organizational situations.

If we accept this conclusion, the next step entails examining the relationship (if any) between individual differences among men in the extent to which they (mis)perceive a woman's friendliness as sexiness, and individual differences in their willingness to tolerate, endorse, or ultimately engage in behaviors that are commonly construed as sexual harassment. Study 5 is an initial attempt to investigate this possible connection.

Study 5: Men's Perceptions of Women's Behaviors and Their Responses to Various Sexual Harassment Scenarios

Subjects and Procedures   Subjects were 108 male undergraduate students. After being (mis)informed that the first part of the study dealt with nonverbal communication, subjects were shown the same videotape portraying the ordinary male professor/female student conversation that was used in Study 3. Following the videotape, they were asked to complete questionnaires that were also identical to those used in Study 3. These responses were used to assess the extent of "sexiness" they perceived in the female student's behavior while she inquired about a possible extension of her term paper deadline.

After they had turned in their completed questionnaires to the experimenter, subjects were then asked to respond to some questions pertaining to 29 scenarios involving male-female exchanges reported in the workplace. Three examples of these exchanges are as follows:

1.   A male supervisor asks a female employee personal questions about her sex life.

2.   A male traveling representative and his female associate are going on a business trip; the male representative requests only one hotel room.

3.   A manager tells his female secretary that she must sleep with him because it is his right—he pays her salary.

The second part of the study was presented to subjects as a *completely different* investigation that was being conducted to examine some of the implications of the tremendous influx of women into various work roles. Informal discussions following the study indicated that subjects accepted our "cover story," and did not perceive any connection between the first and second parts of Study 5. For each of 29 different scenarios, subjects used 7-point scales to respond to six questions:

1. How appropriate/inappropriate is this man's behavior?

2. How would you respond if you overheard/observed a male colleague behaving in this manner?

3. If this woman filed a grievance or law suit and you had observed/ overheard the behavior in question, would you be willing to testify on her behalf?

4. . . . would you be willing to testify in defense of the man involved?

5. If you heard about his behavior while you were interviewing for a job, would it influence your decision to accept the job if it were offered? and

6. How likely is it that you might one day behave in a manner similar to this man?

These six questions were used to assess the extent to which these male subjects were willing to tolerate or endorse (and perhaps even engage in) various examples of sexually harassing behavior. When subjects had completed the second part of the study, they were informed as to the true nature of the research.

Results.   As this book goes into production, we have completed only preliminary analyses of these data. They are, however, encouraging. Perhaps the most informative of these early analyses are the bivariate correlations that were calculated between the four "sexual" perceptions (flirtatious, seductive, promiscuous, and sexy) from the first part of the study and each of the six responses to each of the 29 scenarios in the second part of the study. Of these 696 correlations, 133 (19.1%) are statistically significant ($p < .05$). Although this is not an overwhelming percentage, and most of the significant correlations are in the .2 to .3 range, the likelihood that these significant findings constitute Type I errors because of an inflated experiment-wise alpha level is reduced because *all 133* of the statistically significant correlations were in the "predicted" direction. That is, male subjects who tended to see *more* flirtatiousness, *more* seductiveness, *more* promiscuity, or *more* sexiness reported that they were (1) *less* likely to find the man's behavior (in the scenarios) inappropriate; (2) *less* likely to criticize him; (3) *less* likely to testify in the woman's defense; (4) *more* likely to testify in the man's defense; (5) *less* likely to be dissuaded from accepting a job offer; or (6) *more* likely to engage in similar behaviors themselves.

Further examination of these statistically significant correlations reveals that they are not uniformly distributed across the four "sexual" perceptions (from the first half of the study), across the six responses to each of the 29 sexual harassment scenarios, or across responses to the 29 scenarios (in the second half of the study). Looking first at the four different sexual perceptions, the percentages of significant correlations were as follows: flirtatious—19.5%; seductive—19.0%; promiscuous—15.5%; and sexy—22.4%. Turning to the six responses to the scenarios, the percentages were: appropriate?—37.1%; criticize the man?—15.5%; testify for the woman?—17.2%; testify for the man?—23.3%; dissuaded from job offer?—2.6%; and engage in similar behaviors?—19.9%. Finally, some of the scenarios generated large percentages of statistically significant correlations, while others generated none. These disparities offer additional evidence *against* dismissing these statistically significant correlations as manifestations of an inflated experimentwise error rate.

Discussion.   These preliminary analyses, of course, prove nothing. Even if more complex multivariate analyses reveal that considerably more variance in men's responses to various examples of sexual harassment can be explained by linear combinations of their (mis)representations of women's friendliness as sexiness, this study will still represent only a beginning. Nevertheless, it appears to be a rather encouraging beginning. If, in fact, men who (mis)perceive friendliness on the part of women as a sign of sexiness or sexual availability are more likely to tolerate, endorse, and ultimately engage in sexual harassment behaviors, we will have taken a giant step toward further developing a model of sexual harassment that can contribute to the development of organizational training/orientation sessions that stand a good chance of being acceptable to the organizational personnel involved, and a good chance of reducing or even eliminating the scourge of sexual harassment in organizations that has been revealed through numerous surveys.

CONCLUSIONS

In the first half of this chapter I examined definitions of sexual harassment in organizations, and paid particular attention to how individuals' perceptions figure very prominently in those definitions. I examined survey data, some scientifically sound and some not, and concluded that sexual harassment is indeed a pandemic problem in many organizations, just as Safran (1976) warned more than a decade ago. I also looked at several models or theories that purport to explain sexual harassment, and discovered that those models vary in terms of the extent to which they have received support from empirical research and the extent to which they facilitate the development of organizational intervention strategies designed to reduce or eliminate sexual harassment. Finally, I summarized ways in which practice (in the form of working women and men, as well as federal legislation prompted by their experiences) has influenced those who conduct scientific research into the sexual harassment problem, and ways in which science (in the form of proper sampling and survey procedures, as well as a variety of theoretical models) has influenced practice. Although very few of the scientists and practitioners who contributed to these exchanges were trained or employed as industrial/organizational psychologists, their contributions were similar to those that *could* have been made by I/O psychologists had they been interested, as scientists and/or practitioners, in doing so. I hope that this chapter serves to stimulate more of my colleagues to initiate and pursue research and practice that focuses on the problem of sexual harassment in organizations. In doing so, I suspect that we will generate additional evidence supporting the utility of the scientist-practitioner model for generating solutions to that problem.

Because actions usually speak louder than words, I devoted the second half of this chapter to a description of a research program that has been guided by the scientist-practitioner model and, I believe, offers evidence of the value and viability of that model for tackling important problems in organizations. Each of the studies was predicated on the importance of people's perceptions for understanding sexual harassment; practice (the EEOC's amended guidelines) influenced science. The stimuli for Studies 1 through 5 depicted or evolved from men's and women's actual experiences in work and academic settings; again, practice influenced science. Because women are increasingly moving into higher positions in organizational hierarchies, Study 4 examined the generalizability of the sex differences in perceptions revealed in Studies 1 through 3 to situations where the woman was "in charge"; again, practice informed science.

It remains to be seen whether science, in the form of this research program, will inform practice. At least two conditions will have to be met. First, additional research in the form of replications and extensions of the studies described above will have to be done, and the results will have to provide additional support for the basic hypothesis that perceptual differences can help to explain the extent to which men tolerate, endorse, and ultimately engage in sexual harassment behaviors. Second, scientists will have to convince their practitioner colleagues to develop and evaluate orientation or training programs for reducing or eliminating sexual harassment that highlight the importance of individuals' perceptions and encourage each employee to examine his own proclivity to misinterpret a woman's friendliness as a sign of sexual interest or availability. Of course, the scientist-practitioner might do this him/herself. As Sandroff (1988) acknowledged in a recent article in *Working Woman* magazine, "Sex harassment has developed as one of the great lessons in how education can have an effect on an offensive practice" (p. 73).

In that same article, Sandroff (1988) reported that sexual harassment costs a typical Fortune 500 company approximately $6.7 million every year as a result of lowered productivity, low morale, and increased absenteeism and turnover. Of course, this figure does *not* include the individual costs, both monetary and personal, associated with the psychological and physiological consequences of being victimized by sexual harassment. Clearly this is an area that cries out for the attention of I/O psychologists (and other professionals). Based on the review of surveys and models and the description of the research program included in this chapter, I am convinced that the scientist-practitioner model has tremendous potential for guiding I/O psychologists' work as they strive to understand and eliminate sexual harassment in organizations.

REFERENCES

Abbey, A. (1982). Sex differences in attributions for friendly behavior: Do males misperceive females' friendliness? *Journal of Personality and Social Psychology, 42,* 830–838.

Backhouse, C., & Cohen, L. (1981). *Sexual harassment on the job: How to avoid the working woman's nightmare.* Englewood Cliffs, NJ: Prentice-Hall.

Chacko, T. I. (1982). Women and equal employment opportunity: Some unintended effects. *Journal of Applied Psychology, 67,* 119–123.

Coed complaint: A poet is accused at Harvard. (1982, June 14). *Time,* p. 81.

Dziech, B. W., & Weiner, L. (1984). *The lecherous professor: Sexual harassment on campus.* Boston: Beacon Press.

EEOC. (1980, April). "Title 29—Labor, Chapter XIV—Part 1604—Guidelines on Discrimination Because of Sex Under Title VII of the Civil Rights Act, as Amended Adoption of Interim Interpretive Guideline," Washington, D.C.

Farley, L. (1978). *Sexual shakedown: The sexual harassment of women on the job.* New York: Warner Books.

Fighting its image problem: Congress launches an investigation of sex and drug charges. (1982, July 26). *Time,* p. 12.

Fighting lechery on campus. (1980, February 4). *Time,* p. 84.

Gutek, B. A. (1985). *Sex and the workplace.* San Francisco: Jossey-Bass.

Gutek, B. A., & Morasch, B. (1982). Sex ratios, sex role spillover, and sexual harassment of women at work. *Journal of Social Issues, 38,* 55–74.

Gutek, B. A., Morasch, B., & Cohen, A. G. (1983). Interpreting social-sexual behavior in a work setting. *Journal of Vocational Behavior, 22,* 30–48.

Heilman, M. E., & Herlihy, J. M. (1984). Affirmative action, negative reaction? Some moderating conditions. *Organizational Behavior and Human Performance, 33,* 204–213.

Howe, L. K. (1977). *Pink collar workers: Inside the world of women's work.* New York: Avon Books.

Johnson, C. B., Stockdale, M. S., & Saal, F. E. (1987, August). *Men perceive more sexuality— Except when it's really there?* Roundtable presented at the meeting of the American Psychological Association, New York.

Kirk, R. E. (1982). *Experimental design: Procedures for the behavioral sciences* (2nd ed.). Monterey, CA: Brooks/Cole.

MacKinnon, C. A. (1979). *Sexual harassment of working women: A case of sex discrimination.* New Haven, CT: Yale University Press.

Mead, M. (1980). A proposal: We need taboos on sex at work. In D. A. Neugarten & J. M. Shafritz (Eds.), *Sexuality in organizations: Romantic and coercive behaviors at work.* Oak Park, IL: Moore Publishing Co.

Meyer, M. C., Berchtold, I. M., Oestreich, J. L., & Collins, F. J. (1981). *Sexual harassment.* New York: Petrocelli Books.

Pope, K. S., Levenson, H., & Schover, L. R. (1979). Sexual intimacy in psychology training: Results and implications of a national survey. *American Psychologist, 34,* 682–689.

Ray, E. L. (1976). *The Washington fringe benefit.* New York: Dell.

Rogan, H. (1981). *Mixed company: Women in the modern army.* New York: G. P. Putnam's Sons.

Rosen, B., & Mericle, M. F. (1979). Influence of strong versus weak fair employment policies and applicant's sex on selection decisions and salary recommendations in a management simulation. *Journal of Applied Psychology, 64,* 435–439.

Saal, F. E., Johnson, C. B., & Weber, N. (1989). Friendly or sexy? It may depend on whom you ask. *Psychology of Women Quarterly, 13,* 263–276.

Safran, C. (1976). What men do to women on the job. *Redbook, 149,* 217–223.

Sandroff, R. (1988, December). Sexual harassment in the Fortune 500. *Working Woman,* pp. 69–73.

Sexual harassment charged. (1980, March 14). *United Methodist Reporter,* p. 3.

Somers, P. A., & Clementson-Mohr, J. (1979, April). Sexual extortion in the workplace. *The Personnel Administrator.* pp. 23–28.

State of Illinois. (1980, March 4). *Testimony of Barbara Hayler on research conducted by Sangamon State University and the Illinois Task Force on Sexual Harassment in the Workplace.* Hearings before the House Judiciary II Committee.

Tangri, S. S., Burt, M. R., & Johnson, L. B. (1982). Sexual harassment at work: Three explanatory models. *Journal of Social Issues, 38,* 33–54.

U.S. Merit Systems Protection Board. (1981, March). *Sexual harassment in the federal workplace: Is it a problem?* Washington, DC: U.S. Government Printing Office.

Vogelmann-Sine, S., Ervin, E. D., Christensen, R., Warmsun, C. H., & Ullmann, L. P. (1979). Sex differences in feelings attributed to a woman in situations involving coercion and sexual advances. *Journal of Personality, 47,* 420–431.

Woman demoted for sex overture. (1980, April 9). *The Daily Herald,* p. 3.

Zedeck, S., & Cascio, W. F. (1984). Psychological issues in personnel decisions. *Annual Review of Psychology, 35,* 461–518.

12 Drug Abuse and Drug Testing in the Workplace

Larry D. Reid
Rensselaer Polytechnic Institute

Kevin R. Murphy
Douglas H. Reynolds
Colorado State University

The prevalence of recreational drug use is high, and has been high for some time. Based on surveys of students in high schools and colleges, tabulations from hospital emergency rooms, and self-reports elicited through national surveys, it can be concluded (conservatively) that roughly 10% of the work-force (and a higher percentage of male workers) has or will develop a pattern of recreational drug use that may impede performance on the job. In Newcomb's (1988) sample of young adults, primarily those just beginning their careers, 30% admitted to being "high" on the job at least once, and 8% of the sample reported that they had been "high" on the job more than eleven times during the previous 6-month period, a frequency that was labeled problematic drug use.[1] Our best estimate is that approximately 1 out of 10 prospective or current employees in virtually any job has or will develop a pattern of recreational drug use, including alcohol abuse and alcoholism (AA&A), that is problematic, unless an organization does something specific to change the situation (Tolchin, 1989; Walsh, 1989; see, however, Grabowski, 1989).

One clear threat to our most vital resource, human competence, is posed by addictions to alcohol, cocaine, heroin, and other substances. Although the risks are not as great for younger workers, there are considerable health costs to older workers who are addicted to nicotine. Additionally, we are beginning to realize that we are paying considerable costs associated with marijuana use and use of a variety of other addictive drugs (Kreek, 1987; Mendelson, 1987). Because of the potential costs of drug abuse, the question is not *whether* organizations should attempt to deal with drug and alcohol abuse, but rather *how* they should deal with it.

In this chapter, we examine two facets of an organization's response to drug

---

[1]Excellent reviews and discussions of the effects of drugs and drug testing on work behavior are included in Lorber and Kirk (1987), Newcomb (1988) and Walsh and Gust (1988).

and alcohol abuse. First, we examine the likely effects of drugs on workers' behavior and describe courses of action the organization might take to deal with disruptive drug use. In this first section, we demonstrate that organizations should indeed be concerned with the potential effects of drug and alcohol abuse. Next, we examine the likely effects of drug *testing* on the attitudes and behaviors of job applicants and incumbents. Because there is much less research on these effects, this section of the chapter requires integrating research in several different areas to describe the probable effects of drug *testing* on work attitudes and behaviors. This section shows that organizations that are concerned about drug and alcohol abuse must carefully consider whether a drug and/or alcohol testing program is likely to do more harm than good. In the final section, we suggest ways in which science and practice might be better integrated to design appropriate responses to the problem of drug abuse in the workplace.

DRUGS, ALCOHOL, AND WORK BEHAVIOR

It is clear that the heavy use of drugs and alcohol in the work setting can impair performance, endanger the impaired individual and others, and expose the organization to a wide range of adverse outcomes. The controversy over drug and alcohol testing does not reflect disagreements over this basic fact, but rather over the extent to which the recreational use of alcohol and drugs (in debilitating doses) away from the job is: (a) a valid concern for the organization, and (b) relevant to job performance. The first section of this paper reviews evidence suggesting that the recreational use of drugs and alcohol may indeed affect the organization, even if these substances are never consumed in the workplace.

As our assessments have become more sensitive, it is becoming clearer that recreational use of some drugs is clearly toxic to the brain, particularly certain cells of the brain. Ecstasy (a drug gaining in popularity), for example, is likely to damage the serotonergic cells of the brain (Finnegan et al., 1988). PCP is a potent psychotomimetic (Balster, 1987; Johnson, 1987). Alcohol is clearly toxic to brains of developing babies; the same is true for adults if alcohol is used excessively over a prolonged period (Fischman, 1987). These effects are often irreversible. The child born with brain damage due to alcohol toxicity, for example, is permanently retarded, and will not become fully productive. An adult suffering similar brain damage is also unlikely to be a productive worker.

The side-effects of other drugs may be reversible with cessation of use, but they are nevertheless detrimental. It is becoming increasingly clear, for example, that cocaine use potentiates violent tendencies (Fischman, 1987). It has been clear for some time that the active ingredients in marijuana are related to an amotivational syndrome (Baumrind & Moselle, 1985; Mendelson, 1987; Miller, 1979), and that they retard the transfer of information from short-term memory to long-term memory, a process essential to education. The use of hypodermic syringes and needles by heroin addicts is spreading the deadly disease AIDS.

Reducing recreational drug use (including that associated with alcohol and cigarettes) will nurture competence in general and reduce accidents, criminality, absenteeism, lateness, health care costs, and so forth (Ray & Ksir, 1987). Furthermore, reducing levels of drug use when *not* at work is likely to reduce drug abuse and drug-related problems at work (Newcomb, 1988; Stein, Newcomb, & Bentler, 1988). Because some addictions tend to develop over a considerable period of time (e.g., AA&A) and because the negative consequences become more manifest with aging and become more problematic the longer the addiction is extant, there is a real danger to an organization of promoting someone whose past performance predicts success but whose addiction will interfere with the accomplishment of that success. This is a particularly damaging cost to an organization; an addicted leader is not only apt to be less competent, but may also "defend" his or her addiction by thwarting policies designed to reduce the costs of addictions. Given the high costs associated with drug use in terms of accidents, medical care, and the less obvious but perhaps greater costs involving loss of competence, any organization is apt to profit from instituting a straightforward set of policies that discourage recreational and casual drug use.

Although there are good reasons to believe that drug use will interfere with an individual's performance and effectiveness at work, we know surprisingly little about the *specific* effects of different drugs on work behaviors. That is, we know little about the specific work-related functions that are impaired when drugs are used on the job. As we note later in this chapter, the problem of determining the specific ways in which drugs impair work performance will probably require the joint efforts of researchers and practitioners in several areas, ranging from psychopharmacology to job and task analysis.

Addiction and Compulsive Drug Use

Older theories of addiction stressed the idea that drugs provide relief from drug-withdrawal sickness (or withdrawal anxiety) and from psychological conflicts, and that these negatively reinforcing effects were the prime reason for drug use. Modern theories of addiction (e.g., Bozarth, 1987; Marlatt, Baer, Donovan, & Kivlahan, 1988) do not stress, as an explanatory variable, the idea that drugs are medications for psychological difficulties, or that they are tranquilizers for deep-seated anxieties, fears, worries, or guilt. The idea prevalent now is that drugs are used because they directly excite those areas of the brain that mediate pleasure (i.e., positive reinforcement) (Rossi & Reid, 1976). Recreational drug use is, indeed, a form of recreation, not self-medication. However, characterizing the primary reason for drug use as recreational should not lead us to conclude that drug use is not compulsive. Indeed, the hallmark of addiction is that initially infrequent and casual use often develops into compulsive drug use.

Older theories of addition led to the hypothesis that stress in the workplace was a precursor to drug and alcohol abuse. Recent research suggests that the correlation between the stressfulness of the job and the use of addictive drugs is small (Newcomb, 1988). Job related factors that *are* positively correlated with drug use include opportunities to obtain drugs (e.g., in medical setting) and salary level (which may be an indirect indicator of ability to afford drugs).

The greatest danger associated with casual drug use is that it can lead to compulsive drug use (i.e., an addiction) which, in turn, becomes a highly salient focus of one's life to the exclusion of the ordinary foci of work, family, and friends. This modern characterization of the reasons for drug use has a number of ramifications, including the likelihood that problematic drug use will not be prevented by addressing people's psychological problems. That is, professional counseling is not likely to be an effective program for prevention of drug use and its consequences. Indeed, a case can be made that recreational drug use is an antecedent to many problems that affect workers rather than a consequence of these problems. Programs that prevent recreational drug use may help prevent mental illness.

Predictors of Drug and Alcohol Abuse

There are biological susceptibilities that predispose an individual toward an addiction (Cloninger, Bohman, & Sigvardsson, 1981; Goodwin, Schulsinger, & Moller, 1974; Mello, 1987). On the surface, this may appear to conflict with another conclusion drawn later in this chapter from the literature on drug abuse, that there are no intellectual or personality variables that predict problematic drug use. These ideas are not however incompatible. Presence of individual differences in susceptibility to a particular drug addiction need not mean that the persons who are susceptible are necessarily weak or vulnerable in any other way. Indeed, the particular chemistry that may facilitate an addiction (e.g., alcoholism) may also be a particularly adaptive trait, both now and across the species' history. It is the interaction between the drug and a physiology that is problematic, not the physiology itself. This susceptibility opens the possibility of predicting who is most likely to be at risk (based, for example, on knowledge of blood chemistry).

Although drug abuse can often be predicted, it is sometimes difficult to act on those predictions. For example, a reasonably valid predictor of excessive alcohol use is whether or not excessive alcohol use is common among a person's natural family. Such knowledge, if available, could be used to validly select employees. We have, however, a social standard in our society that a person should be judged as an individual and not on the basis of what his family has done.

There is evidence that one addiction increases the likelihood of another addiction. A person who smokes cigarettes, uses alcohol extensively and marijuana occasionally is more likely to become addicted to cocaine than a person who does not use other drugs recreationally. There are multiple explanations of this tendency, each of which has some data to support it. For example, drug use changes the chemistry of the brain to set the conditions for a new addiction, or drug use puts people in a social circle of drug users, and thereby increases the likelihood of being tempted. Regardless of which explanation one accepts, there is little doubt that drug use of one kind is a good predictor of drug use of another kind (Newcomb, 1988; Ray & Ksir, 1987). A related observation is that more problems are likely to emerge when an individual takes many different kinds of drugs. Drug use begets drug use (Donovan & Jessor, 1983; Huba, Wingard, & Bentler, 1981; Kandel, 1973; Kandel & Faust, 1975) and the more extensive the use of a single drug and the more kinds of drugs used, the greater the likelihood of problems emerging at home and at work. Also, the likelihood that a successful therapeutic intervention will resolve the addiction (or addictions) and its (or their) consequences is lower as the number of drugs used recreationally increases (Mello & Griffiths, 1987).

What is needed is a method of predicting drug use and, more importantly drug use that interferes with day-to-day life. Unfortunately, there are as yet no clear demographic variables (except the possibility that men are more at risk than women) that help identify people at risk. The poor and the rich, the well-educated and the illiterate, those from stable families and those from broken homes, those who profess a variety of political and religious beliefs, and those with different personalities are all approximately equally susceptible. One exception to this generalization, however, is that those who have made strong commitments to religions with unequivocal sanctions against drug use are not as likely to be drug users. However, religious preference is not apt to be a very good predictor of commitment to follow religious dictates.

Scores obtained on intelligence or personality tests, or from biographical questionnaires are not significantly correlated with the development of drug use. Although there are a few studies indicating that a general tendency to be rebellious or impulsive may be related to drug use, these results have not been confirmed by other studies. There is, however, one variable that does predict, future drug use, and that is the level of current drug use (Newcomb, 1988). The more drugs an individual uses *in any setting,* the greater the likelihood that drugs will cause problems at work.

It has been noted that employees who use drugs: (a) are more often late both at the beginning of their work shift and after lunch, (b) are absent more often (i.e., they have a series of short-term absences) especially on Mondays and Fridays, and are more apt to be absent for periods of a week or more, (c) use above-average levels of sick benefits, (d) are more likely to file for workman's compensation, and (e) are more likely to be involved in accidents, especially during the late afternoon or toward the end of the work period (Gardner, 1982; Lodge, 1983; Newcomb, 1988).

Driving while intoxicated within a previous 4-year period is also a reasonable predictor of disruptive drug use at work. Having sold illegal drugs is also correlated with disruptive drug use. In one sample (Newcomb, 1988), over 50% of the individuals reporting these experiences also used drugs at work. This study suggests that knowledge of previous convictions for drinking while driving or for selling drugs is potentially valuable when making personnel decisions.

Frequent tardiness, frequent absences, trouble with the law, heavy use of cigarettes (among young workers), any history of arrests and convictions for drunken driving or sale of illegal drugs, history of "trouble" with supervisors, tendencies toward extroversion accompanied by occasional severe dysphoria, and previous trouble with recreational drug use at work, are all signs of employee drug use. Any cluster of these, combined with urinalysis results indicative of current illegal drug use (typically, marijuana or cocaine use) indicates a potentially serious problem for which we have little remedial or preventive technology. The more of these signs that emerge from an evaluation of an employee, the more likely it is a problem that will arise, and the less likely that an intervention will succeed.

Prognosis for Treatment

We do not have a successful technology for treating addictions, despite the fact that we have a 3-billion-dollar-a-year industry that attempts to implement medical and other treatments, plus a large number of self-help consortia (Marlatt et al., 1988; Miller & Hester, 1986; Nathan, 1986). The mean rate of abstinence 1 year after treatment is approximately 25% (regardless of type of treatment, including no particular treatment). There is considerable variance about the mean that can be accounted for primarily in terms of severity and extent of addictions prior to treatment. Individuals with a single crippling addiction, (e.g., alcohol abuse) who have intact families or other kinds of social support and who are employed are more likely to benefit from treatment. Their rate of abstinence is approximately 50% at the one-year benchmark. Individuals who are polydrug abusers, who have failed to maintain abstinence even after multiple treatments, whose families have abandoned them, and who are unemployed (or have a history of unemployment) are least likely to benefit from treatment. The abstinence rate at 1 year for these individuals is as low as 3%. In brief, the prognosis for successful treatment is often not particularly good, but it is generally good enough to maintain programs until more successful technologies are developed.

Data from longitudinal studies are not sufficient to make definitive statements regarding the life-span chronicity of addictions (Fillmore, 1988). Recreational drug use and extensive use of alcoholic beverages are most common among persons between the ages of 18 and 25 years (Kandel & Raveis, 1989). Later in life, many individuals curb their intake of alcoholic beverages and reduce their use of illegal drugs rather dramatically. There are, however, substantial numbers who do not curb alcohol consumption or drug use, and some who escalate both frequency and the amount of intake over the years. It is estimated that 10% of adults will drink alcoholic beverages to a point where the consequences are clearly noticeable, and that as many as 20% or more of adult men will be so affected. In our society, there is considerable overlap among those involved in alcohol abuse and alcoholism and those using illegal drugs recreationally.

Given the relationship between age and recreational use of alcohol and other drugs, it follows that knowledge of extent of alcohol use and instances of illegal drug use of a person at 20 years-of-age is not likely to be a highly sensitive index of drug use at 40 years-of-age. Knowledge that a person is using illegal drugs and drinking alcoholic beverages frequently and extensively at 30 years-of-age, however, is a solid predictor of such usage at 31 years-of-age, and even at 40 years-of-age.

Organizational Responses to Drug and Alcohol Abuse

Several conclusions can be drawn from research on drug and alcohol abuse, including:

(a) drug use can interfere with competence;

(b) drug use often escalates into addiction;

(c) current prospects for curing addictions are poor;

(d) the prevalence of recreational drug use is high;

(e) drug use can not be justified as a form of self-medication that somehow might thereby improve performance; and

(f) postponing treatment and intervention is likely to make matters worse.

These conclusions have straightforward implications for organizations. One such implication is that an organization should do what it can to:

(a) avoid recruiting people at risk for drug use;

(b) treat drug-using employees as quickly as possible and, if treatment does not succeed, get them out of the organization quickly; and

(c) make all company policies consistent with the idea that casual drug use, alcohol abuse and even cigarette smoking is not acceptable behavior for members of the organization.

It is important to concentrate for a moment on the last point before discussing tests that may predict drug use. There are several organizational strategies for communicating opposition to recreational, or casual drug use. First, statements that drug use is not tolerated should be made often and unequivocally. This is surely easier to do today than a decade ago, since there is now some consensus that illegal drug use is a problem. Second, organizations should enforce regulations against smoking (heavy smoking is one predictor, although a weak one, of drug use). Antismoking policies are relatively easy to implement today because state and local regulations may justify the organization's course of action and because of the increasing unpopularity of smoking. Additionally, an antismoking policy makes it clear that the organization is against recreational drug use in a rather obvious way. Third, organizational social functions should be alcohol-free or, at the very least, alternative beverages should always be available; costs of alcoholic beverages should not be borne by the organization. Fourth, organizations should demand "on-time performance" and monitor absences. Tardiness and frequent leaves for medical reasons are two on-the-job predictors of addiction; implementing strict standards with respect to these behaviors may act to deter escalation of an addiction. And fifth, organizations should reinforce social conventions that are inconsistent with drug use (i.e., strict standards of dress and comportment). This last point may not be so obvious but suffice it to say that drug users are more apt to be displeased with these social conventions and, thereby, not be attracted to the organization [one predictor of drug use is low tolerance for social conventions (Newcomb, 1988; Newcomb & Bentler, 1988), but it is not a strong predictor]. Given the prevalence of recreational drug use, however, these simple policies may not be sufficient; organizations may wish to consider a more controversial approach—the use of chemical assays of blood and urine to detect recent drug use.

Implementing Drug Testing

The first issue that must be considered in drug testing is the accuracy of the tests themselves. The combined accuracy of the current technology for assaying samples, which involves using the cheaper EMIT-test (a test using immunoassay techniques) plus the more expensive tests using mass spectrometers, is almost 100%. However, this level of accuracy is not attained in all laboratories (Marshall, 1988), and relatively small reductions in accuracy can substantially affect the utility of a drug testing program (Wells, Halperin, & Thun, 1988).

If testing is done with current employees, it is good practice to keep the results in a stream of decision making that is relatively separate from ordinary personnel decision making until alternative explanations for positive test results are explored. In other words, initial results should be held in confidence until further testing is done. Initial results could be sent to a medical services unit or an Employee Assistance Program which would hold results in confidence until further assessments were made. This approach would increase employees' willingness to cooperate with a testing program. An organization could establish a yearly medical check-up as a standard practice, during which blood and urine samples are taken, with the understanding that these samples will be screened for drugs. Full disclosure and formal contracts concerning such procedures will also mitigate legal concerns. One complaint directed at drug testing programs is that they focus on illicit drugs and ignore alcohol abuse, even though it is widely known that alcohol abuse is more widespread and serious than most other forms of substance abuse (Newcomb, 1988). There is an emerging technology that will be able to index for alcoholism based on the fact that extensive use of alcohol produces changes in physiology (Tang, 1987). These tests are currently not widely used; several are in various stages of development but they are clearly on the horizon. So, in time, the tests will be more comprehensive.

The greatest fear of nonusers is being falsely identified as a user and being penalized for it. Fortunately, there are ways to protect employees from being falsely labeled. First, any initial sign of drugs (or their metabolites) in urine needs to be verified using a second and more accurate test. Second, the person needs to be questioned prior to testing about the use of prescription drugs. Third, information from urinalysis needs to be held in confidence by a separate group (medical officers or staff of an Employee Assistance Program) until the possibility of a false positive response is thoroughly checked. And fourth, when there is an indication of drug use, other indices such as previous performance appraisals can be used to determine whether or not to alert the employees' immediate supervisors or others making relevant decisions. In no case should such information be distributed except on a "need to know" basis.

A second major complaint directed toward drug testing is that it only indicates recent use of illegal drugs, not whether such usage interferes with job-related behaviors. Some drugs have short-term effects, whereas others do not. A person using cocaine on Friday night may not be impaired by the direct action of the drug on Monday morning. That person is at considerable risk for using cocaine again, however, and escalating his or her use of cocaine to the point of work-day use. There is a post-cocaine depression, following relatively extensive use, that could interfere with performance. Weekend use of marijuana can, however, have effects on Monday morning (Mendelson, 1987). Those who argue that off-duty pleasures should not be of concern to employers assume that the effects of such off-duty pleasure activities can be clearly segregated from on-duty performance (Stein et al., 1988). The case for the ability to segregate the two spheres of one's life can only be made for those who have not yet developed an addiction. Addicted people bring their addiction to work.

Applicant screening is most likely to identify those who do not have sufficient control of their drug use to stop taking illegal drugs a few days or weeks prior to the collection of urine. A strong case can be made, however, that it is those individuals who present the most serious risk of drug-related problems at work, and that a program that merely weeded out such individuals could be very valuable.

Many organizations make treatment for drug and alcohol use available as the first in a series of steps to reduce the chances of problems. As already stated, early intervention has a better chance of succeeding than interventions that occur after the problems have accumulated. Nevertheless, our best treatment programs are not remarkably successful. It follows, therefore, that frequent assessment should be made. Any probation period following identification and treatment of an addiction should last at least 1 year, and possibly longer, depending on the drug.

Once there has been a decision to establish a screening program for use of illegal drugs (or perhaps, for legal agents such as nicotine or alcohol), there is a host of other decisions that must be considered concommitantly. A singularly important decision is what to do when the test tells you an employee is using drugs. The Bureau of Labor Statistics reported that organizations in the private sector who use preemployment screening of urine for illegally used drugs find about 12% do, indeed, use illegally obtained drugs (i.e., the analysis of urine indicates drug use). From over one million tests done of people on the payroll of major private sector employers, it was found that 8.8% had tests indicating use of illegally obtained drugs (Tolchin, 1989; Walsh, 1989). Such data lead to the conclusion that an organization is not going to be faced with dealing with one or two people, but, perhaps, as many as 1 out of 10 employees (but, see Grabowski, 1989).

Is drug screening going to solve an organization's problems with disruptive recreational drug use? The answer is clearly no. Can a drug screening program be an efficient part of a comprehensive program to reduce costs? The answer is "yes," primarily because no other factor predicts future disruptive drug use better than current drug use. Will a comprehensive program be cost-effective? The answer is "probably yes," but as we note in the next section, this is not always the case. The factors making drug testing cost-effective can be only discerned at the local level; the second section of this chapter discusses several of these factors in detail.

PSYCHOLOGICAL EFFECTS OF DRUG TESTING

The debate over employee drug testing (i.e., programs that test current employees and/or job applicants for the presence of illicit drugs in the bloodstream) has concentrated primarily on the effects of testing programs on drug abuse in the workplace (Walsh & Gust, 1988). Legal issues and issues connected with civil rights have also received considerable attention (Lorber & Kirk, 1987). One critical issue that has not yet received sufficient attention is the effect of employee drug testing programs on the attitudes and behaviors (other than drug-related behaviors) of those who are subject to testing. Employee drug testing programs are likely to affect employees' and job applicants' perceptions of the organization, and if testing programs are viewed in a negative light, these perceptions could lead to undesirable behaviors. There is evidence that a variety of personnel practices lead to unfavorable perceptions of organizations, which in turn can affect applicants' decisions to pursue and accept job offers, and can affect current employees' commitment and willingness to remain a part of the organization. Drug testing may, on the other hand, lead to a more *positive* view of the organization, especially if the program appears to the workers to contribute to safety and efficiency in the workplace.

Although it seems likely that drug testing programs will affect variables such as organizational choice, organizational commitment, absenteeism and turnover, little is known about the strength or direction of the effect(s), the circumstances under which they are most likely to occur, or the consequences associated with job applicants' and current employees' perceptions of an organization's personnel practices. Even if drug testing programs lead to lower levels of drug use in the workplace, these programs could still have a net negative effect on the organization if they also lead to unfavorable attitudes and undesirable work behaviors. For example, Bensinger (1987) showed that many potential job applicants who are not drug users object to employee drug testing (see also Murphy, Reynolds, & Thornton, 1989). Testing these applicants may reduce the likelihood that they will accept job offers or new assignments. On the other hand, a testing program that has little effect on actual drug use could still have secondary benefits if it leads to perceptions of a safe and drug-free work environment.

Employee drug testing programs are becoming increasingly common, yet research on the effects of these programs on the behavior of job applicants and incumbents has rarely been attempted. We regard drug testing as an area in which practice has preceded science, and in the remainder of this chapter we suggest some ways in which this might be reversed. Industrial/Organizational (I/O) psychologists may be able to make a unique contribution to the development of rational drug testing programs. The psychological perspective we outline here suggests that we must consider a wide range of consequences in addition to a program's effects on drug use *per se,* and in particular, that we must consider the effects of employee drug testing programs on the attitudes and behaviors of workers.

We use existing research literature to describe the probable effects of drug testing on attitudes and behaviors. First, research reviewed here establishes that employee drug testing is widespread, and that program characteristics vary widely from organization to organization. We then establish that drug testing practices are likely to affect the attitudes of job applicants and incumbents, which in turn affect their work behaviors. The hypothesized link between drug testing practices and work behaviors is supported by: (a) research demonstrating that personnel practices affect worker attitudes, and (b) research demonstrating that these attitudinal effects are linked to work behaviors, and to outcomes such as job choice and organizational commitment. Finally, we discuss methods of increasing the effective interplay between research and application in the area of employee drug testing.

Prevalence and Characteristics of Drug Testing Programs

O'Boyle (1985) reported that 25% of Fortune 500 companies screen applicants and/or employees for illegal drug use. A more recent survey of 378 private-sector firms by Olian and Guthrie (1988) showed that 49% tested for drugs, and that another 5–11% are considering testing in the near future. Surveys conducted by the Department of Labor suggest that the incidence of employee drug testing may be lower in some industries. Nevertheless, it is clear that drug testing is a growing trend, and that very large numbers of job applicants and incumbents are likely to be subject, at some point in their careers, to drug testing. For example, the federal government has developed plans to test over 100,000 civilian employees per year (Walsh & Gust, 1988); the number of employees in federally regulated industries who may be subjected to annual testing exceeds four million (Murphy et al., 1989).

Employee drug testing programs can be characterized in terms of four variables: (a) who is subject to testing, (b) the circumstances that lead to testing, (c) the administrative procedures used in testing, and (d) the consequences of failing a drug test (Lorber & Kirk, 1987). Drug testing is more common for labor and lower management positions than for executive positions (O'Boyle, 1985), and appears to be more likely in jobs that involve high levels of perceived risk to the public (e.g., airline pilots) than in jobs where the hazards associated with drug-impaired performance are minimal (e.g., typist). Drug testing is more common when there is "just cause" or a reasonable suspicion of drug use, but some organizations test all applicants or a random sample of job incumbents (46% of all companies test applicants, 5% randomly screen employees; Olian & Guthrie, 1988). Some organizations (e.g., the military, federal agencies) take elaborate precautions to prevent cheating and screen for a wide variety of drugs, while others employ less invasive or more tightly focused procedures. Finally, the consequences of failing a drug test vary considerably from organization to organization. A single confirmed positive test will lead 69% of the organizations that test to reject a job applicant; 16% of the companies that test will dismiss an employee who fails a single test (Olian & Guthrie, 1988).

Effects of Personnel Practices on Attitudes

Employee drug testing represents one of several personnel practices (albeit, a controversial one) that are used by some organizations. Personnel practices are known to affect employees' perceptions of the organization, and are thought to affect a wide range of work behaviors (Cascio, 1987). Three theoretical perspectives are directly relevant to understanding the links between employees' perceptions of the organization and their work behavior. First, equity theory (Adams, 1965) states that individuals interpret the fairness of their interactions with an organization by comparing the inputs to the outcomes they receive. Employee drug testing can be interpreted as either an input or outcome variable; in either case, the theory predicts that individuals who disagree with an organization's drug testing policy will be dissatisfied unless they are somehow compensated for the perceived invasion of their personal life. Because it is unlikely that organizations will financially compensate employees for participating in drug testing, this compensation is likely to take the form of reduced effort and output, increased absenteeism, or some other outcome with negative implications for the organization. Research by Goodman and Friedman (1971) suggests that equity theory provides a useful vehicle for understanding perceptions of the work environment, and the effects of these perceptions on work behavior.

Social comparison theory (Chadwick-Jones, Nicholson, & Brown, 1982) involves a similar concept, that individuals and groups exchange their effort, attendance, and diligence for a variety of rewards offered by the organization. Introducing a personnel practice that is unwanted alters the prevailing exchange, and workers are likely to reduce their effort, involvement, or attendance, to restore the original perceived equity of the exchange. This approach has been particularly successful in predicting absenteeism (Chadwick-Jones et al., 1982).

Schein (1965) suggested a third theoretical perspective. He argued that employees enter into a "psychological contract" with the organizations they join. This contract, an implicit agreement about the rights and obligations of both parties, develops early in the relationship between the individual and the organization. Psychological contract theory suggest that employees exhibit certain levels of effort, skill, loyalty, and commitment, which they expect to exchange for rewards (financial and otherwise) provided by the organization. If personnel practices are introduced that are viewed favorably, the theory predicts that workers will respond with more effort, performance, and responsibility. Employment practices that are viewed negatively, however, will result in less effort, more absenteeism, less commitment and less interest in one's work.

Applicant perceptions. Outsiders' (e.g., job applicants) perceptions of organizations are particularly likely to be affected by highly visible and controversial personnel policies. Research on job search and job choice has demonstrated that individuals make inferences about unknown or poorly understood aspects of the organization on the basis of whatever partial knowledge they have (Rynes, Heneman, & Schwab, 1980; Schwab, Rynes, & Aldag, 1987; Spence, 1973). Thus, if drug testing leads to either a positive or a negative reaction, that reaction may generalize to the organization as a whole.

Applicants do not object to employment testing per se (Schmidt, Greenthal, Hunter, Berner, & Seaton, 1977), but do object to testing procedures that are seen as unrelated to the job (Lumsden, 1967). A similar phenomenon exists in research on employment interviews. Applicants react positively to interviews that cover relevant qualifications, and negatively to interviews that deal with issues that are perceived to be tangential to the job (Downs, 1969; Matarrazo, Weins, Jackson, & Manaugh, 1970; Thorson & Thomas, 1968). This research suggests that a critical determinant of applicants' reactions to drug testing policies will be their perceptions of the necessity and job relatedness of the testing program.

Schwab et al. (1987) suggested that individuals evaluate organizations by comparing their perceptions of organizational attributes to an internal "attribute preference function." Presumably, reactions to the organizations are a function of the distance between the individual's perception of the actual attributes of the organization and the attributes of an ideal or preferred organization. Because many of these attributes are unknown to job applicants, the effects of recruitment and personnel selection practices on applicants' perceptions of organizations might be especially strong. The personnel practices encountered by a job applicant may be an important basis for the applicant's inferences regarding unknown attributes of the organization.

Behavioral outcomes.   Job-related attitudes have been linked to the work behaviors of job incumbents and to the job search and organizational choice behaviors of job applicants. For incumbents, there is some evidence linking attitudes such as satisfaction with the job and commitment to the organization to levels of job performance (Campbell, Dunnette, Lawler, & Weick, 1970 ; Hackman & Oldham, 1975; Mowday, 1979; Pritchard, 1969). The strongest attitude-behavior links, however, involve absenteeism, lateness, and turnover (Gupta & Jenkins, 1980; Hulin, Roznowski, & Hachiya, 1985; Rosse & Miller, 1984).

Several models of absenteeism cite work attitudes as a critical variable (e.g., Mowday, Steers, & Porter, 1982; Steers & Rhodes, 1978). Research by Mobley (1977) and his colleagues (e.g., Mobley, Horner, & Hollingsworth, 1978) suggests that work attitudes are closely related to intentions to leave the job. Intentions to quit, in turn, are the best single predictor of actual turnover (Michaels & Spector, 1982; Mowday, Koberg, & McArthur, 1984). Attitude-performance relationships are less clear or certain. Nevertheless, it is reasonable to assume that work attitudes will have some implications for job performance.

Research on job applicants suggests that attitude-behavior links are even stronger for applicants than for job incumbents, in part because applicants are not as strongly committed to any particular job or organization (Schwab et al., 1987). This is particularly true of college students, who typically have more job offers, more information about competing organizations, and more time to decide than do other job applicants (Dyer, 1973; Schwab et al., 1987). Professionals and highly skilled workers might also exhibit strong attitude-job choice links; these workers also enjoy multiple opportunities and alternatives to their present jobs (Holden, 1988).

There is no clear consensus regarding the organizational attributes that are most likely to affect job searches and organizational choice. We do know, however, that perceptions of the organization and its environment significantly affect decisions (Powell, 1984; Rynes & Miller, 1983). Research on the effects of the distribution of job attributes (e.g., Rynes, Schwab, & Heneman, 1983; Strand, Levine, & Montgomery, 1981) suggests that employee drug testing policies might, in many cases, have a disproportionate effect on organizational choice. Harn (1987) showed that the range of attributes considered during the organizational choice process affects the relative importance of each attribute in determining choices. For example, if organizations offer widely different salaries, salary may have a strong impact on applicants' decisions. If salary differences are small, this attribute will receive less weight in judgments. Attributes such as pay, opportunities for advancement, and the intrinsic interest of the job itself may not vary substantially for individuals seeking entry-level jobs in the blue collar or white collar work force. If other attributes do not vary, but drug testing programs *do* vary substantially from organization to organization, it is likely that testing policies will have a large effect on job search and job choice (Harn, 1987; Strand et al., 1981).

Research on job-choice strategies suggests that attitudes regarding employee drug testing are more likely to affect choices when these attitudes are negative than when they are positive. There is evidence that applicants follow a search strategy in which they reject unacceptable jobs, and accept the first acceptable offer they receive (Soelberg, 1967). If this is true, the possible beneficial effects of positive reactions to employee drug testing programs may not be fully evident when examining job search and occupational choice, but may be evident in behavioral terms only after the individual has joined the organization.

Job choice and productivity.   It is well known that the use of valid tests in personnel selection can lead to substantial gains in productivity (Hunter & Hunter, 1984). Schmidt, Hunter, and their colleagues have developed and applied methods of estimating the financial value of these gains (Hunter & Schmidt, 1982; Schmidt & Hunter, 1983; Schmidt, Hunter, McKenzie, & Muldrow, 1979); applications of these methods suggest that valid personnel selection can lead to productivity gains of up to $80 billion per year (Hunter & Hunter, 1984; Hunter & Schmidt, 1982).

Murphy (1986) showed that these procedures for estimating utility substantially overestimate the gains associated with personnel selection, because they fail to adequately consider the fact that many individuals decline job offers. Murphy's (1986) analysis showed that rejected job offers are likely to decrease the gains associated with valid selection by 30–80%. More important, this research suggests that the best candidates are most likely to reject job offers, and that the loss in potential productivity is heavily concentrated in a relatively small number of applicants who are best qualified. For example, if a personnel practice results in the top 20% of all applicants who receive job offers rejecting those offers, the organization loses over half of the gain associated with using valid selection tests (as opposed to using invalid or random procedures). Even if the most qualified applicants are only more *likely,* but not certain, to reject job offers, the potential loss in productivity is still extensive. Highly qualified applicants are likely to have large numbers of alternatives to any specific job offer, and are therefore most likely to reject a job offer from an organization whose drug testing policy is regarded as offensive. Thus, a small number of rejected job offers could result in significant losses for the organization. The significance of this finding can be illustrated with an example.

Hunter and Schmidt (1982) estimated that use of a valid ability test to select 2000 workers into an entry-level white-collar job (annual salary—$28,400) would lead to an annual productivity gain of $8,133,012. Murphy (1986) showed that if the top 10% of those offered jobs declined, this figure would be reduced by $2,159,153. If the top 30% of the group receiving job offers declined the offers, the loss in potential productivity would be $5,339,774. These results suggest that procedures that discourage even a small number of highly qualified applicants from applying, or encourage a similar small number to reject job offers, could have a very significant effect on the productivity of the organization.

Research on Attitudes Toward Drug Testing

Although there is an extensive anecdotal literature dealing with attitudes toward employee drug testing, there is little empirical research on this question. A recent study by Murphy, Reynolds, and Thornton (1989) provides some information about college students' attitudes, and suggests that drug testing does indeed affect attitudes, and may affect behaviors.

In many studies, college students represent samples of convenience. In this study, students represented a population whose attitudes should be of considerable interest. As we noted earlier, attitudes toward personnel practices are more likely to affect the behavior of job applicants than that of current employees, and the effects of attitudes will be strongest for applicants who have the largest number of choices, the most time, and the fewest constraints on their decisions. College students fit this description very well.

Murphy et al. (1989) used the four characteristics of testing programs described in Lorber and Kirk (1987) as a starting point, and asked students whether or not they saw employee drug testing as justified: (a) in different jobs (15 items), (b) under different circumstances (12 items), (c) using different procedures (13 items), and (d) resulting in different consequences (8 items). Attitudes toward each program characteristic were measured on a Likert-type scale, where 1 = strongly disagree and 7 = strongly agree with the assertion that the practice described in each item was justified.

This scale was administered to 190 college students; the principal findings of this study are shown in Table 12.1. These results suggest that: (a) drug testing is seen as more justifiable in some jobs (i.e., those that involve possible threats to the safety of customers, coworkers, or the public) than others, (b) testing current employees and testing job applicants was seen as equally justifiable, and (c) comparable consequences of failing a drug test (e.g., loss or denial of job) were seen as less justifiable for current employees than for job applicants.

Our most important finding was the extreme polarization of attitudes toward employee drug testing. For virtually every item on the survey, a large number

TABLE 12.1
Student Attitudes Toward Drug Testing

	Mean	SD
Job		
Airline pilot	6.6	1.2
Air traffic controller	6.6	1.2
Police officer	6.2	1.5
Nurse	6.0	1.5
Truck driver	5.5	1.7
Fork lift driver	5.4	1.7
Machinist	5.1	1.9
Electrical engineer	5.0	1.8
Electrician	4.9	1.7
Professor	4.1	1.2
Accountant	4.0	1.8
Market research analyst	3.9	1.7
Computer programmer	3.8	1.7
Clerk/typist	3.4	1.6
Retail sales	3.3	1.6
Circumstances that Lead to Testing		
All applicants tested	4.0	2.2
Applicants tested at random	3.0	2.0
Test requested by:		
Manager	3.5	1.9
Personnel department	3.4	1.7
Test required because:		
Drug use suspected	4.4	2.1
Known history of drug use	5.0	2.0
Administrative Procedures		
Test procedure:		
Submit blood and urine sample	3.9	2.1
Background check	3.5	2.0
Tests detect:		
All illegal drugs	5.1	1.9
Drugs that impair job performance	4.9	1.9
Illegal drugs and alcohol	4.0	2.1
Test results:		
Kept confidential	5.2	2.2
Given to supervisor	4.8	2.0
Given to personnel department	3.4	2.0
Given to police	2.6	2.0
Consequences of Failing Test		
Job applicants:		
Rejection	3.4	2.1
Lower suitability rating	4.0	2.0
Required to accept counseling	4.9	1.8
Current employee:		
Dismissal	2.9	1.9
Lower ratings	3.8	2.0
Choice of dismissal or counseling	4.8	2.0
Opportunity to accept counseling	5.5	1.8
No action taken on confirmed failure	3.4	2.1

Note. All items assessed on a 7-point scale where 1 = strongly disagree and 7 = strongly agree that the practice is justified.

(typically 20–30%) of students strongly agreed that the practice described was justified, and an equally large number of students strongly disagreed that the same practice was justified. This extreme variability in responses suggests that organizational decision makers who contemplate employee drug testing will be faced with a dilemma—no matter what course of action they take, their policy is likely to be strongly favored by some job applicants and strongly opposed by others.

Implications.   Murphy et al.'s (1989) findings suggest that attitudes toward employee drug testing programs may have a significant impact on college students' perceptions of and behavior toward different organizations. Drug testing is clearly controversial, and is likely to be salient in this population. It is therefore important to determine the impact of attitudes toward employee drug testing on behaviors such as job search, job choice, and job performance.

Several questions require further research. First, we do not know whether attitudes toward employee drug testing are sufficiently strong or salient to affect job choice or work performance. The foregoing study suggests that these attitudes may be extreme, but does not answer the question of how much weight will be given to drug testing when making important decisions about work. Second, we know very little about the consequences of personnel policies that some applicants and employees regard as offensive. As we note in the section that follows, the most important question may be *who* is offended by programs such as drug testing. Finally, none of the existing studies has examined changes over time in attitudes toward drug testing. The implications of these attitudes for organizations will differ, depending on their permanence.

SCIENCE-PRACTICE LINKAGES

Drug testing policies have been shaped by executives and personnel practitioners who have had to respond to organizational pressures, which have in turn been strongly influenced by the national agenda. In the concluding section of this chapter we suggest that there are several issues surrounding drug testing that need to be addressed by scientists and practitioners, so that future testing programs may be better designed and implemented. In the following discussion we suggest that basic research should be conducted to identify the testing circumstances that are likely to affect reactions to the program, and that the relationships between drug use and work behavior should be better specified. Also, we recommend that applied research should focus on the effectiveness of various testing programs in relation to the goals they are designed to accomplish.

Basic Research

The preceding discussion suggests that attitudes toward drug testing may affect attitudes toward other aspects of the organization using drug tests, and may in turn affect work behaviors and preemployment reactions. Preliminary research (Murphy et al., 1989) indicates that attitudes toward drug testing are highly variable; it is therefore very likely that some applicants and employees will react negatively to drug testing. Further research is needed to indicate whether attitudes toward testing are related to such factors as prior and current drug use and actual work performance.

Attitudes may have a considerable effect on the utility of drug testing under some conditions. It can be reasonably assumed that some of the individuals opposed to testing are themselves users and that they therefore perceive testing as a threat. In this case, attitudes toward testing may be' of little consequence, because these applicants are unlikely to be top performers on the job, may be rejected on the basis of results of a drug test, or may choose not to apply to an organization that conducts drug screenings. Moreover, negative attitudes may increase the usefulness of testing programs because they may divert drug users away from organizations that test. On the other hand, if a proportion of high-ability applicants and employees hold negative attitudes toward testing, then those attitudes may lower the utility of the testing program. Researchers need to estimate the relationships between attitudes toward testing, actual drug usage, and work performance to more fully estimate the value of drug testing programs as a selection device.

Murphy et al. (1989) showed that attitudes toward testing are not only highly variable across persons, but are also a function of the characteristics of testing programs. If it is shown that some high quality applicants and employees have strong reactions against drug testing programs, it may still be possible to design effective programs based on procedures that are acceptable to these applicants. For example, Murphy et al. (1989) and others (Blum & Roman, in press; Stone & Vine, 1989) provided evidence that people more strongly approve of drug testing if it is known that the results will be used to aid individuals who test positive; they approve less strongly, however, if positive results lead to punitive action. If reactions to specific program characteristics can be identified, then programs can be better designed to reduce negative reactions. Such programs will fit better within the prevailing organizational culture, and be of higher value as a selection tool. The research cited earlier indicated that both employees and college students perceive drug testing as fair and acceptable under some circumstances; it is up to researchers to more clearly identify the testing conditions that are associated with positive reactions from the individuals likely to be tested. Practitioners may then use this information to design drug testing programs in a manner that is most likely to be acceptable, and likely to fulfill organizational goals at the same time.

Researchers should also continue to address the relationship between drug use and job performance. Evidence of specific performance decrements is lacking in available research, perhaps because it has not been necessary to justify drug testing to the same extent as other selection techniques must be justified. The national *Zeitgeist* against illegal drug use has led the courts to examine issues of unreasonable search and seizure and probable cause, rather than issues of job relatedness. However, it is possible for a job applicant who is refused federal employment on the basis a drug test to claim unfair discrimination under the Federal Rehabilitation Act, if drug use is not demonstrably related to job performance (Angarola, 1986). It is still unclear how the Act will be applied to private employers. When testing is challenged on grounds of job relatedness, it is important to have evidence of relationships between personal time drug use and work time task performance. More research is clearly needed to specify the tasks or behaviors that are most likely to be affected by drug use.

Along similar lines, if drug testing comes to be viewed by the court system as other selection and decision making devices are viewed, it is possible that drug testing may be susceptible to adverse impact suits under conditions where the relationships between casual drug use and performance decrement is perceived to be weak. Research is also needed to determine if the probability of failing a drug test is related to membership in a protected subgroup.

A multidisciplinary approach is needed to adequately assess the job-relatedness of specific drug tests. Physiological psychologists and psychopharmacologists may be able to document the effects of specific drugs on specific behaviors, but this will not be sufficient to establish job-relatedness. The link between specific behaviors and job performance must also be established. I/O psychologists can apply existing methods of job analysis to help establish this link.

Application

Personnel practitioners can add to our knowledge of the actual extent and nature of the drug problem in industry, and can identify procedures and policies that can effectively meet the goals of their organizations. Although drug abuse is thought to be pervasive in industry, actual data regarding incidence levels have been difficult to obtain. Some research has attempted to determine the costs of drug abuse by generally estimating health care expenditures and lost productivity (e.g., Walsh, 1986). These estimates suggest that the costs of drug use can be high. However, the cost of drug screening can also be high (Olian, 1987). Information regarding the prevalence of drug use within specific industries and job classifications could lead to a more cost-effective application of drug testing efforts, by concentrating drug prevention efforts where they are most needed. Personnel practitioners could aid in collecting this information by identifying more sensitive indices of drug use. A procedure as simple as analyzing demographic information kept by existing employee assistance programs (E.A.P.) may permit the identification of subpopulations where drug testing will have the largest effect.

Applied researchers are also in the best position to examine the effectiveness of the organization's substance abuse policies and procedures. In order to estimate effectiveness, it is first necessary to define the specific goals of drug abuse programs. Typically there have been two goals: (a) to reduce the incidence levels of substance abuse in industry, and thereby (b) improve job performance, reduce turnover and absenteeism, improve morale, and generally affect the operation of the organization in a positive manner. The effectiveness of procedures for reducing the incidence of drug use is largely unknown, because the base rates of drug use in the workplace have yet to be clearly established. It is probable that requiring drug testing as a condition of employment will have some effect on the casual user, but the strength and duration of this effect must be estimated if the value of such a policy is ever to be determined. If an organization simply intends to take a stand against drugs in order to reduce incidence rates, then it is possible that simple procedures involving limited testing may be just as effective as extensive screening programs.

When organizations have the specific goal of improving dysfunctional aspects of work behavior, it is important to examine the effectiveness of the mechanisms that have been developed to effect that change. EAPs have been the most common method of improving work performance by reducing substance abuse, and some researchers have estimated that, in about 60% of the cases handled by EAPs, poor performance due to drug abuse can be improved. More research is needed to examine EAP effectiveness, the appropriate linkages between drug testing and EAPs, and the psychological side-effects of EAP referral, before the effectiveness of screening programs as a tool for improving work related behavior can be estimated.

One critical task for practitioners who provide expert knowledge to organizations is to keep abreast of the rapidly developing body of knowledge related to drug abuse and drug testing. For example, new approaches to treating addictions are being developed (Reid, 1989), and these may have implications for the way in which organizations structure and use drug testing programs. Knowledge about the effects of drug testing on work attitudes is quickly accumulating (Stone & Vine, 1989). I/O psychologists occupy a critical boundary-spanning role that makes them an important part of the development, implementation, and evaluation of programs designed to reduce the negative effects of drug and alcohol abuse in the workplace.

REFERENCES

Adams, J. S. (1965). Inequity in social exchange. In L. Berkowitz (Ed.), *Advances in experimental social psychology* (Vol 2). New York: Academic Press.

Angarola, R. T. (1986). Perspectives on legal issues. In H. Axel, *Corporate strategies for controlling substance abuse.* New York: The Conference Board.

Balster, R. L. 1987). The behavioral pharmacology of phencyclidine. In H. Y. Meltzer (Ed.), *Psychopharmacology: The third generation of progress* (pp. 1581–1588). New York: Raven Press.

Baumrind, D., & Moselle, K. A. (1985). A developmental perspective on adolescent drug use. *Advances in Alcohol and Substance Abuse, 5,* 41–67.

Bensinger, C. C. (1987). *Attitudes toward drug screening: Implications for organizational recruitment.* Unpublished master's thesis, Rensselaer Polytechnic Institute, Troy, New York.

Blum, T. C., & Roman, P. M. (in press). Employee assistance programs and human resource management. In K. Rowland & G. Ferris (Eds.), *Research in personnel and human resource management.* Greenwich, CT: JAI Press.

Bozarth, M. A. (Ed.) (1987). *Methods of assessing the reinforcing properties of abused drugs.* New York: Springer-Verlag.

Campbell, J. P., Dunnette, M. D., Lawler, E. E., & Weick, K. E. (1970). *Managerial behavior, performance, and effectiveness.* New York: McGraw-Hill.

Cascio, W. F. (1987). *Applied psychology in personnel management* (3rd Ed.), Englewood Cliffs, NJ: Prentice-Hall.

Chadwick-Jones, J. K., Nicholson, N., & Brown, C. (1982). *The social psychology of absenteeism.* New York: Praeger.

Cloninger, C. R., Bohman, M., & Sigvardsson, S. (1981). Inheritance of alcohol abuse: Cross-fostering analysis of adopted men. *Archives of General Psychiatry, 38,* 861–868.

Donovan, J. E., & Jessor, R. (1983). Problem drinking and the dimensions of involvement with drugs: A Guttman scalogram analysis of adolescent drug use. *American Journal of Public Health, 73,* 543–552.

Downs, C. W. (1969). Perceptions of the selection interview. *Personnel Administration, 32,* 8–23.

Dyer, L. D. (1973). Job search success of middle-aged managers and engineers. *Industrial and Labor Relations Review, 26,* 969–970.

Fillmore, K.M. (1988). *Alcohol use across the life course: A critical review of 70 years of international longitudinal research.* Toronto: Addiction Research Foundation

Finnegan, K. T., Ricaurte, G. A., Ritchie, L. D., Irwin, I., Peroutka, S. J., & Langston, J. W. (1988). Orally administered MDMA causes a long-term depletion of serotonin in rat brain. *Brain Research, 447.* 141–144.

Fischman, M. W. (1987). Cocaine and the amphetamines. In H. Y. Meltzer (Ed.), *Psychopharmacology: The third generation of progress* (pp. 1543–1554). New York: Raven Press.

Hunter, J. E., & Hunter, R. F. (1984). Validity and utility of alternative predictors of job performance. *Psychological Bulletin, 96,* 72–98.

Hunter, J. E., & Schmidt, F. L. (1982). Fitting people to jobs: The impact of personnel selection on national productivity. In M. Dunnette & E. Fleishman (Eds.), *Human performance and productivity: Human capability assessment.* Hillsdale, NJ: Lawrence Erlbaum Associates.

Johnson, K. M., Jr. (1987). Neurochemistry and neurophysiology of phencyclidine. In H. Y. Meltzer (Ed.), *Psychopharmacology: The third generation of progress* (pp. 1581–1588). New York: Raven Press.

Kandel, D. B. (1973). Adolescent marijuana use: Role of parents and peers. *Science, 181,* 1067–1070.

Kandel, D. B., & Faust, R. (1975). Sequence and stages in patterns of adolescent drug use. *Archives of General Psychiatry, 32,* 923–932.

Kandel, D. B., & Raveis, V. H. (1989). Cessation of illicit drug use in young adulthood. *Archives of General Psychiatry, 46,* 109–116.

Kreek, M. J. (1987). Multiple drug abuse patterns and medical consequences. In H. Y. Meltzer (Ed.), *Psychopharmacology: The third generation of progress* (pp. 1597–1604). New York: Raven Press.

Lodge, J. H. (1983, August). Taking drugs on the job. *Time,* pp. 52–60.

Lorber, L. Z., & Kirk, J. R. (1987). *Fear itself: A legal and personnel analysis of drug testing, AIDS, secondary smoke, VDT's.* Alexandria, VA: ASPA Foundation.

Lumsden, H. (1967). The plant visit: A critical area of recruiting. *Journal of College Placement, 27,* 74–84.

Gardner, A. W. (1982). Identifying and helping problem drinkers at work. *Journal of Social and Occupational Medicine, 32,* 171–179.

Goodman, P., & Friedman, A. (1971). An examination of Adams' theory of inequity. *Administrative Science Quarterly, 16,* 271–288.

Goodwin, D. W., Schulsinger, F., & Moller, N. (1974). Drinking problems in adopted and non-adopted sons of alcoholics. *Archives of General Psychiatry, 31,* 164–169.

Grabowski, J. (1989). Drug screening: Behavioral medicine asset or social policy failure? *Psychopharmacology Newsletter, 22*(1), 5–6.

Gupta, N., & Jenkins, G. (1980). *The structure of withdrawl: Relationships among estrangement, tardiness, absenteeism and turnover.* Springfield, VA: National Technical Information System.

Hackman, J. R., & Oldham, G. R. (1975). Development of the job diagnostic survey. *Journal of Applied Psychology, 60,* 159–170.

Harn, T. (1987). *The effect of range of job attributes on their importance in job choice decisions.* Unpublished manuscript. Colorado State University.

Holden, C. (1988). NIH scientists balk at random drug tests. *Science, 239,*724.

Huba, G. J., Wingard, J. A., & Bentler, P. M. (1981). A comparison of two latent variable causal models for adolescent drug use. *Journal of Personality and Social Psychology, 40,* 180–193.

Hulin, C., Roznowski, M., & Hachiya, D. (1985). Alternative opportunities and withdrawal decisions: Empirical and theoretical discrepancies and an integration. *Psychological Bulletin, 97,* 233–250.

Marlatt, G., Baer, J. S., Donovan, D. M., & Kivlahan, D. R. (1988). Addictive behaviors: Etiology and treatment. *Annual Review of Psychology, 39,* 223–252.

Marshall, E. (1988). Testing urine for drugs. *Science, 241,* 150–152.

Matarrazo, J., Weins, A., Jackson, R., & Manaugh, T. (1970). Interviewee speech behavior under different conditions. *Journal of Applied Psychology, 54,* 15–26.

Mello, N. K. (1987). Alcohol abuse and alcoholism: 1978–87. In H. Y. Meltzer (Ed.), *Psychopharmacology: The third generation of progress* (pp. 1515–1520). New York: Raven Press.

Mello, N. K., & Griffiths, R. R. (1987). Alcoholism and drug abuse: An overview. In H. Y. Meltzer (Ed.), *Psychopharmacology: The third generation of progress* (pp. 1581–1588). New York: Raven Press.

Mendelson, J. H. (1987). Marijuana. In H. Y. Meltzer (Ed.), *Psychopharmacology: The third generation of progress* (pp. 1565–1572). New York: Raven Press.

Michaels, C. E., & Spector, P. E. (1982). Causes of employee turnover: A test of the Mobley, Griffith, Hand and Meglino model. *Journal of Applied Psychology, 67,* 53–59.

Miller, L. L. (1979). Cannabis and the brain with special reference to the Limbic system. In G. Nahas & W. Patton (Eds.), *Marijuana: Biological effects.* Elmsford, NY: Pergamon

Miller, W. R., & Hester, R. K. (1986). The effectiveness of alcoholism treatment methods: What research reveals. In W. R. Miller & N. Heather (Eds.), *Treating addictive behaviors: Processes of change* (pp. 121–174). New York: Plenum Press.

Mobley, W. H. (1977). Intermediate linkages in the relationship between job satisfaction and turnover. *Journal of Applied Psychology, 62,* 237–240.

Mobley, W. H., Horner, S. O., & Hollingsworth, A. T. (1978). An evaluation of precursors of hospital turnover. *Journal of Applied Psychology, 63,* 408–414.

Mowday, R. T. (1979). Equity theory predictions of behavior in organizations. In R. Steers & L. Porter (Eds.), *Motivation and work behavior* (2nd Ed), New York: McGraw-Hill.

Mowday, R. T., Koberg, C. S., & McArthur, A. W. (1984). The psychology of the withdrawl process: A cross-validation test of Mobley's intermediate linkages model of turnover in two samples. Management Journal, *27,* 79–94.

Mowday, R. T., Steers, R. M., & Porter, L. W. (1982). *Employee-Organization linkages: The psychology of commitment, absenteeism and turnover.* New York: Academic Press.

Murphy, K. R. (1986). When your top choice turns you down: Effects of rejected job offers on selection test utility. *Psychological Bulletin, 99,* 133–138.

Murphy, K. R., Reynolds, D. H., & Thornton, G. C. (1989). College students' attitudes toward employee drug testing programs. Unpublished manuscript, Colorado State University.

Nathan, P. E. (1986). Outcomes of treatment for alcoholism: Current data. *Annals of Behavioral Medicine, 8,* 40–46.

Newcomb, M. D. (1988). *Drug use in the workplace: Risk factors for disruptive substance abuse among young adults.* Dover, MA: Auburn House.

Newcomb, M. D., & Bentler, P. M. (1988). *Consequences of adolescent drug use.* Newbury Park, CA: Sage.

O'Boyle, T. F. (1985, August 8). More firms require employee drug tests. *Wall Street Journal,* p. 6.

Olian, J. (1987). *Developing methods of bio-testing.* Workshop presented at the Second Annual Convention for Industrial and Organizational Psychology, Atlanta, GA.

Olian, J., & Guthrie, J. (1988, Feb. 17). Personal communication.

Powell, G. N. (1984). Effects of job attributes and recruiting practices on applicant decisions: A comparison. *Personnel Psychology, 37,* 721–732.

Pritchard, R. (1969). Equity theory: A review and critique. *Organizational Behavior and Human performance, 4,* 176–211.

Ray, O., & Ksir, C. (1987). *Drugs, society, and human behavior.* (4th Ed.) Toronto: Times Mirror/Mosby College Publishing.

Reid, L. D. (Ed.). (1989). *Opioids, bulimia, and alcohol abuse and alcoholism.* New York: Springer-Verlag.

Rosse, J., & Miller, H. (1984). Relationship between absenteeism and other employee behaviors. In P. Goodman, R. Atkin, & Associates (Eds.), *Absenteeism.* San Francisco: Jossey-Bass.

Rossi, N. A., & Reid, L. D. (1976). Affective states associated with morphine injections. *Physiological Psychology, 4,* 269–274.

Rynes, S. L., Heneman, H. G., & Schwab, D. P. (1980). Individual reactions to organizational recruiting: A review. *Personnel Psychology, 33,* 529–542.

Rynes, S. L., & Miller, H. E. (1983). Recruiter and job influences on candidates for employment. *Journal of Applied Psychology, 68,* 147–154.

Rynes, S. L., Schwab, D. P., & Heneman, H. G. (1983). The role of pay and market pay variability in job applicant decisions. *Organizational Behavior and Human Performance, 31,* 353–364.

Schein, E. H. (1965). *Organizational psychology.* Englewood Cliffs, NJ: Prentice-Hall.

Schmidt, F. L., & Hunter, J. E. (1983). Individual differences in productivity: An empirical test of the estimate derived from studies of selection procedure utility. *Journal of Applied Psychology, 68,* 407–414.

Schmidt, F. L., Greenthal, A., Hunter, J. E., Berner, J., & Seaton, F. (1977). Job sample vs. paper-and-pencil trades and technical tests: Adverse impact and examinee attitudes. *Personnel Psychology, 30,* 187–197.

Schmidt, F. L., Hunter, J. E., McKenzie, R. C., & Muldrow, T. (1979). The impact of valid selection procedures on work force productivity. *Journal of Applied Psychology, 64,* 609–626.

Schwab, D. P., Rynes, S. L., & Aldag, R. J. (1987). Theories and research on job search and choice. In K. Rowland & G. Ferris (Eds.), *Research in personnel and human resource management* (Vol. 5) Greenwich, CT: JAI Press.

Soelberg, P. O. (1967). Unprogrammed decision making. *Industrial Management Review, 8,* 19–29.

Spence, M. (1973). Job market signalling. *Quarterly Journal of Economics, 87,* 355–374.

Steers, R. M., & Rhodes, S. R. (1978). Major influences on employee attendance: A process model. *Journal of Applied Psychology, 63,* 391–407.

Stein, J., Newcomb, M., & Bentler, P. (1988). Structure of drug abuse behavior and consequences among young adults: Multitrait–multimethod assessment of frequency, quantity work site and problem substance abuse. *Journal of Applied Psychology, 73,* 595–605.

Stone, D. L., & Vine, P. L. (1989). *Some procedural determinants of attitudes toward drug testing.* Presented at Fourth Annual Conference, Society for Industrial/Organizational Psychology, Boston.

Strand, R., Levin, R., & Montgomery, D. (1981). Organizational entry preferences based upon social and personnel policies: An information integration perspective. *Organizational Behavior and Human Performance, 27,* 50–68.

Tang, B. K. (1987). Detection of ethanol in urine of abstaining alcoholics. *Canadian Journal of Physiology and Pharmacology, 65,* 1225–1227.

Thorson, H., & Thomas, W. (1968). Students' opinions of the placement process. *Journal of College Placement, 29,* 80–84.

Tolchin, M. (1989). The government still waits to test millions for drugs. *The New York Times,* March 26, p. E5.

Walsh, D. C. (1986). Some definitional dilemmas. In H. Axel, *Corporate strategies for controlling substance abuse.* New York: The Conference Board.

Walsh, J. M. (1989). Drug testing: A powerful tool. *Psychopharmacology Newsletter, 22*(1), 2–3.

Walsh, J., & Gust, S. (1988). *Interdisciplinary approaches to the problem of drug abuse in the workplace.* Washington, DC: Department of Health and Human Services Publication No. (ADM) 86–1477.

Wells, V. E., Halperin, W., & Thun, M. (1988). The estimated predictive value of screening for illicit drugs in the workplace. *American Journal of Public Health Briefs, 78,* 817–819.

IV THE PAST AND FUTURE OF THE SCIENCE AND PRACTICE OF I/O PSYCHOLOGY

Our final section consists of a single chapter by Joseph M. (Matt) Madden. He examines I/O psychology from the perspective of someone who has been in the field for over 45 years, and suggests directions I/O psychology should take to make a more effective contribution to the solution of problems that are of great societal concern. Matt's function in this book is analogous to that of a senior statesman. His chapter contains fewer references or other academic tricks of the trade, more personal observations, and more wisdom than you will find in the chapters that preceded it. The chapter provides both a summary of many of the points raised by the authors, and a challenge to the field of I/O psychology to go on to bigger and better things.

13 Where Have we Been and Where are we Going?

Joseph M. Madden
Rensselaer Polytechnic Institute

Without question, these are outstanding papers. I have read them with a distinct feeling of pride because most of the authors were my students here at R.P.I. It is hard to believe that the green kids who reported for their first semester in graduate school with so little confidence, such confused looks on their faces, such profound worries about financial survival, wondering if the high tuition at R.P.I. would be worth it and if graduate school would be too difficult and demanding, are now accomplished scholars. In fact, it might be heartening for those of you who are now graduate students to eavesdrop on some of my recollections of these prominent psychologists as they proceeded with their graduate work.

Skip Saal reported in fresh from Vietnam after a tour of duty as an infantry lieutenant. His highest aspiration in life at that time was to achieve a Master's degree in I/O psychology. Early on, he was full of doubts about his ability and preparation to reach such a high level of achievement. He was, as it turned out, an exemplary student, and one of the most meticulous researchers I have ever known. When Skip graduated, my wife insisted that I go to the graduation. I had never attended a graduation for any of my degrees, never worn a cap and gown. I agreed to make the sacrifice, rented a cap and gown and went to the ceremony to honor Skip's graduation. He wasn't there!

I remember Kevin Murphy wore the most disreputable pair of sneakers I have ever seen for his entire tenure here. He must have nailed them down at night. I don't remember his car ever running 2 days in a row. I do remember that before the end of his first year here, he knew more about SPSS than anyone else, including the faculty. Kevin fell in love with the word "robust." Even in the beginning, he had an immense capacity to do an incredible amount of work.

Jean Lapointe was one of our R.P.I. undergraduates and a member of the Naval ROTC. The ROTC gave him a firm limit of one year to complete his graduate work. He had impressed everyone as being very laid back and not the type to make such a superhuman effort. We all thought that 2 years was an absolute minimum to fulfill the degree requirements, and most students had to strain to get it done in that time. Jean did it in a year and remained laid back throughout the whole time. I could never conceive of him in a military role, and after my own 30 years in the Air Force, I regarded him as about as military as a Laborador puppy. His thesis was exemplary. I'll never forget the look of in-credibility on his face as he worked his way through my course in interpersonal relations regarding how inept most of us are in this most important skill area.

Walt Freytag arrived from Brooklyn, New York. When I told him that his heavy accent might have a negative effect on his consulting work, especially in upstate New York, he got an expression on his face that said he had accidentally enrolled in some weird, outer-space institution, and "How do I get out of this foreign place?" However, after some consulting experience in upstate New York organizations, he saw the light and almost completely got rid of the accent. I will never forget the expression on his face for a week or so after he completed the degree requirements. He looked like a canonized zombie who had died and gone to heaven.

Bob Goldsmith was an RPI sophomore engineering major when he came to me and asked, "Is this all there is?" At the age of 18 or 19 he was keen enough to realize that the engineering for which R.P.I. was famous was not for him, and he had a good idea of exactly why. More or less tentatively, he became a psychology major, a strange thing for a student to do at R.P.I. He's one of those people who is so bright that he tends to make others feel a little dull. I always had the feeling that he was a lot smarter than I and a much better student than I had ever been. It seemed easy for him to maintain a close-to-A average as an undergraduate, and graduate school also seemed to be easy for him. Just about everything that could go wrong did so in his thesis work. While I worried quite a bit, he was never even slightly perturbed, and the thesis turned out very well.

When Bob McIntyre arrived he was a highly talented singer. For a while, we thought we could hire him out. But the demands of the program took all his time. For the most part, he even gave up his beloved hunting and fishing. It always appeared to me that each time Bob had a success in his graduate work, which was quite often, he seemed surprised. He would get that, "Did I really do that?" look on his face. However, by the time he finished his graduate work it was more like a "See, I can do anything" look. Bob brings an emotionality to his work that is unusual among scholars, as well as an idealism that I, personally, find laudable.

Bill Balzer did not do his thesis with me, although he did his doctoral work with Kevin Murphy. Since he did his thesis with another faculty member, he doesn't identify as "my" student. He has said that he considers himself a grand-son rather than a son. Nevertheless, I have always felt close to Bill and I remember that, throughout his graduate work here, we had many lengthy conversations on a wide range of topics. I also remember his beard—one of the more outlandish ones that I've seen, even on college campuses. I think he lost 30 pounds when he shaved it off.

Three of these men were married during their work here at R.P.I., and (can you believe it?) are still married to the same women. Diane Freytag, Cathie Saal, and Mary McIntyre have been important positive influences in the careers of their husbands. I am really not poetic enough nor do I have the descriptive talent to do them even minimal justice in these comments. I love all three of them and hold them up to all as examples of what a wife can be.

The other authors are certainly notable scholars. Bob Baron has been Chair of the R.P.I. Department of Psychology for over a year, coming here from a very successful period at Purdue. Already, the department has a new energy. There is electricity in the air. Physical improvements that we have been unable to accomplish for years have been made. The faculty has already been united into a cohesive unit, and even has effective meetings. Attitudes have become very positive among both faculty and students. Everyone has become forward looking and optimistic. The department was pretty much the opposite a year ago, and these changes in such a short time reflect the boundless energy and ability of Bob Baron.

Kevin Williams left RPI over a year ago to join the faculty at the State University of New York at Albany. We were faculty colleagues for about 2 years, but really didn't get to know one another very well. Kevin always has a lot of irons in the fire and is usually surrounded by graduate students.

Larry Reid is a unique person. He has a national and international reputation for his research on addictions. He operates an extremely productive research laboratory with the help of just a few of his graduate students. Dealing with requests for his reprints is almost a full-time job. As one of the nation's leading neuroscientists, he is sought out to give papers and colloquia across the country. His former graduate students are now becoming known and recognized at the national level. Yet, he conceived, planned, obtained financing for, and managed our colloquium in November of 1987 on the topic of "Organizational Behavior, Performance and Productivity: Contributions to Organizational Problem Solving." (This book has emanated largely from that symposium.) The labor and volume of detail involved in such an undertaking is indeed forbidding and, for one on Larry Reid's schedule, a most impressive accomplishment, especially working in a field quite different from his own. As I have said to him, I'm not sure if he is a genius or if there is serious pathology there.

I am not well acquainted with George Thornton or Jan Cleveland. Jan is Kevin's wife and I've met her socially on a few occasions. It is good to see a female I/O psychologist on the scene at meetings traditionally dominated by males! Their topic of simulation, considered in the context of experiential learning theory, is not only timely but one that I predict will receive more and more of our attention.

So these are the people we have just read. These are exemplary scholars, researchers and Industrial/Organizational Psychologists (we made Larry Reid an honorary I/O psychologist). I doubt if one could find a better set of papers, and one would be very hard pressed to equal them.

It seems clear that these authors have demonstrated that we have effectively integrated science and practice. In fact, I think we have been quite successful at this integration for many years. We have seen that science contributes to practice in terms of the way practitioners think about problems, the rigor used in weighing evidence or data, and in the methods used. In fact, it sometimes appears that the practitioner is overly devoted to science and misses some good contributions because they are merely opinion or expert insights and not scientifically sound inferences. It also seems clear that practice keeps the scientists' feet firmly planted on the ground, and helps them avoid the esoteric. Even so, we do see cases of massive theorizing based on a modicum of data, a practice psychologists have been accused of for many decades. For example, any I/O psychologist can open an organizational psychology text and point to topics that are presented as accomplished fact, but are really theoretical positions supported by little or no solid data. (I don't see any such overtheorizing in the present papers; in fact, what we see here is more of an optimal balance.) Our authors are clearly fine scientists as well as fine practitioners. As far as the past and present are concerned, the scientist-practitioner model has been expertly implemented and has led to success in both areas. We no longer see an I/O psychologist, whose graduate training was in experimental psychology, adhering to the scientific method in a rigid, dogmatic way, as we saw in the 1930s, '40s, and '50s. We no longer hear charges of "charlatan" directed toward those who departed too far from the scientific base during the same period. The excesses have faded away and a good balance has been achieved. The question for the future is what to do with our integrated discipline. So let's move on and look at the future.

It seems clear to me that this is a good time to reexamine our purposes and objectives in terms of what we do with this integration and how we implement the scientist-practitioner model in the future. Are the exemplary contributors to this book well utilized? Is there some possibility that our horizons should be widened beyond those depicted in these papers? More caustically, have our authors been so gainfully employed as they might be? Are they doing the most significant work of which they are capable? Is the preparation of papers such as these, fine as they are by our current standards, the best way to utilize such an impressive array of talent? These seem pertinent questions, especially in view of the fact that, in our field, we are much concerned with the utilization of talent.

So maybe this is a good time to consider the future and make some judgments about whether or not we want to continue in the same directions we have pursued in the past. In order to plan for the future, we need a good understanding of the present and the past. But the term "we" suggests a group effort, interaction, meetings, colloquia and seminars. Obviously, such activities are potential events to take place in the future. However, for the present, I would like to offer some personal views that I hope will stimulate the occurrence of such future events. I hope I can be convincing enough to generate some interest and action.

In the distant past, the immediate past, and in the present, I believe we have been and are presently driven by the academic model of scholarship (see McIntyre's chapter in this volume). This is the model to which we must adhere rigidly to succeed in academia. Included here are not only those in academia but also those in industry or non-academic environments. This is because all of us, or practically all of us, want to keep our career options open. It is hard to find an I/O psychologist in a non-academic position who doesn't want to keep the option open for a change of careers into academia. In order to qualify for that career change, the requirements of the academic model must be fulfilled.

Such requirements are well known to all of us. We must produce the required numbers of publications in the "correct" journals, present papers at meetings, give invited colloquia, and attract funding. Emphasis among these requirements may vary from institution to institution, but the uniformity among graduate schools, especially in major universities, is amazing. If we do these things, we will become well known among our colleagues across the country. We will then be promoted to Professor, but the academic model will still drive our behavior because our annual raises are completely dependent on our adherence to the demands of that model. So what? Aren't all these requirements good things to do? Doesn't fulfillment of these requirements gradually increase the general fund of knowledge and eventually contribute to the welfare of man? This question has been argued pro and con, ad nauseum, without really resolving much. But I think all of us agree that there is a significant amount of trivial research produced each year. We all know that there are massive amounts of published research collecting dust on hidden shelves, unlikely to ever see the light of day. Such research is illustrated by studies with such extensive, esoteric, and unusual statistical analysis that the content is obscured; very involved presentations of methodologies with extremely limited application; and trivial variations of previously published work. It does not appear that changes in these matters are likely; it does appear that we will continue to do business as usual for an indefinite time into the future.

I must admit at this point that my personal opinions may have become jaded with time. Perhaps a certain amount of impatience sets in when one realizes, after many years, how slowly things move. Or, looking back, one realizes having made a significant contribution to the contents of those dim, dusty shelves. Or, perhaps the perspective that is tempered by time becomes more realistic. I don't know, but I do have a strong feeling that I have something to say to the authors who have contributed to this book. I wish someone had said it to me at an early stage in my career. I have had the experience of publishing adequate numbers of papers in the correct journals and filling the other squares so that I succeeded in the academic system. For the most part, I was very pleased when my papers were accepted by prestigious journals and felt certain that they would have a major impact on the world. Not very realistic, perhaps, but certainly typical of most of us. Looking back now, I can't help wondering if they had much of an effect at all. I want to be as certain as possible that our authors avoid ever feeling this way in even the slightest degree. At any rate, I'm going to take my best shot, knowing that such an effort is very easy to criticize.

We have seen the success of the scientist-practitioner model reflected in the excellence of these papers and in the careers of their contributors. The authors have learned the model well and have implemented it superbly. The model, when used as a basis for educating graduate students, does produce psychologists who are successful in both academia and other environments. However, I propose that the scientist-practitioner model is incomplete as we now conceive it. It limits our vision. That is, the idea of the scientist-practitioner, coupled with the academic model, is too limiting. The authors of the chapters in this book, typifying the cream of the I/O crop, are too talented to continue to restrict themselves to the limited horizons resulting from the academic model of success. If they do, I suspect that when they reach my stage of life, they will look back and be disappointed. Their potential should be tapped to include a new dimension that will enhance their contributions and broaden the scope of I/O psychology.

I propose a broadening of our horizons. We need to do more than produce publications. We need more definition of problems in terms of social need, for instance, instead of just theory testing. Consider this illustration. In a recent conversation with a U.S. Senator, the Senator informed me that he had never heard of an I/O psychologist. He asked me to explain in some detail how we are educated and what we do. He then listened intently while I gave him a rather detailed answer. As a part of the answer, I described proudly the beneficial effects we routinely have on organizations. He seemed quite puzzled and he then described a serious problem that he and his colleagues deal with on an almost daily basis.

Members of Congress are frequently faced with a difficult dilemma. A bill is proposed that the member thinks would definitely be a good thing for the nation. However, it would not directly benefit the member's constituents and might even result in less government funding, loss of jobs, or have some other negative impact. If the member votes for the bill, the chances of reelection are reduced and, if it happens often, that probability drops to zero. If the member votes against the bill, it amounts to prostitution to constituents—a really serious dilemma. To illustrate how serious it is, the military services have been trying to close hundreds of installations for years. They have not succeeded, essentially because of the situation described above. So the Senator was puzzled because we never work on these serious problems that affect the whole country, whereas our training and interests would suggest that we could and would.

Members of Congress have hundreds of problems similar to the above. Some of them are a result of resistance to change for a variety of reasons, some are due to organizational structure, some are due to power and the struggle for it, and some are due to purely personal motivation. Organizationally, the Congress is the world's worst mess. The problems of communication between a member of Congress and the electors, as well as communication with Congressional colleagues, are horrendous. For instance, voters differ widely in education, income, interests, religion, net worth, age, health, occupation, culture, and many other dimensions. What marvelous opportunities there are here for research on practical problems in communication.

But we don't work on any of these salient problems. We don't apply ourselves to understanding international organizations and their activities such as war, the arms race, genocide, and trade barriers. We don't study the response of nations to air pollution, hunger, the greenhouse effect and terrorism. We don't have a world or even a national perspective. Our perspective is defined by academia and it is a narrow one. Yes, we do work on basics in areas such as communication and organizational structure. But we tend to be working at "micro" levels that sometimes appear far removed from any practical problems. Aren't we applied psychologists? Isn't concern for practical problems one of the things that differentiates us from psychologists in other fields?

We have had a brief look at a situation in only one federal organizational structure. There are hundreds of them. Some of the organizational problems in government are even worse than those in the Congress. And there are fifty states, each with its own dysfunctional governmental organization. Just consider the impact of even a small finding with some generality in terms of application to governmental structures.

The potential impact of research at the federal and state governmental levels is immense. However, it's difficult to conceive of any research or analysis in these organizations being anything but overwhelmingly forbidding. Undertaking research of this type would entail a serious risk of not getting enough publications to make tenure. One might go for years, breaking ground in this stoney terrain, without a positive or publishable finding. One would be unlikely to churn out three or four publications a year. A tenured professor with a serious desire to do something for his country by doing research on problems in government would need to consider the risk of not getting a raise for years. And herein lies our problem. Our current system, mainly exemplified by academia, prevents us from attempting to do something really significant if there is a risk of not getting the "brownie points" that assure a successful career as currently defined.

Research in government would probably require new experimental designs and methods. A Senator is not likely to be a willing subject. Data gathering will probably have to be done in ways different from those used in most psychological research. It may be that new forms of *nonintrusive* data gathering will need to be invented, wherein new types of data will be gathered using *hands off* techniques that allow the collection of meaningful information from a distance. Archival data, for example, may be essential. Even the definition of problems in governmental research will probably be a unique process. For instance, such problems could be ordered in terms of importance based on susceptibility to research, importance to the people being governed, cost-benefit analysis, likelihood of results being publishable in the correct journals, significance for theory development, and feasibility. Selecting problems for research in government based on conventional hypothesis testing and theory development might offer some real challenges. But all of this serves to help make the basic point of these remarks. These difficulties and the necessity for innovation, invention, creativity, and the highest level of competence will require the capabilities and talents of the best people we can find, people such as the authors of the chapters in this book.

It's obvious to the reader by now that this paper doesn't include any references. The reason is not simply the license that an emeritus can claim, but a need for unshackling from the conventional labored approach to which we are so accustomed. We could reference large numbers of papers to support the above remarks. (Some of us claim that in a commentary such as this, references can be found to support almost any comment.) I think that given the present conceptual stage of the ideas presented here, we need a certain freedom, a Jonathan Livingston Seagull state of mind, in order to proceed with the development of new horizons. We need to soar with the eagles for a while. Later, when we get down to the nitty gritty of research, we can get *rigorous* again. But now we need to break some new ground. We have a scientist-practitioner orientation; now we need new conceptions of implementing it. We do not have a laboratory research tradition because organizations have been our laboratories. We can continue to be good scientist-practitioners while exploring uncharted territory in terms of the organizations with which we concern ourselves.

The more I think of it, the more exciting it gets. Let's see now. . . . How would I get some data on effectiveness of various methods for communicating with constituents? Get a Congressman to try several methods on several samples of constituents? What would be the dependent variable? How would I find out how to get acceptance from constituents for legislation that cuts jobs in the state, but significantly reduces wasteful federal spending? Are constituents really as immoral and self-serving as my Senator friend thinks? Maybe some interviews, then a well constructed questionnaire? Is there an agency that would support such research? Maybe there's a foundation. How would members of Congress react to such research? Maybe that's step one. Hmmm. . . .

Author Index

Subject Index